THE ORGANIZATIONAL AND HUMAN RESOURCES SOURCEBOOK

Second Edition

Douglas B. Gutknecht, Ph.D.
Janet R. Miller

UNIVERSITY
PRESS OF
AMERICA

Lanham • New York • London

Copyright © 1990 by

University Press of America,® Inc.

4720 Boston Way
Lanham, MD 20706

3 Henrietta Street
London WC2E 8LU England

British Cataloging in Publication Information Available

Library of Congress Cataloging-in-Publication Data

Gutknecht, Douglas B.
The organizational and human resources sourcebook /
Douglas B. Gutknecht, Janet R. Miller. — 2nd ed.
p.   cm.
Includes bibliographical references.
1. Organizational behavior.   2. Organizational change.
3. Organization.   4. Manpower planning.
I. Miller, Janet R.   II. Title.
HD58.7.G88   1989   658.3—dc20   89–20352 CIP

ISBN 0–8191–7622–2 (alk. paper)
ISBN 0–8191–7623–0 (pbk.: alk. paper)

Dedicated to our colleagues and friends in all organizations, who are working toward more effective and humane organizations. In addition, we thank our families, including Cindy, Marleis, and George, Bob, Tami and Debra for their understanding and patience during the production of this text.

We would like to thank the many colleagues and companies who have shared valuable informationand insights with us. In particular we would like to thank the following individuals who have contributed articles.

Millard M. MacAdam, MacAdam and Associates, 1207 SeacrestDrive, Corona del Mar, CA

Proactive Leadership, in Section One, Chapter Seven.

Sausan Fahmy, President, Advanced Performance Systems, Human Resource Consultants, 198 Avenida Sienega, Anaheim, CA 92807.

The Role of the Compensation Function, Section Two, Chapter Nine.

Richard Y. Chang, Richard Chang Associates, Human Resources Consultants, 41 Corporate Park, Suite 230, Irvine, CA 92714.

Training Needs Assessments, and Learner Focused Methods of Instruction, in Section Three, Chapter Ten.

David M. Gutknecht, Care Systems, 17662 Irvine Boulevard, Suite 2, Tustin, CA 92680.

Organizational Health Promotion: Improving Productivity and the Quality of Life, Section Four, Chapter Fourteen.

THE ORGANIZATIONAL AND HUMAN RESOURCES SOURCEBOOK
Second Edition

TABLE OF CONTENTS

INTRODUCTION 1
    Bibliography 6

SECTION ONE - ORGANIZATION THEORY AND BEHAVIOR 9

INTRODUCTION 11

CHAPTER ONE
ORGANIZATIONAL STRUCTURE 17

  1 ORGANIZATIONAL STRUCTURE. . . Introduction 17
  2 CONTEXTUAL VARIABLES 20
  3 DEPARTMENTALIZATION 21
  4 CENTRALIZATION versus DECENTRALIZATION 23
  5 SIX MODES OF ORGANIZING 24
  6 STRUCTURES IN HIGH TECHNOLOGY FIRMS 26

CHAPTER TWO
CLASSICAL, HUMAN RELATIONS, AND HUMAN RESOURCE THEORY 29

  1 "IDEAL" BUREAUCRACY 29
  2 CLASSICAL ORGANIZATION THEORY OF DESIGN 30
  3 SCIENTIFIC MANAGEMENT 31
  4 HAWTHORNE STUDIES 32
  5 HUMAN RELATIONS THEORY 33
  6 THEORY X AND THEORY Y 34
  7 SYSTEM 4 THEORY 35

CHAPTER THREE
CONTINGENCY AND SYSTEM DESIGN THEORIES 37

  1 TECHNOLOGY AND ORGANIZATION DESIGN 37
  2 STRUCTURE, ENVIRONMENT AND ORGANIZATION DESIGN 39
  3 INFORMATION AND ORGANIZATION DESIGN 40
  4 GENERAL SYSTEMS THEORY 41
  5 CONTINGENCY - SYSTEMS APPROACH 41
  6 OPEN SYSTEMS THEORY 42
  7 SOCIAL ECOLOGY: THEORIES AND PERSPECTIVES 43
  8 POWER, POLITICS, AND ORGANIZATIONS 45
  9 CONFLICT 49
 10 CULTURE 56

CHAPTER FOUR
PERSONALITY AND JOB DESIGN MODELS 65

  1 PERSONALITY THEORIES 65
  2 PERSONALITY AND BEHAVIOR 67
  3 PERSONALITY AND JOB FIT 68

4 CLASSICAL JOB DESIGN: SCIENTIFIC MANAGEMENT 68
5 JOB DESIGN 69
6 JOB CHARACTERISTICS 70
7 JOB ROTATION 71
8 JOB ENLARGEMENT 71
9 JOB ENRICHMENT 72
10 JOB REDESIGN 73

CHAPTER FIVE
CONTEMPORARY MOTIVATION THEORIES AND APPLICATIONS 75

1 A MODEL OF MOTIVATION 75
2 CONTEMPORARY APPROACHES TO MOTIVATION 76
3 HIERARCHY OF NEEDS THEORY 77
4 TWO-FACTOR THEORY 78
5 ERG THEORY 80
6 COMPARISON OF CONTENT MOTIVATION THEORIES 80
7 LEARNED NEEDS THEORY 81
8 EXPECTANCY THEORY 82
9 EQUITY THEORY 84
10 REINFORCEMENT THEORY 85
11 OPERANT CONDITIONING 87
12 A COMPARISON OF MOTIVATION THEORIES 88
13 BEHAVIOR MODIFICATION 90
14 GOAL SETTING 92

CHAPTER SIX
COMMUNICATION SKILLS AND GROUP BEHAVIOR 93

1 COMMUNICATION PROCESS 93
2 BARRIERS TO EFFECTIVE COMMUNICATIONS 93
3 BASIC COMMUNICATION SKILLS 94
4 ACTIVE LISTENING 98
5 GROUPS AND INTRAGROUP BEHAVIOR 102
6 INFORMAL GROUPS IN ORGANIZATIONS 106
7 TUCKMAN MODEL OF GROUP DEVELOPMENT 109
8 GROUPS VERSUS TEAMS 110
9 DIFFERENCES BETWEEN GROUP-CENTERED MANAGERS AND
   TEAM-CENTERED MANAGERS 111
10 COMPARISON OF EFFECTIVE AND INEFFECTIVE GROUPS 112

CHAPTER SEVEN
LEADERSHIP THEORIES, SKILLS AND MANAGERIAL APPLICATIONS 113

1 WHAT IS EFFECTIVE LEADERSHIP . . . Introduction 113
2 BASIC FUNCTIONS OF LEADERSHIP 115
3 TRAIT THEORY OF LEADERSHIP 116
4 BEHAVIORAL THEORIES OF LEADERSHIP 117
5 CONTINGENCY LEADERSHIP MODEL 118
6 PATH-GOAL THEORY OF LEADERSHIP 119
7 ATTRIBUTION THEORY 120
8 SITUATIONAL LEADERSHIP 121
9 A COMPARISON OF LEADERSHIP THEORIES 123
10 TRANSFORMATIVE LEADER MODEL - BENNIS 124
11 LEADERSHIP STRATEGIES AND DECISION-MAKING 125
12 CATEGORIES OF FAILURE OF LEADERS 127
13 A POLITICAL PERSPECTIVE OF LEADERSHIP 128

14 PROACTIVE LEADERSHIP 129
15 LEADERSHIP FUNCTIONS WITHIN HIGH PERFORMING TEAMS 132
Bibliography 133

SECTION TWO -

STRATEGIC HUMAN RESOURCE MANAGEMENT 139

INTRODUCTION 141

CHAPTER EIGHT
STRATEGIC HUMAN RESOURCE ASSESSMENT,
PLANNING, AND MANAGEMENT 147

1 BUSINESS/MANAGEMENT EXPECTATIONS FOR HUMAN RESOURCE
  PROFESSIONALS AND DEPARTMENTS 147
2 THE STRATEGIC HUMAN RESOURCES DEPARTMENT 149
3 STRATEGIC HUMAN RESOURCES PLANNING MODEL 150
4 HUMAN RESOURCE POLICIES 153
5 EQUAL EMPLOYMENT LEGISLATION AND EXECUTIVE REGULATIONS ... 155
6 REASONS FOR ESCALATING COSTS OF ADMINISTERING
  EMPLOYEE BENEFITS PROGRAMS 156
7 WHAT TO DO ABOUT EMPLOYEE TURNOVER 157
8 STRATEGIC PLANNING 158
9 STRATEGIC IMPLEMENTATION 159
10 STRATEGIC THINKING 160
11 STRATEGIC SCANNING 161

CHAPTER NINE
STRATEGIC PERFORMANCE MANAGEMENT 163

1 THE ROLE OF THE COMPENSATION FUNCTION 163
2 PERFORMANCE APPRAISALS . . . Introduction 172
3 PERFORMANCE DIAGNOSIS - IDENTIFYING THE CAUSE
  OF POOR PERFORMANCE 174
4 A SYSTEMATIC PERFORMANCE APPRAISAL PROGRAM 179
5 HOW SMART QUESTIONS MAKE APPRAISALS PRODUCTIVE 183
6 COACHING SKILLS 185
7 PERFORMANCE APPRAISALS . . . POINTS TO REMEMBER 188
8 PERFORMANCE APPRAISAL TRAINING - DO'S AND DON'TS 190
9 PERFORMANCE AUDITS 192
Bibliography 195

SECTION THREE -HUMAN RESOURCE DEVELOPMENT: INTEGRATING

TRAINING, MANAGEMENT AND CAREER DEVELOPMENT 197

INTRODUCTION 199

CHAPTER TEN
TRAINING 205

1 TRAINING . . . Introduction 205
2 THEORIES OF LEARNING AND INSTRUCTION 207
3 LEARNING PROCESS 210
4 LEARNER FOCUSED METHODS OF INSTRUCTION 212

5 THE STAGES OF ACTIVE LEARNING 214
6 ADULT LEARNING STRATEGIES FOR USE IN EDUCATION, TRAINING AND
  DEVELOPMENT ACTIVITIES 215
7 PLANNING FOR TRAINING 217
8 SOURCES OF POTENTIAL INSTRUCTORS 218
9 CHARACTERISTICS OF GOOD INSTRUCTORS 218
10 CREATING A LEARNING CONTRACT 219
11 TRAINING NEEDS ASSESSMENTS 222
12 SYSTEMS APPROACH TO TRAINING 224
13 ON-THE-JOB TRAINING 225
14 PRIMARY OUTCOMES OF TRAINING PROGRAMS 226

CHAPTER ELEVEN
MANAGEMENT DEVELOPMENT 227

1 MANAGEMENT DEVELOPMENT... Introduction 227
2 MANAGEMENT SKILL ASSESSMENTS 229
3 MANAGEMENT DEVELOPMENT DIAGNOSIS 233
4 MANAGEMENT STYLES: AN INTRODUCTION 234
5 MANAGEMENT STYLES: DECISION MAKING 237
6 EIGHT STAGES OF DECISION MAKING 240
7 CREATIVE THINKING AND INNOVATION 241
8 DELEGATION 249
9 TIME MANAGEMENT 251
10 MANAGING STRESS IN OUR PERSONAL AND WORK LIVES THROUGH WELLNESS
   PROGRAMS 256
11 RULES FOR PEOPLE AND PROBLEM MANAGEMENT 265

CHAPTER TWELVE
CAREER DEVELOPMENT 267

1 RECOGNIZING A NEED FOR CAREER COUNSELING 267
2 CHARACTERISTICS OF CAREER STAGES 269
3 FACTORS FOR INCREASED INTEREST IN AN EFFECTIVE CAREER DEVELOPMENT
  SYSTEM 270
4 CAREER COUNSELING FOR MANAGERS 271
5 CAREER PLANNING - IN TODAY'S CHANGING ENVIRONMENT 276
6 CAREER STRATEGIES 281
7 THE MIDDLE MANAGEMENT CAREER PATH 283
8 CAREER PLANNING WORKSHOP 285
9 TRAINING SUPERVISORS AND MANAGERS TO BE CAREER COUNSELORS . 286
10 PREPARING FOR A JOB INTERVIEW 288
11 INTERNSHIPS 295
Bibliography 299

SECTION FOUR-

ORGANIZATION DEVELOPMENT 303

INTRODUCTION 305

CHAPTER THIRTEEN
THE NATURE OF PLANNED CHANGE 309

1 CHANGE... Introduction 309

2 FORCE FIELD ANALYSIS 316
3 CHANGE PLANNING MODEL 317
4 CHANGE PROCESS MODEL 318
5 ACTION RESEARCH MODEL 320
6 CHANGE METHODS 321
7 PLANNING FOR CHANGE 324
8 RESISTANCE TO CHANGE 325
9 IMPLEMENTING A CHANGE OR OD PROGRAM 327

CHAPTER FOURTEEN
ORGANIZATION   DEVELOPMENT INTERVENTIONS 331

1 INTERVENTIONS... Introduction 331
2 SURVEY FEEDBACK 333
3 ORGANIZATIONAL DIAGNOSIS 334
4 TEAM BUILDING...BUILDING A HIGH PERFORMING TEAM 335
5 EFFECTIVE TEAM MEETINGS 339
6 FACTORS CONTRIBUTING TO TEAM DEVELOPMENT AND
   EFFECTIVENESS 343
7 CONDITIONS WHICH SUPPORT EFFECTIVE TEAM PROBLEM SOLVING ... 345
8 COLLABORATION AS A SOURCE OF POWER IN TEAM BUILDING 346
9 MANAGEMENT BY OBJECTIVES 347
10 COLLABORATIVE MANAGEMENT BY OBJECTIVES 348
11 THE MANAGERIAL GRID 349
12 THE SCANLON PLAN 351
13 QUALITY OF WORK LIFE 352
14 PARTICIPATIVE MANAGEMENT 356
15 QUALITY CIRCLES 360
16 MODELING 364
17 PROBLEM SOLVING: DEFINITIONS, ISSUES AND STRATEGIES 367
18 SIX PROBLEM-SOLVING CONTEXTS FOR INTERVENTION
   DECISION-MAKING 370
19 SOCIO TECHNICAL SYSTEMS 372
20 ORGANIZATIONAL HEALTH PROMOTION: IMPROVING
   PRODUCTIVITY AND THE QUALITY OF LIFE 375

CHAPTER FIFTEEN
ORGANIZATIONAL   DEVELOPMENT CONSULTANTS 385

1 BUSINESS MANAGEMENT CONSULTANTS... Introduction 385
2 ORGANIZATION DEVELOPMENT CONSULTANTS -
   WHAT THEY DO 387
3 ROLES OF ORGANIZATION DEVELOPMENT CONSULTANTS 388
4 SELECTING A BUSINESS CONSULTANT 390
5 WORKING WITH THE ORGANIZATIONAL DEVELOPMENT CONSULTANT . 395
6 FAILURE PATTERNS FOR OD CONSULTANTS 397
Bibliography 399

APPENDIX
STRATEGIES FOR ENTERING THE HUMAN RESOURCES FIELD 403

PREFACE

This text will concern itself with many of the organizational and human resource challenges that organizational leaders, managers, staff and employees will face as we enter a more complex and competitive 1990's. We will explore together old and new ideas, frameworks, models, techniques and strategies that we can all utilize to more effectively handle the new demands and dangers that constant change is exposing us to. Our purpose is to help you to think in a more integrative and strategic manner, to improve your ability to become skillful at understanding and using new ideas in management theory, practice, research, to perceive the significant emerging trends, and to learn how to implement strategies for practical improvement of organizations before problems arise and become crises. If none of the above goals were accomplished, we would still feel successful for providing a wide range of resources for managers, consultants and students of organizations to engage in personal and professional growth based upon their own learning agenda.

TEXT OVERVIEW

The second edition has been extensively revised and rearranged. Section One now becomes Organizational Theory and Behavior, which is divided into seven chapters-- (1) Organizational Structure; (2) Classical, Human Relations, and Human Resource Theory; (3) Contingency and System Design Theories; (4) Personality and Job Design Models; (5) Contemporary Motivation Theories and Applications; (6) Communication and Group Behavior; (7) Leadership Theories, Skills, and Managerial Implications. Section Two is now titled Strategic Human Resource Management and is divided into two large chapters-- (8) Strategic HR Assessment, Planning and Management, and (9) Strategic Performance Management. Section Three becomes Human Resource Development: Integrating Training, Management and Career Development, which is divided into three chapters-- (10) Training and Development; (11) Management Development; and, (12) Career Development. Section Four, Organization Development, is divided into three chapters-- (13) The Nature of Planned Change; (14) Organization Development Interventions; and, (15) Organization Development Consultants and the Consulting Process.

In these times of rapid change, many are searching for more humane and productive organizations. This task requires that we tap some reserve of commitment and energy to become more proactive and informed about the emerging possibilities. We believe in the importance of linking personal effectiveness, management and organizational productivity. Since we live in an age of rapid change, increasing international competition, new trends and fads, and an epidemic of mergers, cutbacks and takeovers, we need to know more about what impacts these events will have upon our lives. This time of discontinuity, turbulence, and unpredictable change poses challenges for individual productivity, personal career development, management education, and organization productivity. Yesterday's organizational and management thinking have become increasingly obsolete in a world where constant change is the daily reality.

Please list trends in each of the following areas that are forcing our organizations leaders to consider basic changes in their usual ways of doing business. Use your answers as a pre-test and see how they change after you have completed reading this text.

WORK FORCE

● Increase in highly educated employees who are more concerned with their own values, lifestyles, and rights and are less loyal to arbitrary company policy and traditional motivators.

● _____

● _____

SOCIAL TRENDS

● Aging population requiring increased spending for medical services

● Increased use of litigation in all aspects of work and personal life

● _____

● _____

NATIONAL ECONOMIC ENVIRONMENT

● Increased costs of health care, health benefits, and other social programs

● Falling U. S. dollar and uncertain trade picture

- _____
- _____

NEW CORPORATE STRATEGIES IN RESPONSE TO FINANCIAL PRESSURES

- Acquisitions, mergers, and takeovers
- Increased manufacturing in foreign countries where labor is cheaper
- _____
- _____

MARKET CONDITIONS

- Shorter life-cycle for most products
- _____
- _____

INTERNATIONAL AND GLOBAL ENVIRONMENT

- Political instability and terrorism
- Increased population growth and urbanization in developing countries
- _____
- _____

TECHNOLOGY AND INFORMATION

- The need for large amounts of investment in new technologies, training of the workforce in technological literacy, and managing information more effectively
- _____
- _____

PRODUCTIVITY

- The need for improvement in work and manufacturing quality
- _____
- _____

The signals are becoming clearer everyday-- the old world is dramatically different from the one today and new assumptions and creative responses are now demanded. Today a more comprehensive, systems linked, and flexible strategic model is needed. One that includes the unique dimensions of the individual and a vision of the entire systems' possibilities. This is why creative strategic thinking, planning, and acting is so important today. We need to understand what we are up against in the competitive marketplace; and how to contribute to our organizations's success as it competes locally, nationally, and internationally.

Conventional ideas about how organizations manage changes, new workers and competitive markets are under siege. More voices are being raised to challenge narrow and short-sighted organizational perspectives. The challenge is that we involve our entire system in insuring our quality, productivity and long-term success. This requires that organizations and individuals strategically utilize their most innovative capabilities for constant learning and innovation.

New learning possibilities are pointing the way to a more effective and productive future. Fad formulas provide no security under conditions of fracturing changes and global competition. Organizations need more vitality, flexibility, and diversity to anticipate and prepare for even more rapid changes to come. They must become true continuous learning systems (1) .

Organizations must create an an active and participatory environment that anticipates the dynamics of change. This requires that the organization move away from a functional approach, like training, to a strategic one of ongoing learning. This requires us to strategically select and effectively implement as internal consultants (even as managers) those tasks worth doing. It is the organizations responsibility to teach its employees how to expand the foundation of participation, learning from others and actively supporting effective career growth. When we fail to learn how to effectively plan our future, we lose patience, follow the whims of trend setters and lose our sense of direction and purpose. Piecemeal planning produces unproductive and defensive people and organizations. The primary result is feeling overwhelmed and overstressed by the complexity before us; uncertainty, not confidence, then blocks our every move.

The very pace of change and resulting transitions creates great personal and organizational stress. Organizations become overwhelmed by change, and fail to provide adequate workplace health promotion and transition management strategies to assist individuals to anticipate and handle the negative consequences of change. Organizations ignore how to manage large increases in health care costs, and declining quality and productivity. Complex problems hit us hardest when we are strategically unprepared to anticipate and plan for some of these changes and trends as opportunities for improvement, renewal and excellence.

We are really identifying the need to rekindle the entrepreneurial and innovative spirit by promoting a new philosophy of increased effectiveness and performance. This requires individuals and organizations to work together as part of a learning team. This attempt to strip away the philosophical values, attitudes, and management styles of large sized, rigid, play-it-safe bureaucracies, is needed if we are to promote more innovative, life-affirming, healthy, creative and productive work environments.

Bureaucracy is an enemy of effective, healthy organizations and people. It promotes a lifeless order, rigid control, caution and safe behavior. Old style training and management both exemplify this approach; because they emphasize the domination of employees, which creates passive responses from workers who only learn what is required to survive. Bureaucracy thrives where we rely upon rigid policies, procedures and rules to guide us. Bureaucracy, thus, promotes the fear of risk taking, innovation, flexibility, courage, autonomy, integrity, diversity, resourcefulness, responsibility, synthesis, and other healthy learning values. These new learning values are a strategic threat to bureaucratic dependent behavior.

STRATEGY DEFINED

The need to think more strategically is obvious to anyone concerned with the modern organization. However, the topic of strategy is often applied to everything from remaining competitive in turbulent environments to managing teams and departments more effectively. The key criteria for inclusion under the strategy label are the following: 1) the idea of performance management; 2) an orientation toward what is the normative or appropriate course of action for managers; 3) an emphasis of issues of relevance to top leaders and managers. The latter category often implies issues of general relevance to organizations, and thus, makes strategy important to all levels of management.

Strategy can be viewed in many ways, depending upon ones orientation. For example, Porter (2) views the strategic importance of helping a firm to align itself properly to meet the competition. The key variables are the availability of information, the economic costs of making decisions and acting, the fit of strategy and culture, and the degree to which strategies can be implemented.

Porter's premise is that organizations must strategically align their resources to either the high road of quality or the low road of low cost leadership. To be stuck in the middle area of the product and cost differentiation (market focus) will lead to financial ruin and organizational failure.

Another view of strategy is more of a bottom-up approach. This view of strategy is less dependent upon strategic analysis of economic and competitive forces, or a strategic orientation toward product niches, and instead focuses upon institutional and behavioral factors. Strategy is thus limited by organizational structures which constrain and limit strategic decision making and implementation that it becomes a less than optimum solution. We might say that many productive strategies are at best approximations of optimum decision outcomes; they are often stumbled upon.

Many different combinations of strategy exist, and no one single definition can suffice to explain the empirical diversity of what organizations actually encounter in their strategic attempts to survive. Strategy in varied faces must embrace both the static and patterned elements of planning, as well as the active elements of maneuvering to outwit a competitor.

Another question about strategy is why it is needed at all? The answers are as varied as the definitions of the concept itself. Although overlapping, this question indicates the need to think critically about the type and variety of situations that require good strategic analysis.

THE STRATEGIC CHALLENGES AHEAD

The effects of rapid development and implementation of new technologies, combined with the international character of the marketplace, promises to make the 1990's the most challenging decade in American history since the rise of organized labor. Underlying all change, whether intrapersonal, interpersonal, or organizational is one simple, inherent factor: human beings. Each of us has a basic need to learn how to adapt and create some control over our destiny. We can't really train people to survive change, but we can provide the learning resources to allow workers to actively confront the future. Everyone must learn to become actively involved and support this learning process.

Resistance to change and transition is a short-term, yet sometimes necessary, coping mechanism. However, we must get beyond such resistance. We can do this if we recognize the need to empower people to maintain some control over their destiny through learning. We must each all employees how to read the signs of change and prepare themselves and their organizations. Even normal, healthy resistance can be detrimental to the survival of the organization if not managed properly. The process of managing these responses to change requires strategic thinking, planning, and creativity. Adapting to successive waves of change is likely to overburden both managers and employees' coping skills. The challenge for managers and human resource professionals during the 1990's and beyond will be to understand healthy and unhealthy responses to change, and how to identify and to promote proactive organizational learning.

THE HUMAN RESOURCE CHALLENGE FOR PROFESSIONALS

No list of business trends today would be complete without including competitiveness and its cousin, productivity. It is essential that human resource practitioners present a professional image and an ability to use language to which audiences can relate. They must learn to talk with, for example, financial managers, while avoiding excessive use of their own professional jargon. They must learn to position themselves as internal consultants who know how to assess, plan, implement, and evaluate ideas, needs, and programs of all types. They must learn to listen, communicate, and market their services. And finally, while HR professionals should maintain their generalist knowledge, specializing in a particular field may help them select the most appropriate human resource strategies and work toward an effective integration of human resource systems.

The organization of the future is emerging today. Managers, consultants, and human resource professionals now have the opportunity to demonstrate their ability to develop strategies together that capitalize on human productivity as a means of creating a winning organizations. As the strategic organizations hurry to recover lost and dwindling world markets, the profound importance of tapping the productivity of a healthy, motivated, educated, and caring workforce is still only slightly beyond the stage of lip service. Hopefully this text will provide a framework and sourcebook for more effective actions.

BIBLIOGRAPHY/REFERENCES

INTRODUCTION

(1)   Gutknecht, Douglas B. **Strategic Revitalization: Managing the Challenges of Change** 2nd Edition (Lanham Maryland: University Press of America, 1988)

(2)   Porter, L., Lawler, E. and Hackman, K. **Behavior in Organizations** (New York: McGraw-Hill, 1975)

SECTION ONE

ORGANIZATIONAL THEORY AND BEHAVIOR

INTRODUCTION TO ORGANIZATIONAL THEORY AND BEHAVIOR

Organizational Theory and Behavior looks at the outcomes and actions of organizations as well as the behavior of individuals and groups within an organizational setting. It is the study of the organization, both internally and externally. Internally we view the organization at two levels: structurally (macro), and behaviorally (micro). In Organizational Theory and Behavior, we look at these components separately and as a whole, a system. It also views the systems impact on its own environment, as well as the impact the environment has on it (see Figure 1).

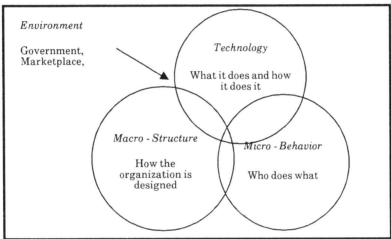

Figure 1. Model of The Modern Organization

Organizational Theory and Behavior should do two things: 1) provide useful, working ideas of how people work and act in organizations and; 2) provide useful methods, strategies and tactics for bringing about concrete organizational change, development and improvement.

Theories or perspectives can provide different angles for improving our understanding and managing of organizations. Without theory we encounter a given situation and believe it either acceptable or confusing merely because we can't place it in some context.   With theory we can break a bewildering situation into meaningful chunks and understandable components (concepts, definitions, variables, hypotheses) which then guide our perception and actions.   Theoretical thinking allows us to sort out a complex array of sensory inputs, and helps us to attend to what is important.

In this section we will concentrate on analyzing an array of theoretical ideas, concepts, perspectives, assumptions, and patterns. By reviewing and thinking about both the classical ideas and modern organizational patterns we will see new ties, connections, and opportunities for synthesis. Our theories can, unfortunately, shield us from the experience of confusion, uncertainty, ambiguity and contradiction. Today, our quest for relevant theory must embrace the search for new forms of seeing, connecting, and integrating.

Lincoln (1) argues that any new paradigm or world view (which reflects our deepest beliefs and assumptions about the human condition) impacts organizational theory development. We observe a shift in the following assumptions:

- from a probablistic world view to one that is complex and diverse;

- from a hierarchically ordered world to one of heterarchy (interactive, simultaneous and mutual influence);

- from a mechanistic to holographic (interconnected network patterns);

- from images of a determinate universe to ones that are more indeterminant;

- from assumptions of direct causality to those of mutual causality;

- from metaphors of assembly (construction of a complex system from a series of simple units) to those of morphogenesis (new form is symbiotically constrained but predictable from elements that make it up);

- from pure objectivity to a perspective or multiple viewpoints model. We might identify the current model as a complex social network in contrast to a complex system.

Today, we can seldom rely upon one perspective or set of assumptions. We need to move between concepts and levels of analysis such as micro and macro, behavioral and structure, theoretical and applied, rational and nonrational, certainty and uncertainty, and theory and practice. Many organizational problems occur because leaders and managers fail to question their old concepts, standard operating procedures, rule of thumb dictates and outmoded models of the organization and the modern world. The modern organizational thinker must also be a doer and problem solver, embracing the realities of complexity, contradiction, uncertainty, ambiguity, value conflicts, life-style differences, perceptual limitations, and environmental pressures from competing constituencies.

Srivastva (2) speaks of four themes common in executive thought and action:

1) **envisioning** - creating in one's mind an image of a desired future organizational state that can serve as a guide to interim strategies, decisions and behavior;

2) **experiencing** and **sense-making** - utilizing processes that give meaning to the environment and that make all human beings a part of the environment simultaneously;

3) **knowing** and **enacting** - continual on-line learning at a personal level. This learning occurs at the interface between desire and reality that forces the executive to reconstruct his or her understanding of the world to account for the discrepancy;

4) **developing the executive mind** through the strengthening of management education.

Bennis and Nance (3) identify four strategies for leading others while managing yourself:

1) attention through vision
2) meaning through communication
3) trust through positioning
4) deployment of self through positive self-regard.

They argue that many organizations are overmanaged yet underled because, while the former means "to bring about, to accomplish, to have charge of or responsibility for, to conduct", the latter means "influencing, guiding in direction, course, action and opinion" (3). The latter entails vision and doing the right thing (effectiveness), while the former involves mastering procedures, routines, and doing things right (efficiency).

A shift in the focus of theory can allow us to downplay the mechanistic, predetermined and routine in favor of the open ended, exploratory, experimental and entrepreneurial. How do we get workers to explore the shift in their own and their organization's behavior - strengths and weaknesses, limits and potentials? Obviously by stretching themselves, allowing them to express themselves in new, creative and perhaps unforeseeable ways.

The study of organizational behavior is a systematic attempt to understand the behavior, attitudes, and performance of people in an organizational setting. As a supervisor, manager, or leader you need to understand your resources, technical and human. If you have a computer system, you would need to know:

1) how it is going to help you;
2) how you get it to do what you need it to do;
3) what to do if it fails, and;
4) what resources you have available should your needs change.

Likewise, if you work with people, you need to know:

1) how can they help you achieve organizational goals;
2) how to get them to want to help you;
3) how to help them succeed or coach them when they fail, and;
4) how to help them learn what they need in order to do their job.

You can see the list is the same -- basically understanding how to utilize your available resources in the achievement of organizational goals in the most efficient manner.

In today's highly evolving technological state, organizations must commit to or reaffirm their interest in human resources -- people. John Naisbett (4) speaks of "high-tech, high-touch", or the need to counter-balance new technology with a human touch. Organizational Behavior is the study of that human touch or the soft side of organizations.

One reason for emphasis on improved models of organizational theory and behavior is the evolution of employee need structures. Postindustrial nations have reached a condition wherein higher-order needs are the prime motivators. In addition, the knowledge society requires more use of intellectual abilities along with the usual manual skills.

The key that unlocks this combination of higher-order needs and intellectual abilities in order to make the system productive, is improved organizational behavior. The human mind is encouraged to be more creative by positive motivation. The promise of more effective organizational behavior is that it motivates people to produce better ideas. There is no apparent limit to what people can accomplish when they are motivated to use their potential to create new and better ideas. The key thought is: Work smarter, not harder.

The behavioral sciences -- psychology, sociology, and anthropology -- are a major contributor to the field of Organizational Theory and Behavior, in the form of emphasis and approach. Through the study of **psychology**, we learn about and develop an understanding of individual behavior, specifically in the areas of motivation and learning. Basic knowledge of human behavior is important to work design, leadership, organizational design, communication, decision making, performance appraisal systems, and reward systems, which are all important aspects of Organizational Behavior.

From **sociology**, we gain knowledge of the impact of group, team and larger institutional structures. Sociology, in dealing with human interaction, plural behavior, and the study of social systems, lends to the field the study of the organization in terms of the variety of people with different roles, status, and degree of authority.

An anthropologist is interested in gaining a better understanding of the relationship between the individual and his or her environment, the culture. Edward Hall (5), an anthropologist who consults with both American and foreign organizations, says, 'American management in the past has been singularly blind to the needs of human beings. Management wants to eliminate the human equation from business'. **Anthropology** can lend us familiarity with some of the cultural differences of employees, which can lead to a greater managerial objectivity and depth in the interpretation of behavior and performance.

We have approached the study of Organizational Theory and Behavior from a multi-level perspective:

- First, we look at **individual behavior**. A worker comes to the organization with a set of characteristics, attitudes, perceptions, motivations, and personality. We address these characteristics by looking at several aspects: personality theories and, types and the relationship of personality to behavior; learning theories and styles, because a worker must first learn his or her job, as well as learn new aspects of the job as it changes; and motivation, which we address from a variety of perspectives and theories, as individuals need to have an understanding of his or her own motivations, as well as the motivation of those around him.

- We then look at **group behavior**, as most individuals work within a group setting. We first address communication and the interactions between peers, superiors and subordinates, top-down communications, and bottom-up communications. A manager needs to understand the dynamics of groups, what happens to individuals within a group, both from the standpoint of managing subordinates, as well as observing, understanding and utilizing knowledge of his or her own individual style within groups.

- Finally, we look at structural and organizational level issues like culture, conflict, power, and leadership.

In this section we have used the concepts of Organizational Theory and Behavior to introduce you to, or reacquaint you with some of the important current ideas in the field. In no way have we attempted to write a full review of these dynamic areas , but rather capsulized on what we consider to be some of the main points.

CHAPTER ONE
ORGANIZATIONAL STRUCTURE

1   ORGANIZATIONAL STRUCTURE... Introduction

Organizational Structure refers to the overall characteristics of the organization, its anatomy. It prescribes the formal and informal roles and relationships that enable people and groups to achieve the mission of the organization. Understanding structure can assist the manager or consultant to take a 'contextual' picture of the organization: it's size, it's technology for getting work done, it's management philosophy and the type of environment in which people work. Structure can also focus attention upon the "departmentalization" of the organization: how work groups are separated, as well as united. Management can view the design of the organization from a range of classical designs, with clear division of work, each being managed by one manager with total authority and responsibility, to contingency designs, where the organizational form is dependent upon differences in technology, environment and information processes.

Organizational Theory studies the structure of the organization, in terms of what work is being done and how it is to be done. It must, however, be sensitive to aspects such as social norms, external competitiveness and the legal climate. It studies job design, including job content, job functions, relationships, task accomplishment and workers reactions to their jobs. Jobs can be designed from simple, standardized, specialized elements, (scientific management), to jobs with much variety which allow the worker responsibility, autonomy, decision making and a sense of achievement (job enrichment). Job design must link with organizational design and other macro structural systems variables (e.g. culture, power, conflict, environment, information).

A simple definition of the organization is a **"goal-directed activity system in which two or more people cooperate"**. The goals include numerous dimensions related to the manufacture of products, services or some combination of products and services for use by the internal subsystems or systems outside the producing organization. Porter (6) defines the following characteristics of organizations:

1) social entities - people and groups acting, interacting and reacting;
2) goal oriented;
3) structure - the way tasks are divided up (division of labor) to achieve the goals;
4) coordination - activities of people in structures (different roles and tasks) must be coordinated to achieve goals;
5) continuity - of activities and relationships over time to indicate a common sense of purpose and involvement, not just an ad hoc group of people.

When building a relevant model of organizations, managerial practitioners must also address the human aspects: the individual human being whose self-concept, attitudes, values, motivation and behavior influences the functioning of all other organizational systems, as well as work units, tasks, and interpersonal interactions; individuals pooling their talents and resources to accomplish group and organizational goals. Some recent theorists and managers appear to have ignored this dimension and the task of managing has, thus, become more problematic. We cover these perspectives of behavior later in this Section.

As stated before, Organizational Structure is the anatomy of the organization, which prescribes formal roles and relationships for people and groups in an attempt to direct work toward accomplishing the goals and mission of the organization (see Figure1-1).

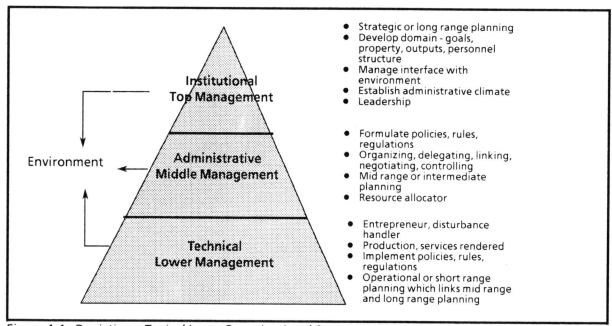

Figure 1-1. Depicting a Typical Large Organizational Structure

There are several key themes that modern managers must confront when thinking about organizational design and structure:

● How to design the organization for effective management of people.

● How to focus the work of top executives, planners and HR executives upon key long-term, strategic issues, while not dissipating commitment and motivation from important short-run concerns.

● How to utilize specialist, technical, and staff roles while still leaving room for managerial flexibility.

● Designing task roles for the strategic group so that they are sufficiently integrated for synergy without suppressing creative problem solving.

● Focusing the organization outward to learn more about its competitive environment.

- Recognizing and managing destructive conflicts before they hurt and demoralize the organization.

- Learning about and using multiple approaches to structuring.

- How to concentrate on critical success areas by involving all levels of management.

- How to encourage and support entrepreneurial and innovative behavior, without bypassing the organization's strengths.

2 CONTEXTUAL VARIABLES:
Size, Technology and Management Philosophy

In combination with environmental factors and organizational structure, contextual variables help explain and predict the functioning and effectiveness of organizations.

Organization Size -

# employees	Small	2-50	Size of organization seems to be
	Medium	50-200	only important when related
	Large	200-1000	other issues
	Huge	1000+	

Technology -

A technology is formed with a particular combination of materials (human and non-human), knowledge, and techniques (processes) in an attempt to produce desired outcomes. There are different types of technology:

Intensive - variety of techniques employed by a team of specialists to solve problems (high interdependence). Example: law, research

Mediating - used to link parties desirous of becoming interdependent. Example: computers, banking

Long-linked - sequential flow of work. Example: machines, assembly line

Management Philosophy -

Management Philosophy is the set of attitudes of the top management toward key aspects of an organizations' competitive environment. As with size and technology, management philosophy is not an independent variable, rather it is influenced by external forces and contextual variables.

Patterns of Attitudes toward the Organizations' Domain -

Traditionalistic - Theory X, profit oriented, results oriented, bottom line, distrustful of environment

Proactive - high regard for employees, quality of life, Theory Y

Individualistic - Growth and power, Machiavellian

3 DEPARTMENTALIZATION

There are four common types of departmentalization found within organizations: Functional, Divisional, Legal, Matrix. The most popular and common form of departmentalization is functional. Following is a description of each and a discussion of the advantages and disadvantages of each.

Functional

The development of units and departments on the basis of specialized knowledge, skill, and action. May be the most popular form in business organizations, and has established our views of line and staff units.

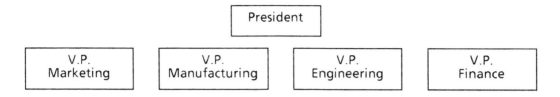

+ Clear task assignments
+ Pool of knowledgeable co-workers
+ Emphasis on technology
+ Vertical focus

- Complex communications
- Could lead to narrow, boring jobs
- Difficult to integrate because of specialized training
- Restricted view of organizational goals

Figure 1-2. Functional Type

Legal

In effect, an organization sets up divisions of autonomous entities composed of several legal entities. The only rationale for this form is to establish a separate unit due to a legal requirement. May occur due to legislation, and is often seen in mergers of huge conglomerates.

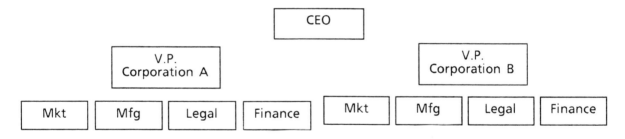

+ Limitation of liability
+ Possible reduction of taxes (particularly for corporations)
+ Appearance of autonomy for various divisions
+ Appears to favor systems survival and growth

- Could be very inflexible
- May limit alteration of programs, personnel, territories, or environment

Figure 1-3. Legal Type

Divisional May be prescribed by the variety of products, clients, or territories within the domain of the organization. *(Units perform almost all the activities needed to produce a product or service.)* Its' hallmarks are:
1) adaptability and flexibility in meeting outside demands
2) greater likelihood of detecting changes in external demands

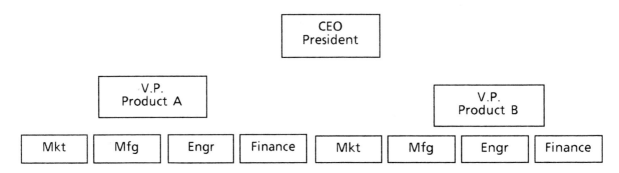

+ Places attention on external conditions, suited to fast change
+ Facilitates integration
+ Decentralized decision making
+ Best in large organizations
+ Best when several products

- Does not facilitate cross-training
- Less attention on efficiency
- Focus on divisional goals
- Difficult to coordinate functions of units concentrating on outside
- Personnel focus may be more external than internal
- May lead to duplication of efforts

Figure 1-4. Divisional Type

Matrix Exists where individuals have two superiors and are members of one administrative unit. More organizations are facing conflicting pressures to use the matrix structure as organizations become larger, technologies more sophisticated and varied, and environments more complex. A unique combination of functional and divisional types. Most often found for special products of limited duration.

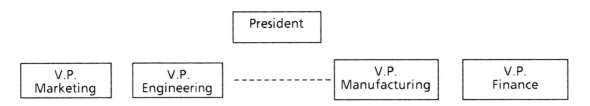

+ Can be used to gain the advantages of two forms
+ Applicable to large organizations where environment is complex and technology sophisticated and variable
+ Facilitates coordination among units

- Unity of command is lost
- Means-end chain becomes muddled
- Expensive method of horizontally linking the actions of various specialists
- Time consuming, requires extensive training, frequent meetings

Figure 1-5. Matrix Type

4   CENTRALIZATION versus DECENTRALIZATION

The issue of centralization/decentralization is somewhat vague, unless one is dealing with a specific topic such as the power to make decisions (See Figure 1-6). When all the decision making power is on the hands of a single, high-level executive, it is a centralized structure. When the decision making power is dispersed among lower level managers, it is a decentralized structure.

To some, the degree of centralization is a rough measure of an organizations' interest in employee-maintenance issues...if employees are considered dynamic, helpful, and generally capable, then decentralization should occur.

DELEGATION

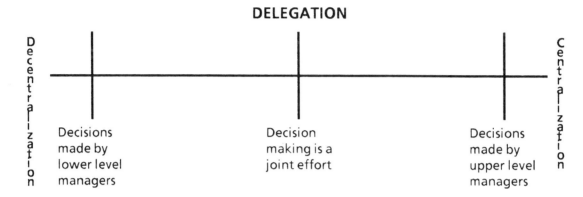

Figure 1-6. Decentralization and Centralization Affecting Delegation

There are two types of decentralization: vertical and horizontal.

Vertical decentralization: dispersal of power down the chain of command

Horizontal decentralization: relates to line and staff relationships

- **Line authority:** when decision making power remains within a particular function
- **Staff authority:** when decision making power flows outside the line structure (such as analysts, support specialists, and other experts)

The decision to decentralize involves consideration of the following:

- **External Environmental Factors** - as the environmental problems faced by an organization become more complex and dispersed, some form of decentralization would follow
- **Growth of the Organization** - the larger the organization, the more need for decentralization
- **Costs and Risk** - the higher these factors, the higher the tendency toward centralization
- **Management Philosophies** - some managers have the habit of making the decisions, and it can be a hard habit to break
- **Locus of expertise** - if the expertise for decision making resides at a lower level, this requires the need for decentralization
- **Abilities of lower-level Managers** - if decisions are made at the top, lower level managers do not develop the ability, nor are young and ambitious managers encented to remain in the organization

5   SIX MODES OF ORGANIZING

Innovations in organizational structure and form have greatly contributed to their improved performance in various industries and environments. The organizational forms of the future will most certainly become more information-based, flexible, and less unitary. Although still appearing to resemble the functional hierarchy, the organization of the future will really behave much differently and require new forms of communication and interaction. Each of the forms below will have different strategic requirements, including information processing needs, which provide unique opportunities and obstacles. The organization that is most exposed to a volatile, changing environment will have more diverse, complex, and diffuse information needs.

Form of organizing	Control and Coordinating Mechanisms	Examples
Integrated Hierarchy	Direct Authority	Single product firm Non-diversified engineering Retailing Aluminum and paper in large firms
Semi-Hierarchy	Arms length control Periodic review	Chemicals, electronics, foods, automobiles
Co-Contracting	Arms length control organization Also mediates relations between co-contracts	Airline manufacturing Joint ventures Air Bus Beijing Jeep
Coordinated Contracting	Agreed specifications and deadlines Long standing trust Quality necessary for continued relations	Construction Japanese automobile Electronic Fashion design
Coordinated Revenue	Formal financial agreements Monitoring of service standards with high quality	Franchises such as MacDonalds
Spotlink or Network	Limited to terms of contract	Stock and international commodity markets

Figure 1-7. Five Modes of Organizing (7)

The first mode is the **integrated hierarchy** where centralized and hierarchical control and coordination resembles the direct authority of the traditionally large and non diversified firm. This most likely will continue to dominate those firms that are small and engage in one primary area of activity. The examples given in Figure 1-7 seem to function with a relatively non-formalized management system.

The second mode is a **semi-hierarchial form** that is exemplified by the multi-divisional firm, the holding company and the parent-subsidary types. This form of diversified, multinational often structures interactions between the corporation and divisions as if they were on a form of internal market with parts competing with one another, which creates a large amount of autonomy for resource bargaining, control and coordination remain hierarchically managed, with informational requirements, particularly financial, diffused. This allows a semi-independent relationship with the parent company. In some new technology areas the degree of strategic independence is quite high in order to take advantage of rapidly changing trends.

The **co-contracting form** is the third organizational pattern that is comprised of a set of independent co-contractors who form a quasi - firm for the purpose of accumulating assets, sharing the advantages of large economies of scale, and reducing dependencies upon key resources. However, as with Airbus Industrie, the large European firm, the political and cultural climate can prevent the organization from merger into one firm. We might also list the joint venture such as Toyota and General Motors as one form of the Co-contracting company.

The **coordinated contracting form** is a quasi-firm that integrates a prime producing contractor with a set of sub-contractors in a relationship that may persist over many years. The insurance industry and Japanese electronics industry provide key examples of the fourth pattern and indicate the importance of product and performance specification agreements for coordinating and integrating sub-contracting vendor relationships.

The **coordinated revenue form** is the fifth and refers to the franchising and licensing arrangements that are rapidly emerging in American Society where the cost of capitalizing any new organization, even the smallest business, is beyond the capability of the average entrepreneur. The Franchise operator's good name is the main asset that is purchased for a franchise fee, but other products and services can be mandated as part of the agreement, which may limit the franchisees' opportunity to run the business in an entrepreneurial fashion.

The **spot network** is the sixth example of a way of structuring organizational activities. It is a form of non-recurring contracting between independent firms or groups that try to leverage the marketplace for short-lived opportunities. The relationship is like a consortium, but is based upon a highly specified contract with very clear tasks, rights, and obligations.

The modern high-technology firm is information intensive and its structure appears more flat, with fewer levels. In this organizational type we need to rethink the idea of levels as merely opportunities for exerting authority and control over decision making. The high-technology firm uses levels as relays for information: collect, repackage and send on information. In this view the idea of span of control (normally six employees in classical theory) is really outdated. The new idea is span of effective communication or the number of subordinates that can be linked and provided information to self-manage effectively.

Control in such an organization becomes a matter of having the right information in a timely manner, not who or how it is provided (see Figure 1-8). If we are getting results than management is doing its job. Information must be timely not because of good principles of time management demand it, but because adjustments can be quickly made if anything is off schedule. Then management is less concerned with reporting why we are failing to deliver on time and more concerned with doing and asking who requires information, when and where to get the job done effectively.

Organizational Features	Bureaucracy	Adhocracy	Organic	High Technology
Job Design	Specialization	Horizontal Specialization	Contributive	Multiple Roles
Department-alization	Formal Boundaries	Fluid	Fluid	Fluid
Coordination Mechanism	Standardization	Mutual Adjustment	Mutual Adjustment	Mutual Adjustment
Role of Staff	Work Standardization	Undifferentiated	Blurred	Support
Hierarchical Disposition	Pyramid	Dynamic	Stratified	Aligned
Grouping Arrangement	Functional	Functional & Market	Network	Hybrid
Decision Making	Top Down	Selective Decentralization	Consultative	Centralized & Decentralized
Control System	Formal Rules	Action Plans	Informal Norms	Cultural
Reward Criteria	Span of Control / Seniority	Expertise	Expertise	Accomplishment / Expertise

Figure 1-8. Contrasting Structural Regimes (8)

Modern technology and information systems can change the shape of organizations because questions about effective performance can be quickly answered with timely and meaningful data. Waterman (9) has recently used the terms, 'friendly facts' and 'congenial controls' because he wants leaders and managers to make the distinction between neutral data and valuable information. The latter should set parameters for more effective strategies and actions. Traditional control strategies are based upon outdated, unprioritized data that feedback irrelevant or garbage signals (reactive use); while modern control strategies prioritize and organize meaningful data (information) to allow us to anticipate change trends and feed forward opportunities (proactive usage).

Some of his suggestions include: cutting costs without lowering quality (need priorities and good facts); using a common fact base for communication about direction and results; treating financial controls as liberating; pushing for better cost information; insisting on comparisons of information -- differences from expectations, historical experience, competitors in same industry, and customer needs; finally, becoming friendly with computer spreadsheets and databases because they provide opportunities to make comparisons (9: 132-135).

The characteristics of high-technology firms (10) seem to showcase the potentials for designing structural characteristics of fluidity, responsiveness and flexibility. Some of important dimensions listed in Figure 1-9 are the following: multiple roles and temporary assignments; project teams and task forces; communication as a key coordinating mechanism; minimum standardization of processes, outputs and skills through traditional staff functions; hierarchical structures so distance is reduced so that top of the leadership structure is flexibly aligned with operating units to effectively communicate and implement new strategic opportunities; grouping of activities due to relatively short product life cycles; organizational control through learning cultural norms (socialization) coaching and professional level performance management systems; decision making is both centralized and decentralized to maximize implementation of new innovations; reward systems that try to maximize the range of innovative rewards (paid sabbaticals, internal management development programs, reimbursement for advanced education, flexible and pleasant working conditions , wellness programs, and exercise facilities) in order to link the individual to the firm.

Structural Characteristics	Specific Features of High Tech Firms
Multiple Roles Temporary Assignments	• Individuals fulfill different roles and are rotated through many assignments in rapid fashion • Fluid boundaries are created and innovation is supported as capability of each individual is leveraged through exposure to diverse learning assignments
Project Teams and task forces	• Special blends of expertise are brought together for different projects • Ad hoc teams and task forces provide for increased commitment and facilitate implementation strategies
Coordinating mechanisms	• Coordination through communication which allows frequency of adjustments • Electronic mail and computerized voice-messaging systems speed up flow of information • Informal interaction through leisure, sports, and wellness programs
Role of Staff	• Staff function kept to minimum • Staff supports line groups rather than self-contained tasks • Staff functions like strategic planning and management development can be temporary assignments for line managers
Hierarchical Configuration	• Structure which allows for quick thinking, planning and action • Strategic apex aligned with operating core • Eliminate intermediate layers to facilitate involvement in planning & implementation
Grouping Activities	• Diversity into related business with short product life cycles • To coordinate 'hybrid' structures are created
Organizational Control	• Control through socialization, learning and performance management that are integrated through values and strategic mission • Convergence of ownership and management controls
Decision Making	• Simultaneously centralized and decentralized • Importance of pathfinding and implementation rather than problem solving through extensive analysis
Reward Systems	• Broad conception of incentives beyond rudimentary monetary rewards • Innovative rewards like paid sabbatical leaves, management development, external education opportunities, flexible working conditions, health and wellness programs

Figure 1-9. Strategic Characteristics of High Technology Firms

CHAPTER TWO
CLASSICAL, HUMAN RELATIONS, AND HUMAN RESOURCE THEORY

1 "IDEAL" BUREAUCRACY

Bureaucratic design, conceptualized by Max Weber, a sociologist, proposed to enable organizations to most efficiently accomplish their goals.

Weber suggests a hierarchy of positions, each with limited authority(see Figure 2-1). Each manager would be held accountable for the actions of his subordinates. There is complete separation of ownership and position, so that individual and organizational concerns are separate. Position and privileges are based on technical competence. Work is divided into specific tasks based on the technical competency required. This model leads to the concept of a hard-worker who ascends the organizational ladder.

Bureaucracy can be seen as a series of reinforcing conditions that stress efficiency, rationality, and security. Impersonality and formal role relationships are stressed.

Bureaucracy works well in situations where the emphasis on stable and routine tasks matches its stable external environment.

Table 2-1 represents a comparison of bureaucratic and non-bureaucratic functions within organizations.

Bureaucratic	Non-Bureaucratic
• Rules Policies, Procedures • Equal treatment based on performance • Division of labor; stress on expertise • Concentration on roles in a hierarchical structure • Career commitment • Separation of ownership and control	• Personal direction by a charismatic leader • Personal, kinship, or emotionally based rewards • Multiple job assignments • Personalities • Temporary association • Individual and organizational concerns are tied

Table 2-1. A Comparison of Bureaucratic Design and Non-Bureaucratic Design

2   CLASSICAL ORGANIZATION THEORY OF DESIGN

The principles of Classical Organization Theory of Design, as formulated by Henri Fayol in the early 1900's, provide guidelines for designing a system of interrelated tasks and authority. The principles are based on the concept that the organizing function involves dividing a task into successively smaller subtasks, grouping tasks into related departments, staffing each department with a manager who has authority and is part of a chain of command (See Figure 2-1).

Fayol proposed five structural principles:

1. The Principle of Division of Work - specialization

2. The Principle of Unity of Direction - one plan, directed by one manager

3. The Principle of Centralization - dependent upon the managers' capability

4. The Principle of Authority and Responsibility - to be given to the manager who is expected to direct the efforts of subordinates

5. The Scalar Chain Principle - communications up and down the chain of command

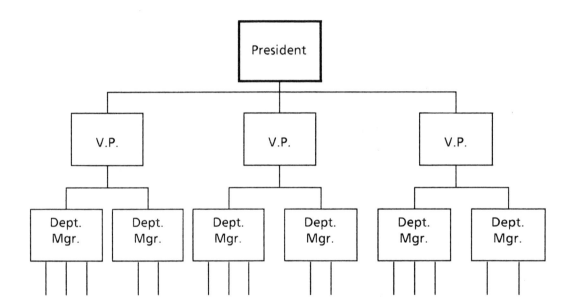

Figure 2 -1. Organization Chart Depicting Classical Organization Theory

3   SCIENTIFIC MANAGEMENT

This theory was developed by Frederick W. Taylor (11), an engineer, in the 1880's, and addresses the study and design of work that maximizes both machines and workers' productivity. The framework was based on a number of premises about individuals in the workplace:

1) The problem of inefficiency is a problem for management, not the worker.

2) Workers have a false impression that if they work too rapidly, they will become unemployed.

3) Workers have a natural tendency to work at less than their capacities.

4) It is managements' responsibility to find suitable individuals for a particular job and then train them in the most efficient methods to do their jobs.

5) Employee performance should be tied directly to the pay system, or an early incentive or piece-rate wage system.

Taylors' four basic principles of management are:

First. Develop a science for each element of a worker's job (this replaces the old rule-of-thumb method).

Second. Scientifically select and then train, teach, and develop the worker.

Third. Heartily cooperate with the worker in order to insure all of the work is being done in accordance with the principles of the science that has been developed.

Fourth. There is almost an equal division of work and responsibility between the management and the worker. Management takes over all work for which they are better fitted than the worker (in the past, almost all the work and the greater part of the responsibility were thrown upon the workers themselves).

4   HAWTHORNE STUDIES

Elton Mayo and his colleagues conducted the Hawthorne Studies at Western Electric from 1927 to 1932. Mayo's student, Fritz Roethlisberger, was actually more actively involved in the conduct of the studies, along with W. J. Dickson, the personnel department's liaison. Western Electric conducted the studies to try to determine how to increase productivity using a scientific management framework, which predicted that increased lighting would increase production. They chose three rooms, progressively increased the lighting in each, only to find no relation between productivity and illumination: there was a productivity increase in all groups. They tried again, this time with only two rooms: the control group where lighting remained the same, and the experimental group where lighting was increased. Again they found no distinction between the groups and productivity increased in both. No consistent relationship, thus, existed between the two variables or lighting and productivity. It appeared that scientific management principles emphasizing the physical determinants of worker productivity, seemed in error. In earlier study, productivity increased even after the lighting was decreased (12).

Mayo and his associates were then called in to conduct a more elaborate study. In one room, they isolated a group of women operators from others doing the same work and introduced changes in lighting, rest periods, hours and economic incentives. According to the theory of scientific management, this was supposed to increase productivity within that group. However, once again, not only did this group experience an increase in productivity, but so did the groups where no changes were introduced. It was concluded that output increased in all groups because of social and psychological factors, workers' participation and social involvement was clearly more important than changes in the physical environment. These experiments have dramatized the inadequacy of a purely economic view of workers, and led to a more holistic view. This research served as a basis for later theories on motivation, job satisfaction and productivity, and quality of work life.

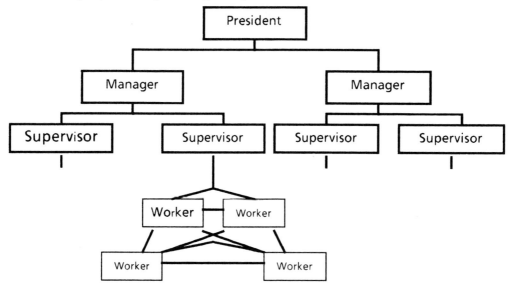

Figure 2-2. Roethlisberger and Dicksons Human Relations Model (13)

Mayo saw that in society, the extended family was becoming the nuclear family, with consequent loss of a larger family-group support system for many (13). He proposed to substitute a new work group for the old family group. The work group was given maximum freedom in controlling their own work. Within the groups, workers could establish their own patterns of coordination (see Figure 2-2).

5   HUMAN RELATIONS THEORY

Human relations theory, 1930's, is the offspring of the Hawthorne studies. It is concerned with attitudes, values, emotions, and more generally, the social psychology of workers and groups. It provides a contrast to classical or scientific management theory, which is more preoccupied with the formal arrangements of departments, positions and division of tasks.

The father of the human relations school as we've seen in the previous document, Elton Mayo, was then professor of industrial research at Harvard Business School. He was concerned with the rootlessness of the industrial worker. Mayo believed that productivity could be increased by involving workers in the decision-making process.

Modern human relations theorists view workers as only marginally controllable by narrow, external and material rewards. Truly effective control comes from internal causes and the emotional and attitudinal dimensions of individual workers. The assumptions of external and manipulatable control arrangements is felt to actually destroy motivation, enthusiasm and worker skill. Instead more complex, dynamic, and democratic social-psychological principles were developed. The emphasis is then upon non-authoritarian leadership style, group participation in decision making, and jobs which truly activate worker interest and involvement (14).

6 THEORY X AND THEORY Y

THEORY X, formulated by McGregor, fits with the human relations and human resource traditions because it is based on the following assumptions (15):

1) The average human being has an inherent dislike of work and will avoid it if he can.
2) Most people must be coerced, controlled, directed, and threatened with punishment to get them to put forth adequate effort toward the achievement of organizational objectives.
3) The average human being prefers to be directed, wishes to avoid responsibility, has relatively little ambition, wants security above all.

Theory X represents the traditional view of direction and control.

THEORY Y, also formulated by McGregor, is based on the following assumptions:

1) The expenditure of physical and mental effort in work is as natural as play or rest.

2) Man will exercise self-direction and self-control in the service of those objectives to which he is committed.

3) Commitment to objectives is a function of the rewards associated with their achievement.

4) The average human being learns, under proper conditions, not only to accept but to seek responsibility.

5) The capacity to exercise a relatively high degree of imagination, ingenuity, and creativity in the solution of organizational problems is widely, not narrowly, distributed in the population.

6) Under the conditions of modern industrial life, the intellectual potentialities of the average human are only partially utilized.

Management by Integration and Self-Control

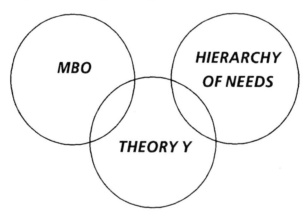

Figure 2-3. (16:61)

The purpose of the model shown in Figure 2-3 is to encourage integration, to create a situation in which a subordinate can best achieve his own goals by directing his efforts toward the objectives of the enterprise. It is a deliberate attempt to link improvement in managerial competence with the satisfaction of higher-level ego and self-actualization needs.

7 SYSTEM 4 THEORY

Likert's theory applies the results of quantitative research to the improvement of management of human resources (17:vii). There are three basic concepts of System 4 management:

● The manager uses the principle of supportive relationships

● The manager uses group decision making and group methods of supervision

● The manager has high performance goals for the organization.

The principle of supportive relationships implies the relationship between superior and subordinate is crucial. The more supportive the superior, the better will be the effect on the subordinates behavior, and in organizational performance. The essential key is the subordinates background, values and expectations, for his perception of the situation, rather than the superiors which determines whether or not the experience is supportive (17: 47-94). This theory proposes utilization of a full range of motives through participatory methods.

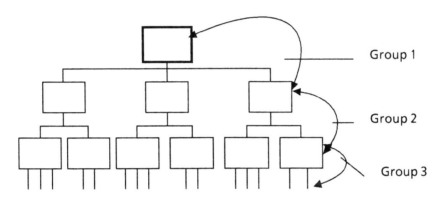

Figure 2-4. Linking Pin Principle

Group decision making implies that each work group is "linked to the rest of the organization by means of persons who are members of more than one group. These individuals who hold overlapping group membership are called 'linking pins'" (17:50). As depicted in Figure 2-4, at each hierarchal level, members of a work group are involved in decision making in issues affecting the group. "The superior is accountable for all decisions, for their execution, and for the results" (17:51).

The communication process should be such that information flows freely throughout the organization - upward, downward, and laterally. The information should be accurate and undistorted.

The interaction process is open and extensive; both superior and subordinate are able to affect departmental goals, methods, and activities.

The goal setting process encourages group participation in setting high, realistic objectives.

High performance, yet realistic goals, should be at every level of the organization. Many studies indicate that along with security, compensation and opportunities for promotion, employees want to be proud of their organization (17:51).   System 4

Theory proposes that through the use of group decision making and multiple, overlapping group structure, the organization sets objectives "which represent an optimum integration of the needs and desires of the members of the organization, the shareholders, customers, suppliers, and others who have an interest". (17:52) Goal setting at each unit allows for high performance goals throughout the organization. The superior recognizes the necessity for making a full commitment to developing, through training, the human resources of the organization.

Supervision is seen as a group, not a one-to-one, superiors-to-subordinates activity. The group is delegated as much authority as possible. The supervisor or manager is seen as a "link-pin" within the hierarchy of levels.

CHAPTER THREE
CONTINGENCY AND SYSTEM DESIGN THEORIES

1 TECHNOLOGY AND ORGANIZATION DESIGN: A Contingency Model

Woodward (18:358) suggests that "Organization structures reflect technology in the way jobs are designed (the division of labor) and grouped (departmentalization)".

The Woodward Research was based on analysis of the structure of 100 manufacturing firms in England. A wide variety of structural differences were found (managerial levels, span-of-control, ratio of individual workers to staff personnel) with no relationship to the type of manufacturing, size, or effectiveness. In studying the types of technology used among the firms, Woodward found a relationship with the structure of the organizations (see Table 3-1).

Types of Manufacturing

Organizational Characteristics	Job Order	Mass Production	Process Manu-facturing
(Median numbers)	System 4	Bureaucratic	System 4
Levels of Management	3	4	6
Executive Span of Control	4	7	10
Supervisory Span of Control	23	48	15
Direct to Indirect Labor Ratio	9:1	4:1	1:1
Industrial to Staff Worker Ratio	8:1	5.5:1	2:1

Table 3-1. Organizational Characteristics and Types of Manufacturing(19)

Affects of technology:

Job-Order firms - produces products or services according to customer specifications. Requires a sensing of market changes and adaptation to those changes (interaction with the environment). Requires high interaction within the organization in the product development stages. Likert's System 4 is the most effective in promoting the necessary interaction within and outside the organization.

Mass-Production firms - standardized products and manufacturing processes. Machines are utilized which are designed and paced by engineering standards. Work flow control is separate from supervision of work force. Bureaucratic design based on the ideas of scientific management and classical organization theory are most applicable.

Process Manufacturing - product development begins the manufacturing cycle. Success lies in finding new products which can be developed utilizing existing facilities, or new facilities once a market is determined. All departments throughout the organization require scientific personnel and specialized competencies. System 4 allows for the adjustment to new scientific knowledge.

2 STRUCTURE, ENVIRONMENT AND ORGANIZATION DESIGN: A Contingency Model

Another more basic explanation for structural differences in organizations is differences in the response to the environment.

The research conducted by Lawrence and Lorsch was conducted in firms in the plastics, food, and container industries. They introduced three key concepts: differentiation, integration, and environment (20).

Differentiation - the state of segmentation of the organizational system into subsystems, each of which tends to develop particular attributes in relation to the requirements posed by its relevant external environment. The concept refers to specialization of labor and degree of departmentalization, and includes the behavioral attributes of employees within the subsystems or departments.

Integration - Process of achieving unity of effort among the various subsystems in the accomplishment of the organizations task. Depends on degree of differentiation.

Environment - the perspective of the organization members as they look outward. Lawrence and Lorsch identified three main sub-environments: market, technical/economic, and scientific. These three sub-environments correspond to marketing, production, and research and development.

Research Findings

- Departments within a single organization are differentiated in terms of organization and behavioral attributes. The differentiation is in response to the departments' efforts to cope with their relevant sub-environments.

- Different departments may find it necessary to organize differently from other departments within one large organization (example production and research).

- The more stable and certain the sub-environment, the more bureaucratic should be the departmental organization structure.

- The more dynamic and uncertain the sub-environment, the more System 4 should be the departmental organization structure.

- Integration between departments should be based on circumstances within the department. Thus, departments with stable and certain market, technical-economic and scientific sub-environments can use classical integrative techniques. Departments with relatively diverse and uncertain environments should use System 4 methods of integration.

3 INFORMATION AND ORGANIZATION DESIGN: A Contingency Model

A key concept related to the synthesis of environment, technology, and organization structure is information. Organizations must effectively receive, process, and act on information to maximize performance. Information flows into the organization from the sub-environments and requires response to market, technological, and resource changes (21, 22).

In classical organization design, information-processing requirements are relatively modest (due to the existence of hierarchical control, rules and procedures, and planning).

In System 4 and other strategic designs, information-processing is imperative in order to process constant and up-to-date environmental changes. The greater the uncertainty of the environment, the greater the amount of information needed.

Managers need to develop strategies to deal with the increasing demand for information-processing. Two general approaches are: 1) reduce the need for information, and; 2) increase the capacity to process information.

Reducing The Need For Information - this can be accomplished by creating slack resources or by creating self-contained units.

- **Slack Resources** -

    - stockpiles of materials, manpower and other capabilities which enable the organization to respond to uncertainty

    - lengthen planning periods, production schedules, lead times

    - reduce the interdependence between units.

    Has some cost considerations and requires a careful balance of relevant costs and benefits.

- **Self-contained Units** -

    - reorganization toward product, customer, or territorial bases

    - each unit provides its own resources

    Cost is lost efficiency

Increasing Capacity to Process Information - invest in vertical information systems or create lateral relationships.

- **Vertical information systems** - computers, clerks, executive assistants
- **Lateral relationships** - joint decision making among functional units, cross-functional task forces and teams

4   GENERAL SYSTEMS THEORY

The genesis of modern general systems theory (GST) was developed nearly fifty years ago by von Bertalanffy, however has only recently been applied in the study of organizations. The purpose was to provide a way of bringing order out of the increasingly diverse approaches to organizational theory . The general systems theory simply states that all parts, components or subsystems of a system are related and dependent upon one another (see Figure 3-1). Each organizational system must

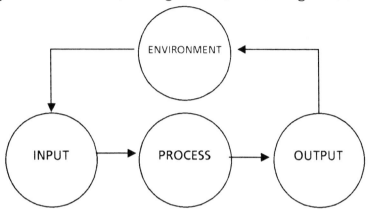

Figure 3-1. General Systems Model

accomplish essential tasks or functions that promote or detract from the survival of the entire system. Each system has its' own boundary and transforms inputs from other systems into outputs.

5   CONTINGENCY - SYSTEMS APPROACH

Due to the vagueness and abstractness of the General Systems Theory, a "mid range approach" or "second-order systems study" has emerged in the discipline of Organizational Theory, referred to as "contingency approach".

Kast and Rosenzweig define the general systems view as seeking: to understand the interrelationships within and among subsystems as well as between the organization and its environment, and to define patterns of relationships or configurations of variables. Contingency views are ultimately directed toward suggesting organizational designs and managerial systems most appropriate for specific situations (23,24).

These theories suggest analyzing organizations from the following approaches:

- Open systems - viewing the organization as being "open" to the influence of the external environment

- System as a whole - view the system not only in each separate component (structure, technology, human resources, environment), but as a whole

- Boundaries - defining the boundaries of the components which delineates the elements belonging to the system and those belonging to its environment

- Equifinality and Fit - a system can reach the same final state through different paths of development

6   OPEN SYSTEMS THEORY

Katz and Kahn (25) propose that the dynamics of organizational activity are seen as a system that involves a complicated exchange of energy. They define energy in terms of a broad set of influences that range from company profits, through authority and role expectations, to factors associated with the job satisfaction of individual workers.

The activities of an open system consist of a series of energy exchanges, cyclical in nature, in which various forms of input are acquired and transformed into units of energy outputs. A prime example of this is the production cycle (see Figure 3-1). The energy obtained from the output system (input) is translated (process-output) through external energy (environment)into a new form of energy, reactivating the cycle.

Closed systems do not recognize external energy as a part of the system, and operate with an internal influencer which moves the system to an end point where it ceases to operate, and the system tends to run down. Open systems do not reach this terminal point, since it acquires new sources of energy from the external environment. Communication with external sources of energy, therefore, is the basic factor that differentiates the open system from the closed system. Katz and Kahn refer to **negentropy** as the opposite of entropy, which is the process that leads a closed system to shut down. The principle source of negentropy is found in the ability of open systems to transform output energies into new forms of input energies that reactivate the system, thereby initiating a new activity cycle.

Each organization must include a negative feedback mechanism that provides the system with information concerning things that produce deviations from desired courses of action. Katz and Kahn refer to this as a state of **dynamic homeostasis**, or achieving a level of constancy in the energy exchange process.

There are certain assumptions surrounding open systems which assist in planning (26):

- Organization members' perceptions play a major role in environmental environment, determining which parts of the environment are attended to or ignored, as well as what value is placed on those parts

- Organization members must share a common view of the environment to permit coordinated action toward it

- Organization members' perceptions must accurately reflect the condition of the environment, if organizational responses are to be effective

- Organizations can not only adapt to their environment, but can proactively create it.

Organizations exist in constant interaction with their external environments, including suppliers, unions, governments, community groups, stakeholders and other relevant sources of inputs and potential users of outputs. Throughout the organizations life cycle the environment changes and, hence, influences the organizations chances for survival and growth. The environment shapes threats and opportunities, limits and challenges, which in turn, influences the organizations energy, structure and processes. The literature on organizational environments characterizes these relationships using various dimensions (See Table 3-2).

Author and Characteristic of Environment		
Aldrich	Pfeffer & Salancik	Child
Concentration/Dispersion - The degree resources are evenly distributed	Concentration - Intent to which power and authority in the environment is widely distributed	Change - Frequency of changes in environmental activities, differences involved at each change, irregularity in pattern of change
Environmental Capability - relative level of responses available	Munificence - the availability of scarcity of resources	Complexity - range of activities relevant to organizational activities
Domain Consensus - degree that organizations' claims to domains are disputed or recognized	Interconnectedness - the number and patterns of linkages	Illiberally - degree of threat resulting from competition, hostility, or even indifference
Stability/Instability - degree of turnover in environmental elements		
Turbulence - extent environment is characterized by increasing interconnection between elements and rate of interconnection		

Table 3-2. Sources: Aldrich, H.E. Organizations and Environments (Englewood Cliffs, N.J.: Prentice Hall, 1979), Child, J. "Organizational Structure, environment and performance: the role of strategic choice" Sociology (1972:6-1-22), Pfeffer, J. and Salancik, G.R. The External Control of Organizations (New York: Harper & Row, 1978)

One concept for understanding the organizations interaction with its environment is the idea of social ecology. **Social ecology** involves a series of exchanges of personnel as they enter, move within and leave the organization; supplies and raw materials which are taken into the organization as inputs and transformed into outputs through a variety of technologies; exchanges of political resources relating to labor markets, unions, laws and social values, the government and community.

These exchanges frame the organizations environmental or ecological "niche", setting the context which situates the organization in a social field or system of dependencies. The environmental field or context frames each organizations unique situation as a configuration of resource dependencies. The environmental space occupied by any organization is modified (expanded or diminished) as the organization struggles to perform effectively and efficiently. Although an expanded niche itself can create problems of overutilization of resources, a problem also arises when an organizations niche shrinks, disappears, or is overwhelmed by the competition.

Today, more than ever before, organizations must understand and monitor performance in close relationship with an environment of organizations, organizational resources and influential stockholders. The organizations performance and reputation is closely aligned with its environmental niche. Each organization must think about its niche and how to defend it. Some theorists suggest a rather passive strategy of coping and adapting because they believe organizations only react to their environments (the contingency model). Other organizational theorists follow a different view: organizations can strategize, control, creatively construct, enact, impose and influence their environment. However, this view does not discount the value of resource sharing, cooperation and other forms of inter-organizational conflict management. In this latter viewpoint, organizations are viewed as a field of social forces and inter-organizational domains. In addition, organizations can create structures and mechanisms to deal with complex turbulent environments, meta-problems and the realities of constant change.

8   POWER, POLITICS, AND ORGANIZATIONS

Introduction

What is power and how does it differ from organizational politics? Why should researchers, consultants, managers, and leaders concern themselves with power? What linkages does power as a theory or variable have with other organizational theories or variables (Systems, Contingency, Leadership Behavior, Organizational Development and Change). Power and politics is important because the basis of group or organizational life revolves around problems of authority, control, participation and policies.

Definitions

Pfeffer (27) defines power as "a property of systems at rest...politics is the study of power in action". Brym (28) defines power as "the structurally determined capacity to control others by deciding issues, by deciding which issues are to be contentions, and by suppressing manifest and latent conflicts". Power can be stated in either a positive or negative manner -- in the former, it includes the ability to initiate and sustain action -- in the latter, the ability to resist or stop action. Kanter (29) defines power as "intimately connected with the ability to produce; it is the capacity to mobilize people and resources to get things done...".

Organizations are, thus, political arenas of member groups actively striving to accomplish the following tasks:

1)   Accumulate and allocate scarce or valued resources (technical, knowledge, expertise, data, funds, space, time) information, and support (enforcement, backing);

2)   Build coalitions by individuals and interest groups (departments, cliques, professional groups, ethnic groups, womens groups, leadership groups);

3)   Establish organizational missions, objectives, goals, agendas for action, and policy decisions, through the processes of bargaining, negotiation and jockeying for position.

The political view of organizations assumes that scarce resources are always a problem for some groups and that power differences and conflict are important dimensions of any organization. Kanter takes a positive view of power and argues that power, innovation and participation fit together (empowerment):

> In companies where there is really no "market" for exchanging or rearranging resources and data, for acquiring support to do something outside the formal structure - because it is controlled either by a hierarchy or by a few people with 'monopoly power' then little innovation behavior is likely...

The political view takes a more realistic, yet sometimes too cynical, position regarding the nature of purely rational authority and the goal setting process. In this view, organizational goals and objectives are not always clear, consistent, agreed upon and unproblematic. The purpose of the organization in the classical model is to enhance rationality and promote unproblematic mission and task objectives. In this view, authority is always at the top, legitimate and responsible for setting organizations goals. However, in the political view, different individuals, groups and coalitions often press alternative goals, objectives, and

45

resource alternatives upon the organization. This process is not always tidy, rational, or even in the interest of organizational survival. It does often appear, in retrospect, to be compatible with democratic values and participation.

Cyert and March's (30) theory of the organization as an arena of coalition formation and bargaining over goal definition was one of the first to identify the positive, pluralistic features of organizational politics. Coalitions actually increase a sense of involvement and participation as they bargain for their pet goals by trading resources, commitment, and side payments such as rewards, personal assistance, recognition and policy promises. In this view, side payments are mechanisms for participation which cuts across and reconciles coalition differences. Power is shared, but not in a manner that assumes full consensus over goals, absence of conflict, fully rational decision making, or the separation of cultural values, such as trust and loyalty, from pragmatic rewards and resources. Power, in this view, becomes a positive source for mobilizing and sharing resources for diverse, pluralistic goal attainment. Power allows the accumulation of resources for worthy task accomplishment.

Kanter defines a similar, positive view of power. The powerful can be masterful change agents and not just destructive authoritarians:

> Any new strategy, no matter how brilliant or responsive...will stand a good chance of not being implemented fully -- or sometimes, at all -- without someone with power pushing for it...Hence the importance of the corporate entrepreneur who remains steadfast in his or her vision and keeps up the momentum of the action team even when its effort wanes.

Also, innovating teams thrive because the organization allows the circulation of power through open communication, networking, the support of coalitions and informal peer alliances and the decentralization or wide dispersal of available resources. Innovative power can be encouraged through human resources policies that encourage job mobility, employment security, rewards for entrepreneurism or risk taking, a team orientation (collaborative and consultative work relations), diffused authority, local access to resources, and a culture of pride in being as good as one can be. Still, one cannot ignore the hard realities of assisting decentralized and entrepreneurial teams to cooperate on issues of importance to the larger organization.

Sources of power

French and Raven have developed six forms of power a manager may possess. These, along with a seventh form (Connection) developed by Hersey, Blanchard and Natemeyer (31), form a discussion of power bases within an organization.

Application: Organization Development and Change

Power in action is politics, the active bargaining for resources and building of coalitions. The use of power always involves some group disagreement, frustration, and failure to mobilize resources or to achieve policy preferences.

The political perspective believes that coalition building and decision making is not entirely rational, nor does it represent organizational effectiveness (goal attainment), the efficient use of resources, or even the human needs of workers. However cynical such a view, destructive power also causes us to recognize that constructive power is possible -- groups and coalitions often need to see their

Legitimate Power

Derived from an individuals position in the structure or hierarchy of the organization. The higher the position, the higher the legitimate power tends to be.

Coercive Power

Based on the ability to control punishment, such as reprimands, demotion, termination. A fear-based power.

Referent Power

Based on attractiveness or appeal of one person to another, personal traits.

Reward Power

Based on the ability to control and administer rewards, such as pay, promotion, or recognition.

Expert Power

Based on a special ability, skill, expertise, or knowledge base.

Information Power

Based on the access to information about particular issues or activities within the organization or about the relation of the organization to the environment. The information is perceived as valuable to others.

Connection Power

Based on connections with influential or important persons inside or outside the organization.

shared interest in avoiding continual and selfish conflict. Thus coalitions can learn to manage conflict and share resources, and authorities can learn to recognize the phenomenon of power-created resistance. Resistance to bargaining, coalition building and participation can actually lead to secondary effects such as worker sabotage, passivity, alienation, increased stress, turnover, and absenteeism. These effects, in turn, will contribute to deterioration of organizational morale, managerial legitimacy, decrease in productivity, and competitiveness.

Power can't be treated as the sole possession of either management or employees. Instead, it must be defined as a negotiated relationship between people, groups and coalitions to accomplish diverse organizational goals. In ignoring these relationships, leaders and managers will downplay their integral involvement with employees and cause them to rely upon a rigid, top down, hierarchical view. The essential point is that legitimate power or authority has both a controlling side and a participatory side. Legitimate recognition and bargaining through coalitions allows potential destructiveness and subversive, covert power to be transformed into organized, manageable bargaining power (opposition).

Finding Power In Organizations

Every organization has two main power systems, the formal and the informal. The formal power system is revealed in mission statements, organizational charts, policy manuals, normal committee assignments and formal job descriptions. The informal power system is revealed in communication links, negotiated relations, face-to-face interaction, the grapevine, organizational assumptions and culture, cliques, in groups and clubs, etc. Both are important to understand in any organization.

The Power and Influence Game

Crozier (32) views society and organizations as power games. The advantage of the game framework is that it focuses attention on the means rather than ends of social action, and removes any negative moral attributes from the process. Life is a game of continuous, strategic negotiation.

We may speak of advantages or handicaps, scarce or surplus resources, and strategies and tactics. The metaphor of the organizational game should thus take the place of the organizational jungle, marketplace or nursery school.
The object of the game is to understand the strategies and tactics that sophisticated social actors invent to achieve their own private and group goals. This view implies that each actor possesses more power than once thought, regardless of position or resource. The power of the game resides in the margin of liberty or freedom to move in ways calculated to enhance their position. Each individual or group is free to become a strategist and choose alternative courses of action in a game or series of games that he or she is constantly playing.

Collective or organizational action is the cooperative behavior that emerges out of the strategies of individual players and groups who are implicated in different games. The idea of the organizational game (politics) can't be proven but seems logical when we observe the daily actions that take place in organizations. The organization is created through cooperative games, which also allow the accomplishment of individual goals, within a larger system of goals. Society and organizations are socially constructed by relatively free individuals who bargain, disagree, choose, manipulate, care, trust, lie, deceive, fall short, try harder, give up autonomy, walk away, and try again. The name of the game is action, both in everyday life and in organizational settings. If you find this argument appealing, expand upon it by observing and writing about organizational games (how many exist, do they differ in their degree of complexity of rules, are the goals of all games the same, which games are more crucial?).

9 CONFLICT

Introduction

Conflict exists within an organization when there is some disagreement about what the organization should be doing; how it should be doing it; what parts of the organization are responsible for which tasks; what parts of the organization should have privileges or rewards. People sometimes question the orders that they get from above, and sometimes do not not follow those orders. People at the top do not always agree on what orders should be given in the first place. There is sometimes antagonisms with other parts of the organization which has conflicting interests. At all levels, employees will resist a particular course of action with which they do not agree.

Conflict manifests itself in several forms: arguments, heated discussions, political maneuvering, abuse, even violence, and exists in any size or type of organization: bureaucracies, enterprises, and voluntary associations. These conflicts severely hinder the organizations ability to operate in an efficient and effective manner. Managing conflict is thus a problem for any organization. The leaders must keep the factions within the organization unified and directed toward the accomplishment of the established goals.

Managing conflict is difficult for some leaders, who would rather replace the original goals with new ones to avoid conflict. However, goal displacement does not allow leaders to act in a powerful manner, and does not set up a way to handle future conflict. The management of conflict is a most important problem for the leaders of any organization.

Bases of Conflict

Conflict arises when the rational organization does not meet the natural organization (33). The rational system model sees the organization as designed like a machine to accomplish a specific purpose. As in Max Weber's Bureaucratic Model, this is a scientific organization, a design to accomplish the goals of the organization. Every department and worker has its place and its fit within the organization chart. Conflict between departments is not expected.

The natural system model however, sees the organization as a set of factors based on the history and experiences of that particular organization, which shape its current behavior. It is a living, open system, which expects conflict to arise as the structure does not reflect a perfect design, but rather the organizations accommodations over time to diverse environmental demands. The natural system would expect conflict between departments that have clearly defined tasks, because each would tend to think in terms of only their function, to the neglect of others.

An example falls within a manufacturing organization, with separate delineations between the manufacturing department and the marketing department. The marketing department wants to exceed its quota of sales for a given month, so it creates a contest for the sales personnel. However, it does not communicate with the manufacturing department, who expects to put out the number of widgits agreed upon originally . The sales people do exceedingly well in this contest, however the manufacturing department finds itself unable to meet the demands of delivery to the customer. Conflict naturally arises due to the structure of the organization -- separate functions with no lateral communications.

Conflict is also built into the organization through the individuals who comprise it. Most organizations include a large diversity of character types and social backgrounds in their personnel. These differences in personality and background possess obvious potential for conflict. In a manufacturing department, typically the "hourly" personnel come from a different social background than the salaried personnel, therefore a source of misunderstanding and conflict is built in.

Conflict can also arise when there is a difference in perception of the proximity to a problem. A worker with an operational function, with hands-on experience, would probably see a problem differently than would a supervisor or manager.

There also appears to be a source of conflict between professionals and nonprofessionals. Professionals are trained not only with a set of skills, but a point of view about problems to be faced and how they are to be handled. When a professional is confronted by a nonprofessional with resistance to that manner of problem solving, the professional may think of the nonprofessional as simply not having the basic competence to decide upon the matter at hand. This leads to conflict, especially when the two types are mixes within a work group.

Another major factor in conflict may be the organizations promotion system. In many organizations a managers promotion may be based on how much improvement takes place in his or her department. This leads to "suboptimization" of situations within the department, emphasizing the part over the whole. This factor of conflict is built into any system in which promotion is based on encouraging department heads to compete for the same resources.

A major source of conflict within organizations arises from struggles over change. Organizations change for many reasons -- new ideology, changed external conditions, new leadership. One of the strongest reasons is a desire for increased efficiency. Let us not confuse efficiency with effectiveness. Effectiveness means achieving the operational goals of an organization; efficiency means doing so by using a minimum amount of resources.

The Value of Conflict

Conflict can have both a positive and negative effect on the organization. Obviously conflict that leads to destructive fighting and political harangue is not going to lead the organization in the direction of achieving its goals in an efficient manner. However conflict that is properly managed, for example competition, can be of significant value to the organization. The critical element is whether the units that are competing are independent or interdependent. In the case of two departments competing for the same resources, where one is a winner and the other a loser, then conflict is destructive. In the case of one group competing with another group, when both are able to reap the same rewards (e.g. sales bonus), then competition is healthy.

Competition will be constructive when: 1) the units that compete are independent rather than interdependent and are not competing for the same resources, and; 2) competition is restrained so that neither party suffers humiliation from defeat.

Destructive competition comes often from lack of identification with other work groups, or departments. If one does not have interaction with other areas, one can tend to think of ones own area as being the only truly important area. Therefore, conflict arises when one group competes for the resources to the detriment of other groups.

This conflict can be avoided by increasing the contact through exchanges of personnel, liaison roles, or joint participation on projects. Socialization outside the work context with those of different groups often cements interdependent work relationships. Encouraging workers to see "the big picture" can be accomplished through courses, training, and feedback on the workers contribution to the organizations mission. Organization members who are given strategic information about the organization and its activities tend to feel like participants in the overall mission, not just their portion of it.

The need to resolve conflict can cause people to search for ways to change the way they do things. Thus, the conflict resolution process can stimulate positive change within an organization. The search for ways to resolve conflict may not only lead to innovation and change, but it may make change more acceptable.

Level of Conflict

The five levels of conflict are **intrapersonal** (within ones self), **interpersonal** (between individuals), **intragroup** (within a group), **intergroup** (between groups), **intraorganizational** (within organizations), and **interorganizational** (between organizations).

Intrapersonal Conflict often occurs when an individual is faced with some form of goal conflict or cognitive conflict. Goal conflict exists when behavior will result in outcomes that are mutually exclusive or have incompatible elements (both positive and negative). The three basic types of intrapersonal conflict are:

- Approach-approach conflict - a choice between two or more alternatives with positive outcomes

- Avoidance-avoidance conflict - a choice between two or more alternatives with negative outcomes

- Approach-avoidance conflict - a choice that has both positive and negative outcomes.

Cognitive conflict at the intrapersonal level exists when individuals recognize inconsistencies in their thoughts. This conflict is usually psychologically uncomfortable for people and usually motivates the individual to reduce the inconsistency (dissonance) and achieve a state of equilibrium (consonance). To achieve consonance, people can: 1) change their beliefs, or; 2) obtain more information abut the issue causing dissonance.

It is believed that the greater the goal conflict before a decision is made, the greater the cognitive dissonance following the decision. This is because typically the chosen alternative has negative (avoidance) elements, and the rejected alternative has positive (approach) elements. The more difficulty in arriving at a decision, the greater the need to justify the decision afterward.

Interpersonal Conflict involves two or more individuals, and the joint outcomes of the individuals as well as the individual outcomes of each person. People respond to interpersonal conflict in at least five ways. Table 3-3 and Figure 3-2 provide a model for understanding and comparing these five interpersonal conflict-handling styles.

51

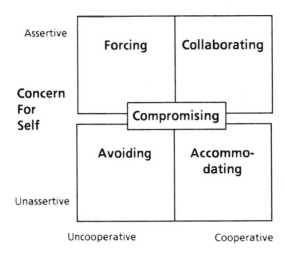

Figure 3-2. Interpersonal Conflict Model

Avoidance	*let the conflict work itself out *minimize the possibility of escalating a conflict *evaluated by others negatively
Forcing	*win-lose (I win - you lose) *evaluated by others negatively
Accommodating	*may represent an altruistic act, a long-term strategy, or submission *evaluated by others favorably, however perceived as weak
Collaborative	*win-win approach *perceived by others as dynamic, very favorably
Compromise	*give-and-take process, involves negotiations and concessions

Table 3-3. Methods for Handling Interpersonal Conflict

Intragroup Conflict focuses on conflict within the group as a whole as well as the individual members. This form of conflict affects the groups processes and outputs.

Studies have shown (34,35) that intragroup cooperation seems to positively affect group processes such as coordination and communication while also improving the quantity and quality of group output, with or without intergroup competition. Intergroup competition seems to stimulate productivity. Competition apparently facilitates performance on some tasks.

Another study (36) shows that conflict within groups is not a simple, single phenomenon. Instead, intragroup conflict seems to fall into two distinct categories: 1) substantive conflict, and; 2) affective conflict).

Substantive Conflict refers to conflict based on the nature of the task or to "content" issues. It is associated with intellectual disagreements among members. Affective conflict derives primarily from the groups interpersonal relations. It is associated with emotional responses aroused during interpersonal clashes. This study suggested that intragroup conflict does not automatically lead to negative consequences, however a group experiencing competition as a form of conflict, may have to work very hard to achieve constructive outcomes.

Intergroup Conflict focuses on conflict between two or more groups. As mentioned before, intergroup competition can stimulate groups to perform better. However, there can be some negative side effects of intergroup conflict.

Typically, when a group is given an opportunity to "win" at some problem is put at competition with another group, group cohesion immediately grows stronger, a group identity develops, and the group becomes closer. The group becomes primarily concerned with task goals, and there is an increased pressure toward conformity and suppression of interpersonal conflict. The feeling in the group is one of "superiority", regarding their group as superior to the other group(s). Hostility developed toward the other groups. Perceptions of the other groups become distorted, inaccurate stereotypes formulate. The intergroup conflict becomes more intensified as the competition grows stronger. When a "winner" is chosen, each group reacts differently. As you might expect, the winning group considers the decision to be fair and just. The winning group becomes even more cohesive. The decision has validated the members' positive view of the group, and the members are self-satisfied. They develop a complacent attitude about future competition (which may mean they do not improve their performance in future competitions). The losing group considers the decision unfair and biased. This group becomes disorganized, and soon unresolved intragroup conflict begins to surface. The group places blame, often within the group. This group can go two ways: 1) in future competitions, this group might reorganize and become more cohesive, it might improve its performance; or 2) it might become demoralized and adopt a defeatist attitude, or even disband.

Managers must minimize any intergroup conflict, if possible, and handle any conflict present with great care.

Intraorganizational Conflict exists in four types:

- Vertical conflict refers to any conflict between levels in an organization, for example superior-subordinate conflict.
- Horizontal conflict refers to conflict between employees or departments at the same hierarchical level in an organization.
- Line-Staff conflict refers to conflict between the people who are directly responsible for some process and the staff who serve an advisory function.
- Role conflict and role ambiguity refers to conflict within an individual or between individuals over the set of tasks one is supposed to handle.

Interorganizational Conflict refers to conflict, or competition between two or more organizations. This is most frequently seen is competing product lines.

Managing Conflict

There are three major approaches to managing conflict:
1) structural methods
2) interpersonal confrontation methods
3) promotional methods

Structural Methods consist of five methods:

- **Dominance Through Position** - managers may simply attempt to resolve conflict within their area of authority by issuing a directive that specifies the course of action subordinates are expected to follow. This method does not always work because a manager cannot always effectively resolve these issues, and the method does not prevent conflict from occurring again. This approach primarily serves to resolve a specific conflict after it already has occurred.

- **Decoupling** - organizations can be designed to decrease interdependence between departments by providing each department with the resources and inventories that are independent of those provided for other departments. This is a costly approach.

- **Buffering With Inventory** - organizations can provide a buffered inventory between two departments that share a work flow.

- **Buffering With A Linking Pin** - the use of an individual to help integrate departments with overlapping activities, understanding the operations of both departments, and coordinating both sets of departmental activities.

- **Buffering With An Integration Department** - a department set up to integrate the efforts of departments with overlapping activities

Interpersonal Confrontation Methods

Confrontation, in this sense, is a process by which parties in conflict directly engage one another, openly exchange information on the issues, and try to work out the differences between themselves to reach a mutually desirable outcome. Confrontation methods assume that all parties may be able to gain something (a win-win situation). The confrontation of conflict depends on the attitudes and goals of the parties involved. If one of the parties adopts win-lose strategies, the interaction is forcing rather than confrontation. Negotiation (a process in which two parties try to reach an agreement that determines what each party gives and receives in the transaction) and third-party consultation (the use of a neutral person) can facilitate confrontation.

Promotional Methods

Promoting functional cognitive conflict may actually be a useful approach to managing conflict.

Dialectical Inquiry Method - the development and recommendation of a course of action by one advocate or group of advocates with the development and recommendation of a contradictory course of action by another advocate or group of advocates. The decision is based on a synthesis of the two conflict viewpoints.

Devil's Advocate Method - a systematic critique of a recommended course of action.

Conflict is inevitable in organizational life, but it need not have destructive consequences for the organization. Depending on how the conflict is managed, the negative effects may be minimized, and positive effects may arise from the conflict. The effective management of conflict is based, in part, on a solid understanding of the different ways conflict emerges and is resolved.

10 CULTURE

Introduction

Organizational culture is a many faceted concept that has gained a faddish popularity in the business literature. However, the importance of the concept resides in its ability to highlight the shadow side of the formal organization -- a unique style, character, energy, commitment, and way of doing things. Researchers also focused upon values, assumptions, informal ideologies, attitudes, myths, symbols, rituals, language, jargon, rumor, prejudices, stereotypes, social etiquette, dress and appropriate demeanor.

Culture is best conceived as the organizations soul, purpose and foundation. It is revealed in the formal charts, policy statements, rules and regulations, machines and buildings. However, it may be in these surface manifestations. The cultural underside must be constantly evaluated, discussed, audited and managed. Left unattended the dysfunctional sides of culture soon becomes dominant.

Organizational culture provides the energy, meaning, direction and commitment essential for doing well the more visible functions like motivating, rewarding, leading, structuring tasks and implementing strategies. It provides both the glue for cohesion and the oil for lubrication - both essential for building effective organizational structure. It can also be, as we have mentioned, a chain on the organizations need to be innovative. However properly trained, it can become a dynamic engine for change.

Culture is both complex and contradictory. The contradictions result from the deeper levels of psyche and society: it reveals the contradictions of human endeavors,the inherent conflicts of interest and values and our lack of self-awareness regarding our own needs, motives, values and assumptions. So again, we return to the idea of an often unconscious, taken-for-granted, fairly stable set of beliefs, values, meanings, assumptions, rituals, myths, and norms which serve as a backdrop for the surface level of daily organizational activity.

The concept of culture is also a product of our academic and managerial culture and thus, becomes a tool for understanding, analyzing, managing and changing the world and our organizations. Some authors use the culture concept as objective, theoretical variable, to build better models of how organizations really work, i.e., integrating culture, motivation, reward systems and strategic planning (37,38). Other researchers (39) view the task as one of engaging in the cultural analysis of organizational life in order to interpret, decode and understand their meaning for modern life. Cultural analysis would be based upon acts of appreciation, critical reading and interpretation, just as we utilize such processes to understand and evaluate music, art, novels, plays, poems, religion or folklore.

Luis (40) defines the three components of culture as:

- First, there is content: the totality of socially transmitted behavior patterns, a style of social and artistic expression, a set of common understandings;

- Second, there is a group: a community or a population, a society or class, a unit;

- Third, there is a relationship between the content and the group.

Anthropologists have focused more on the content and such categories as ritual, myths, folklore, humor, art, religion, etc. Sociologists and organizational researchers focus more upon the latter two categories. The more relevant managerial discussions and applications have focused upon all three levels of analysis.

VanMaanen (41) suggests that culture

> can be understood as a set of solutions devised by a group of people to meet specific problems posed by the situations they face in common.

They have tried to root culture in the historical process of group formation, maintenance and transmission along ecological, temporal and social dimensions. The group has no mind of its own, but the culture might be thought of as inside the groups mind, yet not divorced from the people who carry the ideas. Culture is carried on or transmitted only by free individuals who elaborate, build, extend and create this common legacy. However, as the material and symbolic culture extends its influence we must understand that peoples interactions and choices are also shaped by factors beyond their influence or control -- norms, values, rules, codes, linguistic conventions, behavioral styles. Here again we return to the theme that culture liberates and provides the foundation for understanding ourselves and joining others to achieve our greatest potential, while also constraining, boxing us in, structuring and delimiting our potentials and possibilities.

Table 3-4 capsulizes, by example, the identity and culture of five companies in five different industries. The chart illustrates the difference between identity and culture, and looks at identity's potential influence by considering possible courses of action for each company.

In psychological terms, identity as motivation and culture as response highlight identity's influence on many dimensions of a business -- from how a company is organized, and the kinds of people it hires -- to how decisions of strategy are made.

Hickman and Silva (42) believe it is important to match the three components of strategy (customers, competitors, and company) with the three dimensions of culture (commitment, competence and consistency) to create a nine box model (See Table 3-5):

Kennedy and Deal (43) suggest four culture types:

1) **The tough guy, macho culture** - a world of individualists who regularly take risks and need quick feedback

2) **The work hard, play hard culture** - fun and action are predominant here. Employees take few risks, receive quick feedback and are in constant motion

3) **The bet your company culture** - the key here is the big-stakes decisions which are high in risk and slow in feedback and results

4) **The process culture** - a world of little or no feedback where employees find it hard to measure what they do; instead they concentrate on how it's done. The idea here is the process is out of control (bureaucracy).

Facts about organizational culture to keep in mind:

- Culture left to itself often becomes dysfunctional

57

	BANKING COMPANY	COMPUTER SERVICES COMPANY	CHEMICALS COMPANY	CONSUMER PRODUCTS COMPANY	ENGINEERING & CONSTRUCTION COMPANY
Cultural Themes, Attitudes, Norms	-Expansionist -Power-basing	-Can-do -Achieving mission impossible	-Autonomy rules (no corporate identify, per se)	-Enduring enterprise -Social contribution via business	-Setting precedents
Cultural Behavior and Values	The king and his court (one man rules)	-Entrepreneurial -"Up by the boot-straps" tradition	-Me first -Divisions do their own thing	-Family (home away from home) -Genteel	-Ruggedness; toughness -Marlboro Man philosophy
Strategies, Modes of Action	-Deregulation encourages expansion, thus environment for banks identity is favorable -Hiring should focus on those who'll support leaders vision -Acquisitions-should avoid banks with ambitious management, or be prepared to replace them, strong balance sheet not with-standing	-Despite large size by industry standards, company thrives more as a small business driven by "doing the undoable" -Promotion from within and selective hiring may prove to be far more critical to growth than acquisitions, even though a potential business may fit by definition	-Autonomy precludes cohesive corporate culture; cohesiveness demands biting the bullet: divesting some business, reinvesting in others -Decisions must be based on joint variables: which business have greatest economic potential; which have strongest identity to support corporate growth	-Reason for being in business transcends profit motive -Acquisitions must be products, businesses with some perceived "social benefit" -New hires should seek an extended family and want to make a long-term commitment (opportunists need not apply, talent notwithstanding)	-The higher number of precedent-setting projects, the better in terms of long-range return on people and money -Character, nature of jobs,more important than size -Technicians as well as managers should be highly organized, risk-oriented, innovative

Table 3-4. The Identity and Culture of Five Companies

- Culture needs to be managed, particularly during times of growth, change, transition, crisis, mergers and acquisitions

- Don't confuse the symptoms or surface of culture with the essences of depth

- Often we over emphasize content and forget the process or learning dimension (how it was created or sustained through socialization practices)

- Often times the cultural whole (organization) is confused with the parts (subcultures, company identity, philosophy, climate, management styles, etc.)

- Culture has dynamic consequences for how organizations operate because it suggests how organizations capture and direct the collective will of the organization

- Culture that is moving in the wrong or destructive direction creates <u>ruts</u> or habitual ways of behaving

Strategy	Commitment	Competence	Consistency
Customers	Match organizations collective commitment to culture (purpose) with customers needs	Match competence to deliver superior performance with customers needs	Match consistency in building and sustaining commitment and competence by rewarding product or human resources with parallel efforts to meet customers needs
Competi-tors	Match commitment with organizations strategic methods for gaining a competitive advantage	Match competence with strategic methods	Match consistency in sustaining culture with competitive methods
Company	Match commitment in order to reinforce companys strategic strengths	Match competence with strategic strengths	Match consistency with strategic strengths

Table 3-5. Nine Box Model of Hickman and Silva

- Adaptive or strong cultures are created by surfacing distinctive norms, assumptions, patterns, activating new directions, establishing new norms, identifying cultural gaps or ruts and closing the gaps

- Bureaucratic and old forms of organizational cultures can stifle entrepreneurial and innovative subcultures

- Culture and cultural beliefs help us understand selfish and self-defeating behaviors

- Subcultural groups (professional, technical, exempt, non- exempt, location) exert a powerful influence in most organizations

- Strong cultures and subcultures can create group-think, blind conformity and limited change (pressures to conform) in addition to a sense of community, loyalty, cohesion and high performance

- Culture values and mission statements must be supported by compatible cultural norms if high performance and effectiveness are to be sustained

- Uncohesive subcultures and groups often display mediocre performance as measured by the number of creative ideas produced

- Cohesive subcultures and groups may actually function to promote values not conducive to the organizational values and mission

- Probe whether the organizational norms and assumptions support the mission, encourage adaptive strategies and structures, motivate members to identify and solve complex problems.

How to uncover cultural assumptions

Conduct clinical interviews in order to: 1) avoid subjectivity bias, and; 2) overcome internal resistance. Follow these guidelines:.

1) When entering the organization, focus on surprises - things differing from expected

2) Be systematic when observing and checking - are these patterned and repeatable experiences, not idiosyncratic events

3) Locate a motivated insider who can help you decipher what is going on

4) Reveal surprises and puzzles to organizational members and observe how others respond

5) Conduct joint explorations with members in order to find explanations to divergent interpretations

6) Formalize your hypothesis or educated guess about the type of cultural and subculture

7) Systematically check and consolidate information, hypothesis and hunches

8) Push analysis to the level of assumptions

9) Adjust interpretations as new data surfaces - modify cultural model

10) Write and describe statements and build a cultural model

Interview

Go back over the history of your organization, when it was founded, and events leading up to the present. Who was involved (important founding figures or leaders)? What were the critical problems of getting started (goals, ways of working, key values)? What were the critical incidents in the organizational life (major events that threatened survival, caused reexamination or reformulation of goals or ways of working)?

A DIAGNOSTIC REVIEW OF ORGANIZATIONAL CULTURE

The culture of any organization provides the foundation, direction and energy for building an innovative organization. An innovative and adaptive culture provides the most general and abstract links to the organizations structure, strategic direction, human resource system, including leadership, managerial competence, problem solving and decision making, or group effectiveness, and external environment. Diagnosing aspects of the organizational culture provides clues regarding values, norms, assumptions and other dimensions that must be surfaced, evaluated and regularly monitored to create and support more effective structures, strategies and human resource and performance outcomes. The following diagnostic assessment questions can assist the organization in its cultural evaluation and monitoring process.

Examining organizational values

- Does the organization recognize and discuss the issues or ethics, values, evil, etc?

- Do the organizational leaders comment upon social problems and value trends in the larger society?

- Is the issue of ethics or values included in any management training programs?

- Does the organization always place the blame on someone else when problems occur?

- Does the organization try to discredit outside critics?

- Does the organization have a policy of always firing so called "trouble makers"?

- Does the organization try to consistently suppress information of interest to stockholders, employees and society?

- Does the organization try to cover up and counter significant problems with a major public relations campaign rather than addressing the issue head on?

- Is the organization guilty of constant denial of problems?

- Can you identify value factions between divisions, professions, departments which are becoming dysfunctional for the larger organization?

Desirable behaviors for facilitating positive work values

Organizational values and processes can be evaluated by focusing upon those behaviors desirable in your organization - check the following:

- Working with people who can be trusted and relied upon to pitch in and make a contribution to get the important work done

- Engaging in work activities that really make a difference

- Being in an organization with leaders and managers who desire interaction, treat all workers with respect, understanding and concern

- Being in an organization that recognizes and rewards competence and performance

- Working in an organization that is built upon a belief that long term loyalty and trust will pay off in fair treatment and compensation

- The organization understands the value of team work and cooperative work arrangements

Surfacing organizational stories

Organizational stories can be surfaced by considering the following questions:

- Do certain stories indicate how the company is different from its competitors?

- How do the stories serve the purpose of entertainment, giving information, fulfilling dreams, increasing motivation?

- Are stories used to convey measures to outside stakeholders, in order to elicit their confidence and support?

- Do the experiences of important leaders, past presidents or high officers appear frequently?

- Do stories differ in various organizational sectors?

- Do stories tend to support the belief that in the long-run employees will be dealt with justly?

- Do stories indicate what is of interest to the collective?

Surfacing organizational rituals and ceremonies

- How often does your organization meet in ritualistic or ceremonial occasions -- conventions, stockholders meetings, founders remembrances. Are special costumes, props, preparations and presentations a part of such ceremonies?

- Do you utilize ritual and ceremony to clarify aspects of formal structure?

- Do you use ritual and ceremony to create order and predictability in the face of problems that are complex, mysterious and which create much anxiety in the organization?

- How is humor used or expressed in the organization?

Uncovering organizational myths

- Do our myths express our common purposes, our structure and human resource beliefs?

- Do we utilize myths to maintain solidarity and cohesion?

- Do we utilize myths to legitimize, communicate unconscious wishes and mediate conflicts and contradictions?

- Do we utilize myths to provide a rich narrative to anchor the present in the past and vice-versa?

- Do our myths work too often to protect us from uncertainty and keep in the dark?

Detecting supportive organizational norms

- Do norms support the sharing of information with other groups, departments, or divisions?

- Do norms support innovation, risk taking, provide rewards for creativity?

- Do norms support equality in treatment and reward, trust honesty, and openness in communication?

- Do norms support duplication of work, protection of territory and turf?

- Do norms support the social and expressive needs to allow socializing with ones entire work group, other departments or divisions?

- Do norms allow for the recognition of time for leisure, community service, family and friends as being important as tasks at work?

- Do norms protect leaders and managers from receiving bad news from employees until it is too late because they fear bringing up bad news?

- Do norms encourage waste, laziness, cheating, and lack of discussion of organizational ethics?

CHAPTER FOUR
PERSONALITY AND JOB DESIGN MODELS

1   PERSONALITY THEORIES

Trait Approach

Traits are defined as inferred predispositions that direct the behavior of an individual in consistent and characteristic ways. Traits produce consistencies in behavior because they are enduring attributes, and they are general or broad in scope.

Strengths:
- Provides a catalog which **describes** the individual

Weaknesses
- Does not explain how behavior is causally determined
- Does not offer insight into the development and dynamics of personality
- Is not helpful in predicting behavior across a spectrum of situations

Humanistic Theories

These theories emphasize the importance of how people perceive their world and all the forces influencing them. The theories emphasize growth and self-actualization, the constant striving to realize inherent potential.

Strengths:
- Emphasizes the **person** and the importance of self-actualization to personality
- Recognizes the importance of healthy self-esteem for productive group and organizational functioning

Weaknesses:
- Does not clearly explain the origin of mechanisms for attaining self-actualization
- Negates the reality of functioning in a complex environment

Psychodynamic Theories

Accounts for individual differences in personality by suggesting that people deal with their fundamental drives differently. Freud suggests a constant battle between two parts of personality: the id and the superego, moderated by the ego.
- Id - unconscious part of the personality; operates irrationally and impulsively
- Superego - values, attitudes; corresponds roughly to conscience
- Ego - represents the picture of physical and social reality, consequences; acts as the arbitrator between the id and superego; uses such defense mechanisms as rationalization, identification, compensation, and denial of reality.

Strengths:
- Integrates the characteristics of people and **explains** the dynamic nature of personality development
- Emphasis on unconscious determinants of behavior
- Gave impetus to study of child development
- Psychoanalysis has added to our understanding of how to get people back on the right track toward effective personal functioning
- Recognizes the importance of understanding how repression of our deepest needs can explain conflict

Weaknesses:
- Downplays the importance of cognitive and rational processes in personality and interpersonal malfunctioning
- Ignores the productive role of myths, rituals and other collective forms of group culture that Freud thought reflected collective neurosis or sickness

PERSONALITY TYPES

Receptive - submissive, conforming, dominated

Exploitive - user, manipulative, calculating

Hoarding - miser, possessive, acquisitive

Marketing - trades anything for gain

Productive - creative, adaptive, can be any of the other types when needed

Authoritarian

- The superior/subordinate relationship is important.
- Submissive, super receptive to superiors
- Autocratic , domineering of subordinates
- Rules and regulations very important
- Dependent on structure in organization
- Class differentials
- Ethnocentric, racial distinctions

Machiavellian

- Exploitive type
- Extremely manipulative
- Views others as puppets on a string
- Only interested in means - not ends
- Does not make good decisions
- Prefers con-artistry
- No emotional attachments with object of manipulation
- Does not correlate with any other personality trait or construct
- Does not correlate with I.Q.

66

2   PERSONALITY AND BEHAVIOR

An issue of interest to behavioral scientists and researchers is whether personality factors can predict behavior or performance in organizations. Typically a few select personality factors such as locus of control, tolerance of ambiguity, Machiavellianism, or androgyny are used to examine behavior and performance.

Locus of Control

- **Internal** - believing oneself to be autonomous, master of one's own fate, holding responsibility for what happens to ones self

- **External** - believing oneself to be a helpless pawn of fate, controlled by outside forces over which there is little or no influence

It is generally found that internally controlled employees are more satisfied with their jobs, more likely to be in managerial positions and more satisfied with a participative management style. Studies have shown internalizers perceive less stress and employ more task-centered coping behavior.

Tolerance of Ambiguity

- **Intolerance of ambiguity** - tendency to perceive ambiguous situations as sources of threat

- **Tolerance of ambiguity** - tendency to perceive ambiguous situations as desirable

In various work situations involving change in technology, structure, or personnel the tolerance of ambiguity factor could be significant in understanding or predicting behavior.

Machiavellianism - concern with how people can be manipulated and with what orientations and tactics differentiate those who wield influence from those who are influenced.

Androgyny - refers to the blending of behavior and personality traits traditionally associated with one or the other sexual identity. The androgynous person has both masculine and feminine traits in fairly equal proportions, and is able to respond to situational demands with the most effective behavior for the particular situation.

Studies have shown that androgynous individuals are more independent, nurturant, supportive, have higher self-esteem, social competence and achievement orientations.

3   PERSONALITY AND JOB FIT

Personality plays an important role in the issue of "proper job fit". Obviously, an authoritarian personality type would not fit comfortably into a highly participatory management role, nor a person with a low tolerance of ambiguity fit into a highly unstructured environment. Hence the use of personality tests or profiles as a part of the hiring process.

As individuals, we tend to have a blend of many types of personality, with one strong, dominant type. We also tend to change our personality somewhat to fit our environment. One word of caution, as mentioned in the introduction to this section, personality does interact with other factors in determining behavior of individuals in organizations. Some organizational behaviorists and consultants prefer to emphasize the more surface levels of observable behaviors and management styles, problem solving or leadership. We will explore this theme later in this section.

4   CLASSICAL JOB DESIGN: SCIENTIFIC MANAGEMENT

This theory, first defined by Frederick Taylor, suggests that jobs should be simplified, standardized, and specialized for each component of the required work (44). Organizations utilize this basic work design format by breaking each job into small, workable units (See Figure 4-1), and standardizing procedures for performing, teaching and motivating workers to perform their job tasks under conditions of high efficiency. The assembly line has been the most well-known adaptation of this design.

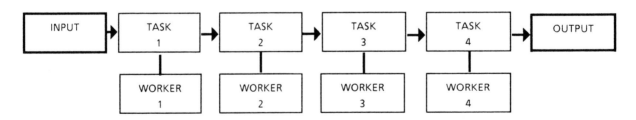

Figure 4-1. Classical Job Design Model

5   JOB DESIGN

According to Hackman and Lawler, "Job design concerns the content, functions, and relationships of jobs that are directed toward the accomplishment of organizational purposes and the satisfaction of the personal needs of the individual job holder"(45).

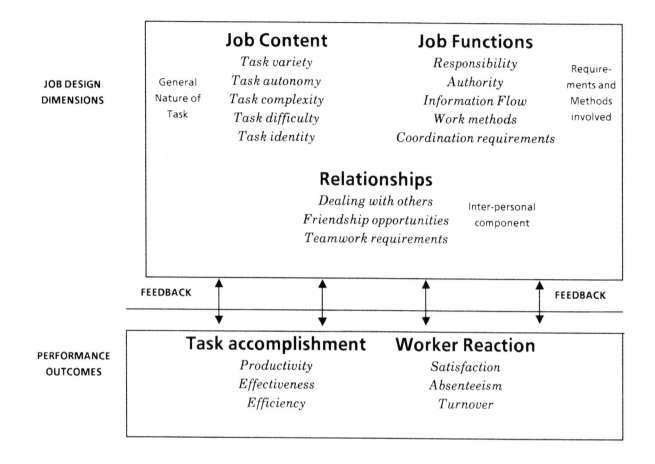

Figure 4-2 A Framework for Job Design

6 JOB CHARACTERISTICS

The most complete and best known theory for explaining worker responses to job characteristics is that presented by Hackman and Oldham (see Figure 4-3). They propose that any job can be described in terms of five core job dimensions (46):

- Skill variety
- Task identity
- Task significance
- Autonomy
- Feedback

These core dimensions are said to influence certain critical psychological states of workers. High levels of critical psychological states will lead to favorable personal and work outcomes.

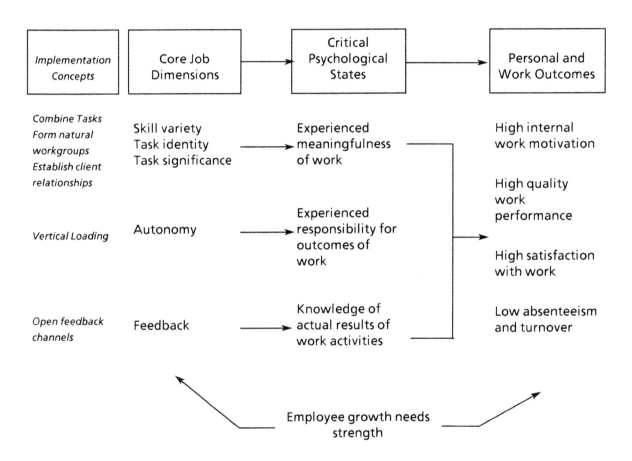

Figure 4-3. Job Characteristics Model

This theory proposes that people with high needs for personal growth and development (GNS) should respond more positively to jobs which are high on the core dimension, than people with low growth needs strength.

7 JOB ROTATION

Job rotation stemmed from problems with the scientific management design of jobs. The premise is that various tasks performed by workers are interchangeable, and workers can be "rotated" from task to task without any major disruption in the work flow (see Figure 4-4).

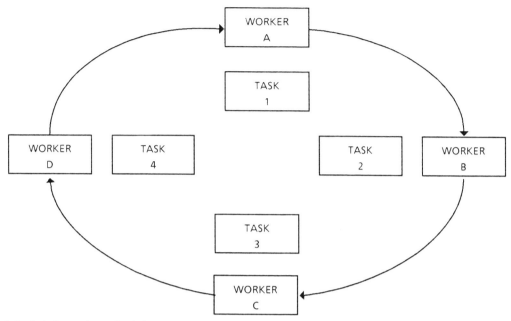

Figure 4-4. Job Rotation Model

8 JOB ENLARGEMENT

Job enlargement also stemmed from problems with the scientific management design of jobs. The basic feature is the horizontal expansion of jobs to include a greater variety of tasks. This involves increasing the number and variety of tasks performed by an individual worker (see Figure 4-5).

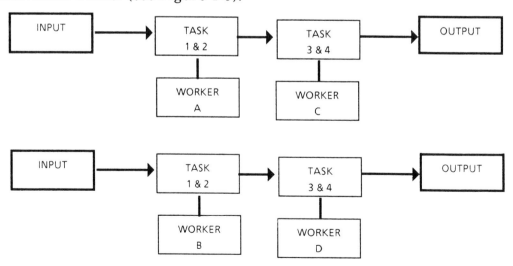

Figure 4-5. Job Enlargement Model

9   JOB ENRICHMENT

Job enrichment is based on Frederick Herzberg's Two-Factor Theory, focusing on "vertical loading" changes to the work itself. The theory is a concept of restructuring and redesigning the activities and elements that make up a job (see Figure 4-6). The starting point are those elements that motivate and satisfy workers.

Some examples of enrichments are:

● **Responsibility** - increase workers responsibility in production, quality control, and maintenance

● **Decision making** - increase workers authority and autonomy

● **Feedback** - provide direct feedback to worker

● **Accountability** - reward on basis of degree to which mutually agreeable performance goals are met

● **Personal growth and development** - provides new learning experiences, elicits workers suggestions, structures career growth

● **Achievement** - comes as a result of the aspects listed above

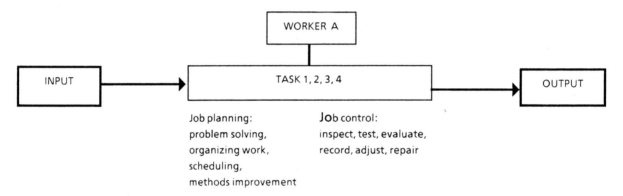

Figure 4-6. Job Enrichment Model

10   JOB REDESIGN

This theory is based on Abraham Maslow's Needs Hierarchy Theory which suggests that some jobs offer workers the opportunity to satisfy material and security needs, social needs, and higher order needs. Job redesign addresses the necessity for an organization to design jobs to fit the important differences that exist among individual employees. Job redesign utilizes Maslow's needs hierarchy by considering two broad need categories:

- **Lower level needs** - safety, security, social
- **Higher level needs** - ego, status, self-actualization

Many organizations already satisfy lower-level needs through highly specialized jobs (scientific management). An effort needs to be made in the design of jobs for employees with higher-order needs to be satisfied.

The following dimensions suggest that for higher-level needs satisfaction:

- The job should allow a worker to feel personally responsible for a meaningful portion of his or her work.

- The job should involve doing something that is intrinsically meaningful or otherwise experienced as worthwhile to the individual.

- The job should provide feedback about what is accomplished.

The following are suggestions for increasing the core job characteristic dimensions:

- Combine tasks - task variety and task identity
- Form natural work units - task identity and task significance
- Establish client relationships - opportunity to increase variety, autonomy and feedback
- Vertical loading - impacts autonomy, variety, task identity, and significance
- Open feedback channels.

A word of caution: Individual characteristics are dynamic and may change over time. Managers should avoid "pigeon-holeing" an employee into a box without readdressing and reassessing at some future point. No manager should attempt to enlarge or enrich the jobs of all employees.

1   A MODEL OF MOTIVATION

Motives are expressions of a persons needs; they are personal and internal.
Incentives are external to the person, a part of the environment; in the work
environment, they are used by management to encourage workers to accomplish
tasks. Figure 5-1 shows the relation of needs to performance.

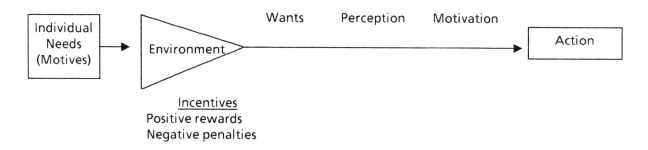

Figure 5-1. A model of motivation (47:43)

Types of Needs.   A simple way of classifying needs is to break them into two
categories:

1) Basic physiological needs (primary) - food, water, sleep, sex, air

2) Social and psychological needs (secondary) - self- esteem, sense of duty,
   self-assertion, giving, belonging, receiving affection.

The secondary needs are more vague because they represent needs of the mind and
spirit, rather than the physical body. These needs are the ones that complicate the
motivational efforts of managers. Nearly any action that management takes will
affect secondary needs. **Therefore, management planning should consider the
effect of any proposed action on the secondary needs of employees.**

Different viewpoints of motivation theorists leads to a number of different
conclusions:

● The analysis of motivation should concentrate on content factors that
   arouse or incite a persons activities (48)

- Motivation is process oriented, and concerns choice, direction, and goals

- Motivation also concerns how behavior is started, sustained, or stopped, and what kind of subjective reaction is present in the person while this is going on (49).

Our discussion of various motivation theories will provide a basic understanding of each as well as some of the advantages and disadvantages of each. The theories included in this chapter are of value to the researcher and practitioner in attempting to develop a better understanding of organizational behavior.

2   CONTEMPORARY APPROACHES TO MOTIVATION

Type	Characteristics	Theories	Managerial Examples
Content	Concerned with factors that arouse, start, or initiate motivated behavior	1. Need hierarchy theory 2. Two-factor theory 3. ERG theory	Motivation by satisfying individual needs for money, status, and achievement
Process	Concerned not only with factors that arouse behavior, but also the process, direction, or choice of behavioral patterns	1. Expectancy theory 2. Equity theory	Motivation through clarifying the individuals perception of work inputs, performance requirements, and rewards
Reinforcement	Concerned with the factors that will increase the likelihood that desired behavior will be repeated	1. Reinforcement theory (operant conditioning)	Motivation by rewarding desired behavior

Table 5-1

3 HIERARCHY OF NEEDS THEORY

Maslow's Needs Hierarchy Theory postulates that people in the workplace are motivated to perform by a desire to satisfy a set of internal needs. Maslow's framework is based on three functional assumptions (50):

1) People are wanting beings whose needs can influence their behavior. Only unsatisfied needs can influence behavior; satisfied needs do not act as motivators.

2) A persons needs are arranged in an order of importance, or hierarchy (see Table 5-2), from the basic (e.g., food and shelter) to the complex (e.g., growth and achievement).

3) The person advances to the next level of the hierarchy, or from basic to complex needs, only when the lower need is at least minimally satisfied.

GENERAL FACTORS	NEED LEVELS	ORGANIZATIONAL SPECIFIC FACTORS
Growth Achievement Advancement	**Self-actualization** *(Fulfill oneself to the highest of ones potential)*	1. Challenging job 2. Creativity 3. Advancement in organization 4. Achievement in work
Recognition Status Self-esteem Self-respect	**Ego, Status, and Esteem** *(Feeling of self confidence and prestige)*	1. Job title 2. Merit pay increase 3. Peer/supervisory recognition 4. Work itself 5. Responsibility
Companionship Affection Friendship	**Social** *(Feeling of belonging)*	1. Quality of supervision 2. Compatible work group 3. Professional friendships
Safety Security Competence Stability	**Safety and Security** *(Need for freedom from threat, protection against danger)*	1. Safe working conditions 2. Fringe benefits 3. General salary increases 4. Job security
Air Food Shelter Sex	**Physiological** *(Basic, primary needs)*	1. Heat and air conditioning 2. Base salary 3. Cafeteria 4. Working conditions

Table 5-2. Maslow's Need Hierarchy

Table 5-2 also shows the general needs of humans grouped in Maslow's hierarchy. Also included are specific organizational factors relating to these needs.

4   TWO-FACTOR THEORY

Based on research with engineers in the late fifties, Frederick Herzberg developed a two-factor content theory of motivation. "The study was designed to test the concept that man has two sets of needs: his need as an animal to avoid pain and his need as a human to grow psychologically" (51). Herzberg based his research on questions concerning what circumstances were in existence when these engineers experienced extreme job satisfaction. He also asked the same question in reverse, when they experienced extreme job dissatisfaction. His studies concluded, unlike other theorists who "assumed that motivation and lack of motivation were merely opposites of one factor on a continuum" (52), that there are two separate factors which influence motivation.

HYGIENE FACTORS VERSUS TRUE MOTIVATORS	
HYGIENE FACTORS	*MOTIVATORS*
Pay Fringe Benefits Good Working Conditions Security Status Company Policies Quality of Technical Supervision Interpersonal Relations	Satisfaction Value Creativity Challenge Contribution Responsibility Achievement Accomplishment Pride/Recognition Work Itself Advancement
External When met = no dissatisfaction When not met = dissatisfaction	Internal When met = sense of commitment and job satisfaction When not met = lack of commitment

Table 5-3

Herzberg calls the first set of factors "motivator needs" or "satisfiers". These produce job satisfaction and motivate the worker to the highest possible level of performance. The motivator needs can only be satisfied by stimulating, challenging, and absorbing work. (See Table 5-3).

The other set of factors produce job dissatisfaction when they are not met. These, Herzberg calls "hygiene" or "maintenance" needs. He found that while these needs, when unmet can produce dissatisfaction, however, when they are met do not produce job satisfaction. When they are met, they merely keep the worker from being dissatisfied.

Motivational factors such as achievement and responsibility mostly are related directly to the job itself, the employees performance, and the recognition and growth

Hygiene Seeker	Motivation Seeker
Motivated by nature of the environment	Motivated by nature of the task
Chronic and heightened dissatisfaction with various aspects of his job context, e.g., salary, supervision, working conditions, status, job security, company policy and administration, fellow employees	Higher tolerance for poor hygiene factors
Overreaction with satisfaction to improvement in hygiene factors	Less reaction to improvement in hygiene factors
Short duration of satisfaction when the hygiene factors are improved	Similar
Overreaction with dissatisfaction when hygiene factors are not improved	Milder discontent when hygiene factors need improvement
Realizes little satisfaction from accomplishments	Realizes great satisfaction from accomplishments
Shows little interest in the kind and quality of work he does	Shows capacity to enjoy the kind of work he does
Cynicism regarding positive virtues of work and life in general	Has positive feelings toward work and life in general
Does not profit professionally from experience	Profits professionally from experience
May be successful on the job because of talent	May be an overachiever

Table 5-4. Characteristics of Hygiene and Motivation Seekers

that are secured from it. Maintenance factors are mainly related to job context, because they concern the environment external to the job. This shows that employees primarily are motivated strongly by what they do for themselves.

Table 5-4 depicts the characteristics of hygiene and motivation seekers.

5 ERG THEORY

This theory, defined by Alderfer, attempts to establish human needs in organizational settings and suggests three basic human needs:

Existence (E); Relatedness (R); Growth (G)

The theory is based upon three major propositions (53):

1) The less each level of need has been satisfied, the more it will be desired;

2) The more lower-level needs have been satisfied, the greater the desire for higher-level needs;

3) The less the higher-level needs have been satisfied, the more the lower-level needs will be desired.

Growth	Creative or Personal	• Development of new capabilities • Challenging work • Autonomy • Creativity
Relatedness	Interpersonal Relationships	• Sharing of feelings • Mutuality of feelings • Emotional support • Respect • Recognition • Sense of belonging
Existence	Physiological hunger thirst shelter	• Pay • Benefits • Physical working conditions • Job security

Table 5-5. Organizational Factors Related to Different Levels of Needs

6 COMPARISON OF CONTENT MOTIVATION THEORIES

This figure depicts the relationship between the three content motivation theories which focus on the question of what it is that arouses, energizes or starts behavior.

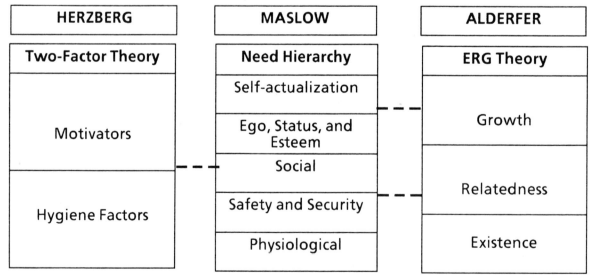

Figure 5-2. Content Motivation Theories (54:94)

7   LEARNED NEEDS THEORY

This theory, as defined by McClelland, proposes that certain needs are acquired (learned) from our culture, three of which are (55):

- Need for Achievement (nAch) - concern for improving performance
- Need for Affiliation (nAff) -   concern   for   establishing, maintaining, and repairing social relations
- Need for Power (nPow) -   concern with reputation, influence and impact

McClelland proposes that when a need is strong in a person, its effect is to motivate the person to use behavior which leads to satisfaction of the need.

Because of the theory that needs are learned, dramatic improvements can occur by stimulating the need for achievement, this approach can have a significant impact on motivation in general. The theory postulates that motivation can be taught in an organizational setting.

McClelland and his associates have developed a profile on high achievers (56):

- High nAch people prefer to set their own performance goals
- High nAch people prefer moderate goals (to easy or difficult goals) which they believe are achievable
- High nAch people prefer immediate and efficient feedback on their performance
- High nAch people enjoy responsibility for solving problems

McClelland suggests the following for developing a positive high need for achievement within workers:

1) Arrange tasks allowing periodic feedback
2) Seek positive models for achievement
3) Develop a positive self-regard
4) Think in realistic terms, plan for the accomplishment of goals.

8   EXPECTANCY THEORY

Expectancy theory, the first of the Process Theories, relates to choice of behavior. Vroom believed that individuals will evaluate various strategies of behavior and then choose the particular strategy that they believe will lead to those work-related rewards that they value.

Vroom (57) explains, as shown in Figure 5-3, that motivation is a product of how much one wants something (valence) and one's estimate of the probability that a certain action will lead to achieving it (expectancy).

VALENCE (strength of one's desire for something)	**X**	**EXPECTANCY** (probability of getting it with a certain action)	**=**	**MOTIVATION** (strength of drive toward an action)

Figure 5-3. Expectancy Model

The valence-expectancy relationship may exist in an infinite number of combinations, as seen in Figure 5-4.

The theory states there are two outcomes to an action: primary and secondary. Primary outcomes result directly from an action. Secondary outcomes follow from the primary outcome. An example is represented in Figure 5-5.

Expectancy

		High	Low
Positive	High	Strong motivation (e.g., .8 x .8 = .64)	Moderate motivation (e.g., .8 x .3 - .24)
Valence	Low	Moderate motivation (e.g., .3 x .8 = .24)	Weak motivation (e.g., .3 x .3 = .09)
Negative	High	Strong avoidance (e.g., -.8 x .8 = -.64)	Moderate avoidance (e.g., -.8 x .3 = -.24)
	Low	Moderate avoidance (e.g., -.3 x .8 = -.24)	Weak avoidance e.g., -.3 x .3 = -.09)

Figure 5-4. Combinations of valence and expectancy

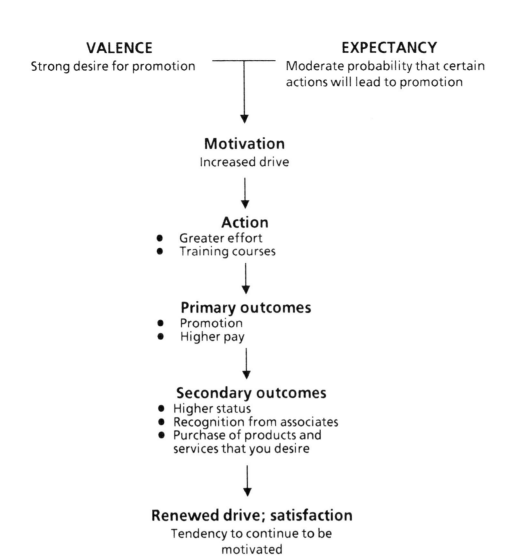

VALENCE
Strong desire for promotion

EXPECTANCY
Moderate probability that certain actions will lead to promotion

Motivation
Increased drive

Action
- Greater effort
- Training courses

Primary outcomes
- Promotion
- Higher pay

Secondary outcomes
- Higher status
- Recognition from associates
- Purchase of products and services that you desire

Renewed drive; satisfaction
Tendency to continue to be motivated

Figure 5-5. Operation of the Expectancy Model (58)

9   EQUITY THEORY

Equity theory (Adams) states that if individuals perceive a discrepancy between the amount of rewards they receive and their efforts, they are motivated to reduce those efforts; furthermore, the greater the discrepancy, the more the individual is motivated to reduce the effort (59). The discrepancy is a perceived one between two or more individuals, and may be based on subjective perception or objective reality.

Figure 5-6 represents a comparison of one individual to another in terms of work efforts and rewards. The satisfaction of Focal Person A is perceived by Focal Person B.

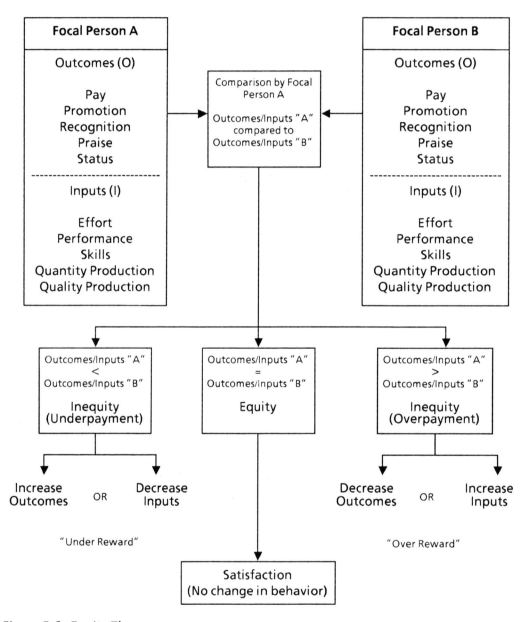

Figure 5-6. Equity Theory

10 REINFORCEMENT THEORY

Types Of Reinforcement

Skinner suggests four types of reinforcement available to a manager for motivating an employee to modify their behavior:

- **Positive Reinforcement** - increases the likelihood that a particular behavior (desired) will be repeated

  Example - a foreman asks a worker to increase his output by ten percent (10%) (**stimulus**), the worker exerts extra energy to do so and is successful (**response**), and in turn, receives a bonus (**positive reinforcement**) (see Figure 5-7).

- **Punishment** - decreases the likelihood that a particular behavior (undesired) will be repeated

  Example - the worker above does not exert the necessary energy needed to increase his output and, in fact, decreases this output (**response**), is called in to the production managers office and is reprimanded (**punishment**).

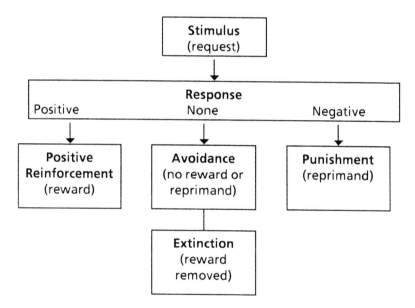

Figure 5-7. Four Types of Reinforcement

- **Negative Reinforcement or Avoidance** - strengthens desired behavior through the workers avoidance of punishment

  Example - the above worker does not put out the extra effort to increase his output, but maintains his current output (**response**) and receives no reward or punishment (**avoidance**).

- **Extinction** - decreases a particular behavior by the withholding of positive reinforcement for a previously acceptable behavior

  Example - the foreman above has rewarded workers for increasing output with a bonus (**positive reinforcement**). This has become too costly to the organization, and the bonus' are removed (**extinction**). The workers reduce their output to normal levels (**response**).

Table 5-6 shows the relationship between the stimulus, response and result of the different types of reinforcement.

Types of Reinforcement	Stimulus	Response	=	Result
Positive Reinforcement- increases likelihood of desired behavior being repeated	Increase output will be rewarded	Worker increases output	=	Reward
Punishment - decreases likelihood of undesired behavior being repeated	Increase output will be rewarded	Worker decreases output	=	Reprimand
Avoidance - increases likelihood of desired behavior by knowledge of consequences	Increase output will be rewarded	Worker maintains normal output	=	No reward No reprimand
Extinction - removal of positive reinforcement to decrease or eliminate undesired behavior	Increase output will not be rewarded	Worker returns to normal output	=	No reward

Table 5-6. Results of Reinforcement

Schedules Of Reinforcement. Two broad classifications of reinforcement schedules (the manner in which reprimands or rewards are given) are identified as continuous and intermittent. In combination, four general types of reinforcement schedules are possible: fixed interval, fixed ratio, variable interval, and variable ratio (see Figure 5-8).

- Continuous - behavior is reinforced at each occurrence
- Intermittent - behavior is reinforced at some occurrences and not others

  - interval schedule - reinforcements are given after a passage of a certain amount of time
  - ratio schedule - after a certain number of occurrences of desired behavior
  - fixed schedule - unchanging format
  - variable schedule - constantly changing format

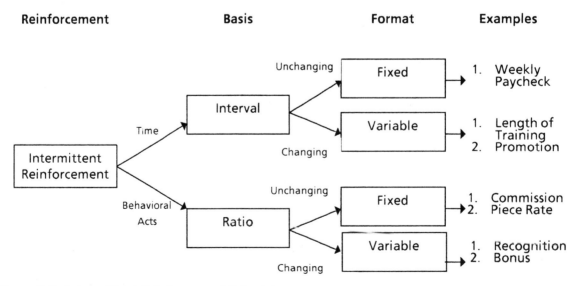

Figure 5-8. Intermittent Reinforcement Schedules

86

11   OPERANT CONDITIONING

Operant conditioning (Skinner) is not a single, accepted theory, but a set of fundamental ideas and principles.

● There is an emphasis on objective, measurable behavior (an example: number of units produced)

● There are contingencies of reinforcement: the sequence of stimulus, response and reward (an example: a foreman telling a worker that if he increases the number of units produced by ten percent (stimulus), he will receive a five percent bonus (consequence); the worker does this (performance/response) and receives the bonus (reward). See Figure 5-9.

● Reinforcement schedule is important: the shorter the time interval between performance and consequence or reward, the greater the effect on behavior (an example: if the above worker receives his five percent bonus immediately, he will more than likely respond positively to the next request). See Figure 5-10.

● Value and size of reinforcement is important: the greater the value and size of the reward to the individual, the greater the effect on subsequent behavior (an example: had the foreman above offered a reward of low value to the worker, he may not have put out the extra effort to achieve it). See Figure 5-11.

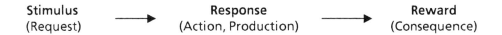

Figure 5-9. Contingencies of Reinforcement

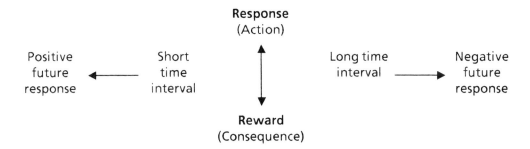

Figure 5-10. Reinforcement Schedule

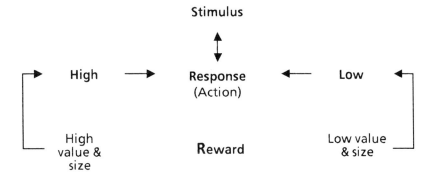

Figure 5-11. Value and Size of Reinforcement

87

TYPE /THEORY NAME	THEORIST	MAIN POINTS	MANAGEMENT USES
CONTENT			
Hierarchy of Needs	Abraham Maslow	• Only unsatisfied needs are motivators • Human needs are arranged in a hierarchical order of importance: Self-Actualization Ego, status, self-esteem Social Safety and security Physiological • Humans advance to the next higher level only when the lower level needs are satisfied	Motivation Job Enrichment Leadership - Participative Open Communications
Two-Factor Theory	Frederick Herzberg	• Humans have two sets of needs: Hygiene Factors (HF) - Pay, security, status, good working conditions, social Motivators (M) - Challenge, responsibility, achievement, accomplishment, advancement HF HF M not met met met ‾‾‾‾‾‾‾‾‾‾‾‾‾‾‾‾‾‾‾‾‾‾‾‾‾‾‾‾‾ - 0 + Dissatisfaction No satisfaction Satisfaction	Motivation Job Enrichment Open Communications
ERG	Clayton Alderfer	• Three basic human needs: Growth - Creativity Relatedness - Interpersonal Existence - Physiological • Levels that are not met are desired • Higher-level needs are desired when lower-level needs are satisfied • Lower-level needs are desired when higher-level needs are not satisfied	Motivation Job Enrichment Open Communications

Table 5-7. A Comparison of Motivation Theories

MOTIVATION THEORIES (continued)

TYPE / THEORY NAME	THEORIST	MAIN POINTS	MANAGEMENT USES
CONTENT (cont'd)			
Learned Needs	David McClelland	• Many needs are learned from our culture - Need for Achievement - Need for Affiliation - Need for Power	Motivation - can be taught Job Enrichment Profile for high achievers Profile for developing a high need for achievement
PROCESS			
Expectancy Theory	Victor Vroom	• Humans evaluate various strategies and choose the one most likely to succeed based on experience	Motivation Path-goal Leadership Goal Setting Management by Objectives
Equity Theory	J. Stacy Adams	• If humans do not perceive the rewards to be great enough, they reduce their efforts	Motivation Equitable pay and reward systems
BEHAVIORAL			
Reinforcement Theory	B. F. Skinner	• Through the use of reinforcement, a manager can increase or decrease the likelihood of behavior being repeated	Motivation Reward system Performance Appraisals Design of system for achievement
Operant Conditioning	B. F. Skinner	• Emphasis on objective, measurable behavior • Utilizes reinforcement contingencies (stimulus-response-reward) • Reinforcement schedule (short time or long time between stimulus and response) • Value and size of reinforcement - must be of value to worker	Goal Setting Management by Objectives Performance Appraisals Reward Systems

Table 5-7 (continued)

89

13   BEHAVIOR MODIFICATION

Behavior Modification is an approach to motivation using operant conditioning as its foundation. The premise of operant conditioning is that desired behavior will be repeated with reinforcement or rewards. Behavior Modification proponents recommend the use of positive reinforcement. The key is that the reinforcer follow the desired behavior as closely as possible.

Behavior Modification, sometimes referred to as OB MOD (Organizational Behavior Modification) assumes that **behavior** is more important than the needs motives, and values of an individual, and focuses on specific behavior, not the intangibles such as self-esteem and personality.

Some key terms used in behavior modification are described in Table 5-8:

Terms	Definition
Operant conditioning	A type of reinforcement to modify behavior by its consequences
Law of effect	Tendency of a person to repeat behavior that is accompanied by favorable consequences and not to repeat behavior that is accompanied by unfavorable consequences
Positive reinforcement	A favorable consequence that accompanies behavior and encourages repetition of the behavior
Negative reinforcement	Removal of an unfavorable consequence that accompanies behavior
Shaping	Successive reinforcements as behavior comes closer to the desired behavior
Punishment	An unfavorable consequence that accompanies behavior and discourages repetition of the behavior
Extinction	No significant consequence accompanying behavior
Reinforcement schedules	Frequency with which reinforcement accompanies a desired behavior

Table 5-8. Key Terms Used In Behavior Modification

A typical behavior modification program is shown in Figure 5-12, and usually follows a specific development format.

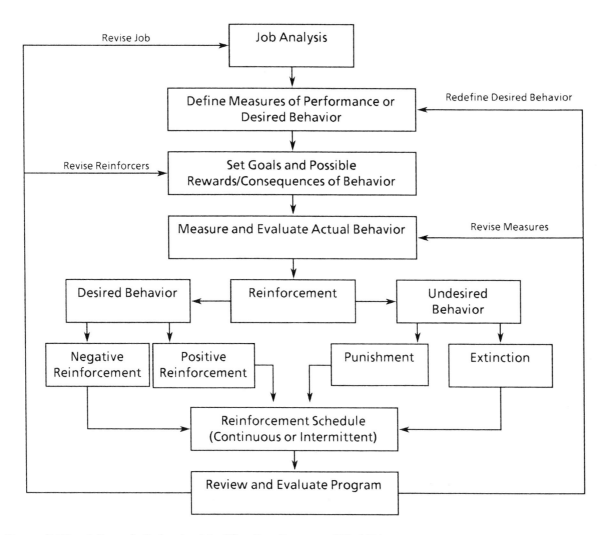

Figure 5-12. A Sample Behavior Modification Program (60:111)

Some guidelines for applying behavior modification are:

- Use positive reinforcement whenever possible.
- Use punishment only in unusual circumstances.
- Ignore undesirable behavior to allow its extinction.
- Use shaping procedures to develop correct complex behavior.
- Minimize the time between the correct response and reinforcement.
- Provide reinforcement frequently.

14 GOAL SETTING

Locke proposed a theory of goal setting that concerns the relationship between conscious goals and task performance (61). Goals are defined simply as what the individual is consciously trying to do. The basic premise of the approach is that an employees conscious goals influence his or her work behavior.

The theory postulates that individual motivation and performance are improved when a worker knows clearly what is expected, and is challenged by what is expected. The goal-setting process requires at least the following factors:

- Proper goal definition - knowing the purpose and necessity of the goal

- Specific, exact goals - definable, measurable, challenging, attainable

- Feedback about progress toward goals - knowing how you are doing in the attainment of the goal.

Goal setting is directly related to each of the three contemporary approaches to motivation.

Theory	Related to Goal Setting
Content	Concerns the needs of the employee. Relating goals to needs and providing the means to attain these goals can result in need satisfaction and improved motivation
Process	Relates to worker outcomes, the valence associated with these outcomes and the process of attaining the outcomes
Reinforcement	Serves as a foundation for the use of reinforcement

Goal setting usually involves five steps as shown in Figure 5-13.

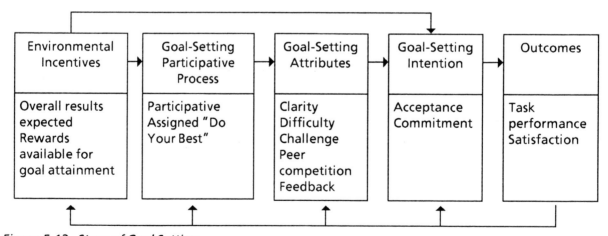

Figure 5-13. Steps of Goal Setting

92

CHAPTER SIX
COMMUNICATION SKILLS AND GROUP BEHAVIOR

1 COMMUNICATION PROCESS

Communication is unavoidable to an organizations functioning; every leader, manager and employee must be a communicator. Despite tremendous advances in communication and information technology, communication between people in organizations leaves much to be desired. Further attention needs to be placed on communicating **effectively**. Figure 6-1 depicts the process of communication from the sender to the receiver via a channel.

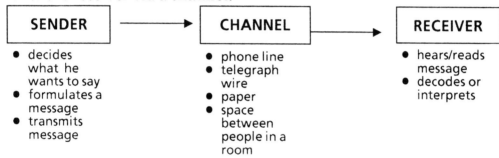

Figure 6-1. The Communication Process

2 BARRIERS TO EFFECTIVE COMMUNICATIONS

Figure 6-2 depicts some of the problems with effective communications between the sender and the receiver through a channel (62).

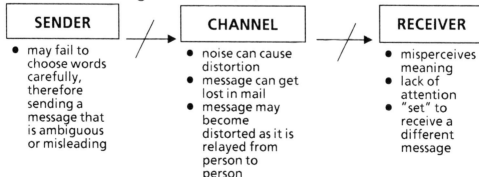

Figure 6-2. Barriers to Communicating Effectively

3 BASIC COMMUNICATION SKILLS

There are several aspects to basic communication skills, which include:

- Listening
- Feedback
- Self-Disclosure
- Problem Solving
- Questioning
- Assertiveness
- Communicating Versus Order-Giving

Listening. Listening involves the ability to understand, acknowledge, and respond to the information being shared by another individual. Effective listening involves:

- An attempt to sense the basic meaning behind what is being said

- Letting the sender of the message know that there is a sincere interest in what is being said

- Attending to the feelings associated with the message being shared

- Avoiding any prejudgment of the senders thoughts and feelings

- Being careful not to intentionally block the sender by moralizing, preaching, interrupting, ignoring, blaming, or humorizing

- An attempt to establish direct eye contact

- An attempt to become aware of the senders nonverbal cues in order to secure additional information

- When appropriate, effective listening requires the restatement of the senders message so that the listener can evaluate the accuracy of his or her perceptions.

Feedback. The receiving of corrective or evaluative information (feedback) is vital to effective communication. It is a skill which provides us with the means for understanding ourselves more thoroughly and accurately. Feedback is often difficult to accept due to its potential impact. Some points on effective feedback are:

- Feedback is most effective when it is given as soon as possible after the behavior occurs

- To avoid miscommunication, feedback should be as specific as possible

- The individual sending the feedback must be willing to take responsibility for what is said

- Feedback should be directed toward behaviors over which the person has some control

- Feedback should be considered as being, in part, a projection of the senders thoughts and/or feelings

- To be most effective, feedback should only be given when the other person has agreed to receive it

- Unless otherwise agreed upon, feedback should be kept in confidence by the individuals involved in the exchange

- Even if the feedback is not well received, it must be given with sensitivity and a respect for the other persons well-being.

Self-Disclosure. Disclosing your thoughts, ideas and feelings allows others to know you as you see yourself. Even though traditionally, little self-disclosure was used in professional settings, self-disclosure is important during certain processes, such as brainstorming, learning, and open communications. The following points will help you increase your ability to share information about yourself:

- Self-disclosure is most potent when an individual is willing to fully examine his or her thoughts and feelings with others
- Self-disclosure should be based upon choice, not upon demand
- Self-disclosure should be related to the topic being discussed or studied
- Self-disclosure is not an all-or-nothing proposition; rather, it can be viewed as being on a continuum, from high to low
- Self-disclosure should never be used to manipulate or coerce others into disclosing
- Whether self-disclosure is given or received, it should be kept confidential
- Self-disclosure is most effective when it is given or received in an environment of trust and support.

Problem Solving. Solving problems creatively and effectively often corresponds to competence in effective communication. Stating the problem accurately, exploring options without undue censorship, examining corresponding consequences, selecting and implementing the choice(s) made, and following up or evaluating are all steps that occur during the problem-solving process. Some points on problem solving are:

- Problem solving often means changing, going beyond habit and routine
- Problem solving demands that an individual expand his or her perceptions, that he or she view a situation from different vantage points
- Problem solving requires that an individual be creative in questioning basic assumptions before moving forward
- Problem solving is often aided by a familiarization with the history of the task at hand: the solutions that have been tried before, the assumptions that have been made previously, the ongoing consequences of the problem
- Problem solving is best implemented in an environment that will support change if the type of recommended change seems reasonable
- Problem solving is often blocked by unrealistic fears and/or expectations
- Problem solving requires a commitment to follow-through and the evaluation of its effects and consequences.

Questioning. Effective questions are well conceived and specific to the area that needs clarification or the information that needs to be obtained. An effective question has a purpose; it is relevant to the situation; it seeks information that the participant is unable, not unwilling, to obtain himself or herself. In developing effective questions, you need to remember several key points:

- Questions should be as specific as possible, and when appropriate, should be related to concrete experiences

- Questions should be asked in the simplest manner possible
- Questions are far more effective if they can be asked as soon as they arise
- Questions should be examined to see if they are disguised statements
- Questions are only effective if a person is willing to listen, without prejudgment, to the answers
- Questions should be asked even when they may be viewed as inappropriate or "stupid"
- Questions, when answered, should be reexamined to see if any points of confusion or doubt still remain
- Questions should not be used for the purpose of manipulating or "leading" another person.

Assertiveness. The ability to stand up for ones needs without violating the needs of others, is an important communication skill. Assertiveness is composed of a variety of skills and strategies, including the following:

- In its most effective form, assertiveness requires the use of the body: a person needs to be in close proximity to the individual being addressed; it is important to maintain direct eye contact, lean forward, and use appropriate gestures
- Assertiveness can be bolstered when a persons facial expression is consistent with the message being sent; for example, laughter is not consistent with the expression of anger
- Assertiveness is more effective when the inflection of a persons voice is forceful and shows no hesitation; it is important, however, to be self-assured without being intimidating
- When a person is assertive, he or she assumes responsibility for his or her own dissatisfaction, i.e., he or she states clearly what he or she finds to be unacceptable, expresses his or her feelings, and lets the other individual know his or her particular needs
- While engaged in assertive behavior, an individual stands up for his or her own needs but also takes into account the needs of the other individual involved in the final resolution or decision
- While engaged in assertive behavior, a person may acknowledge the other individuals message while clearly expressing his or her disagreement with the accuracy of part of all of what the individual has said
- While engaged in assertive behavior, a person may simply repeat his or her concerns or needs until they are finally heard
- While engaged in assertive behavior, a person may meet his or her own needs by using inquiry, instead of argument, to defuse a situation in which he or she is being criticized.

Communicating versus Order-Giving

To make your own leadership, managerial or supervisory approach more positive and truly efficient, stop giving orders and start communicating. Replace confrontation with cooperation.

96

- Speak operationally. Avoid speaking only in abstract terms, such as "trust", "loyalty" and "integrity". Speak in specific terms of behavior you expect. For example, rather than ask an employee to "show enthusiasm" at the next sales conference, ask that employee to "come up with five new ways of looking at the product and present at the next conference".

- When something needs to be done, explain why. Employees who are given orders to do something without the "why" often feel like they are being treated like children or are incapable of understanding the entire picture

- Take responsibility for your own opinions and feelings. Avoid "you" and "we" statements, as they are often offensive to people. Such statements imply that you think you are a superior being who can read their minds and know just what they are thinking and feeling. The use of "I" statements are direct and personal and more readily accepted by employees

- Know what your body language is saying. Be aware of conflicting statements caused by body language

- Hold regular and meaningful meetings. Ask for input into the agenda from employees, and plan time for discussions.

4   ACTIVE LISTENING

One basic responsibility of the manager or executive is the development, adjustment, and integration of individual employees (63). A manager tries to develop employee potential, delegate responsibility, and achieve cooperation. As has been mentioned earlier in this text, a manager must have the ability to listen intelligently and carefully to those with whom he works.

There are many kinds of listening skills, and even some who will say that it isn't a skill at all, but a passive activity. However, effective listening skills to be discussed here will help employees gain a clearer understanding of their situations, take responsibility, and cooperate with each other. "Active listening" is called active because the listener has a very definite responsibility. The listener does not passively absorb the words which are spoken, rather actively tries to grasp the facts and feelings in what he hears, and tries, by listening, to help the speaker work out his own problems.

To be effective, active listening must be firmly grounded in the basic attitudes of the user. Until the listener can demonstrate a spirit which genuinely respects the potential worth of the speaker, which considers his rights and trusts his capacity for self-direction, he cannot be effective.

Active listening is an important way to bring about changes in people:

- clinical and research evidence clearly shows that sensitive listening is a most effective agent for individual personality change and group development

- listening brings about changes in peoples attitudes toward themselves and others, also brings about changes in their basic values and personal philosophy

- people who have been actively listened to become more emotionally mature, more open to experiences, less defensive, more democratic and less authoritarian

- when people are listened to sensitively, they tend to listen to themselves with more care and make clear exactly what they are feeling and thinking

- group members tend to listen more to each other, become less argumentative, more ready to incorporate other points of view

- because active listening reduces the threat of having ones ideas criticized, the person is better able to see them for what they are, and more likely to feel their contributions are worthwhile

- listening provides more information than any other activity, it builds deep, positive relationships and tends to alter constructively the attitudes of the listener.

- By consistently listening to the speaker, the listener is conveying the message that he is interested in the speaker as a person and values his feelings. The demonstration of this message works better than words.

- Listening behavior is contagious, listening can be met with listening.

What to Avoid

When we encounter a person with a problem, our usual response is to try to change his way of looking at things, to get him to see his situation the way we see it, or the way we would like him to see it. We usually respond to our own needs to see the world in certain ways. The major problem for the listener is to free himself from the need to influence and direct others in his own path.

Another problem the listener faces is that of responding to demands for decisions, judgments, and evaluations. The question or challenge frequently is a masked expression of feelings or needs which the speaker is far more anxious to communicate, than he is to have the surface questions answered. Getting to these feelings is oftentimes difficult, yet crucial to full understanding of the message.

Passing judgment, whether critical or favorable, makes free expression difficult. Advice and information are almost always seen as efforts to change a person and thus serve as barriers to his self-expression and the development of a creative relationship. Advice is seldom taken and information hardly ever utilized.

Positive evaluations are sometimes as blocking as negative ones. Encouragement also may be seen as an attempt to motivate the speaker in certain directions or hold him off, rather than as support.

What to Do

Active listening requires that we get inside the speaker, that we grasp, from his point of view, just what it is he is communicating to us. We must convey to the speaker that we are seeing things from his point of view. There are several ways we can accomplish this:

- **Listen for total meaning**. Any message has two components: the content of the message and the feeling or attitude underlying this content. Both give the message meaning. It is the total meaning of the message that we must try to understand.

    Example: A machinist comes to his foreman and says,

    "I've finished that lathe setup"

This message has obvious content and perhaps calls upon the foreman for another work assignment.

    Example: The machinist comes to his foreman and says,

    "Well, I'm finally finished with that damned lathe setup"

The content is the same but the total meaning of the message has changed in an important way for both the foreman and the worker. If the foreman responds by simply giving another work assignment, the employee might feel that he hadn't gotten his message across, that he isn't free to talk to the foreman, that he is going to be more anxious about his next assignment. If the foreman responds with sensitivity to the feelings behind the content of the message, the employee is going to feel that he was heard and understood, that he can talk freely to the foreman, and perhaps build a better relationship with the foreman.

- **Respond to feelings**. In some instances, the content is far less important than the feeling which underlies it. The active listener must respond particularly to the feeling component.

- **Note all cues.** Words alone don't tell us everything that is being communicated. Sensitive listening requires that we become aware of several kinds of communication besides verbal. Hesitations in speech, inflections of voice, facial expressions, body posture, hand movements, eye movements, breathing, can all communicate feelings underlying the content of the message.

Communications

        7%   - words
        38% - tones/inflection
        55% - non-verbal

Testing of Understanding

Because understanding another person is actually far more difficult than it at first seems, it is important to test your ability to see the world in the way the speaker sees it. You can do this by reflecting in your own words what the speaker seems to mean by his words and actions. His response to this will tell you whether or not he feels understood.

Problems in Active Listening

- **The personal risk.** To be effective, one must have a sincere interest in the speaker. Our attitudes always show, and if we only make a pretense of interest in the speaker, he will quickly pick this up, either consciously or unconsciously. He will no longer express himself freely.

  Active listening also carries the risk of the listener being changed, the listener must see himself through anothers eyes -- he must be able to see himself as others see him. It is extremely difficult for a person to free himself from his needs to see things in a way that is comfortable to him.

- **Hostile Expressions.** The listener will often hear negative, hostile expressions directed at himself, which is always difficult to listen to. It is not easy to get to the point where one is strong enough to permit these attacks without finding it necessary to defend himself or retaliate.

- **Out-of-place expressions.** In business and industry any expressions of weakness or incompetency will generally be regarded as unacceptable and therefore will block good two-way communications.

- **Accepting positive feelings.** Negative or hostile feelings or expressions are much easier to deal with in any face-to-face relationship than are truly and deeply positive feelings. This is especially true in the business culture, which expects independent, bold, clever, aggressive expressions and behavior.

- **Emotional danger signals.** The listeners own emotions are sometimes a barrier to active listening.

- **Listening to ourselves.** To listen to oneself is a prerequisite to listening to others. In dealing with the problems of others, it becomes most important to be sure of ones own position, values, and needs.

- **Individual importance.** The kind of behavior which helps the individual will eventually be the best thing that could be done for the group and the organization.

  Groups feel more secure when an individual member is being listened to and provided for with concern and sensitivity. A secure group will ultimately be a better group. When each individual feels that he need not fear exposing himself to the group, he is likely to contribute more freely and spontaneously.

- **Listening and production.** This is no known definite relationship between listening and production, however certain research does point in that direction:

  Employees respond more adequately when they are treated as personalities than as cogs in a machine. If the ego motivations of self-determination, of self-expression, and of a sense of personal worth can be tapped, the individual can be more effectively energized (64).

  Supervisors with better production records give a larger proportion of their time to supervisory functions, especially to the interpersonal aspects of their jobs (65).

- **Maximum creativeness.** The maximum production capacity of employees might be closer to expected heights if we seek to release the motivation that already exists within people rather than try to stimulate them externally.

COMMENTS

We have been communicating since we learned how to get our mothers attention as an infant. As we grew up, our form of communication became more sophisticated. However, as adults communications is one of the major barriers to our effective interactions with others.

This chapter has put forth some ideas, thoughts, and suggestions on how to better communicate.

5   GROUPS AND INTRAGROUP BEHAVIOR

The study and management of groups in organizations is a fundamental concept of organizational behavior. Much of an organizations daily activity and people interactions occur within groups. It is through the actions of groups that many of the managers goals and objectives can be achieved.

In this text we define "a group" as a collection of two or more individuals who are interdependent and interact with one another for the purpose of performing to attain a common goal or objective.

Groups provide the primary mechanism for the attainment of organization goals. In order to provide for effective goal accomplishment, the manager must be familiar with the following group dynamics:

- The process of influencing group behavior toward goal attainment
- The climate for maximum interaction and minimal conflict between group members
- The means for the satisfaction of individual needs within the group.

Group Formation

Some of the reasons groups form within organizations are:

- Task accomplishment - the primary reason for the existence of formal groups in organizations. Some examples are engineering design, maintenance, production, and sales
- Problem-solving - established by the organization for the attainment of some desired goal. These groups are usually temporary and will be disbanded when the problem is solved. Some examples are committees and task forces
- Proximity and attraction - individuals join together if they have similar characteristics, if they interact frequently and if they perceive this interaction to be rewarding. An example is a group of secretaries whose desks are in close proximity
- Socio-psychological - generally occurs when individual needs can be better satisfied in a group. Some of these needs are social, safety, esteem, self-actualization.

Types of Groups

Groups can be classified as formal and informal. Formal groups are those whose primary function is the attainment of organizational goals. Informal groups generally emerge naturally from the interaction of the members and may or may not have goals related to the organizational goals.

Within the organization, the main types of groups are:

- Functional - specified by the structure of the organization. The main factor in this type of group is the relationship between supervisor and subordinates. This type is usually classified as a formal group

- Task or Project - these groups are formed when a number of employees are formally brought together for the purpose of accomplishing a specific task, for a short-term or long-term period. The purpose of the group creates a situation that encourages members to communicate, interact, and to coordinate activities. This type of group also is usually classified as a formal group

- Interest and Friendship - employees form these groups because of common characteristics, such as age, political beliefs, or recreational interests. The groups are formed to attain a common purpose, which may or may not relate to the goals of the organization. Such groups are usually informal and exist until their purposes have been accomplished. However, these groups can form formal groups such as unions, which then become a part of the formal structure of the organization.

There are certain concepts to the discussion of groups and intragroup behavior:

Norms - defined as standards or rules of behavior that are established by group members in order to provide some order to group activities. Norms provide a basis of understanding the behavior of group members and why they initiate their particular action. Norms insure that individual action will be oriented toward group performance.

Norms may apply to every member or they may apply only to some members. Norms may be accepted differently by group members. Different types of norms apply to different positions in the group.

Norm conformity - factors which influence conformity to group norms, and the degree of socialization exhibited by the individual in group activities:

- intelligence - more intelligent individuals are less likely to conform to group norms than less intelligent individuals; more authoritarian individuals are less likely to conform

- situational factors such as group size, structure of the group, and social context of group interaction

- stimulus factors such as clarity of the aspects the group faces at any given time - the more ambiguous the stimulus, the greater will be the conformity to group norms

- intragroup relations include such variables as group pressure, past success records of the group, and group identity

Socialization - the way by which new group members are transformed from outsiders into participating and effective group members. This is important to managers because the way new employees are socialized into the organization will have an effect on the individuals quality of life and level of performance for the organization. There are three stages of socialization in an organization:

- getting in - before entering the organization; includes such organizational programs as recruiting, placement activities which recognize both the needs of the individual and the requirements of the organization, clear discussion of career paths

- breaking in - occurs when the employee enters the organization and attempts to become a participating and contributing member of a work group; includes such programs as orientation sessions, training programs, evaluation systems and work design

- settling - occurs when the employee needs to resolve conflict between work life and home life and conflict between his work group and other work groups in the organization; includes such programs as counseling, flexibility in scheduling and work assignments

Research has identified three individual reactions to socialization:

- Rebellion - the individual rejects and rebels from the norms, values, and procedures of the group
- Conformity - the individual totally accepts all the norms, values, and procedures of the group
- Creative individualism - the individual accepts the basic or most important norms, values, and procedures of the group, but allows some leeway for creative or innovative activity.

Status Systems can clarify the relationships between group members by providing for clear definitions of authority and responsibility. Status is defined as a social ranking within a group and is assigned to an individual on the basis of position in the group or individual characteristics.

Status systems can have a direct influence on group performance through status congruence, which is defined as the agreement between group members on the level of status of individual group members. When there is full agreement, the group is free to accomplish their goals; when there is disagreement on status levels within the group (status incongruence), some group activity is directed toward resolving this conflict.

Roles play an important part in the understanding of group dynamics. Some of the key factors are:

> **Expected roles** - specified by a number of means, including job description, position title, or by organizational structure

> **Perceived roles** - the activities or behaviors in the group that individuals believe they should do

> **Enacted roles** - the way the individual actually behaves

> **Role ambiguity** - lack of clarity regarding job duties, authority, and responsibility which the individual perceives

> **Role conflict** - when multiple demands and directions from one or more individuals creates uncertainty in the workers mind concerning what should be done, when, or for whom

>> **intrarole conflict** - created by multiple directives sent simultaneously to one individual

>> **interrole conflict** - created by many simultaneous roles presenting conflicting expectations.

Group Cohesiveness is regarded as characteristic of the group in which the factors acting on the group members to remain and participate in the group are greater than those acting on members to leave it.

Factors increasing cohesiveness	Factors decreasing cohesiveness
• Agreement on group goals	• Disagreement on goals
• Frequency of interaction	• Group size
• Personal attractiveness	• Unpleasant experiences
• Intergroup competition	• Intragroup competition
• Favorable evaluation	• Domination

6   INFORMAL GROUPS IN ORGANIZATIONS

Human beings are born into a group -- the family. It is within the family and peer groups that we are socialized into ways of behaving and thinking. Our personal identity is derived from the way in which we are perceived and treated by other members of our groups.

Humans have an inherent social nature. People like to be a part of groups, which can have constructive or destructive effects on humans, depending on the nature of the group.

Any effective group has three core activities:

1) accomplishing its goals,
2) maintaining itself internally, and
3) developing and changing in ways that improve its effectiveness.

The Dual Nature of Organizations

Organizations perform two major functions, that of producing a product and that of creating and distributing satisfactions among the individual members of the organization. The first function is called economic and is assessed in terms of costs, profits, and technical efficiency. The second function consists of maintaining employee relations, employee good will and cooperation. This is assessed in terms of labor turnover, tenure on the job, sickness and accident rate, and attitudes. These two functions are interrelated and interdependent.

Informal Groups in Organizations

Many of the actual existing patterns of human interaction have no representation in the formal organization blueprint plans. The formal structure shows the functional relationship between working units but it does not show distinctions of social distance, movement or equilibrium. Formal organizations do not account for the sentiments and values residing in the social organization.

Informal work groups have tremendous power in shaping attitudes, and behavior, and consequently, production. The group determines for the new employees how they feel about management and about all other aspects of organizational life. Individuals perform "role behavior" -- they are expected to do some things and not others by virtue of the position they hold. It is the way that groups work together that either helps or hinders the organizations performance.

The important consideration is the relationship that exists between the informal and formal organization.

Characteristics of Informal Work Groups

Teaching and enforcing groups expectations proceeds in three stages:

1) new workers are told what the situation is, what the group does and likes and what it will not tolerate

2) new employees are observed to see how well they are conforming

3) after an appropriate period of time new workers have either conformed or have not, and appropriate rewards or punishments are accorded

106

Group Cohesion

The degree of closeness of the group is called cohesiveness. The greater the cohesiveness the greater the power of the group over its members to conform. Cohesiveness declines as the group gets larger. Group cohesion needs to be high. Cohesion is based on members liking each other, each members desire to continue as part of the group, the satisfaction of members with their group membership, and the level of acceptance, support and trust among its members. Group norms supporting psychological safety, individuality, creativeness, conflicts of ideas and growth and change need to be encouraged.

Cohesiveness in work groups has a clear positive effect on absenteeism, turnover and tardiness.

High cohesion in work groups stems from two sources:

1) the ability of cohesive groups to reduce member anxiety, and

2) the effectiveness of the group in attaining sources of satisfaction for other needs of its members.

Group Dynamics

Group dynamics refers to the forces operating in groups. The groups to which an employee belongs set standards for their behavior which the employee must accept if they are to remain in the group.

Productivity of work groups can be greatly increased by methods of work organization and supervision that give more responsibility to work groups, which allows for fuller participation in important decisions and which makes stable groups the basis for support of the individuals social needs. Teamwork produces more enduring change because the team provides continuous support and reinforcement for its members.

Groups as Sources of Change

Groups are viewed in three ways:

1) The group is seen as a source of influence over its members. If the group is to be used effectively as a medium of change, then there must be a strong sense of belonging to the same group for those who are to be changed and those who are the influencing factor.

2) The group is viewed as the target of change, rather than the individuals within the group.

3) The group is used as the agent of change. The effectiveness of the change depends on the organization of the group, the members satisfaction and the degree of clarity of goals.

Classification of Member Roles

Group Task Roles: Task roles consist of participant roles that are relevant directly to the task. Their purpose is to facilitate and coordinate the groups effort in the selection and definition of a common problem and the solution to the problem. Hence these roles are identified in relation to these problem solving activities.

Group Building and Maintenance Roles: Roles of this sort are oriented toward the functioning of the group as a group. They are designed to alter or maintain the groups way of working and to strengthen, regulate and perpetuate the group as a group. These roles have the purpose of building group centered attitudes and group centered behavior.

Individual Roles: This role is directed toward the satisfaction of the participants individual needs. Their purpose is some individual goal that is irrelevant to the group task or functioning.

7 TUCKMAN MODEL OF GROUP DEVELOPMENT

Tuckman suggested a developmental sequence -- within both the task realm and the interpersonal realm - of group development. The four stages in this linear, progressive model initially were labeled "forming", "storming", "norming", and "performing". The updated model includes the fifth stage, "adjourning" (66,67). See Table 6-1.

The model is sequential, developmental, and thematic. It is sequential in that the stages occur in a specifically stated order. Each stage will occur naturally, with the timing dependent on the nature of the group, group membership, and group leadership. The model is developmental in that the issues and concerns in each stage must be resolved in order for the group to move to the next stage. The model is thematic in that each stage is characterized by two dominant themes, one reflecting the task dimension and one reflecting the relationship dimension.

Stages of Group Development	Task Behavior	Relationship Behavior
Forming	Orientation - groups task behavior is an attempt to become oriented to the goals and procedures of the group	Testing and dependence
Storming	Resistance or emotional response to task demands	Intragroup and intrapersonal hostility in relationships
Norming	Expression of opinions, cooperation	Development of group cohesion
Performing	Emergence of solutions, problem solving	Functional role-relatedness, group effort is mobilized to achieve group goals
Adjourning	Termination of task behaviors	Disengagement from relationships

Table 6-1. Tuckman Model of Group Development

8 GROUPS VERSUS TEAMS

GROUPS	TEAMS
Members think they are grouped together for administrative purposes only. Individuals work independently; sometimes at cross purposes with others.	Members recognize their interdependence and understand both personal and team goals are best accomplished with mutual support. Time is not wasted struggling over "turf" or attempting personal gain at the expense of others.
Members tend to focus on themselves because they are not sufficiently involved in planning the unit's objectives. They approach their job simply as a hired hand.	Members feel a sense of ownership for their jobs and unit because they are committed to goals they helped establish.
Members are told what to do rather than being asked what the best approach would be. Suggestions are not encouraged.	Members contribute to the organization's success by applying their unique talent and knowledge to team objectives.
Members distrust the motives of colleagues because they do not understand the role of other members. Expressions of opinion or disagreement are considered divisive or non-supportive.	Members work in a climate of trust and are encouraged to openly express ideas, opinions, disagreements and feelings. Questions are welcomed.
Members are so cautious about what they say that real understanding is not possible. Game playing may occur and communications traps be set to catch the unwary.	Members practice open and honest communication. They make an effort to understand each other's point of view.
Members may receive good training but are limited in applying it to the job by the supervisor or other group members.	Members are encouraged to develop skills and apply what they learn on the job. They receive the support of the team.
Members find themselves in conflict situations which they do not know how to resolve. Their supervisor may put off intervention until serious damage is done.	Members recognize conflict is a normal aspect of human interaction but they view such situations as an opportunity for new ideas and creativity. They work to resolve conflict quickly and constructively.
Members may or may not participate in decisions affecting the team. Conformity often appears more important than positive results.	Members participate in decisions affecting the team but understand their leader must make a final ruling whenever the team cannot decide, or an emergency exists. Positive results, not conformity, are the goal.

Table 6-2

110

DIFFERENCES BETWEEN GROUP-CENTERED MANAGERS AND TEAM-CENTERED MANAGERS

GROUP CENTERED	TEAM CENTERED
Overriding concern to meet current goals inhibits thought about what might be accomplished through reorganizing to enhance member contributions.	Current goals are taken in stride. Can be a visionary about what the people can achieve as a team. Can share vision and act accordingly.
Reactive to upper management, peers and employees. Find it easier to go along with the crowd.	Proactive in most relationships. Exhibits personal style. Can stimulate excitement and action. Inspires teamwork and mutual support.
Willing to involve people in planning and problem solving to some extent but, within limits.	Can get people involved and committed. Makes it easy for others to see opportunities for teamwork. Allows people to perform.
Resents or distrusts employees who know their jobs better than their managers.	Looks for people who want to excel and can work constructively with others. Feels role is to encourage and facilitate this behavior.
Sees group problem solving as a waste of time, or an abdication of managerial responsibility.	Considers problem solving the responsibility of team members.
Controls information and communicates only what group members need or want to know.	Communicates fully and openly. Welcomes questions. Allows the team to do its' own filtering.
Ignores conflict between staff members or with other groups.	Mediates conflict before it becomes destructive.
Sometimes slow to recognize individual or group achievements.	Makes an effort to see that both individual and team accomplishments are recognized at the right time in an appropriate manner.
Sometimes modifies group agreements to suit personal convenience.	Keeps commitments and expects the same in return.

Table 6 - 3

10 COMPARISON OF EFFECTIVE AND INEFFECTIVE GROUPS

Effective Groups	Ineffective Groups
Goals are clarified and changed so that the best possible match between individual goals and the groups goals may be achieved; goals are cooperatively structured	Members accept imposed goals; goals are competitively structured
Communication is two-way, and the open and accurate expression of both ideas and feelings is emphasized	Communication is one-way and only ideas are expressed; feelings are suppressed or ignored
Participation and leadership are distributed among all group members; goal accomplishment, internal maintenance, and developmental change are underscored	Leadership is delegated and based upon authority; membership participation is unequal, with high-authority members dominating; only goal accomplishment is emphasized
Ability and information determine influence and power; contracts are built to make sure individual goals and needs are fulfilled; power is equalized and shared	Position determines influence and power; power is concentrated in the authority positions; obedience to authority is the rule
Decision-making procedures are matched with the situation; different methods are used at different times; consensus is sought for important decisions; involvement and group discussions are encouraged	Decisions are always made by the highest authority; there is little group discussion; members' involvement is minimal
Controversy and conflict are seen as a positive key to members involvement, the quality and originality of decisions, and the continuance of the group in good working condition	Controversy and conflict are ignored, denied, avoided, or suppressed
Interpersonal, group, and intergroup behavior are stressed; cohesion is advanced through high levels of inclusion, affection, acceptance, support, and trust. Individuality is endorsed	The functions performed by members are emphasized; cohesion is ignored and members are controlled by force. Rigid conformity is promoted
Problem-solving adequacy is high	Problem-solving adequacy is low
Members evaluate the effectiveness of the group and decide how to improve its functioning; goal accomplishment, internal maintenance, and development are all considered important	The highest authority evaluates the groups effectiveness and decides how goal accomplishment may be improved; internal maintenance and development are ignored as much as possible; stability is affirmed
Interpersonal effectiveness, self-actualization, and innovation are encouraged	"Organizational persons" who desire order, stability and structure are encouraged

Table 6-4

1 WHAT IS EFFECTIVE LEADERSHIP ... Introduction

Leadership is the art and science of getting things done through people. Leaders are the key individuals who must face both outward to read the signs of pivotal changes and trends around them and face inward to empower and energize the organization, management and all employees with vision and purpose. Burns (68:18) has defined leadership in the following way:

> *When persons with certain motives and purposes mobilize, in competition or conflict with others, institutional, political, psychological, and other resources so as to arouse, engage, and satisfy the motives of followers.*

Leadership is the heart and blood of any organization: it pumps vitality into the task and team processes of reading and responding to the challenges that rapid change requires. Leaders are more than managers. They must set the organizational direction with clear purposes and mobilize organizational resources for attaining often divergent goals. Good leaders manage through their follower's point of view (69:27).

Leadership is this view process of gaining our commitment and cooperation, moving various teams or organizational units into action and making sure that team talents and potentials are fully utilized. The effective leader knows how to build morale through this surfacing of latent group talent or underutilized skills. Leadership is certainly important for accomplishing job tasks not just pointing us in the right direction; but visionary enthusiasm, not dominance and control, is the essential driving force.

Effective leaders are able to identify the purposes and motives of employees in a way that also allows them to tie their personal goals with the organizations more abstract mission or purpose. This process is also a great morale builder. Leaders inspire, motivate and leave workers with the feelings of being understood and cared about. Many good leaders are also good managers and they can effectively function in the trenches when they need to.

Leaders create a climate of competence and purpose; they inspire our best efforts. They make us feel confident we are moving in the right direction and we begin to enthusiastically look forward to new challenges and opportunities. They have great powers of imagination and tap a deep pool of experience with a keen sense of timing. They know their professional fields of expertise, yet appear humble as they draw upon diverse sources of information to identify and act decisively upon strategic targets of opportunity. They revitalize both organizations and employees.

The leader must always think and act proactively. This mindset demands that leaders: look to the future for creative opportunities; nurture entrepreneurs and innovators as well as workhorses; feedforward data and ideas for the future, not just feedback rewards for previous success; turn any setback into a positive learning opportunity.

The higher one goes in the organization, the more latitude exists for leading. However, the good leader knows that power is a two-way street. Freedom to control is never without limits; it is always constrained by the actions of followers, a resource base, stakeholder interests, external trends and fluctuating environmental demands. To understand how to lead from the followers viewpoint, requires a good amount of self-esteem, awareness of one's strengths and weaknesses, and confidence that the talent exists within the organization, or through recruiting, to meet the challenges of change.

2 BASIC FUNCTIONS OF LEADERSHIP

Ends and Page (70) suggest there are ten basic functions of leadership:

Establish, communicate, clarify goals

Secure commitment to goals

Define and negotiate roles

Secure commitment to roles assigned

Plan activity and make it clear

Set performance standards and make sure they are understood

Provide feedback to individuals and group

Provide coaching and/or supervision

Provide initiative, enthusiasm, sense of purpose, set an example

Control climate and group process

NOTE: All functions involve interaction with team members individually or as a group

3 TRAIT THEORY OF LEADERSHIP.

Stodgill proposes "there exists a finite set of individual traits or characteristics that can be used to distinguish successful from unsuccessful leaders". Stodgill studied research dating back to 1948 and has identified a leadership classification system with six broad categories (71):

physical characteristics; social background; intelligence; personality; task-related characteristics; social characteristics.

A summary of selected traits within each category is exhibited in Table 7-1:

Physical Characteristics	Social Background	Intelligence
Age	Education	Judgment
Weight	Mobility	Decisiveness
Height	Social status	Fluency of speech
Appearance	Working class affinity	
Personality	**Task-Related Characteristics**	**Social Characteristics**
Independence	Achievement need	Supervisory ability
Self-confidence	Initiative	Cooperativeness
Dominance	Persistence	Interpersonal skills
Aggressiveness	Responsibility need	Integrity
	Concern for people	Power need
	Concern for results	
	Security need	

Table 7-1. Trait Theory of Leadership

Some research findings in this area include:

- A profile of a successful leader shows he or she is concerned with achieving high performance levels, and accomplishes this through integrity, responsibility, seeking behavior, creativity, and concern for people around him or her.

- General appearance, intelligence level, and being in the right place at the right time are of lesser importance than some may believe.

- Recent studies have shown that female leaders have reached executive positions through hard work, persistence, and concern for performance.

- What may be important traits for one occupation may not be important for others.

4   BEHAVIORAL THEORIES OF LEADERSHIP

These theories propose the most important aspects of leadership are not the traits of the leader but what the leader does in various situations. Successful leaders are distinguished from unsuccessful leaders by their particular style of leadership. Two studies are most often referred to in this model: Ohio State Studies -- Initiating Structure and Consideration: and University of Michigan Studies -- Job-Centered and Employee-Centered.

Ohio State Studies

The overall objective of these studies was to investigate the determinants of leader behavior and to determine the effects of leadership style on work-group performance and satisfaction. Two dimensions were identified:

1) **Initiating Structure** - which concerned the degree to which the leader organized and defined the task, assigned the work to be done, established communications networks, and evaluated work-group performance.

2) **Consideration** - behavior that involves trust, mutual respect, friendship, support, and a concern for the welfare of the employee.

University of Michigan Studies - Institute for Social Research

The primary purpose of these studies was to identify styles of leader behavior that result in increased work-group performance and satisfaction. Two styles were identified:

1) **Job-Centered** - focused on the use of close supervision, legitimate and coercive power, meeting schedules, and evaluating work performance.

2) **Employee-Centered** - people oriented, emphasis on delegation of responsibility and a concern for employee welfare, needs, advancement, and personal growth.

The main conclusion of these studies was that the effectiveness of a leader style should not be evaluated solely by productivity measures, but should include other employee-related measures, such as satisfaction.

5   CONTINGENCY LEADERSHIP MODEL

The basic foundation of Fiedler's contingency theory is that the effectiveness of the leader in achieving high group performance is contingent on the need of the leader for structure and the degree to which the leader has control and influence in a particular situation (72). There are four factors which serve as the framework to this model:

Leadership-style Assessment - using a questionnaire, a leader assesses the level of esteem in which he/she holds his/her least preferred co-worker (LPC). According to the model, the lower the LPC score, the greater the tendency for the leader to be task-oriented. The higher the LPC score, the greater the tendency for the leader to be employee-oriented.

Task Structure - the degree to which the group task is routine or complex. The components include: goal clarity; goal-path multiplicity; decision verifiability; and decision specificity.

Group Atmosphere - the degree of confidence, trust, and respect the group has in the leader.

Position Power - the extent the leader possesses, through legitimate, reward, or coercive power, the ability to influence the behavior of others.

Figure 7-1 displays a combination of situations and is arranged in order of favorableness to the leader.

	CELL	1	2	3	4	5	6	7	8
Situational Factors	Leader/Member Relations	Good	Good	Good	Good	Poor	Poor	Poor	Poor
	Task Structure	Structured	Structured	Unstructured	Unstructured	Structured	Structured	Unstructured	Unstructured
	Leader Position Power	Strong	Weak	Strong	Weak	Strong	Weak	Strong	Weak
Situational Favorableness		Favorable			Moderately Favorable			Unfavorable	
Situational Certainty		Very Certain Situation			Moderately Certain Situation			Very Uncertain Situation	
Recommended Leadership Style		Task	Task	Task	Employee	Employee	Employee	Task	Task

Figure 7-1. Fiedler's Contingency Model (72)

6   PATH-GOAL THEORY OF LEADERSHIP

The path-goal model of leadership, developed by House, Evans, and Mitchell, states that the leader's job is to develop more desire for goals and to improve paths toward goals so that goals can be better reached. Leader behavior, modified by the characteristics of the subordinates and the work environment, influences the perceptions of valence and expectancies, which then can result in higher motivation, satisfaction, and performance. Figure 7-2 describes the process:

Figure 7-2. The Path-Goal Leadership Process

A revised theory is composed of two basic propositions (73):

1) Role of the Leader - a supplemental one. The effect of the leader on the motivation and satisfaction of subordinates depends on how deficient the work environment is in other sources of motivation and support.

2) Dynamics of the situation - two main factors are suggested as influencing the situational effectiveness of the leader's behavior:
   a) characteristics of the subordinates
   b) characteristics of the work environment

The theory suggests four styles of leader behavior, as shown in Table 7-2:

Instrumental	Planning, organizing, controlling, and coordinating of subordinates activities by leader
Supportive	Consideration of subordinates' needs, well-being and welfare
Participative	Sharing information with subordinates; consulting with subordinates in group-related decisions
Achievement-oriented	Setting challenging goals, expecting high performance, and continually seeking improvement in performance

Table 7-2. Path-Goal Leadership Styles

7   ATTRIBUTION THEORY.

This theory postulates that a leader does not act from simple observation of a subordinate, but interprets that behavior through a set of causal attributes about why that behavior occurred. See Figure 7-3.

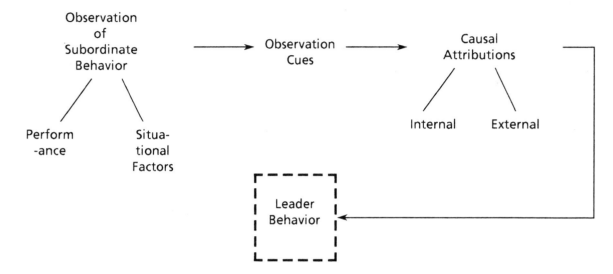

Figure 7-3. Attribution Theory of Leadership

The leader observes the subordinates behavior both from a **performance** standpoint (absenteeism, tardiness, low quality output, conflict), and a **situational** standpoint (equipment, workload, time constraints, coordination needs).

These two observation sets are then interpreted with the use of certain **observation cues**, three of which are:

- Distinctiveness - is this behavior observed across tasks
- Consistency - has the behavior been exhibited over a period of time
- Consensus - do others exhibit the same behavior on the same task.

These cues act as the major input into the actual **causal attributes** held by the person. Causal attributes are categorized in two ways:

- **Internal** - factors which are inherent in the person being observed (lack of ability, low effort, low commitment, laziness),
- **External** - factors beyond the control of the observed person (equipment, excessive workload, manpower problems, unrealistic deadlines).

These causal attributes may lead to the actual behavior of the leader.

8   SITUATIONAL LEADERSHIP

This model, first developed by Paul Hersey and Kenneth Blanchard (74), and more recently updated by Blanchard, is a concept which is based on a relationship between 1) the amount of direction and control (Directive Behavior) a leader gives; 2) the amount of support and encouragement (Supportive Behavior) a leader provides; and 3) the competence and commitment (Development Level) that a follower exhibits in performing a specific task.

Directive Behavior -- the extent to which the leader engages in one-way communication; spells out the follower's role and clearly tells the follower(s) what to do, where to do it, how to do it, when to do it, and closely supervises performance.

Supportive Behavior -- the extent to which a leader engages in two-way communication, listens, provides support and encouragement, facilitates interaction, and involves the follower(s) in decision making.

Development Level -- defined as 1) the follower's job knowledge and skills (competence) and 2) the follower's motivation and/or confidence (commitment). The more competent and committed, the more responsibility the subordinate can take for directing his/her own behavior.   It is important to remember that development level is task specific.

THE FOUR LEADERSHIP STYLES

Directing -- Leader provides specific instructions (roles and goals) for follower(s) and closely supervises task accomplishment.

Coaching -- Leader explains decisions and solicits suggestions from follower(s) but continues to direct task accomplishment.

Supporting -- Leader makes decisions together with the follower(s) and supports efforts toward task accomplishment.

Delegating -- Leader turns over decisions and responsibility for implementation to follower(s).

See Figure 7-5 for the model.

Situational Leadership II demonstrates there is no one best style of leadership. People in leadership and management positions become more effective when they use a leader style that is appropriate to the development level of the individual or group they want to influence.

FOUR LEADERSHIP STYLES

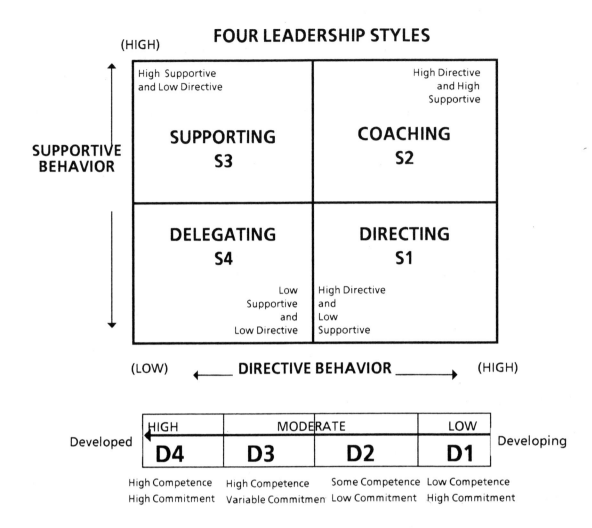

To apply, correspond Development Level (D) with Leadership Style (S)

Figure 7-5. Situational Leadership II

122

THEORY NAME	THEORIST	MAIN POINTS
Trait Theory	Ralph Stodgill	• There are a finite set of individual traits and characteristics which can determine successful leaders: - physical, social background, intelligence, personality, task-related, social skills
Behavioral Theories	Ohio State Studies	• The most important aspects of leadership are what the leader does • Initiating Structure - organized and defines task, assigns work, establishes communications networks, evaluates performance • Consideration - trust, mutual respect, support and a concern for employees
	University of Michigan Studies	• Job Centered - close supervision, use of power, meeting deadlines, evaluating performance • Employee centered - delegation of responsibility, concern for employee

Contingency Leadership	Fred Fiedler	• Effectiveness is contingent on need of structure of leader, and degree of control and power of leader
		• Four factors:
		  - Leadership-style assessment
		  - Task structure
		  - Group atmosphere
		  - Position power

Path-Goal Theory	Robert House
	Martin Evans
	Terence Mitchell
		• Leaders role is to create desire for goals and improve path for reaching goals
		• Four styles:
		  - Instrumental-planning, organizing, controlling, coordinating
		  - Supportive - consideration of employees needs, well-being
		  - Participative - sharing information, consulting
		  - Achievement Oriented - set challenging goals, expect high performance, seek continual improvement

Attribution Theory	Terence Mitchell R.W. Wood	• Leader response to worker's behavior is based on observation of worker's behavior, processing that behavior through observational cues, and interpreting causal attributes of the behavior

Situational Leadership	Paul Hersey
	Kenneth Blanchard
		• Leadership style depends on development level of followers
		• Four styles:
		  - Directing
		  - Coaching
		  - Supporting
		  - Delegating

Table 7.3. Comparison of Leadership Theories

"Leadership requires the ability to harness diffused power - and to empower others to translate a vision into reality. The vision must leave room for creativity" (75). Bennis refers to "transformative power- the essence of what it originally meant to be a leader", as the ability to translate an idea into reality and sustain it.

Bennis sees leadership and management as different, in that leaders are concerned with the organization's basic purposes, why it exists, and its general direction (**effectiveness**). Managers, on the other hand, are concerned with the nuts and bolts, the translation of the vision into reality (**efficiency**).

Bennis sets out certain characteristics which are possessed by successful leaders:

- **Vision** - the capacity to create and communicate a compelling vision of a desired state of affairs.

- **Communication and alignment** - the capacity to communicate their vision in order to align the support of others.

- **Persistence, consistency, focus** - the capacity to maintain the organization's direction.

- **Empowerment** - the capacity to create environments that can harness the energies and abilities of others.

- **Organizational learnings** - the capacity to allow the organization to receive feedback and alter its course if necessary.

11 LEADERSHIP STRATEGIES AND DECISION-MAKING

There are many strategies a leader or manager can use in the process of making a decision. The following is a discussion of several strategies which can be employed, followed by questions regarding the certain factors of the decision to be made.

Orton (76) suggests that by reviewing the strategies and factors influencing the decision, a situational approach can be utilized in the organizational setting.

Strategies

- "I'll go it alone" - the manager takes complete responsibility for the decision.

  ex: when determining a salary increase for an outstanding employee within company guidelines

- "Answer my questions" - the manager needs specific information and solicits it from specific individuals to help in making the decision.

  ex: asking an employee about the department's travel expenses during a particular month

- "Give me the benefit of your thinking" - the manager elicits information and analysis from individuals on an individual basis, then makes the final decision alone.

  ex: asking an employee about their travel expenses for a particular month and asking how he sees that changing over the next few months

- "Let's discuss it" - the manager shares information in a group setting, eliciting open discussion, then makes the final decision alone.

  ex: manager needs to cut expenses and needs input from the group on ideas as to how to accomplish his goal

- "The decision is ours" - the manager allows the group to discuss the alternatives and make the decision by consensus.

  ex: manager shares with the group the problem "we need to cut expenses", uses group decision in decision making

Decision Making

Certain factors affect the quality of the decisions or the commitment of people involved.

- Does the quality of the decision really made a difference?
- Do I have all the information I need to make the decision alone?
- Do I know what I'm missing? Do I know where to find the information? Will I know what to do with the information I am given?
- Do I need anybody's commitment to make sure this succeeds?
- Can I gain commitment without offering participation in the decision?
- Do those involved in the decision share the organization's goals?
- Is there likely to be conflict over the available alternatives?

Situational Approach

To determine which strategy is the most viable, one approach is:

- Determine the characteristics of the situation
- Eliminate approaches that will be ineffective
- Assess the impact of time
- Commit to an effective but practical approach

12 CATEGORIES OF FAILURE OF LEADERS

A study conducted at the Center for Creative Leadership by McCall and Lombardo identified ten basic reasons why leaders often fail (77):

1) Insensitive to others: abrasive, intimidating, bullying style

2) Cold, aloof, arrogant

3) Betrayal of trust

4) Overly ambitious: thinking of next job, playing politics

5) Specific performance problems with the business

6) Overmanaging: unable to delegate or build a team

7) Unable to staff effectively

8) Unable to think strategically

9) Unable to adapt to a boss with a different style

10) Overdependent on advocate or mentor

The following are ten mistakes often made by leaders who have or are failing.

1) Failure to develop and maintain basic management and leadership skills

2) Permitting poor employee selection techniques

3) Failure to discuss expectations or establish goals which have been mutually set.

4) Inattention to the training and development needs of team members.

5) Failure to advocate, support and nurture team building activities.

6) Preventing the involvement of team members in any activity where they could make a contribution.

7) Failure to provide and receive feedback from the team.

8) Allowing conflict and competition to get out of control, or trying to eliminate it altogether.

9) Depending on someone else to recognize and reward the team and its' members.

10) Failure to send players who have not responded to coaching back to the "minor leagues".

13　A POLITICAL PERSPECTIVE OF LEADERSHIP

As we have already noted in our discussion of power and politics in the previous section: "Political skills are needed to organize others and win support for visions. They are increasingly critical in organizational life because of major changes in organizational environments and work characteristics"(78). Here are five political perspectives that have great implications for the task of leading organizations today:

- **Standing still means losing ground.** No longer can a manager acquire skills, gain a position, and sit back. Resources become worthless over time in increasingly turbulent environments. There is more competition in all areas: there is a continuing need to produce more. Entrepreneur skills, marketing skills, needs assessment skills are necessary, as well as the ability to continually demonstrate improved performance.

- **Investment in the future is essential.** Because the future will be different from the past, with fewer sources of stability, managers will increasingly turn to forecasting and strategic planning as important functions of their jobs. Flexibility now becomes more of a necessary skill: the ability to modify plans in the face of new developments. Each function and each individual must learn to think with long-range planning skills and try to identify and predict the important influences upon organizational survival.

- **Selling is characteristic of more and more work.** There are fewer jobs where selling is not necessary in order to get work done. Automatic authority no longer carries the unquestioned status. Competition and more innovative approaches to problems, the entrepreneurship attitude, exists in today's organizations. The decline of the traditional organization chart makes unchallenged authority obsolete. Matrix organizational design, allowing workers to report to two managers, one for their function and the other for their product, makes authority negotiable.

- **Team work is characteristic of more and more work.** Very few jobs are done alone anymore: jobs now exist as part of task forces or teams. Success increasingly involves knowing how to build the right team to do the job, how to take advantage of all available resources.

- **Others below you and others around you in the organization need and want more power and autonomy.** Decentralization and delegation are inevitable, power sharing seems increasingly characteristic of the new organization. Participatory management is now mainstream. The younger worker is bringing to the organization a need for challenge, responsibility, power, autonomy to the job. Productivity issues encourage participation and power sharing.

14   PROACTIVE LEADERSHIP

Organizations that want to insure their profitability over all prosperity, and longevity during the decade ahead, need to focus on developing proactive leaders throughout all levels of the organization. It is these kinds of leaders that will be able to help develop an enhanced capability on the part of the organization itself, its work teams, and its employees at all levels to function more effectively and efficiently.

To try to achieve greater profitability and stability, many executives and managers have initiated organization development interventions of four dimensions; maintenance, installation, alignment and transformation.

Maintenance interventions are usually training programs designed to help people do what they are already doing better. **Installation** interventions are organization development interventions that often place a new procedure, technology or operational policy into place without carefully analyzing the appropriateness or potential impact on the organizations's goals. An **alignment** intervention also places new procedures, technology or operational policies into place. However, alignment is done with careful consideration of the organization's vision, driving values, mission and goals that are part of its strategic plan. **Transformation** is an organization development intervention that begins with the evolvement of a new vision, new or revived driving values and a new or revised mission with new goals. It is a series of interventions that literally cause the people in the organization to transcend the old reactive and unproductive ways of doing business and begin anew in actions, spirit and direction. This intervention calls for a commitment from everyone in the organization to develop and provide skillful leadership in different situations and at all job and management levels.

To many executives and managers who are trying to keep up with the latest leadership and managerial theory in order to more effectively develop the capacity of their people and their organizations to perform better, the literature sometimes seems confusing than enlightening. In addition to reflecting differences of opinion and semantics, it generally comes to the reader with an emphasis on one or two specific aspects of leadership and managerial practices.

The purpose of the Proactive Managerial Functions Assessment Chart (See Table 7-4) is not to give you as an executive or manager any new information about the critical tasks and functions of managing the enterprise, but to help you put the pieces together in such a way that you can begin to assess the managerial functions holistically. When this is done, you can determine what skill areas are in need of polishing and/or developing.

Introspection is essential for building and using effective leadership skills. The degree to which you are able to understand and manage yourself effectively correlates directly with your ability to manage others - peers, subordinates, bosses, and customers - at higher levels of effectiveness. This understanding of the importance of good personal functioning is basic to avoiding the oscillation and chaos that come from reactive, hip-shooting, and fire-fighting kinds of management behaviors.

There is a distinction between leader and manager. The terms are not used here interchangeably. An effective manager will function as a skillful leader, as well as being effective at introspection, conceptual thinking, and administration of executive affairs. It is not leadership, in the general sense, that we are dealing with here, but

RESOURCES	TASKS	CONTINUOUS FUNCTIONS	SEQUENTIAL FUNCTIONS
SELF	**Introspection** - Open investigation of self. Behavior Feelings Self Concept Truth Option Values	**Analyze Behavior, Feelings, Values**- List actions, ascertain causes, solicit feedback, and develop effective responses	**Self-Centering, Balancing** - Focus mentally and intuitively on aspects of self. Create balance; set goals and objectives for personal behavior; act; monitor; adjust; and evaluate
IDEAS	**Strategic Thinking** - Forecasting, conceptualizing using left and right brain and intuition	**Problem Solving** - Gather facts, ascertain causes, and develop alternative solutions	**Planning** - Set vision, values, goals, objectives, driving force, budget, time lines, procedures and policies.
THINGS	**Managing**- Coordinate details of executive affairs. Develop organization's purposes, structure, rewards systems, helpful mechanisms and relationships	**Decision Making** - Arrive at conclusions and judgments. Use decision matrix. Balance degree of authority with degree of responsibility for each staff member.	**Organizing** - Coordinate tasks to achieve goals and objectives: create job descriptions/standards; assign work; orchestrate change; facilitate relationships; and reduce conflict
PEOPLE	**Influencing**- Motivate people to get quality results related to goals/job tasks. Use the adaptive skills regularly and effectively. Flex leader styles. Select appropriate sources of power.	**Communicating** - Get understanding. Flex communication styles. Listen actively. Check for understanding - paraphrase, perception check. Remove roadblocks. Use four part "I" messages. Use pacing skills.	**Staffing** - Secure can do/will do people to do organization's tasks: select; orient; train; and develop competencies. **Leading**- Get action to achieve goals and objectives: tell, sell, participate, and delegate; monitor; give feedback; and initiate needed changes. **Controlling Work Outcomes** - Achieve objectives; develop performance standards; measure results; reward; and use ProActive Super Vision.

Table 7-4. Proactive Managerial Functions Assessment Chart

leadership as a function of management. We are not dealing with administration in general but, again, as a function of management.

Let's use the following definitions for clarity and simplicity:

Management - Achieving vital goals and objectives through others.

Administration - Managing the details of executive affairs.

Leadership - Influencing people to accomplish the desired objectives.

It is hoped that this assessment of management tasks and functions will help you and your management team produce a variety of benefits such as:

- Help experienced managers make personnel assessments of job functions to begin establishing targets for personal/professional development

- Help new managers see the "boundaries of the ballpark" and sense the sequential relationship of certain functions and interrelationships

- Provide a positive model for integration of self and job role expectations

- Provide a model for fitting together all generally accepted tasks, functions, and activities of management

- Provide a clearer distinction between the leadership, administrative, and strategic planning functions of management

- Identify and relate such activities as problem analysis, management of change, and management of differences.

The chart gives equal space to "behaviorist" and "humanist" functions of management. It provides a foundation from which specific performance guides or job descriptions can be developed. It also serves as a starting point for exploring the specific skills needed to support the managerial tasks and functions at a more refined level. It provides a starting point for determining specific individual and management team performance strengths and short suits from which to establish your personal and your management team's professional development objectives and coaching needs.

15 LEADERSHIP FUNCTIONS WITHIN HIGH PERFORMING TEAMS

The role of the leader within high performing teams is very important. Certain leadership functions can be shared among team members; others can only be performed by a designated leader. The leader of the group is the person with primary responsibility for linking his work group to the rest of the organization (79); the leader has full responsibility for the group's performance and for seeing that the group meets the demands and expectations placed upon it by the rest of the organization of which it is a part. Members will share in both responsibilities, but the leader cannot avoid full responsibility for adequate performance of the team.

There are certain qualities, which we have mentioned throughout our discussion of Team Building, that a leader must possess to function effectively in a high performing team. Some are:

- Listening well and patiently.
- Not being impatient with the progress being made by the team, particularly on difficult problems.
- Accepting more blame than may be warranted for any failure or mistake.
- Giving the group members ample opportunity to express their thoughts.
- Being careful never to impose a decision upon the group.
- Putting his/her contributions often in the form of questions or stating them speculatively.
- Arranging for others to help perform leadership functions which enhance their status.

This leader is "group-centered" as opposed to "employee-centered" and utilizes these skills to enhance the effectiveness of the team.

BIBLIOGRAPHY/REFERENCES

ORGANIZATION THEORY AND BEHAVIOR

INTRODUCTION

(1)   Lincoln, Yvonnas (Ed.) <u>Organizational Theory and Inquiry: The Paradigm Revolution</u> (Beverly Hills, CA: Sase Publications, 1985)

(2)   Srivastva, Suresh and Associates. <u>The Executive Mind: New Insights on Managerial Thought and Action</u> (San Francisco, CA: Jossey-Bass Publishers, 1983)

(3)   Bennis, Warren and Nannus, Bert. <u>Leaders: The Strategies for Taking Charge</u> (New York: Harper & Row, 1985)

(4)   Naisbett, John. <u>Megatrends, Ten New Directions Transforming Our Lives</u> (New York: Warner Books, 1982)

(5)   Hall, Edward T. "The Translator" <u>Science 85</u>, (July/August 1985)

CHAPTER 1

(6)   Porter, L., Lawler, E. and Hackman, K. <u>Behavior in Organizations</u> (New York: McGraw-Hill, 1975)

(7)   Child, John. <u>Information Technology, Organization and the Response to Strategic Challenges</u>

(8)   Carroll, Glenn R. 'Stratocracy in High-Technology Firms' <u>Organizational Approaches to Strategy</u> (Cambridge, Mass:Ballinger Publishing Co, 1989)

(9)   Waterman, Robert. <u>The Renewal Factor</u> (New York: Banham Books, 1988)

(10)   Carroll, Glenn R. 'Stratocracy in High-Technology Firms' <u>Organizational Approaches to Strategy</u> (Cambridge, Mass:Ballinger Publishing Co, 1989)

CHAPTER 2

(11)   Taylor, Frederick. <u>Scientific Management</u> (New York: Harper & Row, 1911)

(12)   Roethlisberger, F.J. and Dickson, W. <u>The Management and the Worker</u> (Cambridge: Harvard University Press, 1939)

(13)   Sashkin, M. "An Overview of Ten Management and Organizational Theorists", in Jones, J.E. and Pfeiffer, J.W. (Eds) **The 1981 Annual Handbook for Group Facilitators** (San Diego, CA: University Associates, 1981) pp. 212-214

(14)   Mayo, E. **Human Problems of an Industrial Civilization** (New York: MacMillian, 1933)

(15)   McGregor, Douglas. **The Human Side of Enterprise** (New York: McGraw-Hill, 1960)

(16)   McGregor, Douglas. **The Human Side of Enterprise** (New York: McGraw Hill, 1960)

(17)   Likert, Rensis. **The Human Organization: Its Management and Value** (New York: McGraw-Hill, 1967)

CHAPTER 3

(18)   Gibson, James, Ivancevich, John and Donnelly, James Jr. **Organizations** Fourth Edition (Plano, Texas: Business Publications, 1982) pp. 358-364

(19)   Woodward, Joan. **Industrial Organization: Theory and Practice** (London: Oxford University Press, 1965)

(20)   Lawrence, Paul R. and Lorsch, Jay W. **Organization and Environment** (Homewood, IL: Richard D. Irwin, 1969)

(21)   Galbraith, Jay. **Designing Complex Organizations** (Reading, MA: Addison-Wesley Publishing, 1973)

(22)   Galbraith, Jay. **Organization Design** (Reading, MA: Addison-Wesley Publishing, 1977)

(23)   Kast, F. E. and Rosenzweig, J. E. "General Systems Theory: Applications for Organization and Management" **Academy of Management Journal** (Vol 15, 447-465, 1972)

(24)   Kast, Fremont E. and Rosenzweig, James E. **Organization and Management: A Systems and Contingency Approach,** 3rd Edition (New York: McGraw-Hill, 1979)

(25)   Katz, D. and Kahn, R.L. **The Social Psychology of Organizations** (New York: Wiley, 1978)

(26)   Cummings, T. and Srivastva, S. **Management of Work: A Socio-Technical Systems Approach** (San Diego, CA: University Associates, 1977)

(27)   Pfeffer, Jeffrey. **Power in Organizations** (Marshfield, MA: Pitman, Publishing Co., 1981)

(28)   Brym, R. J. **Intellectuals and Politics** (London: George Allen and Unwin, 1980)

(29)   Kanter, Rosabeth Moss. **The Change Masters: Innovation for Productivity in the American Corporation** (New York: Simon and Shuster, 1983)

(30)   Cyert, R.M. and March, J.G. **A Behavioral Theory of the Firm** (New York: Prentice Hall, 1963)

(31)   Hersey, Paul, Blanchard, Kenneth and Natemeyer, Walter. "Situational Leadership, Perception and the Impact of Power", published for **Center for Leadership Studies** (San Diego, CA: Learning Resoruces Corporation), 1979)

(32)   Crozier, M. and Erhard, Friedberg. **Actors and Systems: The Politics of Collective Action** (Chicago: University of Chicago Press, 1980)

(33)   Scott, W. Richard. **Organizations: Rational, Natural, and Open Systems** (Englewood Cliffs, NJ: Prentice - Hall, 1981)

(34)   Deutsch, M. "A Theory of Cooperation and Competition", **Human Relations** (2, 129-152, 1949), and Deutsch, M. "An Experimental Study of the Effects of Cooperation and Competition on Group Process" **Human Relations** (2, 199-232, 1949)

(35)   Julian. H.W. and Perry, F.A. "Cooperation Contrasted with Intragroup and Intergroup Competition" **Sociometry** (30, 79- 90, 1967)

(36)   Guetzkow, H. and Gyr, J. "An Analysis of Conflict in Decision-Making Groups" **Human Relations** (7, 367-381, 1954)

(37)   Cummings, L.L. and Stau, Barry (Eds.) **Research in Organizational Behavior** Vol. 3 (Greenwich, CN: JAI Press, 1981)

(38)   Schwartz, Howard. "Matching Corporate Culture and Business Strategy" **Organizational Dynamics**, (30-48, Summer, 1981)

(39)   Smircish, Linda "Is the Concept of Culture a Paradigm for Understanding Organizations and Ourselves" in Frost et al (Ed) **Organizational Culture** (73-94)

(40)   Frost, Peter J., Moore, Larry F. Reis, Luis, Merley, Lundberg, Craig C. and Martin, Joanne. **Organizational Culture** (New York: Sage, 1985, p. 74)

(41)   VanMaanen, John and Barley, Stephen R. "Culture Organizations: Fragments of a Theory" in Frost et al (Ed) **Organizational Culture** (31-54)

(42)   Hickman, Craig R. and Silva, Michael. **Creating Excellence: Managing Corporate Culture, Strategy, and Change in the New Age** (New York: New America Library, 1984)

(43)   Deal, Terrence and Kennedy, Alan. **Corporate Cultures** (Reading, MA: Addison-Wesley, 1982)

CHAPTER 4

(44)   Taylor, Frederick. **Scientific Management** (New York: Harper & Row, 1911)

(45)   Szilagyi, Andrew and Wallace, Marc. **Organizational Behavior and Performance,** 3rd Edition, (Glenview, IL: Scott, Foresman and Company, 1983) pp 124-127

(46)   Hackman, J.R. and Oldham, G.B. "Motivation Through the Design of Work: Test of a Theory", **Organizational Behavior and Human Performance** (16, 250-279, 1976)

CHAPTER 5

(47)   Davis, Keith. **Human Behavior at Work, Organizational Behavior** (New York: McGraw-Hill, 1981)

(48)   Atkinson, Joan. **An Introduction to Motivation** (Princeton, N.J: Van Nostrand, 1964)

(49)   Jones, M.R. (Ed.) **Nebraska Symposium on Motivation** (Lincoln: University of Nebraska, 1955)

(50)   Maslow, Abraham H. **Motivation and Personality** (New York: Harper & Row, 1954)

(51)   Herzberg, Frederick. **Work and the Nature of Man** (Ohio: The World Publishing Company, 1966)

(52)   Herzberg, F., Mausner, B. and Synderman, B. **The Motivation to Work** 2nd Edition (New York: Wiley, 1959)

(53)   Alderfer, Clayton P. **Existence, Relatedness, and Growth** (New York: Free Press, 1972)

(54)   Szilagyi, Andrew and Wallace, Marc. **Organizational Behavior and Performance** 3rd Edition (Glenview: IL: Scott, Foresman and Company, 1983)

(55)   McClelland, David. "Business Drive and National Achievement" **Harvard Business Review** (July/August, 1962)

(56)   McClelland, David. **The Achievement Motive** (New York: Appleton-Century-Crofts, 1953)

(57)   Vroom, Victor H. **Work and Motivation** (New York: Wiley, 1964)

(58)   Davis, Keith. **Human Behavior at Work, Organizational Behavior** (New York: McGraw-Hill, 1981)

(59)   Adams, J. Stacy. "Toward an Understanding of Inequity", **Journal of Abnormal and Social Psychology** (November, 1963)

(60) Szilagyi, Andrew and Wallace, Marc. **Organizational Behavior and Performance** 3rd Edition (Glenview: IL: Scott, Foresman and Company, 1983)

(61) Locke, Edwin A. "Toward a Theory of Task Motivation and Incentives", **Organizational Behavior and Human Performance** (1968)

CHAPTER 6

(62) Dessler, Gary. **Applied Human Relations** (Reston, VA: Reston Publishing, 1983)

(63) Rogers, Carl R. and Farson, Richard. "Active Listening", in Sigband, Norman. **Communications for Management and Business** (New York: Scott, Foresman and Co., 1976)

(64) "Productivity, Supervision, and Employee Morale", **Human Relations** Series 1, Report 1 (Ann Arbor, MI: Survey Research Center, University of Michigan)

(65) Kahn, Robert. "The Human Factors Underlying Industrial Productivity", **Michigan Business Review** (November 1952)

(66) Tuckman, B.W. "Developmental Sequence in Small Groups" **Psychological Bulletin** (1965, 63, 384-399)

(67) Tuckman, B.W. "Stages of Small-Group Development Revisited" **Group and Organizational Studies** (1977, 2, 419-427)

CHAPTER 7

(68) Burns, James McGregor **Leadership** (New York: Harpar & Row, 1978)

(69) Zierden Anthony. "Leading from the Follower's Point of View" **Organizational Dynamics**, 1980

(70) Ends, Earl and Page, Curtis. **Organizational Team Building** (Massachusetts: Winthrop Publishers, Inc. 1977)

(71) Stogdill, Ralph M. **Handbook of Leadership** (New York: Free Press, 1974)

(72) Fiedler, Fred E. **A Theory of Leadership Effectiveness** (New York: McGraw-Hill, 1967)

(73) House, Robert J. and Mitchell, Terence R. "Path-Goal Theory of Leadership" **Journal of Contemporary Business** (Autumn, 1974)

(74) Hersey, Paul, Blanchard, Kenneth and Natemeyer, Walter. "Situational Leadership, Perception, and the Impact of Power", published for **Center for Leadership Studies** (San Diego, CA: Learning Resources Corporation, 1979)

(75)   Bennis, Warren. "Leadership Transforms Vision Into Action" **Industry Week** (May 31, 1982)

(76)   Orton, Ann. "Leadership: New Thoughts on an Old Problem" **Training** (June, 1984)

(77)   McCall, Morgan, Jr. and Lombardo, Michael. "What Makes a Top Executive?" **Psychology Today** (February, 1983)

(78)   Kanter, Rosabeth Moss. "The Meaning of Influence Skills in Today's New Corporation", published for **Goodmeasure**, Inc. (Cambridge, MA: 1981)

(79)   Likert, Rensis. "The Nature of Highly Effective Groups", **New Patterns of Management** (New York: McGraw-Hill, 1961)

SECTION TWO

STRATEGIC HUMAN RESOURCE MANAGEMENT

DESIGNING GLOBAL HUMAN RESOURCE, MANAGEMENT, AND LEARNING STRATEGIES

Global management is the word today. When news on the other side of the world is beamed live by satellite into our homes on the six o'clock news, it is obvious that we live in a global economy. The "soft" side of business--management style, ethics, motivation, understanding corporate cultural values--are relatively new to the business milieu and have evolved out of a need for increased productivity in today's competitive international market. What happens today in China, India, Saudi Arabia or South Africa is likely to have an effect on our business strategies tomorrow. Organizations must become sensitive to the possible impact of its decisions, policies, and processes upon all aspects of survival.

There is also a greater cultural diversity within the business community, both at home and abroad. Today, foreign companies are setting up shop on U.S. soil, combining their native management style with American employee expectations. Assignments abroad for American executives and their families require that they learn to adapt--and quickly--to cultures, languages, religions, and beliefs that are truly foreign to their experience. Managing on a such a global basis in the 1990's will require more strategic training training .

Organizations may be viewed as an orchestra of groups, each of which often plays its own tune at the expense of the organization. This cannot continue. Senior management's strategic job is that of a conductor, providing the music for synchronizing the differing units of the organization into one harmonious song. In reality, this communication frequently is faulty, resulting in costly turf battles between groups and producing a raucous noise instead of strategic music. All too frequently the conductors react to this chaos by frantically examining their musical players without examining sheet music, failing to lift their eyes to see that it is often not the music out there which is at fault, but their failure to provide direction.

Management strategies are so very crucial when managing teams or working with groups. By becoming more sensitive to energizing group development issues and process we can tap a rich source of talent for succession planning and other strategic personnel needs. By practicing a positive emphasis, whether identifying successes or failures, we are saying that we can bring out the productive potentials of those around us. The basis of this vision is the belief that anyone can become a proactive leader in their own life. Each of us can achieve our most productive and self-affirming opportunities by actively contribution to a larger purpose, and through such a vision inspire the meaningful growth of others and the need for a humane form of work relations.

In today's turbulent world, the issue is how to construct more adaptable, flexible, creative and strategic organizational systems. In this view, the daily management of

141

task processes must not become separated from strategic and creative thinking about all relevant organizational systems and the external environment.

In light of the tremendous pace of change, revitalization and renewal can no longer be thought of as a luxury. External and internal consultants can help call attention to the need for better strategy. However, organizations need to better educate their leaders and managers to think like consultants. This task involves strategically thinking, integrating various operational dimensions, planning for personnel needs, and training for change and transitions management. This strategic framework allows us to move to any level of analysis, depending upon the organizational issues we need to address. The key is not to become locked into a single rigid perspective, framework, or system level. We must recognize the need to open our viewpoints and challenge outdated assumptions; even those that appear to be working for us in the short-run. The goal is to integrate business thinking with human resource strategies for more flexible and innovative organizational structures, processes and reward systems that improve quality, productivity and personal performance.

FROM STRATEGIC PLANNING TO STRATEGIC FLEXIBILITY

The old paradigm of strategic planning has recently come under fire in many articles. The model has served us well through the late 60's before the forces of international competition, inflation, deregulation and other problems that threaten the very survival of firms. The classic models of strategic planning, like the Boston Consulting Group's 4- box Product Mix and Experience Curve have become too mechanical and often failed to evolve with the new conditions organizations faced. The old questions about our current line of business, what we should be doing, in what direction we should be going, proved to be less relevant in a world where any delayed answers were irrelevant because the questions were changing on a daily basis.

Traditional, strategic planning is still a valuable tool in the arsenal of strategic management. However, its failures often result from too narrow emphasis upon such traditional tools as corporate portfolio management, narrow return on investment assumptions, management by numbers, mergers and paper entrepreneurism. These should only serve to compliment more comprehensive strategic analysis and flexible planning,

Strategic planning in an ideal world allows the organization to clarify goals, values and culture; define the mission or purposes; and creatively examine the external environment, devoid of rush. This process is much easier in a stable, unchanging or regulated environment. This analysis should ideally produce a strategic plan to guide the organization, but often fails to adequately integrate a more flexible and organic view of how the social, cultural, technical, administrative and environmental systems will really impact organizational survival.

The traditional approaches to planning can be appropriate in certain situations, but such scenarios seldom embrace all the contingent situations that modern markets, technologies and environments are imposing. The speed of change in most situations can often disconfirm, the value of a formalized planning posture. More proactive approaches are seeking to identify the least probable outcomes with the highest impacts. It is feasible to consider some mix of the two approaches in most organizational situations.

Robbins (1) contrasts strategic planning with the evolutionary, flexible and spontaneous mode of strategy. If the old model explores the current situation in order to formulate a planned set of guidelines for achieving where one wants to go then the new model doesn't rely solely upon systematic or rigorous plans that often just sit on the shelf after they are completed.

The former model has been gaining some favor because it includes dimensions that are more dynamic and flexible. In this perspective, the competitive environment sets the parameters that often requires a quick and creative response, not well-thought out plans. The old view supported the acquisition of assets through mergers and often overwhelmed the structures ability to manage the diverse sectors of the new conglomerate.

In contrast, the new view underscores the attempt to create true productive value which can be managed, even in turbulent situations. Although there are numerous differences in old and new models, the important point is the fact of change and and which model allows us to anticipate and effectively respond to rapid change.

An effective strategy in today's highly turbulent world depends upon the fit between strategy, processes, structure and environment. Organizational processes, such as human resources and information systems, can lend support to innovative and flexible organizational structure. Some label these tasks strategic thinking, issues management, strategic outlook or strategic self-renewal management.

Much old literature on strategic management and planning, in contrast, is guided by mechanistic life cycle assumptions. Many companies believe product lines will always follow a natural cycle of growth and decline. The problem with such a view does not reside with a general model of organizational life stages (cycles), but in the application of rigid, mechanistic and deterministic assumptions. The stages of infancy, innovation & growth, maturity & stability, bureaucracy & decline are not sequential or inevitable; nor are they incapable of reversal through strategic actions. Any business or organizational unit can experience life cycle rejuvenation and reversal through planned self-examination and new strategic interventions (2).

An example from the Japanese will highlight this contention. Why did many Japanese electronic companies not give up on the radio, a product seeming to lag in its technological potential, and in the sunset of its life cycle? The answer lies in how the Japanese defined the product and its potentially new and promising markets. Instead of defining it with a 4-box product portfolio (BCG) as a cash cow existing in declining product market, they defined it as a potentially more exciting line of audio entertainment and continued to invest money in developing it. The very successful walkman and watchman are the result. Many organizations are today displaying the same innovative and strategic thinking that allowed the radio to retain its profitable product potential. More organizations must follow the path of these groundbreaking companies in order to save declining products and see their new uses.

Good strategic thinking involves an exploratory, creative and futuristic orientation. This strategic focus allows the organization to target its resources to those things worth doing, with as little waste as possible. Effective organizations must learn to anticipate problems and trends by asking questions regarding emerging market segments and customers, not what has made them successful in the past. Formal strategic planning mechanisms don't, themselves, provide the certainty that management will always be focused upon the right things in a complex and changing world. New environmental forces, stakeholders, assumptions, products, market segments, competitors, opportunities and threats must be constantly monitored. Organizations must devote continuous efforts to strategic thinking and flexible, organic planning. The process is as important here as the products. The key is not just to own a strategy but to be able to easily give one up as the situation warrants. Organizations are capable of evaluating important trends and strategic issues, and exploring favorable future options through a systematic process that senses the future, evaluates changing environmental and social forces, and actively anticipates both opportunities and threats. Environmental scanning and issues anticipation can be used to build scenarios of the future. Such scenarios help the organizations gain clarity regarding the strategic consequences of various courses of action, and prepare the organization to quickly embrace alternative strategic responses.

The ideas on the following pages will assist the reader to better perceive the challenges ahead by exploring diagnostic skills, creative thinking, new ideas, and more innovative models about the complex organization world that today's manager, HR professional, and consultant faces every time they roll out of bed in the morning. As Peter Drucker has often reminded us, we do live in an Age of Discontinuity. American Society for Training and Development (ASTD) lists fourteen trends that they expect to have the most impact on doing business in the U.S. in the next three to five years. The list is striking for the number of trends that are global. Eight of the fourteen trends concern areas external to any particular business. The organizational professional should be positioned to function as an educator, a resource, and a management facilitator to meet the training and education requirements that these trends suggest.

We must also Increase human resource professional's personal power in order to develop their own proactive career and performance edge. HR practitioners must stop blaming and complaining about their lack of influence and power and accept responsibility for influencing their organization through their strategic business knowledge. They must proactively seek organizational power by educating themselves about the fundamental forces and trends impacting their organization and its industry.

At the same time, they must better understand the nature of how any business functions--such as marketing, finance, production, information and technology. They must come to see and learn that the important consumers of human resource programs and ideas are managers and their employees. It is imperative that they promote the view that the organization is a continuous learning system and succeeds through the process of generalist learning and teaching by example. The consumer or customer, in this case line managers, are the primary benefactors and users of this information, so make it timely, and relevant to their needs.

And if my organization is going to push learning further down, lower- level workers must be able to respond to new demands. Part of the of the problem in many organizations today is the illiteracy and the lack of training of our lowest-level workers. HR professionals become more innovative when developing competency-based professional development programs for all levels of the organization. These programs must look toward training workers in the primary technologies used to produce quality and innovative products and services.

The idea of good strategic management must begin with our understanding the importance of building and maintaining the self- esteem of every worker. A working definition of self-esteem is that deep feeling of certainty regarding one's own worth or value. This idea of self-worth is based upon self-awareness, a positive self-image and self-acceptance. It is a composite measure of our perception of our unique strengths and weakness, which either creates feelings of security and confidence or insecurity and lack of self-confidence.

What does a damaged sense of self-worth look like in the workplace? The self-deprecating doormat type is easy for most people to recognize due to the need to please everyone. A bit more subtle is the super- responsible one who won't delegate, who insists that no one else can do it "right"--and "right" is only his or her way--this manager is afraid of losing control. This person may also be a workaholic, a perfectionist who fails to treat employees as respected contributors to the organizations ultimate success.

The message that an individual is indeed competent, worthwhile, and has much to offer is not determined solely by such factors as wealth, education, parent's occupation, religious beliefs, or where one lives. Instead, self-worth comes from the quality of interaction and communication that exists between the individual and important people in the environment. This message of quality relationship is the crucial ingredient of mental health, even when the individual experiences momentary failure.

Proper development of our workers is an important strategic objective. It means having self-esteem, confidence, and skill to examine ones job and career prospects. This development does not inevitably come with time and tenure in poorly run organizations. The issue is less of one working more but more one of working smarter. We all, thus, have the potential to evolve toward a more complex understanding of the organization, its environment and unique challenges. However, since the latter stages of career and personal development require a more sophisticated interest in learning, which build upon earlier experiences and stages, organizations must make a strategic and early commitment of resources to this type of continuous learning environment.

Sometimes during the process of development, we are concerned with issues of personal career growth; at other times we are exploring issues of interest to our relations with the wider world. This alternating movement of priorities is really about our ability to better balance various dimensions of our personal and work lives. As we move beyond areas of personal growth, we each must find new ways to relate our personal career goals to the strategic needs of the organization. As we achieve personal and interpersonal balance, we can then continue to see new opportunities to redefine ourselves in ways that confirm our newly emerging strengths.

Such actions require a sense of self-confidence and self-esteem that allows us to take risks and search for creative new growth opportunities. As we expand our boundaries and strive toward balance among the complex dimensions of our personal and work lives, we rely upon the self-esteem already earned as our foundation to carry us to places less clearly defined by the conventions of others in our organization. This involves us in the search for more creative and innovative solutions to organizational problems and includes a higher sense of responsibility, goal direction, self-control, and discipline. This reaching beyond our traditional boundaries is highly beneficial for creating more knowledgeable and cooperative workers who can function as members of temporary teams and projects.

These more responsible workers are better able to nurture the organizations' human resources. They begin to understand the importance of helping others to develop confidence in themselves. Learning to meet these human needs is essential for the optimum development of individuals, organizations, and society. Developing good self-esteem results in all of us becoming better transition managers. This process should be one of ongoing self-examination for awareness, understanding, renewal, and growth. Such examination builds character, in addition to improving one's skills. The modern organization must become more active in directing this process.

Research indicates that organizations which promote the value and attitude of strategic and continuous learning also improve the quality of work life. We can observe this process in those individuals who actually improve their lives and increase their energy by increasing the number of priority activities that promote the organizations success. A commitment to a more productive life is really a statement about our strategic belief in people. Each of us must accept the challenge to view any

145

obstacle to our esteem and development, or those of the organizations for we we work, as learning opportunities.

In addition, obstacles or blockages provide the nourishment for re-charging and run down mental, emotional, and human resource batteries. Thus, we need the world of obstacles and challenges to provide us the testing ground for measuring our degree of commitment, caring, integrity, skills, awareness, knowledge, and maturity. It is not by accident that the process of building both a personal mission and strategic organizational purpose requires that we make some fundamental perceptual shifts from action to reflection and back again.

Throughout our lives, each of us must learn to utilize our own experiences to gain insights for renewing our fundamental connection with the work that is important to us. The well-managed personal life is the foundation for all meaningful activity; it focuses us on those projects worth pursuing and strengthens our mission actively seek the pursuit of those work and organizational values that make a difference in our lives. Organizational excellence is fundamentally the process of building upon the potentials of our most precious human resources. The strategic challenge is to support this process in new ways that bring results.

CHAPTER EIGHT
STRATEGIC HUMAN RESOURCE ASSESSMENT, PLANNING, AND MANAGEMENT

1 BUSINESS/MANAGEMENT EXPECTATIONS FOR HUMAN RESOURCE PROFESSIONALS AND DEPARTMENTS

- Understand how to recruit, staff and compensate and get the right people in the right jobs

- Creatively help solve personnel and business problems

- Make sure that the compensation/reward system (benefits, health care, vacation) is administered effectively and fairly

- Diagnose and monitor problems, issues and concerns of organizational members and create programs to resolve these concerns before they create a crisis

- Engage in anticipative and collaborative human resource planning to support the organization's strategic business plan

- Provide change, integration, coordination and transition management skills when needed

- Provide training and development programs to ensure that employees are receiving the most relevant and specialized information about how they might do their job more effectively (e.g. computers, listening skills, communication skills, time management, planning skills)

- Maintain their credibility and influence as an important source of internal consulting and professional expertise regarding people, processes and systems

- Provide leadership, expertise and legitimacy for various programs of equal employment opportunity for women, minorities and the handicapped

- Record and have available adequate documentation concerning the administration of the human resource system in order to meet both organizational and governmental requirements

- Support employee relations and career development, including health, safety and wellness

- Maintain a system of positive worker, labor and union relations

2 THE STRATEGIC HUMAN RESOURCES DEPARTMENT

- Learns thoroughly the traditional functional areas of personnel -- compensation, benefits, recruiting, staffing.

- Supports a holistic and multi-perspective view of the internal organizational system -- structure, processes, culture, boundaries.

- Monitors the stakeholders and forces operating in the organization's external environment (government, regulation, unions, quality conscious customers).

- Incorporates a more dynamic view of organizational design and planning to strategically integrate the business and human resource plans, including performance measures, assessment of organizational talent and the firms internal capabilities.

- Responds to the realities of organizational politics and power (the ability to accumulate and delegate resources to accomplish innovative tasks) in order to increase the influence, visibility and thus legitimacy of Human Resources Department (particularly at the senior management level).

- Integrates OD assessment, intervention, evaluation, execution and other relevant change-management skills that propel the HR professional beyond a narrow functional orientation to one of internal consultant, problem solving diagnostician, and strategic planner or thinker.

- Focuses upon the context of business-management effectiveness and meaningful problem solving involving people, and not just isolated people problems, divorced from the context of the particular organization.

- Incorporates the skills of creative thinking, and a long-term perspective, with a practical, bottom-line orientation.

- Fully understands the modern realities of the work place and return on investment (ROI) criteria in hiring, relocating, training employees, retaining an increasingly diverse and educated work force. In addition understands the demand for personal challenge, fairness, promotional opportunities, special needs of groups like women, minority, older and handicapped workers, the need to attract and nurture skilled and innovative management to lead the organization in the future, and the need for integrating quality, customer service and productivity.

3   STRATEGIC HUMAN RESOURCES PLANNING MODEL

Human Resource Planning (HR Planning) is the process of evaluating, analyzing and estimating the human resources requirements of the organization:

Work Force Analysis

- How many people do we have that can potentially staff various positions identified in human resource needs assessment?

- Discuss obstacles, difficulties and costs associated with recruiting outside the organization and opportunities for recruiting and promoting from within.

- If employees cannot be found internally or externally, how will this effect the HR plan and ultimately the organization's strategic plan?

- What skill requirements, leadership and managerial needs can be met by training and development programs? To what extent must outside consultants be relied upon? What kinds of lead time will be necessary to meet all plans with built-in contingencies?

- Securing the employees that the organization needs, when it needs them, thus, lessening the losses associated with failing to fill key vacancies in a timely fashion

- Anticipation of the necessary current skill levels and inventory of people who can fill such key positions

- Providing lead time for recruiting, training and development

- Focusing on how any expansions or reductions in operations, technological changes and external forces will impact the organization in the future

- Allowing the organization to anticipate needs to shift employees, cut back on recruitment, anticipate retraining programs for layoffs

- Establishing a framework for successful planning which facilitates the retention and development of key future leaders and long-term strategic forces.

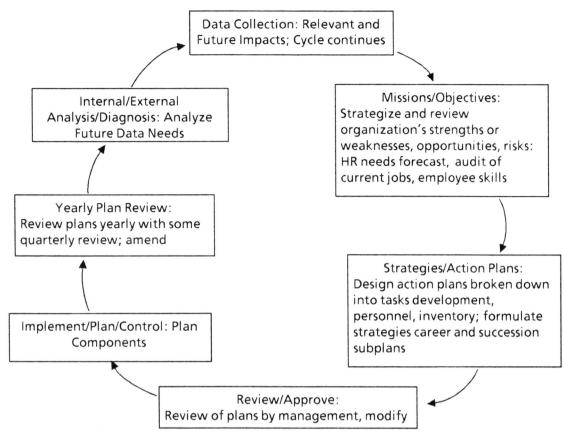

Figure 8-1. HRM Planning Cycle

ANALYSIS OF HR NEEDS AND SYMPTOMS OF PROBLEMS	Training Manage ment Develop ment	Recruit- ing Orienta- tion	Manage ment Systems and Process	Manage ment Develop ment	Compen sation Benefits	Labor Relation	Em- ployee Relation	OD	HR Forecast ing
High turnover Absenteeism	X	X			X		X		
Career stagnation Dead end jobs Loss of talent			X	X				X	
Workers bringing personal problems to work			X				X		
Manpower - Shortages in key areas	X	X		X	X				X
Communication problems between line and staff and key interface units			X	X		X		X	
Lack of management depth		X		X				X	
Key managers being recruited by head hunters			X	X	X			X	
Compensation problems		X		X	X				
Performance evaluation	X		X	X					

Table 8-1. Human Resource Needs Analysis for Determining Plan Requirements

4   HUMAN RESOURCE POLICIES

Policy Issues

1. Absenteeism
2. Benefits
3. Jury Duty
4. Discipline
5. Equal Employment Opportunity Policy and Procedure for Complaints
6. Employee Operation
7. Relocation
8. Leave of Absence
9. Pay, Hours of Work, Records
10. Temporary Employment
11. Performance Appraisal
12. Promotional Transfer
13. Health and Safety
14. Training and Development
15. Educational Assistance - Reimbursement
16. Unemployment Compensation
17. Workmen's Compensation
18. Vacations, Sick Leave

Policies Should Be

- Short . Simple . Don't talk down, preach or dictate

- Revised periodically to reflect current leadership and climate of company

- Evaluated constantly to determine whether the policy enforces, or hinders operations

- Consistent with the company's strategic and business plan

- Helpful or hurtful to morale

- Communicated clearly

- Administered fairly and consistently

- Explained to all workers as an attempt to: state the company position on this important issue; provide uniform guidelines and standardization for all personnel decisions; establish responsibility for administering personal policy and procedures; help in the auditing of the human resource function; assist in the process of employee counseling; protect the company in the face of litigation

- Located in a personnel policy manual or separate manuals, for example, salary and wages, benefits, etc.

Effective Policies Are:

1. Communicated between managers/supervisors and workers at least quarterly and reviewed yearly during performance evaluation

2. Published in employee newsletters or magazines through issues and personal ties that feature the importance of following policy

3. Reviewed in employee orientations and other corporate media

4. Linked to the larger issue of employee development -- the worker and the organization as partners (must reflect the factual situation)

5. Reinforced in speak-up breakfasts, luncheons or dinners

6. Acknowledged through a question box or hotline, in order to encourage dialogue on the effectiveness of policies

7. Reviewed with members of work teams as they impact task assignments and execution

8. Used during social and recreational activities (sports, clubs, craft faire) as a means of employee communication

9. Encouraged through many vehicles, for example: start an employee speakers bureau for communicating company purpose and mission (through policy) to community groups, external constituents and vendors, as well as internal groups.

5 EQUAL EMPLOYMENT LEGISLATION AND EXECUTIVE REGULATIONS

ACT, YEAR	KEY PROVISIONS
Equal Pay Act, 1963	Equal pay for men and women performing the same general work
Title VII, Section 703A - Civil Rights Act as amended by the Equal Employment Opportunity Act, 1972	Prohibits employment discrimination that is based upon considerations of race, religion, color, sex, or national origin. Who is covered: all private employers of 15 or more persons; all educational institutions (public and private); state and local government; public and private employment agencies; labor unions with 15 or more members; joint labor-management committees for apprenticeships and training
Executive Order 11246, 1965; 11375, 1967; 11478, 1979	Federal contractors and subcontractors must utilize affirmative action plans to eliminate current and prior discrimination practices. Order 11478 applies to postal workers
Age Discrimination in Employment Act, 1967 - amended 1978	Outlaws discrimination against any person 40 - 70 and prevents the use of mandatory retirement standards, except where "bonafide occupational qualification" is established
Pregnancy Discrimination Act, 1978	Prohibits discrimination against women affected by pregnancy, childbirth, or related medical conditions
Vocational Rehabilitation Act, 1973 and 1974	Outlaws discrimination against handicapped individuals for employers with federal contracts over $125,000
Vietnam-Era Veterans Readjustment Act, 1974	Requires affirmative action plans for and outlaws discrimination against Vietnam-era veterans

Table 8-2. EEO Legislation and Executive Regulations

6 REASONS FOR ESCALATING COSTS OF ADMINISTERING EMPLOYEE BENEFITS PROGRAMS

- An increasing holistic concern with the value of human resources for long-term organizational efficiency and effectiveness.

- Increase cost of new medical technology.

- Increase in governmental legislation and involvement (Employee Security Act) - ERISA passed in 1974, Pregnancy Disability Act in 1978

- Increasing liberal treatment of vesting requirements.

- Basic benefits are expanding to include such areas as dental, vision, insurance, scholarships for employee's tuition, tuition reimbursement, annual physical exams, better food services, more paid personal business days, relocation expenses, paid parking, matching donations to colleges, universities, stocksharing, social and recreational programs, day care expenses, counseling services and other employee related assistance programs.

- Increasing sense of entitlement on the part of a diverse and educated work force.

- Failure on the part of the work force to understand the costs of specific benefits.

7   WHAT TO DO ABOUT EMPLOYEE TURNOVER

As a supervisor, you can directly influence employee turnover. What you do, or don't do, makes a difference. Studies consistently show that the relationship between the supervisor and the employee is among the top three factors that determine whether an employee stays or leaves (3).

The Hiring Process:

1) **Find out the applicant's needs, wants, and goals.** Ask questions during the interview, to learn more about the applicant as an individual.

2) **Tell the applicant what you want to accomplish and explain how you do things.** During the interview, explain the goals you have set for your group and yourself. Describe how you communicate, how you wish to be communicated with.

3) **Let the applicant know the philosophy and goals of the company.** A prospective employee needs to know as much about the company as possible.

4) **Tell the applicant about any policies or procedures that would directly affect him or her.** Give the applicant a chance to ask questions.

5) **Provide a written, up-to-date job description.** Go over it in the interview with the applicant.

6) **Show the applicant the kind of work he or she would be doing and what his or her work area would be like.**

7) **When possible, take all applicants to meet and talk to some of the people they would be working with.**

After The Hiring Decision Is Made

1) **Make sure the new employee is well launched.** Look for areas where further orientation or training is needed. Be alert for problems the employee may be having in adjusting. Be especially diplomatic if you must point out mistakes.

2) **Work at keeping in touch.** Be available to help or listen.
3) **Recognize achievements.** Employees are eager in the beginning to know how their work is evaluated; use praise plentifully.

4) **Run interference.** Keep management informed about the concerns your people have.

5) **Be the main source of company information.** Relay vital information about company policies and procedures - particularly impending changes that will directly affect them. Be honest with your employees about your information base.

6) **Show a willingness to work things out.** Make sure your actions demonstrate that you are aware of what is happening in your area, that you are consistent and fair.

8 STRATEGIC PLANNING

Sound implementation of strategic plans depends on having adequate performance management, career development and management succession systems in place. These help the strategic plan survive and support the structural planning that is initiated by others in the organization (4).

There are three reasons why strategic planning is an appropriate Organization Development activity:

1)   It requires the successful facilitation of a group process without becoming entrenched within one functional discipline.

2)   It supports the core OD tenet that key executives' active participation in a process heightens client ownership of the plan and awareness of the discarded alternatives, thus reducing anxiety and resistance.

3)   It is a natural offshoot of other OD assignments/projects.

The consultant contributes to strategic planning by being responsible for the "how", while the client is responsible for the essential grounding -- who, what, when, where, and why. While the consultant offers objectivity, the client contributes historical perspective and overall awareness of the organization.

It is suggested that strategic planning be participated in by key executives, support personnel as needed, and consultants (internal and external). The session(s) should be held off-site, for a minimum of two days with multiple sessions. Pre-session preparation is needed to acclimate the members to the process.

Some components of strategic planning are:

•   Mission statement - the organization's priorities and emphasis;

•   Domain identification - reflect the external environment and genuine values of the organization;

•   Domain analyzation - reflects the environment, current activities, future perspective, inconsistencies with the mission statement, the ideals, action plans;

•   Objective statement - clear and succinct strategic objectives, to include identification of major resources, major activities needed, schedule and responsibility;

•   Development of systems to manage plans.

Strategic planning must occur at the corporate level initially, then at division and unit levels. Broader mission statements can then test the legitimacy of division and unit planning.

CEO/LEADERS ROLE	CHARACTERISTICS AND ASSUMPTIONS	STRATEGIC QUESTION
Commander	--Rational --Excessive linear thinking --Easy implementation --Top-down strategies more likely to succeed --Centralized information needs --Under control of leader only-little sharing --Splits firm into thinkers and doers	• How do I formulate the optimum or one best strategy?
Change Architect	--Behavior can be molded or manipulated to achieve compliance with plan --Ignores problems by obtaining accurate information --Still somewhat top down --Trades off strategic flexibility for normative strategy	• I have a strategy in mind; now how do I implement it?
Collaborator-Coordinator	--Trust to get input by brainstorming and other group dynamic techniques --Utilizes dialectal inquiry and teacher mode --Sometimes sacrifices economic rationality for team commitment	• How do I involve top management to get commitment to strategies from the start?
Cultural-coach	--Leaders guided by communicating and instilling a vision or overarching mission --Once game plan set, the CEO or leader acts as coach in giving general directions, encouraging managers and others to determine the operating details --Focuses on entire organizational system, goals and values --Culture and strategy go together --Requires a great deal of time to implement --Assumes uniformity and sometimes resistance to differences and new ways of doing things --Assumes informed and intelligent people and sufficient organizational slack to absorb costs of implementing cultural, HRM and educational strategies	• How do I involve the whole organization in implementation?
Precisive, Premise-setter and Judge Advocate	--Strategy should derive upward from the firing line rather than downward from the top --CEO or leader sets decision premises and defines organizational purposes broadly enough to encourage risk taking and innovation --Supports some degree of autonomous strategic behavior --Without local or managerial involvement find energy wasted upon hiding pet projects, bending rules, biasing data, and creating new norms for circumventing work tasks felt to be arbitrary and irrelevant to work unit realities --Willingness to relinquish control, delegate partial responsibility for strategy and tactics --This model fits well with organizational theories of transformative leadership, agency theory and organizational creativity	• How do I encourage managers to come forward as champions of sound strategies?

Table 8-3. Models of Strategic Implementation (5)

STAGE AND DEFINITION	CHARACTERISTICS
Assessing the situation - organizing and making sense out of what is happening - tells us what is happening and why	• choose variables or indicators which provide boxes into which phenomenon can be classified - prices, competition, consumer needs • choose measures for variables relating to amounts, higher, lower, etc. • source of variables can be heuristics (rules of thumb, personal experiences, business or behavioral science disciplines, knowledge of strategy • variables might include scope (product, markets, price/quality, market position); competitive edge; specifications (market share, return on equity, technical innovation, conflict resolution); dynamics (timing for achievement of objectives); risk (probability of gain and win or loss); deployment of resources (among human, capital and liquid categories); synergy (joint efforts sought); environment (analyze supporters, customer/client suppliers, union, end user of service, community perception) • variable should be chosen to link one's assessment to personal experience and sound organizational theory; should permit the gathering of data; should provide insight into underlying patterns and relationships in the situation; should allow one to communicate the assessment to relevant others • model building is the first stage of the assessment process • generalize from the variables (sales are falling) to the variable itself (sales) - this level is called description • determine the relationships among variables and state these relationships as conditions - this level is called conjecture and suggests how the variables might influence each other • the movement to the second step requires creativity skills because we are moving from concrete facts to a situation of other possible influences and states as the variables interact upon each other
Identifying and analyzing problems - tells us what is wrong and should be changed - problems are identified from an assessment by formulating strategic objectives and analyzing gaps in the achievement of objectives	• problems are uncovered by the assessment but now must be interpreted in light of one's objectives (is declining GPA's a problem relative to desired clientele); in other words a gap between the actual situation and the desired situation - a short fall, discrepancy or variance • not all gaps are problems that must be solvable (feasible to close gap) and include our desire or intention to solve • objectives thus help us to see problems as we learn where we want to be • objectives can be formulated through following acceptable business/organization practice (norms), in response to what one does or doesn't want, or through creative processes • problem analysis is now required to explore the gap between assessment (the actual situation) and objectives (where we want to be) • strategy -- steps to close the gaps which are identified as significant problems; next all variables are examined for their influences on closing the gaps and variables most directly influenced by management are identified; next, alternative solutions are designed by specifying changes in the states or variables influenced by management; alternatives are evaluated, finally, alternatives are chosen which appear to yield the best results
The synthesis - executives and managers are reasonably certain about what the problems are and how to solve them - the dialectical method is used to create synthesis by, introducing uncertainty in order to achieve a better solution	• delineate the strategy advocated by various participants and identify the problem which the strategy is intended to solve • find the conditions sufficient for the strategy to be implemented • determine conditions necessary for the strategy to work and reframe those conditions through assessment • gather date to support the conditions and screen conditions • repeat all the above steps for each strategy • develop counter conditions and support these conditions with data • confront conditions and counter conditions with data and then reframe conditions • develop the best strategy under the various circumstances

Table 8-4. A Model of Strategic Thinking (6)

11   STRATEGIC SCANNING

In order to strategically plan for organizational change in a world of increasing uncertainty, scarce resources, global competition and unrecognized stakeholders, it is essential for all organizations to track or scan their environment (7). Boundary spanners, issues managers, in-house futurists, strategic planners and OD specialists can anticipate important trends, forces, issues, resource scarcities, sources of uncertainty, possibilities, opportunities and threats before they arrive.

- Scan any relevant source of information - movies, books, videotapes, audio tapes, magazines, newspapers, annual reports, specialist publications, in order to identify current economic, technical, social, and political developments.

- A scanning or strategic action committee can divide responsibilities for various information and media arenas. Each person can be made responsible for shifting through the information and selecting only the most meaningful materials to bring back to the entire committee.

- Scan a broad range of both personal and organizational activities based upon an agreed set of important indicators or base line trends important to the organization.

- Passive scanning can be important. Emphasize that everyone in the organization gather some relevant material continually. This scanning can relate to the relationship of each individuals interests, goals, values and career objectives as they dovetail with the organization. Many organizations fail to utilize creative sources of information and selectively ignore much useful data. The criteria for this type of scanning need not be rigorous and can remain obscure and ad hoc.

- Active scanning requires a more rigorous organizational commitment and the information search process requires more systematic attention and more formalized mechanisms. Here the information resources monitored are selected and evaluated according to organizational relevancy and urgency. The focus moves to the "interesting" future where issues, trends and events may have a potentially important and practical impact upon the organization. Organizations with scanning committees must become more aware of how to build upon their passive scanning skills to include more relevant, systematic and creative criteria. In addition, the organization must learn to identify those individuals adept at spotting trends, issues, opportunities, threats, seeing that the source of innovation can often lie in the unexpected success. (See also strategic planning in this section.)

CHAPTER NINE
STRATEGIC PERFORMANCE MANAGEMENT

1   THE ROLE OF THE COMPENSATION FUNCTION

This text addresses many theories of organizational development, and styles of management as they relate to organizational success (8). Another area of Human Resources which merits review in this chapter is the compensation function which revolves around directing employee performance toward achieving organizational goals.

In this chapter, we will focus on compensation as a direct reward system which is used to attract, retain, and motivate qualified individuals to achieve organizational goals. The emphasis will be on the management of base pay and performance management.

In recent years compensation has expanded beyond the direct wages for hours worked to encompass both money, non-financial rewards, and performance management. It is no longer purely an economic concept which entails a price for hours of production. It is also a psychological concept which addresses how theories of motivation can be applied to management practices in order to increase employee productivity. For example, Victor Vroom's and Frederick Herzberg's theories of human behavior and motivation have frequently been applied to reward systems.

Compensation has also become, among many other Human Resources functions, a legal concept. Both state and federal legislation have impacted compensation practice in several areas, such as job status (exempt vs. non-exempt), overtime pay, equal pay for equal work, record keeping, minimum wages, wage controls, prevailing wages, and taxation.

The development of a base compensation system involves many stages: job analysis and the writing of job descriptions, job evaluations, salary surveys, a pay structure, and a performance management program. There may be additional elements of the compensation system, such as bonuses, lump sum pay, and commissions. However, they are not addressed in this section.

Since compensation is a reward system, its successful management should be based on an understanding of motivation. One of the most recognized theories in this field is Victor Vroom's theory of motivation which takes into account a person's expectations for success. According to Vroom, motivation will occur if the following occurs:

- The "valence" or value of the particular outcome (such as a promotion) is very high for the individual; and

- If the individual feels that there is a likelihood of accomplishing the task and obtaining the outcome.

Effort leads to accomplishing -->	Person sees that accomplishing task leads to desirable outcome task such as status or recognition.	-->	Motivation will take place

Frederick Herzberg's Motivator-Hygiene Theory divides Abraham Maslow's hierarchy of needs into lower level (physiological, safety, social), which he calls hygiene factors, and higher level (ego, self-actualization) needs, which he calls motivators. Herzberg considers hygiene factors as poor motivators because they are quickly satisfied, then the only way to continue motivating the person is to offer more of them, in an endlessly escalating process.

The higher part of the hierarchy, on the other hand, includes the true motivators. According to Herzberg, the right way to motivate someone is not to give more money or a raise, but to arrange the job in such a way that the person gets a sense of achievement out of doing it.

Herzberg's theory suggests a program called "job enrichment." This program would include five basic actions which a manager can take to enrich jobs:

1. **Form natural work groupings**. Structure each job to entail working with a specific group of individuals or departments. For example one Human Resources Representative would be assigned to a single unit or division, instead of all the Representatives supporting all the units or divisions.

2. **Combine tasks**. Form a total process instead of disjointed steps. This entails assigning the person in the job a whole and meaningful process.

3. **Establish client relationships**. Let the employee have as much contact as possible with the "client."

4. **Vertical Loading**. Let the employee assume the responsibility of planning and controlling his or her own job.

5. **Open feedback channels**. Provide an opportunity for the employee to get immediate feedback on performance.

DEVELOPMENT AND IMPLEMENTATION OF A COMPENSATION PROGRAM

The success of any compensation program or an element of it depends to a great extent on whether all levels of management, including supervisors believe in it and are willing to implement and maintain it. Approval of top management alone is not sufficient.

Program success also depends on clear and frequent communication with employees concerning the philosophy of the program, why it was developed, and how it will affect them.

Programs which are developed, communicated, and maintained solely by the Human Resources department will be ineffective, no matter how solid their theoretical basis. Therefore, it is important to involve different levels of management as early as possible, whenever a program is being development. The following steps help ensure the success of the program being developed.

- Explain what you are attempting to develop to management and employees and invite them to provide you with input concerning their needs and opinions.

- Involve all levels of management and supervision in the development steps.

- Train all managers thoroughly in the philosophy of the program, how it relates to the organizational goals, its impact on different areas, and how to administer and maintain it.

- Encourage management's ownership of the program and ensure that they are the primary administrators.

- Communicate frequently with employees regarding the philosophy of the program and how it affects them.

Another element in the compensation program's success is the development of a compensation philosophy, mission statement, and goals, which are compatible with the overall organization's mission and goals. The goals should include a definition of what each component of the program is expected to accomplish. For example, a job description can be used for many purposes; such as recruitment, compliance with government regulation, motivation, evaluation of performance, position evaluation, training, and several other objectives. The design of the contents of the job description should then be based on the uses or functions which it expected to perform. The following is a list of the most typical uses of the different elements of compensation system:

- Evaluating jobs.

- Deciding on pay.

- Hiring.

- Promotions.

- Performance management.

- Motivation, development.

- Discipline.

- Training.

- Organizational design and staffing.

- Safety and health.

- Federal Legislation against discriminatory practices.

Now, let us review the different areas of Compensation which are included in developing a base pay structure: foundation work, job analysis, job descriptions, evaluations, market surveys, salary structure development, and a performance management program.

Since this is a brief review of the different elements of a base compensation system, only the most common uses of each element will be listed. They will be based on certain assumptions which may not be clear to the reader. However, if the compensation professional defines his/her own uses for the element before development and implementation, the format will be self evident.

The Foundation:

Before the compensation program is developed, it is imperative that those involved in the development understand the organization's mission, philosophy, culture, values, and the existing compensation structure. The compensation program must be an expression and a reinforcer of these areas.

In some organizations, these are clearly spelled out and practiced, while in others they can be inferred from the "way things are done around here."

Studying and understanding these elements should lead to the writing of a statement which defines the Compensation department's direction and its place in the organization.

Once the compensation professional achieves an understanding of the current conditions and develops the company's compensation mission statement and goals, it is appropriate to begin the development of the new program from the most basic unit, which is the job.

Job Analysis. Involves the identification and description of what is happening on the job. It identifies the major responsibilities and tasks, the knowledge, and the skills necessary for performing them, and the conditions under which they must be performed. It includes:

1. The activities performed in the job.

2. The organizational structure which the job is a part of.

3. The tools, materials, and equipment required for the job.

4. The outcomes of the job.

5. The knowledge, skills, and abilities needed to perform the job.

6. The job environment, such as working conditions.

7. The performance standards; what constitutes good, poor, and superior performance on the job.

Process of Job Analysis:

- Determine the organizational use of the job analysis.

- Learn about the mission, structure, operation, and jobs of the organization.

166

- Formulate a plan of action with a budget, methodology, and forms. It should be based on the organizational use of the job analysis.

- Communicate and carry out your plan of action.

Methodologies of Job Analysis:

- Interview

- Questionnaire

- Observation

- Diary/Log

- Combination

Job Analysis is the process or collecting information and data on characteristics of a job that make it different from other jobs (9).

Key Data Events
.   Job duties, responsibilities and relevant work activity
.   Behavior required and performance expected
.   Working conditions
.   Interaction with others and supervision given and received
.   Reporting relationships
.   Skill requirements
.   Effort needed, equipment used.

Methods of Data Collection

1. **Observation** - <u>Continuous</u> observation may occur as the manager or job analyst takes notes to describe the job over a period of time. The <u>work sampling</u> method allows the analyst to statistically sample certain work actions throughout the work cycle, rather than observing each detailed action.

2. **Interviews** - Conducted on a one-to-one basis with job incumbent at each job site. Can be structured using a semi-structured, focused format. The supervisor or manager must also be interviewed to give a complete picture.

3. **Questionnaire** - A survey instrument is developed and given to employees. The employee and supervisor can complete the questionnaire together or independently of each other. Discrepancies and contradictions can be highlighted through interviews. A minimum of one employee evaluation per job is needed, but more than one is more advantageous.

Functional job analysis (FJA) (10) is a system of analyzing the component tasks or responsibilities involved in any job. For example the Dictionary of Occupational Titles (DOT) is a standardized data source that lists jobs by a code which includes: occupational code, title, industrial designation in the first three digits; the next three digits indicate how it is marked on a numerical scale concerning the degree to which a person has responsibility for more comprehensive and tasks dealing with data, people and things. The final three digits indicate the alphabetical order of titles within the occupational group with the same responsibilities and judgments. (manager; personnel - 166. 117.-018):

4th Digit 1 DATA	5th Digit 1 PEOPLE	6th Digit 7 THINGS
0 Synthesizing	0 Mentoring	0 Setting up
1 Coordinating	1 Negotiating	1 Precision working
2 Analyzing	2 Instructing	2 Operations-Controlling
3 Compiling	3 Supervisors	3 Drivers-Operators
4 Computing	4 Diverting	4 Manipulation
5 Copying	5 Persuading	5 Tending
6 Comparing	6 Speaking-Signalling	6 Feeding
	7 Serving	7 Handling
	8 Taking Instructions-Helping	

Job Description. The role of the job description is to define the major aspects of the job, so that both the incumbent and the company have a clear definition of the job. It is the end product of the job analysis.

Elements of the job description include:

1. **Identification information.** Includes the job title, job status (exempt versus non-exempt), a job code which permits easy referencing, the date the description is written, the writer(s) of the description, the plant/division and department/section name, and the title of the immediate supervisor.

   Other information which may be included in this section; such as grade, points, or approvals.

2. **Job Summary.** A brief description which delineates the general characteristics of the job, listing only major functions or activities which outline the primary reason for the existence of the job. This section is usually used for job matching in surveys.

3. **Job Responsibilities.** This section includes the major responsibilities of the position. They are the broad categories of work activities that, in total, define the scope of work assignments. Responsibilities include tasks or duties, which are separate activities, the sum of which produce an identifiable outcome. An example of a major responsibility is recruiting candidates. This responsibility may include several tasks or duties; such as advertising the position, reviewing resumes, interviewing candidates, and recommending the most appropriate candidate for the job.

   This portion of the job description is usually the longest and the most difficult to write. The challenge is to ensure tasks or duties are grouped under the appropriate major responsibility, instead of listing isolated and scattered actions. There is usually a tendency on the part of the incumbent to list as many tasks and duties as possible, believing that the more of these that are the listed, the higher the value of the job. The ideal number of job responsibilities for most jobs is 7 to 10.

4. **Job Standards.** This is a crucial part of defining the job which is rarely included in job description. It defines the desired results or outcome of performing the major responsibilities of the job. It should include quality, quantity, time, and

168

cost requirements. It may also outline desired job-related behaviors, only when listing the outcome is not sufficient.

5. **Job Requirements.** Includes basic requirements for knowledge, skills, experience, education, and any special training.

Once jobs are defined, job hierarchies can be established through job evaluations or based on a market comparison.

Job Evaluation. A process which establishes the relative internal worth relationships of the job. Worth in this case signifies the importance of the job or its contribution to the overall attainment of the goals and objectives of the organization.

Since the job evaluation is used to establish the internal value of the job, it is important to reconcile it with the organization's methods of establishing its external or competitive position in the market. In today's changing environment, many organizations are experiencing great difficulty in following an internal evaluation method which tells them that an engineer's job has the same internal value as an accountant's, yet the market place tells it that there is a difference of $5,000 to $10,000 between the two positions. Concern over this discrepancy leads many managers and compensation professionals to "back into" an incorrect evaluation which would justify the market difference.

Others may assign the appropriate value, yet slot the engineer's job, for example, into a higher salary range than the accountant's, in order to comply with market demands. Both methods corrupt the integrity of the evaluation system. It may be more appropriate in some cases to make a decision to be purely market driven and base the salary structures on market data, rather than internal job evaluations.

The job analysis and job description provide the information necessary for the job evaluation. They report the work activities and worker requirements. However, the evaluation process determines which aspect(s) of work activities and/or which worker requirements are to be used.

Job evaluations can be seen in two dimensions:

1. What comparison standard will be used to weigh the relative worth of the job?

2. Is the technique used quantitative or nonquantitative?

This can be represented in the following matrix:

Comparison

	Job to job	Job to Standard
Nonquantified	Job Ranking Method	Job Classification Method
Quantified	Factor Comparison Method	Point Method

169

The matrix demonstrates that the answer to the first questions should address whether each job will be evaluated based on a comparison to other jobs in the organization or to predetermined standards/compensable factors.

In the job to job comparison method, the job is rated based on a comparison to another job(s) in the organization; such as comparing a secretary's job to an assembler's.

In using compensable factors, they are defined as criteria or generic areas on which the organization places a value across jobs. Examples of compensable factors are knowledge, decision-making, and problem-solving. This method entails setting up predetermined job grades and slotting jobs into them based on the weight of their compensable factors.

The answer to the second question determines the other dimension in job evaluation category. A nonquantitative method has no numeric values assigned to the job or the standards. There is no distinction made of how much more one job is worth than the another, nor how much of a compensable factor exists in a job. The job ranking and job classification methods are considered nonquantitative.

On the other hand, the point and the factor compensation methods entail a determination of a numerical value to the weighing criteria.

Salary Surveys. To establish an organization's competitive position in the market, and maintain external equity, an organization needs to acquire information about market pay practices. This information can be obtained through salary and benefit surveys.

There are many published surveys which if used properly can provide an organization with vital information about the market. However, complete reliance on these surveys is not advisable. First, there is always a need for the organization to conduct its own survey to validate the published surveys.

In addition, every organization has positions which are typically not included in published surveys.

In conducting market surveys, it is important to take the following into consideration:

1. Identify the geographical location of your labor market. The lower the level of the jobs to be surveyed, the closer the labor market to your company's location. For example, clerical positions are usually filled from a pool which is within 10 to 20 miles from your organization, while top management positions could be filled with candidates from any where in the US.

2. Decide on the companies to include in the survey. These should include competitors in the same industry as the surveying organization, and other organizations which are sources of potential employees or possible employers of the organization's current employees (those you can get employees from or lose employees to.)

3. Decide on the appropriate size of the organizations to survey. Again, this is dependent on which companies you may lose employees to or be able to attract employees from. The size of the surveyed organizations, however, needs to be reasonably close to your company's size.

4. Prepare a written list of positions to be surveyed and all necessary questions, even if the survey is to be conducted by telephone. The list should be

comprehensive and address all the relevant data to serve the purpose of the survey. For example, when surveying hourly positions, questions regarding the amount of overtime worked and shift differentials should be included. Benefits are also becoming a major concern and may need to be included in the survey, along with salaries.

Survey data should be updated at least once-a-year and in volatile markets or for jobs which are in high demand the updates should be made every six months.

Salary Structure Design. Based on a determination of both the internal and external value of positions, a salary structure can be developed which defines the following:

1. Job hierarchies

2. Minimum and maximum levels of base pay for each job based on the organization's decision regarding its competitive position in the market.

How a Pay Policy line is Developed:

1. Establish the lowest and the highest rates of pay for the organization and draw a line connecting them.

        or

2. Obtain the market or going rate of pay for the lowest-paid and highest-paid jobs. Connecting these two points will also give you a first approximation for a pay policy line.

3. Most organizations follow this:

   - Identify the market rates of various benchmark jobs that cover the entire pay spectrum from the lowest to the highest rates of pay.

   - Plot on a chart the pay-rate information obtained through the survey, thus producing a scatter diagram or scatter plot. Each point represents a job. The paired coordinates for locating each point are the evaluated score for the job and its actual pay. An indicator of job worth on the horizontal axis (X) and the dollar value of the job on the vertical axis (Y).

   - Use the pay policy line to set midpoint values for all their jobs.

The point method assigns points for each amount of a compensable factor, then the points are added to determine the total value of the job. This method compares the relative magnitude of differences between jobs across the compensable factors.

2   PERFORMANCE APPRAISALS ... Introduction

The most important asset of any company is its people. Peters and Waterman (11) state, "Although most top managements assert that their companies care for their people, the excellent companies are distinguished by the intensity and pervasiveness of this concern ... we are talking about a tough-minded respect for the individual and the willingness to train him, to set reasonable and clear expectations for him, and to grant him practical autonomy to step out and contribute directly to this job".

Surveys have shown that American workers want to do their best but feel that management and "the system" keep them from it. Managers often create, with the best intentions, the very conditions that lead to poor morale and low productivity. To perform at one's best, it is essential to feel good about one's self and one's job. If the message from management is one that indicates a lack of caring about the individual, only concern about getting the work done, quality will slip. If a worker is unclear about what is expected of his/her in his/her specific job, it is likely that performance will not be very high.

$$p \quad = \quad m \quad x \quad a$$

Performance = Motivation x Ability

There are three typical reasons why people do not perform well: they don't know how to do their job; they don't know exactly what is expected of them; or they simply don't want to.

Most workers want to experience "job satisfaction". If you follow Maslow's premise, employee's derive this satisfaction if they can continually meet one or more of the following:

    Survival. . .basic work, base salary
    Security. . . continued employment, fringe benefits
    Belonging. . . compatible work groups, professional friends
    Prestige. . . title, merit increases, responsibility
    Self-Fulfillment. . . challenge, creativity, advancement.

It stands to reason that if an organization is to provide the atmosphere where workers can meet these needs, performance and productivity will be high. It does mean that supervisors and managers must be prepared to take on more "humanistic" roles such as: coach, counselor, teacher, leader of employees to challenges, provider of honest, timely and direct feedback, and the ability to make people feel good about themselves.

EXAMINE YOUR EXPECTATIONS.

Along with the need to satisfy the above-mentioned motivating factors, two things are important to high performance in individuals: the ability to see the end result of their efforts; and the ability to know exactly what is expected of them and how they are performing against those expectations. Additionally, when an employee has as sense of how their work fits into the overall scheme of the organization, it allows them to feel a sense of pride in their work.

Do you expect your employees to put out a high level of productivity if they don't feel involved in the end product? Do you expect your employees to just "know" what your expectations are of them, or how you perceive their performance? Do your employees

172

know what the organization is trying to accomplish, and how it is meeting (or not meeting) its goals? Are you setting aside quality time on a regular basis with your employees to discuss their performance?

Peters (12) says "Performance Appraisals should be ongoing, based upon a simple contract between the person being appraised and his/her boss".

In this section we discuss Performance Appraisal Systems, Performance Diagnosis, Performance Audits. As throughout this text, sections and topics are overlapping, and you will find other related discussions, such as job design models, motivation theories, communication skills, and career counseling relevant to performance management. Hopefully, these discussions will provide you with the basis for creating a strategic performance management system.

3   PERFORMANCE DIAGNOSIS - IDENTIFYING THE CAUSE OF POOR PERFORMANCE

A performance appraisal will highlight performance which does not meet standards, however will not uncover the reasons why. A typical manager will feel the reason is based upon the subordinates characteristics, such as laziness or carelessness. This, however, is usually not the true cause for poor performance. Lack of or poor training, undeveloped skills, circumstances beyond the employees control could all contribute to poor performance. If the Performance Appraisal does not identify these causes, managers must use other methods for uncovering them.

Performance Diagnosis is a method of revealing causes for poor performance. There are three basic questions a manager must ask of an employee whose performance does not meet standards:

- What is going wrong when someone is not performing well?

- What type of performer is this employee?

- What, if any, skills are in need of development?

Job performance is the culmination of three elements working together: skill level, effort level and external conditions. Does the employee have the necessary skills to perform the job adequately? Is the employee motivated to exert the effort to perform the job adequately? Are the external conditions (such as economic conditions, working machinery, adequate supplies) favorable to the employee performing the job adequately? If any of these three elements are deficient, the employee cannot perform to meet standards.

Performance diagnosis calls for rating the employee as either high or low in the three elements above. The employee will then fit into one of the types of performers listed in Figure 9-1 and briefly discussed below.

TYPE	SKILL	EFFORT	EXTERNAL CONDITION
Stars	High	High	Favorable
Victims	High	High	Unfavorable
Coasters	High	Low	Favorable
Quitters	High	Low	Unfavorable
Long Shots	Low	High	Favorable
Wheel Spinners	Low	High	Unfavorable
Lottery Winners	Low	Low	Favorable
Deadwood	Low	Low	Unfavorable

Figure 9-1

174

- Stars are skilled, motivated, and in the right place at the right time. They usually have no performance problems.

- Victims are skilled, motivated, and not in the right place. An example of this is a good sales person not meeting his/her targets due to a poor economic situation. The manager must find a way to remove the unfavorable external conditions for this employee.

- Coasters are skilled, however unmotivated, and lucky enough to be in a position where much effort is not required. The example here is the talented sales rep who is successful due to a lot of "bluebirds", and does not make the effort to increase his new prospects. The employee should be encouraged to increase their effort level, as they may not be so lucky to always have favorable external conditions.

- Quitters are skilled, unmotivated, and in unfavorable conditions. They have given up. The above mentioned sales rep now finds him/herself in a territory requiring much work and tough customers. The manager must remove the unfavorable external conditions and encourage the employee to put forth more effort.

- Long Shots are not very skilled, however are highly motivated and in the right place. An example here is a new sales rep who is willing to put in the hours, and has a good territory which pays off. This employee should be trained to maintain high performance, both in their current situation, and in the event their external conditions change.

- Wheel Spinners are not very skilled, not in the right place, however are highly motivated. The example here is the new sales rep who isn't trained and doesn't have a good territory, but is willing to put in effort. Due to the unfavorable conditions, he/she is not performing well. The manager should provide training to increase skills, and remove the barriers to a favorable condition.

- Lottery Winners are not particularly skilled or motivated, however have found themselves in a "lucky" situation. They may not be diagnosed with poor performance (the sales rep in this situation has a good territory which yields good sales performance), however should be trained to increase skills, and encouraged to exert more effort.

- Deadwood employees are unskilled, unmotivated, and in unfavorable external conditions. Perhaps the most challenging , the manager will need to provide training, coaching, and perhaps job reassignment.

Performance diagnosis can assist the manager to find the underlying causes for poor performance. It can also eliminate wasted efforts and money (for example providing additional training to a "victim", or coaching a "wheel spinner"). Performance diagnosis can provide a basis for a realistic performance appraisal discussion and the creation of a solid developmental action plan.

Performance diagnosis utilizes three types of performance appraisals, 1) results-oriented appraisals, where bottom-line results are measured against a standard, 2) behavior appraisals, where an employee is appraised by what he/she does, and 3) proficiency tests, where skills relating to the job are measured. See Figure 9-2 and discussion below for the sequence of performance diagnosis.

Results-oriented appraisals are a combination of the three previously mentioned elements, while behavior appraisals look at skill and effort. Proficiency appraisals look at skill only. The difference between results-oriented and behavior appraisals is

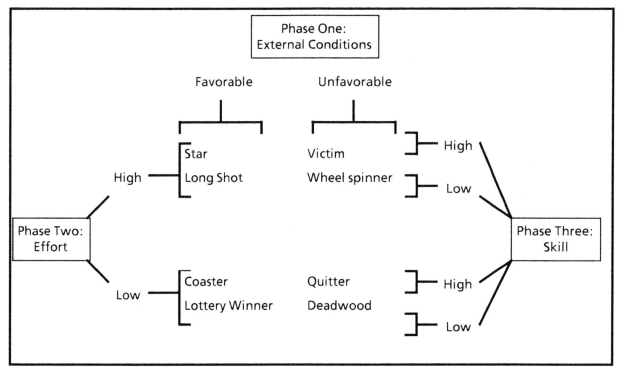

Figure 9-2

external conditions. Performance Diagnosis calls for a review of the three elements of job performance.

Phase I: **External Conditions** is a comparison of results-oriented and behavior appraisals, which will show the impact of external conditions on performance. If behavior is appraised as high and results are high, probably no performance problems exist. If behavior is high and results are appraised as low, the variable is unfavorable external conditions. If behavior is low and results are high, favorable external conditions prevail. Low behavior and low results indicates unfavorable external conditions.

BEHAVIOR	RESULTS	EXTERNAL CONDITIONS
High	High	Favorable
High	Low	Unfavorable
Low	High	Favorable
Low	Low	Unfavorable

Phase II: **Effort Level** is a comparison of behavior and proficiency appraisals, which will show the impact of effort on behavior. If proficiency is appraised as high and behavior is appraised as high, no effort or ability problem exists. If proficiency is high and behavior is low, effective behaviors are not being performed. If proficiency is low and behavior is high, the employees efforts make up for low skills. Low ratings of proficiency and behavior indicate low efforts on the part of the employee.

176

PROFICIENCY	BEHAVIOR	EFFORT
High	High	High
High	Low	Low
Low	High	High
Low	Low	Low

<u>Phase III: **Skill Level**</u> calls for an examination of proficiency test scores. This determines what an employee can do, not what they are doing. Phase III simply records proficiency scores.

This quantitative method of performance diagnosis is beneficial to both manager and subordinate in the creation of an accurate and fair performance appraisal. Each phase narrows the set of potential performance problems, allowing the manager to more accurately assess the situation.

To extend Performance Diagnosis to the final step, one must go beyond high or low ratings. You will see in Figure 9-3 a three rating scale for the three performance appraisal systems: Does not meet standards, Meets standards, and Exceeds standards. After an employees results, behaviors, and proficiencies are determined, they are rated using the five point scale. The three areas are then compared and transposed onto the chart.

	DOES NOT MEET STANDARDS (1)	MEETS STANDARDS (3)	EXCEEDS STANDARDS (5)
RESULTS			
BEHAVIOR			
PROFICIENCY			

External Conditions:

Negative Number = Unfavorable

Positive Number = Favorable

—————— —— —————— = ——————
Results   Behavior   External
Score   Score   Conditions

Effort Level:

Negative Number = Low

Positive Number = High

—————— —— —————— = ——————
Behavior   Proficiency   Effort
Score   Score   Level

Skill Level:

—————— = Skill Level
Proficiency
Score

1 = Below Standard

3 = Standard

5 = Above Standard

Figure 9-3

This systematic approach to Performance Diagnosis removes some of the subjectivity in identifying the cause of poor performance. It also opens up avenues to providing effective remedies to these performance problems.

4   A SYSTEMATIC PERFORMANCE APPRAISAL PROGRAM

The Performance Appraisal has three purposes (13):

1. To help improve performance by identifying strengths and weaknesses and by getting things done which will develop the former and overcome the latter.

2. To identify those with potential for greater responsibility, now or in the future, and to provide guidance on what should be done to ensure that this potential is realized.

3. To assist in deciding on pay increases which fairly equate the level of reward with the level of performance.

While assessing an employees performance is one of the most important aspects of management, it is also one of the most resisted. Managers tend to resist the conventional Performance Appraisal programs, even though they may agree with the concept. Some reasons for this resistance are:

● Most managers dislike criticizing a subordinate and fear having to justify their opinion.

● Lack of training and skill development needed to conduct the Performance Appraisal interview

● Mistrust of the appraisal instrument, especially in non-objective areas such as attitude

● Time involved in the process of evaluation, discussion, and action plan development.

Subordinates tend to dislike the conventional Performance Appraisal programs, feeling

● the general appraisal instrument is not adequate or accurate for their specific jobs;

● the manager is not capable of accurate assessment of the more technical areas of their jobs;

● the manager is unable to relay criticism in a positive and constructive manner, keeping the discussion to specific performance and behaviors, not personality;

● the manager plays favorites;

● the amount of salary increase is determined by factors other than performance;

● the Performance Appraisal is not tied to on-going reviews and discussions.

As a result, in many cases the Performance Appraisal is written and delivered in a less than satisfactory method, the subordinate does not leave the session feeling adequately and/or accurately assessed, and does not have a definite developmental action plan in place to correct any necessary areas.

The following represents the steps to an *objective* and *systematic* performance appraisal system.

Step 1. Review and Appraise Performance Since the Last Appraisal

A. In preparation for this performance appraisal, your major task is to collect three kinds of information; (a) all goals, objectives, or levels of performance that were agreed to at the start of the period being reviewed, (b) your subordinates actual performance results for the period, in all aspects of performance for which goals were set, and (c) your subordinates self-assessment of his/her performance results against the objectives defined at the beginning of the period.

B. The above data should be for the period covered by the appraisal, and for this period only. A major source of data for (a) could by your records of previous feedback and coaching sessions during the period.

C. Your next task is to compare actual performance (b) with goals and objectives (a) and the employees self assessment (c) in order to determine where the employees performance has either fallen short of or exceeded goals. You should also attempt to identify areas where performance is either on an improving trend or is deteriorating.

D. Now you must do some hard thinking about your subordinates past and current performance and about his or her potential for improvement. You should then prepare a formal "performance appraisal" (using the company's standard format if one exists) for the period just finished.

E. Your appraisal of the employees overall performance should be fair and impartial, and unbiased by personal feelings toward the person being reviewed. The appraisal should be behavior-based and use examples of performance to substantiate any overall ratings assigned.

F. Your appraisal should also consider whether factors outside the control of the employee could have caused a shortfall from the specified goals or output levels; such as, reallocation of resources to other projects, or new work assignments that could have diverted the persons efforts away from the original goals.

Step 2. Prepare Employee Development Plan and Tentative Goals for the Next Review period

A. Looking ahead now, you should prepare a program of training and development for your employee for the next six months or year. Request input into this developmental plan from the employee at the same time as he/she provides the self-assessment of their performance (Step 1, A). The plan at this point is tentative, and will be firmed up after discussion with the employee.

B. The development plan should contain Performance Objectives, a set of goals, targets, or improvements in performance during the period ahead. These performance objectives should be challenging yet attainable. The improvement goals should consider the persons past performance, current performance, and your assessment of the employees potential for improvement.

C. The Performance Objectives should be related to the overall objectives of your department, or section, as well as related to the organizations goals.

D. The development plan should consider the relative costs, benefits, and availability of formal training, college tuition plan courses, special development assignments, and home study by the employee.

Step 3. Provide Feedback on Performance

A. You should by now be well prepared for the feedback session with your subordinate. Your task now is to meet with the employee, first notifying him/her in advance of the meeting about the time, place, and purpose of the conference. (A sudden surprise meeting can defeat the purpose of your review.)

B. You should set and maintain a constructive tone throughout the meeting, in order to encourage full participation and input by your employee. Your task now is to discuss the persons performance results as compared with the goals and output requirements set at the beginning of the period.

C. Your review meeting should be held in a quite setting conducive to a constructive dialogue between you and your employee, free from the daily distractions of the workplace.

D. You should actively encourage your employee to offer his/her own views on past and current performance, and to state his/her own reasons why the goals may not have been met.

E. Your own feedback to the employee should be given in a positive manner, with emphasis on the good parts of the persons performance, on the persons job strengths, and on improvement areas during the recent period.

F. Try to keep the discussion focused on the work and the persons work performance, and not get into non-productive talk about personalities, attitudes, and personal traits.

G. Before leaving the discussion about past and current performance, make certain that the employee understands fully what your appraisal is, and how you arrived at it. It is not necessary that the employee agree fully with your appraisal - however he/she should understand your reasons for it.

Step 4. Agree on New Goals and Final Development Plan

A. At this point, your task is to, along with your subordinate, look to the future, by reviewing the proposed Performance Objectives and tentative employee development plan. These will include both your ideas, as well as the employees.

B. Through a process of negotiation on those performance objectives that are negotiable, you should reach agreement on final goals and output requirements for the next six or twelve months. Limit the number of goals to the four to six most meaningful goals - the ones with the most effect on output and results.

C. You should also mutually agree upon the development plan. The final development plan should be put in writing, and a copy given to the employee.

D. As a result of the discussion, you may decide that coaching is needed (he/she may not know how to perform the work properly). Or you may decide that career counseling is needed (he/she has indicated a desire for more challenging work).

E. Before closing the formal appraisal session, you should recap the key points discussed, restate the new goals, and make sure you and your subordinate have a good and full understanding.

F. You should bring the meeting to a close by expressing your appreciation for the persons past efforts, and confidence in his/her ability to meet the new goals.

G. Finally, you should formally document the total performance review and appraisal.

Keep in mind some of these ideas when designing your performance appraisal system.

1) Tie the subordinates job to the organizations goals. If an employee knows exactly where and how they (their job) contribute to the corporate goals, they can gain a sense of ownership of their part of achieving those goals. This can lead to improved performance and productivity, reduced turnover, and increased employee satisfaction.

2) Allow the subordinate the opportunity to provide input into their Performance Objectives. Once the employee sees how their job plays a role in achieving corporate goals, he/she can better understand the pieces of their job. He/she should carefully review their own strengths and weaknesses and develop specific plans for meeting these Performance Objectives.

3) Manager and subordinate should mutually agree on the Performance Objectives. The subordinate is more likely to "buy" these objectives, given the chance to have a say in their creation.

4) In the situation where the manager is not as technical as the subordinate, and is unable to accurately provide a fair assessment, utilize a third person. This may be a "lead" person, a technical support person, someone within the organization who can assess technical skills. The manager incorporates this technical assessment and provides feedback in the area of performance and production.

5) Reassess the conventional appraisal instruments and eliminate subjective elements, such as attitude, dress (unless there is a specific dress code required to perform the job), personality, looks, etc.

6) Tie the Performance Appraisal system to performance, which is tied to the organizations goals. Reward performance which helped meet those goals.

By implementing a systematic Performance Appraisal program, the manager can move from a judicial role to a coaching role. The subordinate is held accountable and responsible for his/her performance, and knows that he/she is the principal participant in his/her own development.

5   HOW SMART QUESTIONS MAKE APPRAISALS PRODUCTIVE

Smart questions turn performance appraisals into a prime motivational tool (14). Questions are a tool to help both the manager and subordinate prepare for the performance appraisal session, and clarify thinking during it. Smart questions have a lot of benefit to the manager:

● By asking questions, you talk less and therefore obtain more information.

● You can lead the discussion without appearing to do so (because the other person is doing most of the talking).

● Questions put responsibility on the other person by forcing them to provide specific information.

● Using questions keeps both manager and subordinate from becoming defensive.

● Questions encourage both to be more objective, as opposed to getting caught up in personal value judgments.

● Questions let you deal with a persons behavior - what they have done and what they are going to do - not with the person him/herself.

As a manager in a performance appraisal session, you may feel the need to justify your ratings and opinions, therefore you may tend to do most of the talking. You are in a judicial role. With well-planned questions, you can accomplish the same goals (letting the employee know your assessment of his/her performance), with more involvement from the employee. This can move you into a coaching or consultative role.

Openers

Rather than giving the positive feedback, then zapping the employee with negative feedback, establish a positive tone for this meeting with a few opening questions, such as:

"Is there any special place you would like to start this discussion?"

"How would you like this appraisal to work for you?"

"How would you like to feel at the end of our session?"

"What information would you like to have?"

"Of the objectives we agreed to at our last review, which is the one you'd like to start with for discussion?"

Exploring Questions

Employees will usually be critical and objective and give an accurate assessment of their performance if they feel they are not under fire and don't have to defend themselves. By using some of the following questions, you set the tone for this objective discussion:

"How well is this current project being done?"

"How could it be better?"

"Tell me how you feel about what you've accomplished and what still needs to be done?"

"One of your objectives was to improve communication with data processing - how did that go?"

Expanding the Appraisal

With the tone set, you can now expand the performance appraisal into an opportunity to build motivation:

"What do you consider your main accomplishments this year?"

"What obstacles were most serious for you?"

"What did you do to deal with them?"

"What could you do in the future to deal with them more effectively?"

"Where do you think you could improve?"

"How could I help you more?"

"If you could redo this year, given the same circumstances, what would you do differently?"

Setting Goals

The final stage of the performance appraisal session is the goal-setting for the next period. These questions can lead the discussions:

"What do you hope to accomplish during the next six months or a year?"

"What can you do this coming year that will make a noticeable difference - to your department and the organization?"

"How do you see yourself achieving your goals?

"What can I do to help you achieve your goals?"

"What further training or skill development do you feel you need to achieve your goals?"

6 COACHING SKILLS

One of the skills a supervisor or manager must have is Coaching Skills, or the ability to provide initial on-the-job training (OJT) and remedial or corrective training for the improvement of performance. OJT is mandatory for all new employees within a department or group, and is either provided by you, the supervisor or manager, by someone you delegate, or by the company's training specialists. Coaching is a discretionary activity that involves management judgment as to when it is required, and how it is to be delivered.

Coaching is used when feedback fails to correct an employee's sub-standard performance. It backs up verbal feedback with action to correct performance deficiencies. The following is a comparison of Performance Appraisal versus Coaching.

COMPARISON OF...	APPRAISAL	COACHING
1. Purpose	Measurement and Control	Planning and Development
2. Time Orientation	Past	Future
3. Manager's Role	Judge presents Verdict	Helper
4. Manager's Interview Style	Tell and Sell	Problem Solving
5. Subordinate's Role	Reactive	Interactive
6. Subordinate's Behavior Options	Accept or Reject	Modify, influence outcome, share in planning
7. Motivational Impact	Provide recognition; show fairness	Show concern, Achievement, Growth

Table 9-1

Coaching can benefit you and your group by:

- increasing the productivity of your group, reducing unit costs, improving quality of output,

- bringing the performance of individual workers up to and above the standards of their jobs, thus increasing job satisfaction, and

- demonstrating to the individuals in your group that you are concerned about their ability to effectively improve their performance.

Coaching will not work if 1) the problem is caused by factors outside of the control of the worker, such as defective tools, or faulty instructions, 2) if the individual does not have the capacity to learn from coaching or the desire to improve his or her performance, or 3) the workers do not have a high level of trust with the manager and see this as only another manipulative tool.

Coaching skills are key leadership skills. When you provide coaching that is positive, constructive, and reinforcing, the performance of your subordinates will meet and exceed the standards of the work. When the coaching you provide is given with sensitivity and awareness of each individual's abilities and work interests, your employee's will be motivated to strive for improved performance.

The following are guidelines to effective coaching.

Step 1. Confirm a Need for Coaching.

Some observable signs for a need of coaching are:

- You observe an employee using an incorrect work method, and/or
- the employee's output or quality is seriously below the standards for the job,
- you have provided corrective feedback without results, and
- you have eliminated other possible causes of low output, such as defective materials, tools, equipment.

You should confirm the need for coaching, and decide whether coaching can remedy the employee's performance deficiencies by:

- review the employee's work history, corrective feedback you gave earlier, previous coaching, etc., and
- discuss the need for remedial on-the-job training with the individual.

Based on this, you can decide whether the person has the ability to learn from coaching and whether he/she has the desire to improve performance.

Step 2. Prepare to Coach the Employee

In preparing to coach an employee, you must define the content of the coaching. To do this, you should gather information about a) the person's actual job performance and results, b) the job standards, and c) the employees performance deficiencies (b - a = c)

Next you must identify and list the areas of performance which coaching can improve, and which are most urgent.

Select the best time for the coaching session, based on your workload and that of the employee, as well as the need for immediate action (as in a safety or health situation). Also select the best location. You might want to do this in public, if other group members could benefit by it, or in private, if it might prove to be embarrassing to the employee. Notify the employee of the time and place.

You must also select the coaching method, depending upon the situation. Some methods for consideration are demonstration by yourself, demo by someone else, formal instruction, workshop, observations of others doing the task or job.

A word of caution: you must know the proper procedures and methods yourself before you provide remedial training to others. If you are not current and up-to-date, you might either consult standard practices, other managers, or have someone else conduct the coaching.

Step 3. Provide Coaching to Employee

You should begin the coaching session with a review of the employee's performance, maintaining a constructive tone during this discussion. Actively encourage participation in this session by the employee, having them focus on why their performance is not meeting standards.

All discussion should focus on the employee's deficient performance, and relate to output requirements or standards. Discussing attitude or personal traits at this time would not be beneficial or productive.

You can now move to the actual coaching, where you or a delegate instruct or demonstrate the correct method of performing the task. You will want to make sure that it is designed to be easily followed by the employee, and meets with his/her learning capabilities.

You then check with the employee to determine their understanding of the correct method, either by asking them to demonstrate back to you, or some other method. If someone else performed the actual training, you should ask to see the demonstration, as you are responsible for the coaching results.

You finalize this session by making follow-up plans with the employee, to ensure correct performance the next time the work is done. You should encourage the employee to come to you (or a designate) with any questions, and express confidence in the person's ability to master the task.

Your final task is to document the key points of the coaching session, according to company policy.

Points to Remember about OJT and Coaching

- On-the-job training (OJT) is personalized on-site instruction in proper work methods.

- OJT is mandatory whenever an employee is new to the job, or the work is new to the employee.

- The purpose of OJT is to bring an employee's output up to or above the standards for the job.

- Coaching is remedial on-the-job training, intended to correct performance deficiencies and bring output up to standard.

- Coaching is needed whenever an employee's work output is seriously below standard, and/or the person is following an incorrect work method or procedure.

- Coaching is the second step in the remedial process - you should always give corrective feedback on performance first.

- OJT and coaching are important contributors to the productivity of your group, and to the motivation of its members.

- OJT and coaching need not always be given personally by a supervisor or manager, but may be delegated to a competent fellow worker who has some talent for instructing. However, the manager of the group always remains responsible for coaching results.

7 PERFORMANCE APPRAISALS...POINTS TO REMEMBER

- Performance appraisal (PA) is the center-piece of any integrated human resource management system. It is an important responsibility and obligation of every manager - and a vital motivational tool.

- PA systems should measure and reward the processes, goals, behavior, and tasks that are part of the strategic direction of the organization.

- The effectiveness of any PA system is judged by both appraisers and appraisees.

- The PA should focus on job performance and job content that is important to both appraisers and appraisees; take place over an extended period of time, selected in advance; include an employee's self-appraisal; involve discussions of salary, and pay decisions; be focused on mutually agreed upon MBO or other work related problem solving goals; thoroughly document and recognize the subordinates' performance; provide subordinates with specific development information and support services that can be utilized to improve performance.

- PA system should not be used to discipline or punish harshly. The primary purpose of a formal review and appraisal is to motivate the employee to upgrade overall performance. A performance appraisal should emphasize an employee's strengths, not weaknesses; this is not a time to "hash over" the person's past work errors and failures.

- PA should not be based upon vague personality traits, or ill-defined qualities such as: reliability, initiative or even leadership, should focus upon concrete behavior and results related to the job under review.

- Evaluation appraisers should be trained in the use of the PA system and how it was designed to facilitate the organization's strategic direction. The training should include discussion of the limits of standard systems and leave room for individual judgment. In fact, training and career development should be one aspect of any PA system.

- Performance appraisal is one of the most demanding of all managerial/supervisory responsibilities in terms of human relations; it must be done with sensitivity and skill in order not to damage the employee's motivation or impair your relationship with the employee.

- PA systems can often effectively rely upon peer and team or group evaluations to provide supplemental information.

- Any PA system must meet various legal standards and requirements including statutes, constitutional provisions, executive orders and federal guidelines (to the VII or 1964 Civil Rights Act, 1978 EEOC guidelines, 5th and 14th Amendments, Civil Rights Statutes 42 USC 1981, 42 USC 1983, Execute Order, 11,246, Amended by EO 11,375).

- PA rating instruments are more consistent and valid when they are based upon measurements with five to nine rating categories; consistency among raters drops significantly when there are less then four or more than ten categories.

- Valid ratings occur most often at the extremes of outstanding or very poor performance. However, it is the middle range which most PA systems must address. Here we find much rater bias, reluctance to be honest, fear of negative feedback, problems of varying standards, recent problems (giving greater weight to more recent events than earlier performance), harshness or leniency of rater pattern, and halo effect (higher ratings on all items because of one favorable characteristic, trait, interest or skill).

- All evaluators should be rewarded for enhancing the developmental and career growth of their workers.

- Appraisers should clearly separate their evaluation role from their helper/developer/assistance role.

- PA systems should not overwhelm the supervisor or managers with paperwork and irrelevant administrative tasks. Policies, forms, and procedures should be reviewed often and streamlined for simplicity, relevance and effectiveness.

- Performance appraisal requires a high degree of communication skill and leadership. Done well, it can energize all employees to strive for excellence; done badly, it can cause grievous personnel problems.

- Remember: The clarity of purpose in the PA system should be addressed in the beginning. It must meet business growth, legal requirements and win the support of workers and managers. It must focus upon collaborative, mutual goal setting, accountability, awareness and recognition of contributions, self- reliance (internal motivation) and career development.

8   PERFORMANCE APPRAISAL TRAINING - DO'S AND DON'TS

Do's

- Plan PA training with executives, managers, and supervisors in order to insure that the program meets the strategic needs of the organization.

- Train managers with supervisors and employees in order to create a set of common and consistent appraisal practices throughout the organization. A highly collaborative and participant appraisal will clarify expectations, increase motivation and increase the skills to use it in a meaningful way.

- Balance the content of the PA training to ensure that participants:

  1) Understand PA as a tool for maintaining and improving performance and their own careers;

  2) Can write good concrete, measurable, behavioral performance objectives;

  3) Understand and can utilize knowledge about the strategic plan, political-cultural realities, and the management system, in order to make sure the PA system has a real chance of working;

  4) Role play and practice the appraisal interview.

- Rely upon experienced managers with good communication skills as trainers. The emphasis should be upon developing a collaborative, exploratory problem- solving approach to make the PA system effective and useful for both managers and employees. Also involve groups of managers to assist in the instruction. These groups can share their expertise and experience.

- Spread out the delivery of PA training over several weeks and months; try and link the content of training to current on-the-job activities and requirements.

Don'ts

- Introduce a PA training program with an elitist, disciplinary, or administrative bias (We'll Get Them Now attitude).

- Try to focus on low level basics and the view of the PA task as a necessary evil. The PA task should be understood as an important management skill and tool.

- Ignore the importance of the initial design of the PA system because good training with poor content can lead to a disaster. Soon managers and supervisors start turning off worker potential or people learn how to beat "this inept system".

- Failure to honestly communicate to trainees and ultimately every worker that no PA system is perfect. All systems have some weaknesses because they are designed with several goals in mind -- productivity improvement, worker self-guidance, employee development, quality control, increase in pay. Also in many organization's different groups are involved with different goals and needs. Genuine PA is not a list of personality traits but an attempt to provide measurable performance standards, develop mutual planning skills (supervisors and subordinates), give regular and systematic feedback, provide personally meaningful goals and career directions for all workers.

- Ignore middle and senior managers in the training process and think just first and second-level supervisors benefit.

- Expect all training participants to instantly embrace the PA process with heartfelt gratitude. Try to deal with their fears, insecurities and resistance to doing interviews, by focusing on the specific skills they need and the importance of sharing information about the strategic direction of the organization. Impart the idea that each worker can share in the feeling of success through the increased mastery of work related skills. Both extrinsic and intrinsic rewards can be emphasized. Try to deal with the attitudes of resistance by using positive factual examples of the way it can or is working in other organizations. Point out potential problems in any organization with little or no formal PA procedures.

9 PERFORMANCE AUDITS

The performance audit is a comprehensive examination of an organization's task activity, conducted by an independent assessor who analyzes how well results match intentions, or how well resource utilization matches results.

Individual Performance Audits (I.P.). Focuses upon the instructional outcomes on individual competence gained. The auditor looks for discrepancies between current performance and expected performance outcomes.

Organizational Performance Audits (O.P.). Focuses on organizational outcomes and overall organizational competence and productivity. The two types of O.P. audits are management audit, and program audits
.

Management Audits. Focuses upon the efficient use of resources (land, capital, time), policy or procedural standards, common business practices, industrial averages, or current academic research findings. The audit compares the relationship between the organization's inputs and outputs; the present conditions and desirable results or outcome standards.

Program Audits. Focuses upon the criteria of effectiveness or goal (objectives, intentions, standards) attainment (15). The audit attempts to indicate the relationship between the organization's stated mission or cultural goal and its accomplishments in such areas as: **finance** (return on investment, profit and loss; **technology** (new inventions, innovations, impacting industry; **social** (contribution to community or social equality and justice; **economic** (market share, dominance); **human resource** (employee satisfaction, low turnover, affirmative action record; and **business strategic** (long- term objectives).

Select	Select Appropriates
Normative Criteria (What Should Be Source of Information)	Measurement Methods Comparing Condition to Criteria/Outcome/What Is
Source of Normative Data	Possible Methods
. Government Documents and Agency Information . Industrial Research Standards, and Trade Information . Academic Research . Legal Information	Systems Analysis Linear Programming Path Diagram Analysis Multiple Regressions Survey Research Cost/Benefit Analysis Network Analysis Accounting Methods Flow Charts

Table 9-2. Performing Audit Tests

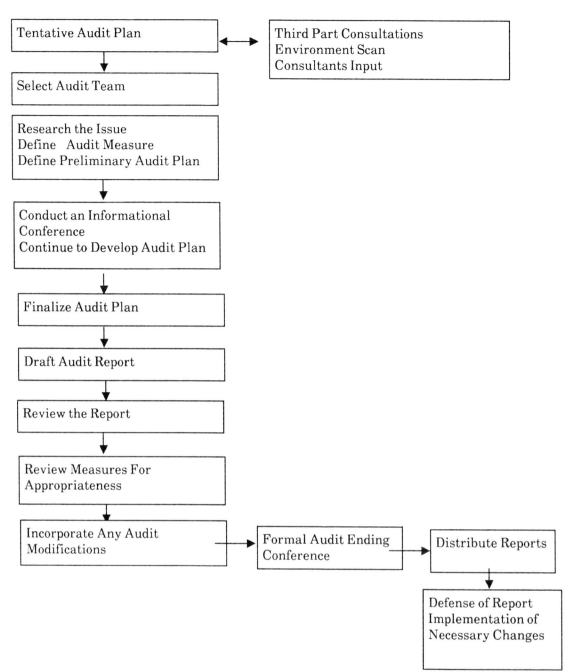

Figure 9-4. A Model of Performance Audits

193

BIBLIOGRAPHY/REFERENCES

STRATEGIC HUMAN RESOURCE MANAGEMENT

INTRODUCTION

(1)   Robbins, Steven P. **Organization Behavior** (New York: Prentice Hall, 1983:95)

(2)   Adizes, Ichak. **Corporate Lifecycles: How and Why Corporations Grow and Die and What to Do About It.** (New York: Prentice Hall, 1988)

CHAPTER 8

(3)   Triplett, Jan F. and Diener, Daniel. "What Can You Do About Employee Turnover?" **Practical Supervision** (Round Rock, Texas: Professional Training Associates, Inc., Number 30, May 15, 1985)

(4)   Rogers, Thomas H. "Strategic Planning: A Major OD Intervention" in French, Wendell and Bell, Cecil, Jr. and Zawacki,Robert. **Organization Development. Theory, Practice and Research**

(5)   Adapted from: Bourgeois, L.J. and Brown, David R. "Strategic Implementation: Five Approaches to An Elusive Phenomenon" **Strategic Management Journal** (Vol. 5, 241-264, 1984)

(6)   Resources Available: Aquilar, F.J. **Scanning the Business Environment** (New York: MacMillian, 1967), Renfro, William L. and Morrison, James L. and Boucher, Wayne Z. **Applying Methods and Techniques of Futures Research** (San Francisco: Jossey-Bass, 1983), Nanus, Burt. "QUEST - Quick Environmental Scanning Technique" **Long Range Planning** (Vol. 15, No. 2, 1982)

(7)   Dessler, Gary. **Applied Human Relations** (Virginia: Reston Publishing Co., 1983)

CHAPTER 9

(8)   Article written by Susan Fahmy

(9)   Sources - Yoder, D. and Heneman, H.G. (EDS) **ASPA Handbook of Personnel and Industrial Relations** (1982) **Vol.1 Staffing Policies and Strategies** (Washington, D.C.: Bureau of National Affairs, 1979); Arvey, R.D. et al. "Narrative Job Description vs Potential Sources of Job Analysis Ratings" **Personnel Psychology** (35, 618-629, 1982); Jones, A.P. et al. "Potential sources of Basis Job Analysis Procedures" **Academy of Management Journal** (35, 813-828, 1982)

(10)   Source U.S. Dept. of Labor. **Dictionary Occupational Titles,** (Washington, D.C.: Government Distributing Office, 1977)

(11)   Peters, T. and Waterman, T. **In Search of Excellence: Lessons from America's Best Run Companies"** (New York: Warner Books, 1982)

(12)   Peters, Tom. **Thriving on Chaos** (New York: Harper & Row, 1987)

(13)   Armstrong, Michael. **A Handbook of Human Resource Management** (New York: Nichols Publishing Company, 1988)

(14)   Leeds, Dorothy. **Smart Questions: A New Strategy for Successful Managers** (New York: McGraw Hill, 1987)

(15)   Sources: Herbert, L. **Auditing The Performance of Management** (Belmont, CA.: Lifetime Learning, 1979); Rummler, Geary "The Performance Audit" in **Training and Development Handbook**, R.T. Craig (ED) 2nd Edition, (New York: McGraw Hill, 1976); Gibbert, Thomas F. **Human Competence: Engineering Worthy Performance** (New York: McGraw Hill, 1978)

SECTION THREE

HUMAN RESOURCE DEVELOPMENT : INTEGRATING TRAINING, MANAGEMENT AND CAREER DEVELOPMENT

The topic of human resource development (HRD) will help us to learn more about the ways we can more effectively structure and manage today's organization by investing in employee development. Chalofsky and Reinhard (1:xiii) define the HRD function as follows:

> The organizationally based unit responsible for providing planned adult learning activities, services, and programs to members, individual and collective, of the organization, for job or skill training, education and development.

The HRD field and function is certainly on the move and becoming more important to the strategic perspective we have discussed throughout this book. Chalofsky and Reinhard (1:4) cite the following evidence as support for the enhanced HRD function in organizations today:

- Management has become convinced that education drives the business

- A stepchild until recently, the training function is now seen as essential to the company's strategic goals

- Developing our people is now the heart of our business strategy

- Training departments used to be wiped out by recessions, but few were in the recent one.

The changing face of the modern world, and increased pressures on organizations and managers to find efficient, cost effective modes of operation, have placed increased emphasis on the need for the modern organizations to be just that: modern and efficient.

Webster defines proactive as "involving modification by a factor which precedes that which is modified." This idea is compatible with the need for learning as an everyday part of all jobs career growth, and not just through job-specific skills training. This also supports cross training which is closer to learning for breadth in professional and work unit activities. This also includes the fact that workers should teach each other and have numerous cross-department or work unit experiences through teams, task forces, project groups and other forms of goal focused activity. Largely because such learning fosters adaptability, we regard a broad or generalist education as the best possible foundation for effective management learning.

One of the key elements to improving the efficiency of any organization lies in the ability of its individual members to work effectively together as partners in learning and growth.

Managing and leading for the future does not mean we must throw away all our existing management tools, but rather that we re-examine our own perceptions, our values, our attitudes, our assumptions about how people work best. To learn how to be a better manager in turbulent times, we must first question our own feelings about change and toward learning itself. Before we can successfully implement any participative learning environment, we must have the clear commitment of top management for supports and resources.

The responsive organization and its managers must understand the focus of change and where the trend lines are moving. A manager's job is to get things done through others. In that very light, understanding people within the organizational setting becomes extremely important. Because a manager's job is typically so fragmented with such a variety of non-routine tasks, time must be spent on communicating effectively, understanding the needs, values, ana motivations of others, as well as understanding one's own personality, motivations and managerial or leadership style.

Self-Management Skills

Chalofsky and Reinhart (1:129) argue that the HRD function of the future must be 'more creative and flexible in supporting personal development ... We may be approaching breakthroughs in human learning that will enable us to make enormous leaps in knowledge acquisition ...' With a more highly educated work force whose variety of needs are being met, employees' growth toward self-development should become a priority. Mature adults want to be in control, to make choices. Unfortunately, many of us have been taught that our careers are mere artifacts of external forces of business survival. Instead of strategically striving to build a repertoire of new skills and anticipating future learning and career opportunities, many organizations continue to think about the world in old ways.

They continue to design career systems and strategies that fit the assumptions and practices of yesterday and today, not tomorrow. This is a strategy for disaster because it is fundamentally reactive rather than proactive. The proactive person and organization knows that the time to rethink strategy is today, before the situation gets out of hand. It is imperative that we take another look at the data and begin to ask strategic questions when things are still going well. We must learn to attack from a position of strength, when time, energy and patience are still on our side.

Definition of Management Development

House (2) defined management development as, 'any planned effort to improve current or future manager performance by imparting information, conditioning attitudes, or increasing skills. This definition implies that the results of development must be defined in terms of measurable change in either learner states or learner performance'.

Assumptions of Management Development

There appear to be two major underlying assumptions concerning management development. The first assumption is that of careers being managed to meet organizational needs. This suggests the need for establishing management succession schemes, linking development actions to the organization's strategic and tactical plans, job rotation and transfer actions to provide inter-functional and multi-location experience, planned and structured training programs, selective assignment of employees to university management development or executive development programs, and so forth. This assumption is consistent with a paternalistic or bureaucratic approach to management.

The second assumption is that of careers being planned and developed by individuals. This suggests that the individual, rather than the organization, is responsible for identifying both present and future development needs, identifying actions that will provide the necessary development experience, initiating job assignments and transfers to provide needed development, arranging for additional education and training (often at the individual's own expense), and so forth. This assumption is consistent with a humanistic approach to management, that is, an approach that assumes that individuals are responsible for and can act to change their own situation.

Many organizations do not consciously articulate their dominant assumption, and one may find that that assumption varies from department to department, division to division, and from manager to manager. Expressions such as, 'the cream rises to the top", 'initiative and being a self-starter is important', suggest situations in which the individual is responsible for their own development. 'It's time to move Jane to an office with a different client mix', or 'Tom's abrasive style requires some counseling and probably some sensitivity training', are more typical of situations where the manager feels responsible for guiding, directing, causing employee growth and development. Lack of a common organizational commitment to one assumption may result in visible friction between different parts of the organization due to very different handling of management development issues. An effective management development program might well consist of a blending of the organization-responsible and individual-responsible assumptions into a **shared responsibility** model.

Career Development and Management Development

Budget support for career development programs usually indicates management support of on-going management development. The responsibility for administering career programs is most often assigned to the personnel department. The responsibility for career development in general is seen as a shared responsibility between the personnel department and the manager. The proactive organization, however, places a large part of the responsibility into the hands of the employee.

Morgan et al (3) drew the following conclusions concerning the state of career practices within organizations:

- Career programs are not new

- Many of the career programs are informal

- The responsibility for career development is shared

- The supervisor should be a career specialist

- Career program objectives are viewed in terms of an organization, not an individual

- There is a paucity of efforts to evaluate the effectiveness of career programs

201

- Unrealistic expectations on the part of participants are a major problem

- Both large and small organizations can implement effective career programs.

Management Training and Organization Development

Management development programs often utilize management training and may utilize organization development. Fiedler and Garcia (4) reviewed studies that have evaluated organizational improvement programs and came to some interesting conclusions concerning organization development (OD) and structured management training (SMT):

> SMT will almost be less expensive than OD... the effects of SMT tend to be consistent. The effects of OD depend on the skill of the particular consultant and, therefore, are less predictable. There may be occasional failures with SMT, but these methods are not highly dependent on the skill and sensitivity of the consultant, and it is easier to maintain quality control.

> While a well validated structured training program is a cost-effective choice for many organizations, OD seems well-suited for problem solving at upper management levels, with minimized cost. Although SMT also has been successful with top management, it is most economical at lower levels of the organization.

Career Programs

Morgan et al (3:24-28) identified steps that firms should be taking in terms of career development. They explicitly recognized needs varying with different career stages.

> We should not plan large, formal career development program ... let your career activities grow as they need to, but avoid developing a major career program just for the sake of having one... The best way to keep your career activities from outgrowing the needs they serve is to focus on the immediate supervisor. The supervisor probably has more impact on the person's career than any other person ... If the major unit for career development is the employee and the immediate supervisor, this suggests that the personnel specialist should not be directly involved in this process, for at least two reasons: 1) if the personnel specialist becomes too involved, this may take the supervisor 'off the hook', and 2) no company, regardless of size, has enough personnel resources to provide individual career counseling in the personnel department ... As part of the information-gathering process in career planning activities, you should be sure to provide realistic company opportunities to employees ... Provide for different needs in different career stages. People have different needs for development at different stages in their careers. ..

Conditions for Management Development to be Effective

House (2:18) identified the conditions required to induce change through management development (see Figure 1).

	Change in knowledge	Change in attitude	Change in ability	Change in job performance	Change in operational results
		(Conditions in Cols. 1 & 2)	(Conditions in Cols. 1, 2, & 3)	(Conditions in Cols. 1, 2, 3 & 4)	(Conditions in Cols. 1,2,3, 4, &5)
	Col. 1	Col. 2	Col. 3	Col. 4	Col. 5
Participant characteristics	Sufficient IQ Sufficient motivation	Flexible attitude on part of participants Agreement with spirit of the material to be learned	Non-conflicting habits or personality traits		
Learning effort	Direct method of instruction (programmed learning, lectures, films, reading) Competent instruction	Discussion of on-the-job applications and personal benefits	Practice of desired abilities Corrective training to correct undesirable habits and behavioral patterns	Opportunity for on-the-job practice of newly acquired abilities	
Leadership climate		Neutral or positive attitude of superior toward development	Superior's attitude and example consistent with desired change	Coaching, counseling, and periodic performance review by superior consistent with desired performance	Performance appraisal by the superior based on practices taught in the learning phase
Organizatio nal climate		Goals, top-management philosophy, and policies consistent with learning phase		Philosophy, practices, and precedents of the policy-making executives consistent with desired manager performance	Top management active support in development Incentive system designed to reward practices taught in the learning phase
Organizational culture		Cultural conditions and social beliefs consistent with desired attitudes		Informal group rules and standards consistent with desired change	Positive employee and informal group attitudes toward desired change

Figure 1.

203

We will like to conclude this section with another insightful quote from Chalofsky and Reinhart (1:136) that raises key questions for those charting the future course of HRD, rather than provides easy answers:

- If more employees start working at home, what will be the impact on identifying training needs? Or scheduling and delivering development activities?

- How will artificial intelligence research contribute to adult learning? (Xerox has just established an Institute for Research and Learning to study specific questions.)

- How will the next several rounds of technological advances (holographic projection, pocket TV's and telephones, libraries on line to main frame computers, voice activated computers) affect instruction?

- What will be the effect of robotics on the HRD field?

- How ill the next evolutionary step toward a more spiritually oriented 'peak performer' affect training and development?

- What will happen if we find a method of implanting learning directly into the brain?

Here we can once again see the need for educating leaders and managers to be creative thinkers and rigorous analysts. Thinking leaders must dispel the myths about how organizations can work. We must find ways of educating the whole manager-person in order to view behavior as a function of consciousness, of meaning and purpose, and not just behavior and consequences. We can learn about leading and managing by exposing ourselves to this rich heritage of liberal studies. Managing knowledge workers requires thinking leaders who are able to probe the deepest and richest sources of human motivation.

The educated manager and leader of tomorrow needs to understand the complexity of theories, perspectives and strategies in order to tap the organizations' potential, create effective corporate cultures, engage in complex problem solving, and embrace new challenges. Work today is no longer motivated by a narrow view of monetary compensation but is closer to an extension of our deeper selves, a reflection of our life-style choices, and only satisfactory to the degree that our unique learning or problem solving styles are recognized and appreciated. It his this very shift in perspective and point of view that has become the driving issue of how we will develop our human resources in the future.

CHAPTER TEN
TRAINING

1 TRAINING ... Introduction

In today's corporate environment, the success of business is directly tied to its ability to manage change. Constant change in technology, products, markets, jobs, and competition has brought about an increase in the importance of training, especially a new approach, one of continuous learning. Conventional approaches called for a one-time training of a specific skill or piece of equipment, today's more strategic approach is necessary to allow employees to keep up with, and organizations to manage, change.

Today's training demands that everyone in the organization - employees, line managers, supervisors, and technical personnel - become more actively and continuously involved in expanding their skills. Learning becomes an everyday part of the job, rather than being confined to a classroom; employees learn the skills of others in their work unit, as well as those related to their own jobs, and employees teach, and learn from, one another.

Work in America Institute conducted a three year national study, "Training for New Technology", which examined organizations that had adopted successful training strategies (6). The study identified five major forces affecting corporations and their implications for training:

1. **Increased global and domestic competition** is leading to a greater need for competitive strategies, which often include training as an essential element.

2. **Rapid changes in technology** result in changes in operations, products, and processes; job design; work flow; and skill requirements. These changes, in turn, create an acute need for people with specialized technical skills.

3. **Widespread mergers, acquisitions, and divestitures**, which realign corporate structures and functions but not necessarily the ability of people to carry them out, require long-term training plans that are linked to decisions about the business future.

4. **A better educated workforce**, which values self-development and personal growth, has brought about enormous learning needs plus a growing desire for participation at work.

5. **Occupational obsolescence and the emergence of new occupations** - resulting from the changing nature of the economy, the shift from manufacturing to service industries, and the impact of research, development, and new technology - require flexible training policies to prevent increased turnover and lower productivity.

Organizations must align their training strategy to the corporate goals, in order to gain quality and results from training. Those who are in the training department must be made aware of the overall goals of the organization, so that their training programs can help meet those goals. Training must assume a more central, strategic role within the organization, and training requirements must be driven by the changing needs of the organization.

Training is a part of effective supervision and management. A manager must do many things at once, all of which are important. However, nothing is more important than training. The management of people determines organizational success. Training cannot wait until "the manager gets around to it" or "when time permits". Training must receive a high priority from management. The highest levels of management must agree on the importance of training and allocate time and resources for it to be done well. No manager can train in a vacuum. Top management must endorse the value of training and employees must be convinced of what training will do for them.

Some employee benefits from training are:

- Personal knowledge that you are doing a good job
- Higher chances for wage/salary increase and promotion
- Less anxiety about performance evaluations
- Fewer customer complaints
- Feeling of being a "professional"
- Higher respect/esteem from customers, peers, and your boss
- Job enjoyment
- Less on-the-job accidents
- Less on-the-job boredom, less tiresome work
- Improved teamwork
- Reduced work related stress and job related disabilities
- Improved organizational health and ultimately lower health care costs

2   THEORIES OF LEARNING AND INSTRUCTION

THEORIES OF LEARNING

Pedagogy. Learning is a process of giving or receiving information. More a theory of instruction than learning, it dates back to medieval universities. It suggests that the purpose of learning is to absorb information, that learning is a linear, one-way process of communication and change. To foster learning, information must be presented in an organized manner from least to most difficult, from previously known to unknown, from past to present. This type of instruction will most be found in the academic environment.

Behaviorism. Learning is an association of a series of stimuli and accompanying responses. Advocates of this theory use psychological research to derive principles that explain and predict relationships between stimuli (the means to induce behavior), behavior (observable actions that are in response to stimuli), and consequent conditions (rewards or punishments for action). This theory suggests that:

1) the focus of learning should be on present behavior, not on past determinants of it,
2) the focus should always be on the external and observable (thinking and feeling have relatively little to do with learning because they are internal, thus unobservable, and only indirectly measurable), and
3) behavioral goals or objectives of learning should be specified prior to instruction and should be measurable.

Theorists in this area include John B. Watson, Ivan Pavlov, Edwin Guthrie, Edward Thorndike, B. F. Skinner, and Clark Hull.

Cognitivism. Learning is a result of insight, perception, and other internalized phenomena. Based upon the Gestalt school of psychology, these theorists emphasize the uniquely personal side of learning, since it is essentially a process of individuals discovering relationships. Individual change results from acute awareness; an emphasis on perception as fundamental to learning. Theorists in this area include Edward Tolman, Kurt Lewin, Wolfgang Kohler, and Jerome Bruner.

Developmentalism. Learning is a means of meeting human needs. Theorists stress the human capacity to act on the environment rather than merely react to it. It proposes that people learn in order to satisfy their needs, they are inclined to seek greater freedom and to strive to become what they are capable of becoming. Theorists in this area include Jean Piaget, Carl Rogers, and Malcolm Knowles.

The following table is a review of the major components of these theories, and an introduction to the area of theories of instruction.

Theories of instruction are based on theories of learning. There are four general theories of instruction. These theories are not mutually exclusive and within each one there are alternative approaches.

THEORIES OF INSTRUCTION

Subject-Centered Instruction. Based on pedagogical principles, it focuses on what will be taught. Advocates of this theory believe instructors should:

207

THEORY	DEFINITION OF LEARNING	HUMAN NATURE	ROLE OF INSTRUCTOR	ROLE OF LEARNER	GENERAL TYPE OF INSTRUCTION
Pedagogy	General awareness of knowledge; information received	Passive, reluctant learners	Crucial	Unimportant	Subject centered
Behavioral	Conditioning	Influenced by environment	Model	Shaped by environment	Objectives centered
Cognitive	Development of internal classification schemes	Influenced by individual interpretations of external events	Provides environment suitable to learning	Crucial	Experience centered
Developmental	Problem-solving; influenced by stages of development	Active, eager learners	Facilitator	Crucial	Opportunity centered

Table 10-1. Theories of Learning and Instruction

- Plan instruction carefully, sequencing information according to the logic of the material.
- Ignore or discount the value of learner experiences.
- Assume learners will understand that what they learn will have future uses not readily apparent to them now.
- Assume that the learner is dependent on the instructor for guidance.
- Use strong discipline to force learning when students lack motivation.
- Be expert of the subject to be taught, not necessarily on facilitating learning.

Objectives-Centered Instruction. Based on behaviorism, it focuses on observable and measurable outcomes of instruction. Advocates of this theory believe instructors should:

- Reinforce learner behavior which is desired; ignore or fail to reinforce inappropriate behaviors.
- Encourage repetition of acts performed correctly.
- Give frequent examinations to gather feedback on learning progress.
- Emphasize ways to elicit numerous correct responses from learners.
- State objectives clearly in advance. The instructor should know what responses should be elicited from what stimuli.
- Provide many different variations of the same stimuli, because each stimulus-response bond is unique.
- Use such secondary reinforcers as praise, grades, and challenging assignments to encourage learning.
- Define, in behavioral terms, what learners will be able to do after instruction.

Experience-Centered Instruction. Based on cognitivism, it focuses on what learners experience during instruction. Advocates believe instructors should:

208

- Structure learning problems so that learners perceive the most important features first.
- Emphasize the meaningfulness of the learning event and its importance in achieving desired goals.
- Provide frequent feedback to learners to confirm appropriate responses or correct inappropriate ones.
- Allow learners to establish or participate in establishing instructional goals.
- Encourage creative thought as much as logically correct thought or appropriate performance.

Opportunity-Centered Instruction. Based on developmentalism, it focuses on matching individual needs to appropriate instructional experiences. Advocates believe instructors should:

- Be aware of the learner's stage of development and cultural background.
- Provide challenging learning experiences that will allow both assimilation and accommodation.
- Provide a supportive climate for individuals and/or groups.
- Help learners clarify their own needs.
- Encourage students to think for themselves through diligent but reflective questioning.
- Provide groups of learners with every opportunity to pool individual experiences and insights.
- Assess the readiness of individuals to learn by analyzing problems that learners are facing in their careers or work at present.
- Pose instruction in the form of problems, rather than just transmit information.

3   LEARNING PROCESS

Learning can be defined as the process by which a relatively enduring change in behavior occurs as a result of practice.

There are certain concepts for understanding types of learning:

- **Drive** - the aroused condition within a person
  - Primary Drives (example: hunger) - unlearned
  - Secondary Drives (example: becoming anxious over an encounter with a supervisor) - learned

  Once a drive is learned, it serves to trigger behavior

- **Stimulus** - a cue that elicits a response; sometimes clearly obvious, other times obscure

- **Response** - behavioral result of stimulation

- **Reinforcer** - an object or event that serves to increase or sustain the strength of a response.

$$Drive -> Stimulus -> Response -> Reinforcer ->$$
$$\uparrow \qquad\qquad\qquad\qquad \leftarrow$$

Figures 10-1, 10-2, and 10-3 are examples of types of learning:

a) Classical Conditioning - Pavlov

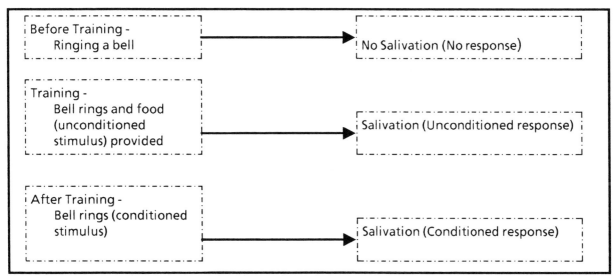

Figure 10-1. The Pavlov Procedure for Classical Conditioning

b) Operant Conditioning - Skinner

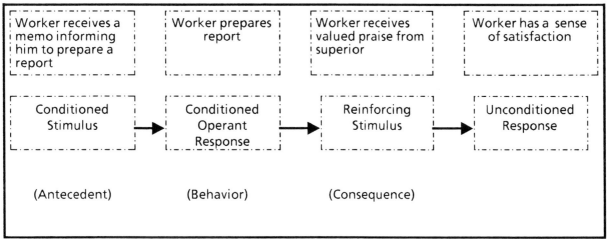

Figure 10-2. An example of Operant Conditioning

c) Observational Learning - Modeling

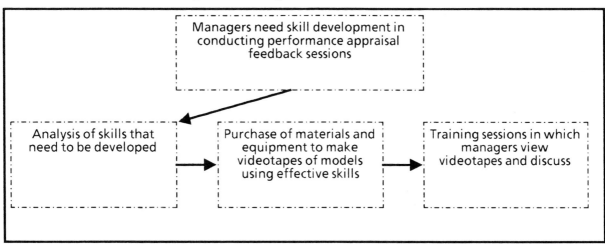

Figure 10-3. An example of Modeling

4   LEARNER FOCUSED METHODS OF INSTRUCTION

Training and Development practitioners are responsible for facilitating the content, process, and environment of a learning situation. For this reason, it is very important that professionals with classroom training responsibilities be skilled in utilizing a variety of effective presentation techniques which enhance participant interaction and involvement.

Participative learning takes into consideration the following set of assumptions:

- that individuals learn best when they are personally involved in the learning process
- that knowledge has to be discovered by the learner if it is to mean anything to them or make a difference in their behavior
- that a commitment to learning is highest when individuals are free to set their own learning goals and actively pursue them within a given framework

According to Kolb's (7) analysis, participative learning involves the following four stages:

- **Concrete** - concrete personal experiences
- **Passive** - observation; reflection; examination
- **Abstract** - formulation of abstract concepts, rules, and principles
- **Active** - personal theory to be tested in new situations

Whatever training methodology is used, it is important that the techniques be directed toward facilitation of the learning process. The following basic learning principles should be incorporated:

- **Repetition** - retention of new information/skills by repeated practice
- **Reinforcement**- positive consequences for trainee's behavior resulting in repetition of such behavior

- **Association** - enabling learning connections between different bases of knowledge
- **Senses** - involving various sensory systems (e.g. sight, speech, sound, touch, and smell)

When To Use Participative Learning Methods

In order to enhance the learning process, it is important for trainers to identify when it is appropriate to use a participative learning method. Some sample situations include:

- As a session ice-breaker...used to catch the group's attention at the beginning of a training session.
- To involve participants...may involve trainees in various physical, intellectual, or verbal exercises.
- As an illustration...provides a change of pace for the trainees using examples/illustrations of different contexts.
- As practice...provides opportunity for immediate feedback on performance.
- As a session closing...used to summarize session and may facilitate the transfer of learning.

Some Examples of Participative Learning Methods

1. **Role-Playing/Practice Demonstrations** - Depiction of characters, both in terms of actions and feelings, in scenarios for illustrative purposes. The outcome is not predetermined, and the situation is not rehearsed. Initial instructions are given and the participants determine what happens.

2. **Case Study** - Through the case study method, the participant learns in several different ways including: problem identification, problem analysis, problem solving, and decision making. The case study method is more concerned with factual data and the analytical thinking process.

3. **Brief Exercises** - These serve as helpful tools to stimulate quick participant interaction and may include: ice-breakers to begin a training session, interactive exercises during sessions to stimulate discussion, and small group activities.

4. **Games** - May be thought of as competitive encounters between individuals which involves some degree of skill and/or luck. These may attempt to develop such skills as: negotiations, decision-making, interpersonal communications, business strategy, etc.

The use of participative learning methods helps to shift the responsibility for learning from the trainer/instructor to the trainee/participant which is the underlying premise of adult learning principles.

5   THE STAGES OF ACTIVE LEARNING

Learning can be viewed as being composed of a series of stages that are fluid or cyclical in nature. The better we understand these stages, the better equipped we become to master any topic under investigation.

Assessment - awareness of self, others and the environment to determine strengths, weaknesses, and needs. Assessment enables us to learn the knowledge and skills needed to become high performers.

Goal Setting - based on your assessed needs and present abilities, represents the starting point from which you can measure your future progress. Chose goals which are compatible with your abilities to perform the actions necesary to achieve them.

Integration - the combining, selecting and processing of information and experiences that produces some decision and motivation to change or improve behaviors. Integrating new information and experiences requires time, skill development and the ability to examine one's actions and insights concerning the new information and experiences.

Implementation - transfer learned information to your real life situation. Sort through the information gathered and consolidate and maximize its effectiveness.

Feedback - receiving evaluative or corrective information on how your actions have fared. The usefulness of feedback is contingent upon your awareness, receptiveness to its informational content, and your objectivity concerning what is presented.

Resource Identification - resources that can offer support for the ongoing development of the learning you have received. Resources include such items as self-awareness, positive change skills, health informtion, informal contacts, materials, and technology.

Evaluation - of the information received as to its meaning, quality, relevance, application, and impact. The evaluation may be as simple as a mental checklist about new information gathered or as complex as a quantitative analysis.

COMMENTS

Learning occurs within the organization as an individual is hired and must learn: 1) the organization (formal); 2) work habits (informal), and the job itself. Throughout a workers career, learning takes place as the job, technology, organization and environment change. We all learn at different paces, and in different manners. Some of us like "hands-on", some of us prefer lectures and reading. As a supervisor or manager, understanding the learning process can add to your knowledge of people within the organizational setting. Training in the professional setting will be discussed later in this text.

6 ADULT LEARNING STRATEGIES FOR USE IN EDUCATION, TRAINING AND DEVELOPMENT ACTIVITIES

- Share something of value -- a mutually credible, intense experience, your involvement with subject matter, or something about your real self

- When issuing mandatory assignments or training requirements, explain your rationale

- Eliminate or minimize negative conditions that surround the subject -- reduce pain, fear and anxiety, frustration, humiliation, and boredom

- Ensure successful learning through group study procedures, textbooks, workshops, programmed instruction units, computer assisted instruction, audio-visual methods, tutorial help -- set clear standards of mastery and excellence; avoid inter-learner competition; break down material into smaller units of learning; frequently use nongraded evaluation

- Make the first experience with the subject matter as positive as possible

- Positively confront the possible erroneous beliefs, expectations, and assumptions that may underlie a negative learner attitude -- tactfully find out what the learner may be telling her/himself that leads to a negative attitude; point out how negative feelings would naturally follow from this belief; offer and encourage more positive assumptions and beliefs that might facilitate learning

- Associate the learner with other learners who are enthusiastic about the subject

- Encourage the learner through recognition for real effort -- minimize mistakes while the learner is struggling; emphasize learning from mistakes; demonstrate a confident and realistic expectation that the learner will learn because he/she has the capacity

- Promote the learner's personal control over some aspect of the learning context -- allow them to plan and set goals and make choices about what, how or when they will learn something; allow self-evaluation procedures; assist learner assessment of personal strengths and abilities; let the learner log personal progress and analyze potential blocks to progress; use prompt feedback

- Announce the expected amount of time needed to study and practice for successful learning

- Use confronting methods -- contracts should include what the learner will learn (goals or objectives); how the learner will demonstrate learning (performance tasks or exam); the degree of proficiency expected (evaluation or evidence of accomplishment); choice of resources and activity alternatives for learning; and target dates for completion

- Use imagery techniques to help learner clearly remember specific problems or tasks that are relevant to the knowledge or skill being taught

- Introduce the unfamiliar through the familiar

- Create components in the learning environment that tell learners they are accepted and respected participants -- learn names; use seating arrangements where people can see and hear each other; interview each member personally; designate course and training responsibilities from each member of the group

- When appropriate, plan activities to allow learners to share and publicly display their projects and skills which appeal to their curiosity, sense of wonder, need to explore

- Provide variety in personal presentation style, methods of instruction and learning materials -- body movement (how often do you move? in what direction?); body language (gestures used, animation, smiling) ; vocal (tone, pitch, use of voice to convey emotion, emphasis); pauses (when and how often, periods of silence); eye contact; selectively change channels of communication (auditory to visual or tactile); when making a change, vary the process of learning to support different activity

- Introduce, connect and end learning activities attractively and clearly -- ask provocative questions (how many have ever...?, when was the last time...?); call on learners to become active (ask them to help, move, observe, evaluate, remember, lead); create anticipation ("I've been looking forward to doing this exercise"); relate the learning activity to contemporary culture and work; review basic concepts or skills; allow for clarification, feedback, opinions, or evaluations

- Relate learning to adult interests and the advantages that will result

- Use humor, emotions, examples, stories, memories, comprehension or thinking questions, unpredictability (to a reasonable degree)

- Selectively use application, analysis, synthesis, and evaluative questions -- e.g. "using two troubleshooting strategies, correct the errors in this case study" (solve, classify, choose, select, use, employ); "why do you think managers fail to delegate responsibilities when they are overloaded" (analyze, conclude, infer, distinguish, deduce, detect, why); "given this list of client needs, design an appropriate system for ---" (predict, draw, construct, produce, originate, propose, plan, design, synthesize, combine, develop, create); "in your opinion why have Japanese management techniques been oversold in America" (judge, argue, decide, appraise, evaluate)

- Create opportunities and conditions for the following experiences - challenging, meaningful, flexible, broad range of challenges (8).

7 PLANNING FOR TRAINING

The following ten examples are why proper planning for training programs is so important:

1. The trainer "forgot" that training was to take place.

2. As a trainee or student, you were uncertain about what you needed to learn.

3. The training was often interrupted because of outside priorities.

4. The quality of training was lowered by the lack of supplies or unavailable equipment.

5. The training was not conducted in a setting conducive to learning.

6. The procedures taught by the trainer were not consistent with the written or audio visual materials, what others told you to do, or what you saw others do.

7. The training was unorganized, there was no sense to the flow of information.

8. The trainer was ineffective because of attitude or lack of knowledge of the subject or skill being taught.

9. There were no written or other materials to help you learn.

10. Training was done "only when there was time" and was fragmented.

8   SOURCES OF POTENTIAL INSTRUCTORS

SOURCE	ADVANTAGES	DISADVANTAGES
Professional Training and Development Staff	• Possess professional training related knowledge and skills • Can provide guidance/support to other instructors within the organization • Expertise to create new programs	• Amount of direct in-classroom time is limited • Expensive overhead for the training and development department • If not a subject-matter expert, could reduce credibility
Management Personnel Within The Organization	• Related direct operational experiences resulting in greater credibility • Enhances competence of management/personal development • Increased commitment to concepts/ideas presented back on the job • Reduced training department expenses	• Possibly less skilled at instructing/facilitating • Loss of management time back on the job • Frequently it's the least competent managers who can be spared from current responsibilities to handle training
Technical Experts	• First-hand experience with the job or technology assigned to teach • Subject matter expertise • Increased exposure within the organization	• Possibly less skilled at instructional facilitating • May need to provide train-the-trainer programs • Reduced time back on the job
Educators	• Well grounded in instructional methods and skills • May possess some referent credibility due to affiliation with college/university	• Lack of organizational knowledge (e.g. products, services, employees, etc.) • May be too theoretical in approach
"Expert" Consultants	• Highly experienced in specific skills/topic area • May possess "mystical" expertise as an outsider	• Very expensive • Lack of organizational knowledge (e.g. products, services, employees, etc.)

Table 10-2. Sources of Potential Instructors

9   CHARACTERISTICS OF GOOD INSTRUCTORS

The following are some characteristics and qualities of a good instructor:

1. The trainer must have an interest in training.
2. The trainer should have a sense of humor.
3. The trainer must be a good communicator.
4. The trainer must have patience.
5. The trainer must have the time to train.
6. The trainer must have the respect of colleagues.
7. The trainer must be enthusiastic.

10   CREATING A LEARNING CONTRACT

A learning contract (also called training, education, project management, or performance contract) is negotiated between two individuals (one a manager, teacher, project manager and the other a worker-subordinate, student or project team member) for the purpose of achieving learning, educational and performance goals. The process begins with a discussion of who the student is, what the student's goals and objectives are, why the student needs or desires to study a particular skill or content area, how the learning will be accomplished, what resources will be utilized, how the learning will be assessed and evaluated or measured and the amount of credit to be awarded in the case of academic learning. The teacher, trainer or manager may discuss their own expertise, alternative ways that learning can be accomplished, the range of resources available for learning, and the level of performance expected. The process should be one of open and active negotiation between two involved.

The outcome of this negotiation is a contract of written agreement that includes some variations upon the following four areas (see sample contract, Figure 10-4):

● the learner's specific objectives for the learning period under discussion

● the learner's long-range purposes, goals, objectives

● the learning activities to be completed, include: a description of the content and/or skills to be mastered; the techniques of study, training or research; an outline of the learning resources to be used or tried; and the amount of credit earned upon fulfillment of the contract

● the criteria and methods of evaluating performance.

Learning contracts allow for individualized learning activities through consideration of the following items:

● **where** learning will take place -- formal classrooms, work, internships, mediated courses, workshops, conventions, special training sessions, correspondence courses, field placements, travel study

● the **time** involved -- whether spread over long periods of time or concentrated, full time or part time, interspersed with other activities or task specific

● learner's **objectives**, purposes, goals, needs, wants

● **content** of learning situation organized into disciplines, perspectives, theories, paradigms, themes, problems, interdisciplinary, professional or vocational, theory, practice or integration of theory and practice

● **Learning activities, methods and procedures** -- books, magazines, lectures, audio-tutorial, television, films, self-directed programmed materials, simulations, interactive video, computers, field experiences, journals, internships, discussions, conference workshops, using mentors, attending professional meetings, joining special interest groups

● **evaluation** -- should focus upon: methods, paper, oral examination, performance, display, field observation, journal, simulation, group presentation, film, videotape; criteria indicates the standards that will be used to judge acceptable performance; and <u>indicators</u> or evidence that criteria have been satisfied.

The following is a sample group learning activity.

Phase 1 Conduct individual needs analysis, goal setting and planning. Individuals discuss purposes, anticipated outcomes, learning activities and evaluation strategies in groups. Groups of learners share plans in order to clarify, focus or expand individualized plans.

Phase 2 Discussion and development of a group plan. With leader, the group presents several ideas and tries to synthesize the common aspects of individual plans in order to develop a group plan. Roles and responsibilities must be clarified and the project name decided upon. Questions of resources and methods can be explored by breaking larger groups into smaller groups.

Phase 3 Information core. Lectures by faculty, individual reports by small groups to larger group and discussion.

Phase 4 Small task force work. Research by all common interest task forces. Leader can participate as internal consultant and other outside speakers can be brought into the learning situation.

Phase 5 Presentations are given and each student should have the opportunity to be questioned by other students, to hear criticisms and be evaluated by their peers.

Phase 6 Wrap up and evaluation. Final conclusions are offered in a form of group synthesis of material. Individual and small group meetings are scheduled to discuss the work presented by the students, discuss the evaluations of each other's work and receive the leader's evaluation.

LEARNING CONTRACT EXAMPLE

I.   Student's General Purpose:

To earn a bachelor of science degree with a concentration in reliability and quality control.

II.   Student's Specific Purpose:

In this contract, Mr. Smith seeks to:

1.   Study the principles of reliability theory and sampling methods;

2.   Carry out an in-depth study of an actual reliability-quality control problem at his place of employment.

III. Learning Activities:

1.   Mr. Smith will enroll and complete CASM 761, Reliability, at Rochester Institute of Technology.

2.   Mr. Smith will prepare and teach a course in quality control sampling methods at the corporation where he is employed. He will provide his mentor with an outline and a brief written summary of the course.

3.   Mr. Smith and his mentor will examine in detail a reliability/quality control problem(s) associated with Mr. Smith's work. In this study they will define the problems involved, critically examine the work already done, propose new approaches, and review the results. They will pay close attention to constraints such as cost, time, personnel, etc. Mr. Smith will prepare periodic written summaries of the status of the problem(s) and his evaluation of the progress of the work. He will hold extensive regular discussions of this problem with his mentor. At the conclusion of the project he will prepare a summary report describing the problem, conditions for a solution, approaches attempted, results and suggestions for how the process could have been improved.

IV.   Methods and Criteria For Evaluation:

1.   The instructor will evaluate the reliability course. A grade of C or better will be considered passing.

2.   The mentor will evaluate the learnings Mr. Smith has gained through teaching quality control acceptance sampling. Specifically Mr. Smith is to show in his summary and outline that he can select topics in acceptance sampling and present them in a clear, logical manner.

3.   The reliability project will be evaluated by the mentor. Mr. Smith will be expected to develop his skills at problem analysis and definition, test design, and date gathering and analysis. He is to be able to identify and work within economic, technical and time constraints and to develop his own style of solving difficult engineering problems.

Student_____

Date_____

Mentor _____

Date _____

Assoc. Dean_____

Date_____

Figure 10-4. Sample Learning Contract

11 TRAINING NEEDS ASSESSMENTS

Three primary functions of a Training and Development department are:

- Provide programs, services, and activities which help the organization achieve its strategic business goals and objectives

- Ensure that the right programs and services are introduced into the organization at the right time.

- Assist the Training Department to become perceived as a proactive, needs driven, internal consulting group.

As a result, the needs assessment process must take into account many different variables such as: economic factors within the organization; social factors; technological trends; organization size; internal political issues; and manpower support to name a few.

There are basically four different, but complementary, types of needs assessments (9). They are:

1. **Organization Needs Assessment** - Viewing training and development needs from a global perspective. Organization needs are difficult to assess since they emerge from a combination of organization goals, objectives, priorities, and cultural environment.

2. **Group Needs Assessment** - Somewhat easier to conduct than organization needs assessment, since you are able to more closely relate to specific jobs and/or classifications of employees. Group can either be comprised of homogeneous job functions (e.g. secretaries, programmers, etc.) or heterogeneous (e.g. a project team comprised of an engineer, accountant, production supervisor, buyer, and administrator).

3. **Individual Needs Assessment** - Typically easier to conduct than group needs assessment since you are able to readily identify personal characteristics such as education level, experiences, knowledge and skills, and career desires. Individual needs assessments would take into consideration the job the individual is currently doing, potential future assignments, and individual development goals.

4. **Job Needs Assessment** - Depending upon the job being assessed, job needs assessment can be either the easiest or most difficult to define. Operational jobs (i.e. assemblers, tellers, stock clerks, etc.) are relatively easy to analyze in terms of task behaviors. Process oriented jobs (i.e. supervisory and managerial positions), on the other hand, are much more difficult to assess since job requirements are not as observable.

Methods of Assessment

There exist a wide variety of methods and approaches to conducting needs assessment effectively. The challenge facing the training and development practitioner is to select the method(s) which is(are) most likely to provide reliable and timely data at a reasonable expense to the organization. Some possible methods may include:

- **Attitude Surveys** - Can provide feedback and information relating to broad areas of employee satisfaction and dissatisfaction. It is important to remember that attitude surveys provide **indications** of training needs rather than a determination.

- **Inventories/Questionnaires** - Involves the use of an inventory or questionnaire that identifies the skills and abilities of a specified homogeneous work group (e.g. secretaries, supervisors, engineers, etc.). A tabulation of individual scores determines a rank order which reflects the relative importance for training which focuses upon those particular skills and abilities.

- **Interviews** - One-on-one interviews conducted with members of a target population can provide additional information regarding training and development needs. It is also useful to interview superiors and subordinates of the target population for additional insights.

- **Advisory Committees** - Committees comprised of representatives from different organizational levels and functional areas can provide valuable information regarding training needs. In addition, the committee can provide input relating to support and priorities.

- **Reviewing Business Plans** - Make a concerted effort to meet with department heads and executives within the organization, to review operational and long-range business plans. Linking those plans to training and development plans is very important since programs and activities should support the goals and objectives of the organization.

- **Performance Reviews** - If you are able to gain access, they may provide additional insight into training needs within the organization. Often times, personal development plans and career aspirations are noted on the performance review forms.

- **Job Descriptions** - Typically, job descriptions identify the skills, knowledge, and abilities required to perform successfully in particular jobs within the organization.

There exist many other possible methods and approaches to assessing training needs within organizations. When conducting a needs assessment, it is important to utilize more than one method in order to gain support for the findings. Whereas formal needs assessments are carefully planned projects, informal needs assessment is an on-going process where trainers are constantly looking for program opportunities.

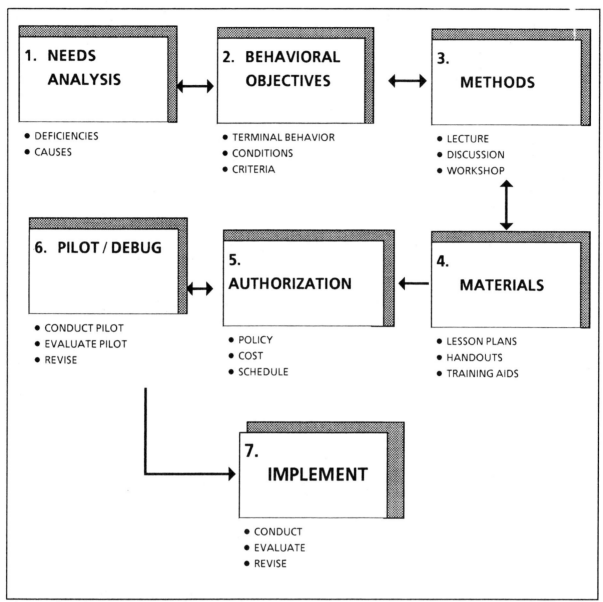

Figure 10-5. Systems Approach To Training

13   ON-THE-JOB TRAINING

On-the-job training (OJT) is the most popular method of training, especially in small organizations. OJT is simple, if planned correctly. OJT can be successful if the basic training principles are utilized to this method of training, as are used for group training, otherwise it can be a waste of time. The following is some basic information about on-the-job training.

- Pre-planning is necessary. Task lists, task breakdowns, performance standards, training plans, and training lessons should be developed before OJT is used to train new employees.

- Trainer selection is important. The trainer must want to train, have adequate job knowledge, and understand and use basic training principles.

- Written materials such as task breakdowns, operating procedure manuals, and handbooks can be helpful to reinforce what the trainees learned.

- Time for training must be provided. It is usually not adequate to simply allow a trainee to "tag along" with a more experienced employee as work is performed.

- Before demonstrating a work task, it is essential to prepare the work area, collect all appropriate tools, supplies, and any other necessary items.

- Evaluation is an integral part of on-the-job training. This should be considered as the program is planned. Some evaluation is necessary both as the program evolves and at the time of its completion.

- Even if the training is delegated by the supervisor to another subordinate, it is important for the supervisor to remain involved with training progress.

- A basic understanding of the current level of knowledge of the trainee is important. An initial study of the task list along with a demonstration of work required for some tasks can clear the way to emphasize activities with which the trainee is unfamiliar.

Purpose of Training Program	Program Examples	Knowledge Acquisition	Skill Building	Attitude Change
Prepare people to do their jobs	1. Entry-level management training program 2. New worker orientation program 3. Formal apprenticeship training program	Management trainee will be able to describe the seven primary functions of management	Management trainee will be able to prepare a workable budget for a six-month period	Management trainee will display the qualities and behavior of a good 'team player'
Improve present job perform-ance	1. Workshop on stress management for management-level personnel 2. Communication skills workshop for secretaries and receptionists 3. A skills update on the new components of the packaging machine	Manager will be able to define the terms conflict and conflict management	Manager will be able to demonstrate at least two alternative ways for handling a specific conflict situation	Manager will demonstrate through both behavior and specific actions that he or she is not afraid of handling a conflict situation
Assist depart-ments and whole organiza-tions to grow	1. A weekend conference retreat for all mid-level managers in Division A 2. A one-day workshop on improving effectiveness and efficiency for all grade 6 secretarial personnel 3. A quality circles program for all line supervisors	All of the supervisors in Division A will be able to define and describe the process of conduct ing quality circles	All of the supervisors in Division A will be able to effectively lead a quality circle	All of the supervisors in Division A will display through their behavior a belief in the use of quality circles as one way to improve performance

Table 10-3

CHAPTER ELEVEN
MANAGEMENT DEVELOPMENT

1 MANAGEMENT DEVELOPMENT... Introduction

Management Development can be defined as increasing managerial skills and abilities through organized training and relevant job experiences. The organization itself must build a management team to run the organization successfully over time. The task of management development requires a dynamic systems view of the related human resources, organizational and managerial components - policies, procedures, selection, recruitment, training, supervision, performance evaluation, rewards, promotion, transfers and career development (10).

Career Development is a sequence of job assignments, training courses and other activities armed at achieving career goals.

Training is the process of teaching the skills needed to do the organization jobs, and move into new jobs at the same or a higher level in the organization.

Development is the process of minimizing weaknesses and trying to build upon and enhance strengths. Training rarely completely changes weaknesses and rarely builds new strengths, but it does allow the individual to meet needs and seek new and better ways of doing the job. Development requires more self understanding in order to enhance abilities and expand one's potential. Both require motivation and goal setting. All workers need to feel that effort will result in obtaining the incentives desired -- a basic level of ability is present and the rewards are desirable.

Managerial Career Development is anticipated and facilitated by the following techniques:

- **Selection:** candidates are subjected to a rigorous selection process...candidates who receive job offers are made to feel part of an elite group; thus their sense of self-confidence is increased

- **Realistic Job Previews:** these previews include information about job duties, promotion, and transfer opportunities. Their purpose is to reduce reality shock

- **Management Orientation:** an introduction to organizational policies and procedures which contribute to organizational loyalty and group cohesiveness

- **Assignment to a New Group**: as newcomers work together, group norms and identification with the group and organization develop simultaneously

- **Technical Training**: information about, and training in skills required for specific job functions which contribute to role clarity

- **Apprenticeship**: learning the ropes with an experienced manager generates group cohesiveness, realization of expectations, and reduced reality shock

- **Bottom Up Experience**: management recruits are assigned to menial line positions that require them to learn the business at the most basic levels

- **Mentor Programs**: newcomers meet periodically with higher-level managers during first years to discuss experiences and organizational conditions. This practice encourages role clarity and prevents reality shock

- **Performance Feedback**: frequent reviews of performance during the first year or so in management, properly done, perhaps quarterly, can build newcomers' confidence in themselves and their newly developed skills

- **Competition**: newcomers are measured by a succinct set of criteria, so that it is easy to compare them to each other in the same area of a business. Such comparison also highlights the importance of achieving visible results, although it has the potential disadvantage of generating intraorganizational conflict

- **Departmental Meetings**: In many organizations, departments have meetings away from the office, often in remote locations, to discuss departmental goals, progress, and other issues. Departmental meetings generate a sense of belonging and a basis for shared experiences

- **Assignments to Special Projects**: this practice establishes feelings of personal importance, intrinsic motivation and achievement

- **Assignment to Undesirable Tasks**: this "hazing" works because people rationalize their experience as a reflection of their commitment to the organization

- **Exposure to Company Folklore**: sharing company folklore enhances newcomers' commitment and provides a model for individual work goals.

2 MANAGEMENT SKILL ASSESSMENTS

The following are various Management Skills, presented in a format for you to be able to conduct a self-assessment. While these do not represent the entire scope of management skills necessary to be effective, they are representative of some of the most important.

PLANNING. Planning is the thinking that precedes the work. If planning is not done, time and effort is usually wasted. Effective Planning includes the following elements. Check your proficiency level for each.

SKILL	DO WELL	NEED IMPROVE MENT
1. Interpreting goals which are passed down as the result of planning at higher levels.		
2. Articulating organizational needs (including those of the team) into team goals and objectives.		
3. Formulating implementation plans by examining alternatives and selecting activities which lead to successful results.		
4. Identifying resources needed to achieve goals (people, time, money, materials, and facilities) and insuring they are available.		
5. Establishing time lines and completion target dates.		
6. Determining standards of performance and how results will be measured.		

ORGANIZING. Once planning is underway, organizing becomes important. Resources - people, capital, raw materials, and technology, must be coordinated effectively to achieve team goals. Some key aspects of organizing are listed below. Check your proficiency in each.

SKILL	DO WELL	NEED IMPROVE MENT
1. I can divide work into logical tasks and groupings.		
2. I know how to secure the resources required to achieve goals.		
3. I am comfortable assigning tasks, resources and responsibility to team members on the basis of functions and skills.		
4. I can establish guidelines in order to coordinate activities between team members and other groups involved with the outcome.		
5. I make it a practice to design information systems which assure appropriate feedback as the work progresses.		
6. I can establish communications networks to insure there is a free-flow of information up, down, and across organizational lines.		

229

MOTIVATING. People work for a variety of reasons. Motivation is personal and managers must get to know individual employees in order to learn what motivates them. A manager must be sensitive to recognize these employee needs, and design ways to meet them while achieving the goals of the organization. No single technique works for everyone. When the following elements are combined, both individual and team success is possible. Check your proficiency below.

I AM PROFICIENT AT:	DO WELL	NEED IMPROVE MENT
1. Insuring each employee knows what is expected and how performance will be measured.		
2. Getting to know employees as individuals to learn their needs.		
3. Providing the training and supervisory assistance necessary for each employee to achieve mutually established objectives.		
4. Providing the resources required to perform the job.		
5. Guiding and encouraging personal growth for individual employees.		
6. Recognizing and rewarding good performance and correcting, or eliminating poor performance when it occurs.		

CONTROLLING. A part of project management is to establish a control system to make sure it will progress according to plan, and the ultimate objective will be achieved. Controls should be established during the planning process, and be as simple as possible. Some important aspects of controlling are listed below. Check your proficiency in each area.

I NORMALLY:	DO WELL	NEED IMPROVE MENT
1. Establish control elements as part of the project plan		
2. Set up time schedules and check points to measure progress.		
3. Encourage feedback from team members throughout the project.		
4. Evaluate problems or deviations from plans, and then construct a new action plan which is timely and appropriate.		
5. Adjust objectives, plans, resources or motivational factors as required to meet the organizational goals.		
6. Communicate progress and plan changes to those who need to know.		

HIRING. Human resources are the most critical part of any organization's success. Good people help insure profitability, productivity, growth and long term survival. As a manager and team leader, it is essential for your team members to work well together. Some critical elements in employee selection and placement are listed below. Check to see how well you perform in this area.

SKILL	DO WELL	NEED IMPROVE MENT
1. I analyze job requirements thoroughly before beginning the selection process.		
2. I always probe for objective evidence of an applicant's skills; knowledge; past successes and failures; dependability; and attitude toward work, co-workers, supervision and customers.		
3. I describe my idea of teamwork to applicants and ask them to assess how they would work under these team conditions.		
4. I make sure each applicant understands the job requirements and expected standards of performance.		
5. I evaluate facts carefully and avoid making premature conclusions or stereotyping while making a selection decision.		
6. People I hire are placed in positions where there is a potential for success.		

TRAINING. Training is an important part of a manager's job. Your attitude, knowledge and approach will influence what is learned and how well it is applied. Here are some suggestions to improve your training methods.

I NORMALLY:	DO WELL	NEED IMPROVE MENT
1. Review performance against expectations with each employee periodically, and jointly identify training that will strengthen results.		
2. Listen to an employee's growth objectives, and support them when it is appropriate to do so.		
3. Talk in advance to employees selected for training to reinforce the importance of the training to their jobs.		
4. Have an employee's work covered by others while they are in training so they can concentrate on what is being taught.		
5. Help employees develop an action plan to apply their training to the job.		
6. Ask the employee for an evaluation of the training program and whether it would be suitable for other members of the team.		
7. Assign work to employees that allows them to apply new techniques and methods learned during training.		
8. Compliment employees when they apply their newly acquired skills.		

EVALUATING. A good leader maintains control but strives to establish an environment in which team members will exercise self-control. Evaluation is the means by which positive discipline is implemented through clear communication and good feedback. Indicate your proficiency with each technique below.

TECHNIQUE	DO WELL	NEED IMPROVE MENT
1. From the outset, make sure team members understand what is expected of them and what standards are to be met.		
2. Teach team members how to fulfill expectations and achieve standards.		
3. Encourage team members as they make progress toward attaining company goals.		
4. Compliment team members when standards are achieved and expectations are realized.		
5. Re-direct inadequate or inappropriate performance when it occurs, and repeat 1-4.		
6. If the inadequate or inappropriate performance persists after a reasonable period of time (and step 5 has been applied), bench or trade the player. He or she hasn't made the team.		

3   MANAGEMENT DEVELOPMENT DIAGNOSIS

London (10) suggests ways of diagnosing an organization's philosophical commitment to Management Development by asking the following questions:

* To what extent are employees treated as corporate assets?

* Does the company want to develop generalists, or specialists within departments?

* Who has control over promotion and transfer decisions?

* To what extent does the company depend on promotion from within to fill vacancies?

* To what extent are bosses responsible for assisting subordinates in career planning?

* Should there be (in your opinion) a comprehensive manager development program encompassing many career development components, or should efforts be limited to separate programs operated on an as-needed basis?

* Is it beneficial to identify high-potential employees and put them on a fast-track advancement program, separate from those with average potential who are on a standard career track?

* To what extent should the organization designate specific career paths?

4   MANAGEMENT STYLES: AN INTRODUCTION

There are four basic management and follower styles that can be easily recognized when we learn to be "people watchers". Watching people, understanding their different styles, and acknowledging their styles as having worth gives us the critical knowledge and advantage needed to better manage and influence them.

Let's call the four broad and general styles directing, influencing, supporting, and delegating (see Figure 11-1). We can determine our basic style by sensing where we fit between relationship-oriented and open to task-oriented and self-contained, and between being indirect and slow-paced to direct and fast-paced.

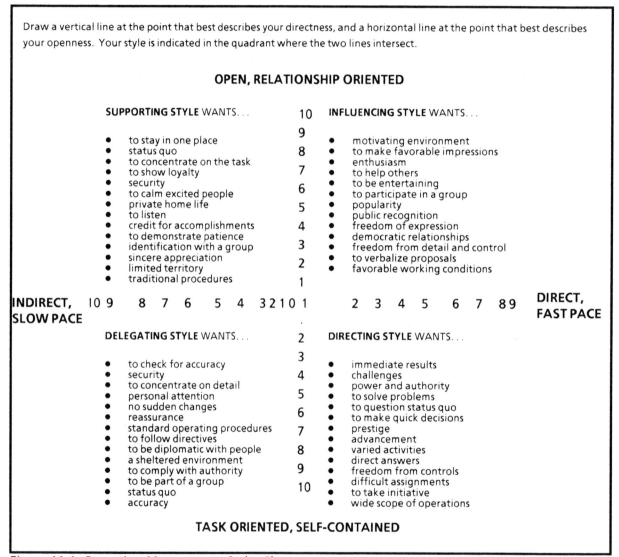

Figure 11-1. Proactive Management Styles Chart

How do your individual management style and the styles of others influence these tasks and functions? We all exhibit a set of behaviors representing our personal styles and preferences for living and working. These styles are observable and remain predictable over a lifetime. Your management style is a vehicle for conveying knowledge, feelings, values and perceptions - a vehicle for managing and influencing others to help you achieve your vital goals. For you to effectively carry out the tasks

234

and functions previously discussed, you need to understand and acknowledge your own style and those of your peers, subordinates, bosses, and customers.

Look back over the last week and try to identify some situations where you had easy times and hard times influencing other people. Why is it that sometimes it is difficult to influence some people, and at other times you instantly hit it off with someone you have just met and get the results desired? There seems to be something that creates a basis of understanding and trust that is more than can be explained by common background or related profession. Understanding and trust often occur because of a congruence between the operating styles of two or more people during a given meeting.

These manager and follower styles influence our interpersonal relationships and our ability to manage proactively, ultimately influencing our personal success and corporate achievement. Consider these points:

- Everyone uses a blend of all four styles

- Despite using a blend or style mix, each person relies heavily on a primary or dominant style

- Under significant stress, a person's style may change

- Each person's style is manifested in his or her behavior and may be observed

- An individual's lack of effectiveness often represents an overextension of his or her strengths due to fear, lack of acknowledgement, or under use in creative and productive ways

- People are most receptive to and understanding of persons whose styles are similar to their own styles

- Effective managers develop the strength and skills to shift their styles and use their short suits in order to accommodate themselves to the situation. They acknowledge the other person's needs in order to influence that person.

Understanding, acknowledging, and holding a high regard for your own style and the styles of others can culminate in understanding and trust.

When we are blocked from expressing our true styles, we often overextend our strengths to the point of being reactive, and our strengths become overbearing liabilities.

Figure 11-2 shows some techniques you can use with people who have different behavioral styles.

BEHAVIORAL FLEXIBILITY WITH INFLUENCERS	BEHAVIORAL FLEXIBILITY WITH SUPPORTIVES
Support opinions, ideas and dreams	Support feelings and interpersonal relationships
Do not rush the discussion	Project personal interest
Try not to argue - you can't win	Get him to spell out objectives
Summarize everything in writing	Be sincere and personable
Be entertaining	Move along in an informal, slow manner
Be stimulating	When you disagree, discuss personal opinions and feelings
Move quickly	Provide personal guarantees and assurances
Provide testimonials	Do not rush him - guide

BEHAVIORAL FLEXIBILITY WITH DIRECTORS	BEHAVIORAL FLEXIBILITY WITH DELEGATORS
Support goals and objectives	Support organized and cautious approach
Keep relationship businesslike	Demonstrate through actions, not words
Get to the point	Be prepared, systematic, and organized
Argue facts, not feelings	List advantages and disadvantages of any plan you propose
Be precise and well-organized	Do not rush decision-making process, but do gently nudge
Provide alternatives for decisions	Avoid gimmicks
	Provide guarantees

Figure 11-2. Behavioral flexibility with Different Styles

5   MANAGEMENT STYLES: DECISION MAKING

One thing that all managers have in common is - they all must make decisions. These decisions are crucial because they affect individual, group, and organizational performance. Decision-making is not a science, because each manager's personal motives, values, and perceptions play an integral part in the process. Knowledge of decision style theory can help managers and leaders strengthen their decision-making abilities. It can help them also better understand their subordinates and improve subordinates' performance by matching the individual employee's responsibilities with her or his decision style.

A decision style is a learned way of processing information and making decisions. It is a habit acquired through past experiences. The process of decision-making differs among people in two key dimensions: complexity and degree of focus. Complexity means the amount of information used in reaching a decision, focus refers to the number of alternative solutions generated from the information. The complexity of a person's decision process increases to the degree that more information is utilized and a greater number of solution alternatives are generated. Person A may make use of only half of the information available to reach one conclusion, while Person B may utilize all information available to reach several alternative solutions.

Extremes in either complexity or focus are usually undesirable. Too much information can be overwhelming and lead to confusion and chaos. Too little information may not provide an adequate basis on which to make decisions. An extreme number of multiple focuses can lead to problems of over analysis in which so many conclusions are considered that none are executed.

In Figure 11-4 you will see a matrix to identify the four decision styles. The decision styles represent pure types, and some people predominantly use one style, while others frequently shift among several styles. These styles are shown in order of ease of use with decisive being the simplest style, integrative the most complex decision style.

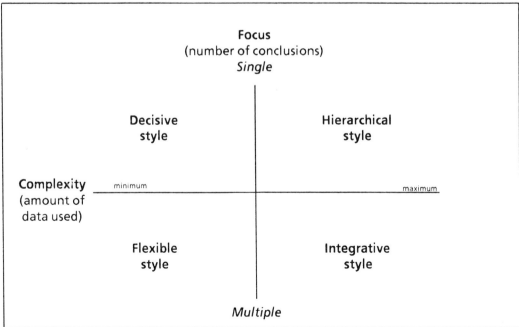

Figure 11-4. Decision Styles

Decisive style is one that uses a minimum amount of data to arrive at one "satisfactory" decision.

Flexible style relies on a minimum amount of information, but shifts focus repeatedly over time, reinterpreting data and continually generating different conclusions.

Hierarchical style uses large amounts of data, which are analyzed to generate one optimum decision.

Integrative style uses maximum data to generate several different feasible conclusions.

When there is an abnormal oversupply or undersupply of information on which to base a decision, or if there are severe time pressures, people tend to shift to a back-up style. The most common back-up style is either the decisive or the flexible because these styles require the least amount of information and are, therefore, faster.

DECISIVE	HIERARCHICAL
Present action conclusions first	Respect other's control values
Avoid detail	Relate suggestions to other's preferred
Be positive and avoid criticism	method
Be firm and appear certain	Present both your data and conclusions
Be punctual	Expect other to "correct" your proposals
Produce results	never "win" an argument
Don't expect friendliness	Don't make quick replies
Keep things impersonal	Try for zero defects
never go over other's head	make informed comments
	Listen well
FLEXIBLE	**INTEGRATIVE**
Show initiative	Present problems
Suggest new ideas	Refrain from offering solutions
Be fast	Have a variety of data sources
Don't overkill a topic	Avoid absolutes
Don't be too personal	Strive for cooperation
Keep detail out	Communicate hunches
Stay loose	Perform your own control
Keep an open mind	Be ready to shift topics
Don't ask for long-term commitment	Be open

Figure 11-5. Coping Effectively with Other Styles (Manager's course of action)

No decision style fits all jobs or situations equally well. Any given style works best when there's an appropriate match or congruence between the job and the individual. A decisive style is best for highly programmed jobs that require speed and consistent behavior based on specific procedures. The flexible style would be more effective for jobs that require speed, ingenuity, and adaptability. The integrative style is more successful in highly complex and rapidly changing situations.

Figure 11-5 shows some coping techniques you, as a supervisor, manager, or leader can use to effectively deal with other styles.

CHARACTERISTICS OF EACH DECISION STYLE

STYLE	ADVANTAGES	DISADVANTAGES
Decisive Style	+ Concerned with speed, efficiency, consistency + Action and result oriented + Plans are short-range and deadlines critical + Prefers hierarchical organizational structures with short, clear spans of control + Tends to ignore long, detailed reports + Accepts authority based on position + Motivates through a rigid reward/punishment system	- Rigid mind set - Avoids introspection - Low self-concept - Avoids change - Unreceptive to complex data
Flexible Style	+ Values action, speed, adaptability, variety + Prefers not to plan + Uses their intuition + Tends to pursue self-oriented goals + Prefer loose, fluid organizations with little structure or rules + Prefer brief, concise communications and reports + Likes spontaneous interaction between people	- Shallow mind set - Has an inability to concentrate - Is too fascinated with variety - Unwilling to accept structure - Poor planner - Appears to be flippant
Hierarchical Style	+ Values perfection, precision, and thoroughness + Likes to be in control + Likes thorough, long-range planning + Prefers intricate hierarchical organizational structures with broad spans of control and elaborate policies and procedures + Motivates by providing others with relevant information + Influences others by using logic and analysis	- Suppressive or tyrannical attitude - Perfectionist - Inability to delegate - Argumentative nature - Not willing to share credit
Integrative Style	+ Generates long-range plans based on detailed analysis of data + Prefers loose, fluid organizations that can be adapted to the demands of various circumstances + Communications are long and elaborate + Influences with their information processing skills + Allows all concerned to participate in decisions that are based on feelings, facts, and opinions	- Indecisive nature - Unable to meet deadlines - Avoids detail - Passive attitude - Places overemphasis on process instead of results

Table 11-1

239

6 EIGHT STAGES OF DECISION MAKING

1. Listening and observing all the possibilities, options and choices involved in the issues

2. Sustaining a free flow of feelings and thoughts about each of the possible choices

3. Observing thoughts and feelings about each option

4. Relating choices to established priorities

5. Coming to a conclusion / designation

6. Registering the decision

7. Investing the decision with committed feelings, thoughts, time and energy

8. Translating decisions into optimistic action

DECISION BLOCKERS	SECRETS OF SUCCESSFUL DECISIONS
Losing touch with feelings Resignation and avoidance of potential conflicts Having no priorities Lack of confidence / poor self esteem Hopelessness / depression Unrealistic image of self Inappropriate dependency upon others Obsessive quest for mastery and applause Perfectionism Chronic belief in "grass is greener" or something is better Imagination rules Fear of bad choice Option blindness Time pressure Impaired judgment Procrastination	Know your priorities Establish realistic goals and expectations Know there is always a price to pay Self-confidence, know your assets and don't fear failure, handle insecurity, and accept others for who they are Know and explore your style Often easier to leave than stay Know that conditions are always imperfect Recognize that moods make a difference Accept ambivalence Value concentration Profit from others' experience, expertise, help Delegate Use time effectively Use insight and discipline Be able to postpone gratification Value struggle

Table 11-2

7   CREATIVE THINKING AND INNOVATION

INTRODUCTION

Creativity simply refers to the ways of generating new, more unique, or novel ideas and solutions to problems. The failure to find more creativity in organizational life is the result of blockages, and communication gaps, not the lack of high IQ workers. Innovation is simply the application of creative ideas to the development and implementation of new and profitable processes, products and services.

If we really accept the view that creativity is only for some, then the message is clear: don't risk effort because you will surely fail, and maybe even humiliate yourself in the process. If this happens, then innovative and entrepreneurial thinking will also surely dry up. Creativity is not related to special personal traits or characteristics, according to many experts in the field.

THE DIMENSIONS OF CREATIVITY AND INNOVATION

Creativity includes such components as imaginatively generating original or novel ideas, utilizing knowledge (gather as much relevant information and other resources as possible) to evaluate the ideas, and finally, working to insure their implementation. People may be creative in any of the key dimensions, but the success of any creative project or product demands that we integrate all these dimensions. For example, we must first develop potentially original ideas. We cannot, however, generate good ideas while saturated with the fear of breaking the organizations cultural beliefs that promoting safe and noncontroversial ideas is the only way to get ahead.

Second, any organization must create procedures to systematically evaluate these potentially unique ideas. This helps us to insure their high quality application to the particular practical problems, or products we are currently exploring.

Third, highly original or quality ideas once evaluated must then become implemented by management, if they are to make a difference. This task requires good planning, communication and change management skills. Many individuals forget that reducing the resistance to creative ideas and fostering their implementation through innovative services or products is as important as generating good ideas in the first place.

Workers in uncreative, unproductive, and highly bureaucratic organizational cultures often learn that doing nothing, obstructing innovation, or avoiding risks are the rewarded behaviors. Remember, any positive change must be reinforced through the reward system (compensation, performance appraisal, bonuses, recognition) and modeled by respected leaders and managers. When this doesn't happen, it is customary for workers in such situations to avoid any innovative or entrepreneurial behavior.

Innovation requires that change become the norm, in opposition to the established, habitual, and routine ways of operating. Innovation is built upon the creative process and results in marketable products or services.

A primary task of anyone trying to use creativity to harness innovation is to sort out those situations which are crucial. It is easier to build relevance into a creative idea than vice-versa, because the first key process is breaking through the barriers.

241

Good management, human resource development, training or even health promotion, is really concerned with opportunities for practicing creativity on the firing line. Creativity can support some very practical goals which will help us to improve our personal effectiveness and organizational productivity. But we need to know how to use our creative skills to manage and develop people and systems by removing the blocks to creative thinking and innovative action.

OVERCOMING OBSTACLES TO CREATIVITY AND INNOVATION

Why aren't leaders, managers and workers more creative? The answer is not because they are incapable. Instead, we need to look at those learned habits that have become blocks to our natural creativity and openness to different ways of viewing the world around us. By understanding some of these blocks, we can better prepare to learn some creative techniques for improving the personal well being of workers, as well as increasing organizational innovation.

Ask yourself, "how do I perceive the situation?" Perceptual blocks are like invisible walls that keep us from seeing all the possibilities in the situation. For example, do you check your style of communication when others fail to seem to listen and follow your instructions?

The perceptual block lies in our inability to observe deeper or more basic issues than those that first appear on the surface (the presenting problem in the language of employee relations counselors). For example, you think your subordinates need to listen to directions, when the deeper issue might be that you have a need to control everything. This simple reality may obscure the clarity and real sincerity of your message.

Creativity requires a good amount of preparation and stimulation, as well as times of diversion and intellectual rest. First, stimulate your mind with ideas by saturating it with information. You can use techniques like brainstorming, asking twenty questions, reviewing ideas, using checklists, conducting interviews, and listening to those around you. Second, after you have gorged yourself for a while on this information feast, just relax, and wait while you try a different activity. This is called incubation because we keep potentially good ideas alive and growing, like something that is nurtured in an incubator.

Practice deferring judgment or evaluation and try to become more alert to the unexpected. Don't be afraid to challenge your first perceptions and expectations; embrace non traditional ideas for the sake of changing your angle of vision. A little playfulness and just plain foolishness is a prescription that might produce some unique thoughts. Humor can provide a sudden shift of focus and the surprise twist essential for creativity and a fresh approach to old problems.

Another block to creativity is emotions which sometimes limits our ability to stretch the creative imagination and think about problems in new ways. For example, excessive commitment to our work, or winning at any cost, can cause us to be perceived as self centered. Workers can learn the wrong lessons from this behavior and become emotionally incapable of working with others and building effective workteams.

Today, the name of the game in business and almost any activity is teamwork. Our actions can teach others how to tolerate ambiguity by eliminating the excessive need for censoring the seeds of good ideas before they have an opportunity to sprout and grow. The key is learning how to remain open emotionally to new opportunities and possibilities.

242

Try being supportive and enthusiastic. And remember that your critical side can dominate your imagination and is affected by such emotions as the fear of failure. Be open, take risks and feel the joy of being absorbed with new people, ideas and possibilities.

Cultural blocks can limit our creativity by constricting behavior to what is socially acceptable. People locked into their own cultural viewpoint are called ethnocentric. Organizational expectations can also block creative exploration and expression. By rejecting exploratory behavior in ourselves, we are prematurely preventing the opportunity for others to exercise their creative capacity. Practice doing things your organization ignores, like spending time at work relaxing your mind, generating as many ideas as possible, and ignoring the need for any solution; unclutter your day from detail and deadlines.

Intellectual blocks to creativity occur as a result of faulty information gathering, formulation, and processing strategies. Individuals with preferred modes or styles of thinking about problems may display inflexible behaviors, and ignore their weaknesses. But, merely having information and expertise does not guarantee that ideas will be used imaginatively. Without knowledge, imagination cannot be productive, and without imagination, even the most well prepared minds cannot help us to perceive potentially innovative paths or entrepreneurial opportunities.

Sharpen your sense of problem assessment. Practice asking questions, and develop curiosity about how and why things go wrong more often than they might. Listen to the ideas of others, and jot down your ideas about how things can be improved. Ask questions and develop sensitivity to the problems festering below the surface. Don't always accept at face value the surface or presenting problem. Broaden or narrow the problem in order to consider a wider range of possibilities.

Formulate the problem by asking the right questions. This reframing process is an important aspect of creativity. Be independent and courageous in your thinking. Practice extended concentration so that distractions and interruptions do not effect your ability to work anytime.

Stress is another major obstacle to creativity. We can define stress as the arousal of the mind-body system which, if prolonged, can fatigue or damage the human system to the point of disease. Stressors are the physical, social, and psychological conditions or situations that cause the onset of stress. Stress is the body's nonspecific response to any demand placed upon it, whether pleasant or unpleasant. In fact, a moderate amount of stress is necessary to facilitate any meaningful task, including work and creativity.

Creativity begins when we learn self-regulation strategies through relaxation, in order to gain more balance and control over stress. Excessive tension and worry prolongs stress. These tensions are actually locked into our constricted thinking patterns, and prevent us from getting outside our old, narrow perceptions and attitudes about situations and people.

Here are some strategies to help you to take charge of your stressors. Get to know your stressors and how you respond to them over time in in various situations. Determine what factors or situations seem to impact you chronically or severely. Exercise regularly and non-competitively for about three half-hour sessions a week to give you a surge of energy and increase your well being. Eat a balanced diet and reexamine your life and work priorities. Allow yourself the luxury of making some mistakes, and learn to forgive others for being less than perfect. Put perfection, guilt and anger in perspective, and learn how to appreciate and celebrate success and failure, victory and defeat in more humble and constructive ways.

243

The final block to creativity is organizational structure: constraints over control, tight deadlines , poor communications between units, and ineffective project management.

These can be overcome by fostering a sense of personal control, access to resources and sponsors, good project management skills, high trust, low levels of red-tape, acceptance of failure as part of the entrepreneurial process, and open communications. Some ideas for removing these structural blocks and supporting innovation are listed below. You should try to identify creative talent and understand how to develop, use, and reward this talent once identified. Here are some questions to ask:

1. Who are our creative people, and how do we know that they are creative?

2. What opportunities exist for creative people in our organization?

3. What barriers have we managers placed in front of creative type employees and innovative behavior?

4. In what ways do we reward creativity?

5. Do we embarrass, ridicule, and reject those workers who experiment and try new approaches?

6. How do we specifically encourage or promote experimentation and independent thinking?

7. Do you as a manager usually make all the important decisions? What types of decisions do you encourage your subordinates to make?

8. Are staff and committee meetings, round table discussions, and small group meetings always agenda bound, tightly structured, time constricted and dominated by critical, control orientated managers who cannot tolerate deviation or getting off the path (11)?

TECHNIQUES FOR ENHANCING CREATIVITY

The task is to set the climate for exploring our creative processes and getting in touch with our imagination, intuition, and divergent thinking processes. Our goal is to get out of our critical, analytical left brain for a while. Remember, we are ultimately interested in using both sides of the brain and associated processes.

Be Receptive To New Ideas

The key is learning how to see connections within data that do not appear at first blush to contain information relevant to your task. Acquiring data is only the first stage because we are most interested in those ideas that can truly make a difference.

We need to become more aware of excessive criticism in the early stage of generating ideas. Just because we've often been taught at school and conditioned at work to evaluate ideas, doesn't mean we can't decide upon the best times and places to critically evaluate. Each of us must learn to suspend our critical capabilities when we're trying to generate creative ideas and alternatives.

In addition, we must push beyond the logical limits of the immediately relevant to the more fuzzy boundaries of the only approximately relevant. This is because

244

reasoning with analogies (approximately relevant) enables individuals to work on problems without feeling the stress of practicality, the intimidating eye of relevancy, or the fear of our internal censor.

Being receptive to creative ideas means challenging old thinking habits, reflecting about obstacles to the creative process, and not getting bogged down trying to work with only bits and pieces that must logically resemble the topic or problem. It also means patiently getting into new situations and listening, observing, and risking with a non judgmental attitude.

Use Checklists

Osborne (12) offers the idea of getting a list of topics or words and consider them in light of the key topics or subjects about which you're trying to generate some creative angles. The list could include any of the following :

* Adapt? Put to other uses? New ways to use as is? Other uses if modified? What else is like this? What other ideas does this suggest?

* Modify? New style? Change meaning, color, motion, sound, odor form, shape? Other changes?

* Magnify? What to add? More time? Greater frequency? Stronger? Higher? Longer? Thicker? Extra value? Duplicate?

* Minify? What to subtract? Smaller? Condensed? Miniature? Lower?

* Substitute? Who else instead? What else instead? Other ingredients? Other materials? Other processes, powers, places, approaches?

* Rearrange? Interchange components? Other pattern, layout, sequence? Transpose cause and effect? Change pace? Change schedule?

* Reverse? Transpose positive and negative? How about opposites? Turn it backwards? Turn it upside down? Reverse roles?

* Combine? How about a blend, an alloy, an assortment, an ensemble? Combine units, purposes, appeals, ideas?

Incubate Ideas

This strategy is to establish the proper conditions for making new or unexpected connections. Try to immerse yourself in a situation, issue or condition; daydream, play music, exert yourself to your limits, as you wait for revelations, connections, and implications. Patience and timing are key virtues here, and their diligent cultivation will produce creative results.

Now back off and change directions by doing the opposite and let data and ideas mix below the surface of awareness. Read anything to stimulate your imagination. Don't expect some grand illumination, just be aware of less dramatic insights and connections, which can be constantly built upon.

Remember, waiting for great leaps of imagination can create excessive stress and performance pressure. Accept the fact that the kernels for all new ideas are laying around everywhere. We can actively learn anytime by modifying, borrowing, combining, synthesizing, evaluating and recognizing the fertile, historical soil of former innovations or inventions.

Listing Attributes

Crawford (13) first developed this technique for stimulating creativity. The process is a special type of of checklist where you list all the attributes of any product, idea, situation, or problem. Next, take each attribute and probe it, as it contains some essence and possible clues about the creative potential of the product, idea, or service change under consideration.

For example, after listing the attributes of an effective team or group, one then evaluates each attribute separately in order to improve upon the idea. If we stated that work groups require cohesiveness, goals, norms, leadership, interaction, and roles, then we might focus on just one attribute in order to improve them.

Let's take group cohesiveness as the attribute that we are going to analyze in order to improve work groups. We might begin with a definition of what cohesiveness is: the characteristics of the group in which the forces acting on the group members to remain and participate are greater than those acting on members to leave it (14:144). Using this definition as a starting point, how could we improve the process of building group cohesiveness?

Let me suggest several possibilities from my own brainstorming of alternatives derived from the above definition. Establish common interests and participate in extracurricular activities together in order to improve the chances of agreeing on important group goals to work toward. Increase the frequency of positive interaction and informal visiting and interaction at the worksite. Introducing some type of intergroup competition because groups will increase cohesiveness when they identify a common enemy.

And finally, hire people with similar characteristics because they will function more like us and probably support our group goals. The basic idea behind this generating lists technique is to probe each component and ask, "How can this be done differently or viewed from a more productive angle?"

Forcing Relationships

The idea here is to force a relationship between two previously unrelated things, concepts, or products. The forced relationship is established using such items as catalogs, magazines, books, or dictionaries, and selecting an idea or subject of interest for new possible combinations.

Next, the second word or subject is also mechanically selected, and the two elements are considered together to evoke original thoughts derived from the forced associations. The process is really to force associations between the old and the new, the mundane and the extraordinary; what you know and what you need to speculate about.

Alternation Principles: Thinking/Judging, Solo/Team, Involve/Detach

Thinking/Judging is the principle that suggests we generate ideas first and then judge them. Thinking for increasing our creative output requires that we record every idea, whether good or bad, without initially judging or evaluating them.

Ideas themselves become the stimulus for other ideas. By giving our ideas the green light, and deferring judgment, our mind begins to move faster, rapidly generating new ideas without slowing down for fear of the detours ahead. Associations spring to life more fluidly and naturally as this free association process taps into the deeper sources of the unconscious.

Deferring judgment has also been called divergent or lateral thinking (15). Lateral thinking helps us challenge assumptions in ways that logical thinking does not. This occurs as the mind interrupts its habitual, organized thought process and leaps "sideways" out of its ingrained patterns. When this happens, the brain often links unrelated neural patterns and synaptic connections, helping us to see problems in new ways. Any time you find yourself reacting to an idea as it seems to float into awareness, just jot it down.

The method is first formally identified by Alex Osborn in 1938 as **brainstorming**. This long available technique was first practiced in India as part of a Hindu religious ceremony called Prai Barshana, which means outside yourself questioning. It became the technique for using the brain's capabilities for intuitive insight in the right hemisphere to create elements for a more creative approach to solving problems. A more formal definition is the uninhibited development of ideas, suggestions, and insights by individuals or groups.

The first thing we need to remember is to suspend our judgmental attitudes and critical, left.brained censor. Be prepared to record all ideas generated without evaluating their relevance, usefulness or validity. Watch for nonverbal put-downs such as a snicker, rolling eyes, or condescending humor; and verbal put downs such as "that will never work" or "top management will never approve of that." Remember, you are trying to suspend your preconceived ideas and generate as many ideas as possible over a short, fixed time span.

Let's now review the stages of brainstorming.

1. **Free Wheel.** Generate as many ideas as possible on a topic, problem, situation or attribute. The ideas should not be criticized or evaluated. Set an initial time limit of approximately THIRTY minutes.

2. **Record.** The ideas generated should be recorded on a chalk board or notebook.

3. **Rest And Incubation.** About halfway through the time frame ask participants to close their eyes, fold their arms in a relaxed way, and rest their heads. Suggest that they reflect uncritically on the ideas already generated.

4. **Resume Freewheeling.** The group recorder (who may also be the group leader) can now resume the recording of ideas as they are generated during the remaining FIFTEEN minutes. The leader/recorder should try to facilitate, not directly control or dominate the free association process and remind the participants of the rules.

5. **Combine And Evaluate.** After the ideas have been generated and recorded the group should then try to combine, categorize, or organize the ideas produced. Here the facilitator can direct a discussion and evaluation about the ideas listed. Participants can add more ideas. Through these discussions the scope of the situation or problem can be clarified, and possible solutions generated.

6. **Return To Free Wheel.** You can return to the free wheel brainstorming of ideas if at any time the group decides to expand upon one key idea or solution.

Solo/team alternation of effort suggests that some people work better together as individuals, while others improve their work when they join a team or group effort. However, for the type of complex problems that most individuals and organizations

247

are facing today, the advantages of pooling one's resources, talent, knowledge, and expertise is obvious.

The alternating principle of involvement/detachment is a psychological dimension of the last idea. Sometimes we need to not only leave a problem by departing a group or leaving our office; we also need to depart consciously. People often get so overloaded, burned out, frustrated and intense that they need a mental, emotional and physical break. Relaxation and rest away from any situation can provide needed time to gain a new perspective.

CONCLUSIONS

Creativity is the ability to produce something of innovative beauty through imaginative skill. We must all learn the three attributes of the creative process: sensitivity to problems often overlooked by others; fluency in generating ideas when faced with difficult situations or problems; and finally, flexibility to examine many alternatives and to determine the most beneficial and innovative outcomes.

Creative leaders, managers, and workers can work together to help establish more innovative organizations. They can support a climate for creativity to flourish. One key for a company's long-term survival is the ability to manage the challenges of change and proactively master new competitive situations. Managing change is such an important skill because it requires modifications and significant departures from the organization's established operations and procedures. Most managers can improve their general performance by understanding at least some principles of creativity.

The truly creative organization is one where both innovative and adaptive behavior are nurtured, supported, and rewarded. By recognizing the potential contributions from both styles of management, organizations can build more balanced, creative management teams which can ultimately enhance the organization's effectiveness .

We can support this mission by valuing creativity and innovation because the success of any enterprise is tied to its quality of people and their skill in thinking and applying the results. As we build a culture of accomplishment, experimentation and pride in innovation through these creative techniques, the organization will flourish. This type of organization is quick to give credit for creative behavior in order to sustain a climate of excellence through innovation.

Workers need to feel wanted, appreciated, and successful. Innovative organizations get excited about the challenges ahead. They recognize that down cycles are inevitable, but success over the long term is their goal. These organizations don't interfere with the creative process because they respect their workers and believe that they are striving to produce the best possible outcomes, given the current conditions, personnel, and resources. They appreciate mistakes because they know that only in such an open and experimental climate can creativity and productive innovation flourish.

There is creative potential in virtually all of us, although it emerges and shows itself in different ways. Let's get on with important work and eliminate the excuses that block our path and traps us in creative immaturity. While we whimper that we are not capable enough to sustain creativity in a manner that is only reserved for some artistic elite, the everyday competitive world is banging at our door.

248

8 DELEGATION

When a supervisor or manager does not use delegation, certain results are evident within the department or work group:

- Schedules and deadlines are often hard to maintain
- Employees tend to feel under-utilized
- There are few opportunities for skill development or advancement
- Nearly everyone feels stressed

If you can answer "yes" to any of the questions below, you probably have room for improvement in the area of delegation (16).

Do you spend time nearly every day on routine or repetitive work?

Are you often interrupted with detailed questions about assignments or current projects?

Do you have to struggle to get things done on time?

Do you feel you put in longer hours and work harder than most of those you supervise?

If something happened to you today to keep you away from work for several weeks, would your department have trouble maintaining a high level of productivity?

Some common excuses which keep managers from delegating effectively are (17):

- "I can do it better". This may be true, but is "better" necessary? Can a subordinate do an adequate job?

- "I'm afraid my subordinate will fail". Realize that calculated risk is both necessary and desirable. Some employees are motivated by new challenges and are thankful for more responsibility. Delegating does not mean giving up all control, you still oversee the project, thereby reducing the risk of delegating.

- "I enjoy doing this task". Even though you might be comfortable with the task, determine if it is necessary for your future growth, attaining your goals.

- "It has to be done right now". Time management is the answer. Plan ahead, organize your time to delegate.

- "I don't want my people to think I'm a tyrant". Egalitarianism is a persistent theme of modern management.

What to delegate

1) Delegate jobs that your employees can do as well as or better than you. Reserve for yourself those tasks that require your experience, skill and training.
2) Delegate duties and tasks that are temporary or that come up infrequently.
3) Delegate the preparation of rough drafts of written material, such as policy statements, reports, or proposals.
4) Delegate problem analysis and solution gathering.
5) Delegate tasks you would find routine but others would find challenging.

How to delegate

1) Delegate fairly and consistently. Give all your employees opportunities to show off their competence and receive recognition for doing well.
2) Match the individual to the task. Assign projects based on a person's strengths, but also be aware of areas in which improvement is needed. Look for opportunities to provide a challenge.
3) Communicate clearly about the assignment, stating your desired results and time frames. Let the employee know if there are alternative ways to accomplish the same results.
4) Be sure to delegate authority as well as responsibility. Let employees know what your are delegating, and then let them make their own decisions.
5) Don't overrule decisions, resist the temptation to reverse the decision. When you must intervene, allow the employee handling the assignment to announce any changes.
6) If a problem arises, don't solve it yourself, simply offer your help.
7) Delegate each assignment to the lowest level. Make sure everyone knows the reporting structure, if several employees are involved on one project.
8) Follow up on what you have assigned. Establish a system for getting regular progress reports. Do not wait until the deadline to check on the status of the project. Remember, you are still held accountable for the project.

9   TIME MANAGEMENT

Time has the potential to be a positive or negative factor in our lives. It is positive when <u>we</u> manage <u>it</u>, a negative when <u>it</u> manages <u>us</u>. How we manage time plays heavily on our productivity, our stress control, how we balance our work and family lives, our time for play, and our ability to work on our personal development.

We all have the same amount of time in any given day. What we do with that time can determine our priorities, our future opportunities, our career options, and help determine how successful we are.

The key to time management is setting priorities. It is a good business practice to keep a calendar of appointments and a "to do" list. It is most helpful to dedicate time each day, either early morning or late evening, to planning our schedules and working on the prioritization of our list.

Alan Lakein suggests using an ABC priority system (18). The "A" is for activities with the highest priority, "B" is for medium priority, and "C" for low priority. Lakein suggests breaking this down even farther to A1, A2, A3, and doing the same for the Bs and Cs.

The idea is to work on the As during your peak hours of performance. Lakein suggests that some people try to do as many things as possible on their list, without priority given to the importance of the tasks. Therefore, while they have a high percentage of items crossed off, their effectiveness is not necessarily high, as many of the tasks may have been C items. Other people tend to start at the top of the list and work their way down, again with little regard to the importance of the task. "The best way is to take your list and label each item according to ABC priority, delegate as much as you can, and then polish off the list accordingly" (18:65-66).

TIME MANAGEMENT HELPFUL HINTS:

How to be on time

- Motivate yourself to be punctual. List all the benefits of being on time.

- Focus on the starting time. Make your starting time as important as your project due date or arrival time. Calculate how long it will take to get somewhere, or how long it will take to finish the project, and add a cushion of extra time.

- Set an early deadline. Start work earlier and do everything possible to complete the project at the earlier due date.

- Make it a goal to be early. Promise yourself a reward for being early.

- Make a list of what you need to do before you leave. Begin a checklist far in advance of your departure time.

- Notify people if you are running late or going to miss a deadline, as soon as you are aware of it.

What to do if you are kept waiting

- Hold people accountable. Ask if they are positive they will be at an appointment at the agreed upon time. Ask them to call you if they know they will be late. Let them know that you expect them to be on time.

- Be firm and consistent in your time management, even though others who do not subscribe to your standards might label you inflexible or uptight. You will set a good example by respecting your time, and they may begin to value time more highly.

- Call ahead to remind people about important meetings. Call before you leave for appointments to make sure others are on schedule.

- Avoid setting ambiguous deadlines. Be specific about date and time.

- Set unusual meeting times, such as 11:07 instead of 11:00 or 11:15. This emphasizes the fact that you mean business and that you expect punctuality. It may arouse their curiosity enough to have them be there on time to see if you are.

The following ways can help you to improve your time management. Check the one that would help you most:

_____1. Eliminate my persistent time wasters.

_____2. Improve my attitude towards interruptions.

_____3. Take more time to plan.

_____4. Use a prioritized "To Do" list every day.

_____5. Delegate more work.

_____6. Keep interruptions short.

_____7. Organize my desk or work area.

_____8. Systematize my paper processing.

_____9. Concentrate on one project at a time.

_____10. Avoid crises by getting ahead of deadlines.

1. Write down one action you can take to improve. And write down when you will do it.

   Will do:

   _____

   _____

   _____

   Date: _____

2. Write down one thing you can stop doing that will help. Date it.

   Will stop doing:

   _____

   _____

   _____

   Date: _____

3. Give a copy of this to a couple of your friends, and ask them to check up on you every week for the next month.

4. Offer to do the same for them.

A Summary Of Time Savers

Goal Setting, scheduling and planning

Establish goals and priorities
Daily to-do list
Prioritize items on list
Frequently ask: "What is the best use of my time now?
Emphasize priority items
Ask:"Would anything happen if I did not do this?"
Put signs in your office to remind you of your priorities
Clear expectations
Know when to stop a task; don't overdo it
Make sure you have proper tools to accomplish goals
Do one thing at a time
Reserve some time to do nothing
Use time-logs and idea files
Set aside time for uninterrupted concentration
Let people know your scheduling needs and allotted times to interrupt
Use yearly, monthly, weekly, and daily calendars
Group related tasks together
Use "prime time" appropriately
Deadlines
Analyze current time use
Expect things to take longer than anticipated
Leave early for appointments
Eat light lunches
Exercise at lunch
Long-range planning
Careful action planning

Correspondence and Paperwork
Write responses right on the letter or telephone back
Form letters and standard paragraphs
Short letters and memos
Use diagrams and charts instead of drawn out papers
Generate as little paperwork as possible. Don't do unless necessary
Touch each paper only once
Dictating machines
Speed read

Delegate
Use a set time for correspondence
Use phone instead

Filing
Color code
Weed out regularly
Well organized record system

Telephone

Group your calls
Plan what you'll say
State purpose of the call early
Use squawk box
Use secretary to screen calls
Use a message recorder
Arrange definite times to call or get back to callers

Environment and Work Space

Reserve work space for work - socialize on neutral grounds or parts of office space not dedicated to work
Throw away what you don't need - a work space is no place for clutter, storage, or status symbols
Proper arrangement of work space
Clear desk top except for tasks at hand
Keep items off work space until you are ready for them
A place for everything
Have a comfortable, pleasant space with easy access to necessary tools
Remember a work space is a place for receiving and processing information

Decision Making and Overcoming Procrastination

Get interested in your work
Clear statements of problems to be solved
Challenge yourself with deadlines
Avoid perfectionism
Realistic deadlines
List benefits of doing unpleasant tasks
Don't needlessly complicate tasks or problems
Put reminder of task in center of desk
Make an appointment to discuss what you are avoiding

Ask: "What am I avoiding?"
Regular time every day for doing
unpleasant task
Write out your plan
List consequences of not doing the task
Before breaking establish the next step

Meetings and Appointments

Listen carefully
Only invite necessary people
Clear purpose
Time limit
Schedule meetings before lunch or near
quitting time
Reduce time used for thinking in groups
Start on time
Agendas with time allotments
Priority items first and information items
last
Subgroups or committees
Close the door
Don't make everyone talk unless necessary
Request an agenda from the leader
Pre-meeting position papers, reading, or
discussions
Redirect discussion back to the topic
Only hold a meeting or attend if necessary

"Dead Time" and Slow Time

Slow down when blocks result
Try and work on a project of satisfaction or
accomplishment
Have something you can do while waiting
Take work to do while flying
If you can stall write down problem and
clarify what is blocking progress

Resource Utilization

Hire good people
Delegate whatever you can
Watch upward delegation
Say "no" skillfully
Don't reinvent the wheel; research existing
possibilities
Training

Interruptions and Excessive Talkers

Meet in the lobby if possible
Summaries

Stress and How It Affects Us

We can define stress as the arousal of the mind-body system which, if prolonged, can fatigue or damage the system to the point of disease. **Stressors** are the causes of stress -- physical, social, or psychological conditions or situations that trigger a stress reaction and outcome.

Stress outcomes are either physiological or psychological. We can call the former psychosomatic, which includes emotionally caused physical disorders, such as backache, skin disorders, peptic ulcers, migraine headaches, respiratory disorders, and the latter physiological disorder, where anxiety, anger, fear and frustration actually increase body's vulnerability to organic diseases. The former involve organ damage but not infection or degeneration, the latter include infection and degeneration.

Stress is the body's nonspecific response to any demand placed upon it, whether pleasant or unpleasant. Our goal in life should not be to try to completely avoid or eliminate stress, but to learn to recognize our typical response patterns and whether they are causing us problems. If we observe negative stress patterns, we should try to change them.

What happens to our bodies when we encounter stressors? The physical reaction is rather simple, although variations in the strength and effect of hormonal reactions vary. The activator stressors signals the hypothalamus in the mid-brain. It is yet uncertain whether the signal comes from frontal or cortex or elsewhere. The hypothalamus activates the interior pituitary, or master gland, in the adrenal cortex and the sympathetic, or automatic nervous system, including the adrenal glands on top of the kidneys, which regulates catechamines, adrenaline (epinephrine) and nonadrenaline (nonepinephrinie).

People under stress also feel a wide variety of subjective states and behave in many ways that indicate stress. Some people look, feel, and act agitated, nervous, hyperactive, fidgety or shaky. Others feel depleted, enervated, drained and depressed. Many react with anger and often appear like they are out of control or sinking into oblivion. Others find the sensations and moods difficult to pin down or label, but they know one thing - they feel different than usual.

What is "too much stress"? This depends on the individual and his or her capacity to cope. One person may be able to handle large amounts of long-term stress before developing problems, whereas another individual may manifest symptoms after only a short time period.

Life is a constant process of managing and deciding how to solve problems which create stress. We search for information and identify problems out of curiosity to explore the possible consequences of troublesome situations. Then we must decide how to implement a strategy, program, or solution to the potential or current problem. Solving work and relationship problems requires much experience, information, awareness and social skills. The inability to solve our problems, or at least to reasonably manage them, creates stress in our lives. When we fail to solve problems, we end up feeling even more anxiety, insecurity, uncertainty, frustration and ultimately, low self-esteem. Our low self-esteem is thus tied to our weakened intellectual grasp of our situation and our increasing fear of failure.

Stress decreases as a result of our ability to interpret, organize and solve life's personal, social and intellectual problems.

Excessive worry can prolong stress and contribute to the failure of our problem solving strategies. Muscle tensions are actually locked into problem solving strategies, because we utilize mental images in our memory to reconstruct the problem situation. Since our bodies and mind are linked, so do our mental and actual physical images become linked through memories of the problem situation. Positive mental strategies allow the mind to scan the world for patterns of information. Humans utilize strategies such as trial and error, learning, dreaming, daydreaming, and fantasy to deal with the unknown. Excessive muscle tension can be produced by negative images of problem solving, when insufficient information, low self-esteem or confidence, and few social and cognitive skill strategies appear available. The individual's tension level increases as the negative images of failure become more vivid in the mind. The mind then becomes fixated or preoccupied with sensations of uncertainty.

A Proactive View of Stress and Wellness

Stress is truly a product of our mind-body link. However it begins in our minds with our hopes and dreams of enjoyment, satisfaction, stability, friendship, success, etc. How we interpret opportunities, risks and obstacles can challenge us to perform, or overwhelm us with the consequences of stress. Stress is the legacy of each individual and becomes dysfunctional only as each of us decides certain circumstances are interfering with our hopes and dreams. But we still don't know why certain things are stressful at one time and not stressful at another.

The answer in our view is a proactive and preventative wellness strategy. In this view we must learn new informational, cognitive and other social skills which bolster our sense of self-esteem and mastery of modern, complex situations. The basis of this proactive wellness strategy is intellectual or cognitive curiosity. The curious person has an engaged or activated intellect which tries to organize, make sense of, and create meaning out of anything that is unfamiliar and interesting in his or her environment. The curious intellect is poised to explore the unfamiliar, in order to determine how to restore harmony, reestablish meaningful events, and modify expectations, perceptions, hopes, desires, beliefs to a more realistic sense of the situation. The key is thus intellectual curiosity, meaningful social perception, and social and cognitive skills, which thrive upon the process of long-term exploring and learning, not just make-shift and short-term outcomes.

Stress management strategies in any integrated wellness program involve three key dimensions: 1) personal life management, 2) social supports and networks, and 3)system wide organizational development. The first category includes dimensions like nutrition, diet, physical, relaxation, biofeedback, meditation, pain control, time management, goal setting, therapy, hypnosis, behavioral modification and assertiveness training. The second category includes goal setting, time management, group problem solving, support and self-help groups, stress counseling, community change, team building, work affiliations, conflict management, role and job analysis and restructuring. The third category includes time and stress management, team development, changing jobs, altering work ecology, altering work unit interaction, delegation, company-wide employee relations programs including smoking, weight reduction, and substance abuse counseling.

It is preferable to take a proactive approach to stress and wellness and intervene before the stressors take their toll on our lives. However many times we become aware of stressors during or after stressful events. Most stress techniques can be adapted for use in personal, community, group and organizational programs, either before or after problems arise. In most cases, we often reach a threshold level, where certain stressors overwhelm us, before we act. For some, the initial stressful events and reactions are enough to prod the individual into a more proactive stance. However, many individuals and most organizations fail to build programs that move beyond reactive strategies to embrace a viable, proactive strategy. A proactive strategy can produce long-term benefits such as increased energy, work effectiveness, improved problem solving and decision making, and increased physical and mental health functioning. These benefits also impact upon improving the financial bottom-line.

Wellness and stress management programs in organizations need to include a major dimension of personal involvement, ownership and responsibility. Each individual's self-esteem, personal worth, and perceived feeling of control over impinging stressors is at stake. The goals of any stress management program should be operationalized to reflect concrete and specific aspects. Goals should be specific and realistic:

- reducing by 10% the number of days absent from alcoholism
- reducing by 5% the number of smokers in your unit
- reducing by 10% the number of those who are 25 pounds overweight
- involving 10% of the work force during the first year.

It is, thus, preferable for a stress management program to be part of a total wellness program.

STRESS MANAGEMENT STRATEGIES

Assessment Of Stressors

Medical conditions and habits which increase chances of <u>heart disease</u>:

Heredity - parents, grandparents, brothers, sisters who have had a heart attack and/or stroke

Tobacco Smoking - if you inhale deeply and smoke a cigarette down close to filter

Lack of Exercise

Cholesterol or Saturated Fat Intake - lard, cream, butter, beef and lamb fat

Blood Pressure - if it is too high

Sex - men have from 6 to 10 times more heart attacks than women of childbearing age

Diabetes - particularly when present for many years

Character, Personality and the Stress under which one lives

Vital Capacity - the amount of air you can take into your lungs in proportion to the size of your lungs - the less air you can breathe, the higher your risk

Electrocardiogram - if certain abnormalities are present in the record of the electrical currents generated by your heart

Gout - caused by a higher than normal amount of uric acid in the blood

Physiological Warning Signals of Stress

The healthy personality or informed person can analyze him/herself of the warning signals of stress:

1. overweight
2. shortness of breath
3. insomnia
4. pains in arm, neck, or chest
5. drinking too much
6. excessive cigarette smoking
7. menstrual problems
8. crying spells
9. fits of depression
10. teeth grinding
11. excessive sleep
12. stomach pains
13. headaches
14. diarrhea
15. constipation
16. false pregnancy
17. problems conceiving
18. high blood pressure
19. hay fever, allergies
20. asthma

Stress Changes and Problems

Physiological
(Body)

Hypertension
Heart Attack
Stroke
Diabetes
Cancer
Fatigue
Ulcers
Emphysema
Accidents
Gastrointestinal
Colds
Headaches
Backaches

Psychological
(Emotions)

Excessive Anger
Despair
Guilt
Compulsiveness
Depression
Withdrawal
Authority Problems
Excess Anxiety
Passivity
Confusion
Aggressiveness
Shock
Worry
Lack Confidence
Fears

Social Intellectual
(You & Me)

Marital
Parenting
Employer
Employee
Loss of Friends
Phoniness
Sexual
Withdrawal

(Thoughts)

Preservation
Boredom
Confusion
Apathy
Illogic
Forgetfulness
No Imagination
Obsessive Thinking
Lack of Creativity
Indecisiveness

STARTING A CHANGE PLAN

Know What Your Stressors Are. Some might choose to avoid and others welcome certain ones. Determine "who you are" at any given point, what you want and what you do not want for yourself.

Review and Use Preventative Approach. "Today is not tomorrow". You are changing and you need to know that as much as possible.

Look at Patterns of Behavior. It is not so much a single piece of behavior, but the patterns that our lives take on that are important.

Tune Into How You Feel. You are the best judge of how you feel but allowing yourself to hear the impressions of those who care about you can help safeguard the future and save valuable time.

Exercise Regularly and Non-Competitively. Often competition can result in more problems than we imagine. About three hours of weekly exercise with physician's approval helps maintain a sense of physical and emotional well-being.

Eat a Balanced Diet. Despite our taking our diets for granted, we know that a healthy diet enables us to feel, look and function more effectively.

Learn to Do Things That Develop a Positive Attitude. Taking regular breaks in your job and personal roles to become positively refreshed is effective. Even "too much of a good thing" can be a negative.

Take Regular Vacations. Taking a vacation alone or with family <u>when</u> <u>needed</u> is valuable. Become exhausted doesn't allow us to respond as well to vacations.

Define Expectations Clearly. Responsibility doesn't mean "obligation" or "perfection". Use the gauges of WANT TO and HAVE TO to determine what you and others can expect of you.

Create Fluid Means of Communication. Holding feelings in will result in a heavier price. Learn to trust and express feelings in an assertive, meaningful manner and you will be well on your way.
Don't Necessarily Associate Tension With Workload. It is how we handle ourselves, our jobs and our relationships that make the difference.

Re-Examine Priorities. Nothing is written in stone with regard to stress/tension. As situations change, so can you.

Create a Sense of Sharing and Involvement. "Going it alone" will result in a sterile lifestyle.

Learn How to Listen. Slow down, look <u>at</u> and <u>with</u> the person you are communicating and <u>hear</u> them - a real positive!

Develop a Sense of Humor. Learn to laugh at yourself so that you do not take yourself so seriously, and you will appreciate your uniqueness and humanity tenfold.

Try Touching People. Those who can touch and be touched by others feel better...feeling expressions work wonders too.
Relaxing Is a State Of Body and Mind. Practicing relaxation methods that help us feel good helps us use our time effectively.

Allow Yourself to Make Mistakes. Mistakes are part of life. You won't die if you make them, and others who "practice humanity" will understand as well.

Learn How to Forgive. Forgiving oneself is primary before we can effectively forgive others.

Put Guilt and Anger in Proper Perspective. There is no need for guilt to be the method of leading our lives, and unexpressed anger can turn a rock into a boulder.

Learn How to Celebrate. It is not only the eating and drinking, but the people that make a celebration a celebration.

We Can't Change Everything. Learn to differentiate those things that can be changed from those which cannot. Save energy!

No Man is an Island. The dilemma of our individuality vs. others must be pondered. Balance and Perspective.

Feel the Pain. Understanding our pain and its origin enables growth, character and maturity to take place in our emotional lives.

TIPS TO REDUCING STRESS

At Work

- If you are bored with your job, change your routine or do something innovative. you might try a new restaurant for lunch

- See what new positions may be opening up in your company. See if you qualify for any of those openings

- Take challenging evening courses or work toward a degree to give you better job opportunities
- Write a list of things you would like to accomplish each day, then set out to do them

- Seek to accomplish one task at a time whether at work or at home. Do the most important task first

- Get involved in a regular exercise workout

- Equalize your pressures by balancing difficult tasks with less demanding ones

- When pressures begin to mount, take a break or something similar to take your mind off the present matters

- Stop rushing; pace yourself better. Needless hurrying burns up energy

- The next time something irritates you, ask yourself, "It it worth getting upset over?"
- Develop assertiveness -- the ability to say "no" without feeling guilty

261

- Time management -- organize your time effectively

- Reduce interruptions -- don't allow people to interrupt you frequently

- Delegate to others rather than take a lot of responsibility on yourself

- Be flexible

- Reward yourself with relaxation behaviors

- Schedule lunch hours and other activities strategically to avoid crowds

- Take frequent mini-vacations rather than a once-a-year long one

- After a particularly stressful day, use physical exercise to relieve the tension

- Avoid business talk at lunch hours on a regular basis

- Imaging yourself handling a difficult situation rather than anticipating failure

- Develop a relaxation routine after you leave work

- Use relaxation techniques like deep breathing and visual imagery throughout your day

- Do a five- minute revitalization exercise -- sit at your desk with your eyes closed and pay attention to your breathing. On each inhalation say the word "I" to ourself and on every exhalation say the work "Am" -- this exercise helps quiet your mind and store energy and maintain a state of inner calmness

- Break large jobs down into small components

- Do neck rolls throughout the day

- Avoid being a perfectionist -- put your best effort into whatever you are doing, then rest and relax and don't worry about the results

Personal

- Keep physically fit through regular exercise and healthy diet

- Accept yourself and be good to yourself

- Maintain a confidante to discuss problems with

- Maintain stability zones -- keep some aspects of your life unchanging and stable

- Set realistic expectations of yourself

- Think positively
- Learn your stress signals and do something about them early

- Develop hobbies and interests totally unrelated to your job

- Take time for humor

- Participate in clubs, social groups. Take a night class

- Maintain an active religious affiliation

- Get up 15 minutes early in morning to reduce the rush and have time to enjoy something like reading the paper or talking with a family member

- Have some "alone" time every day

- Plan some idleness every day

- Listen to others without interruption

- Read books that demand concentration

- Learn to eat slowly and savor food. Never sit on the edge of your chair to eat

- Avoid irritating, overly competitive people where possible

- Plan leisurely, less structured vacations

- Live by the calendar, not the stop watch

- Be aware of your surroundings -- get "into" walks and conversations

- Organize time to be with your spouse or children and remember, the quality of time spent with them is better than quantity

- Plan ahead -- get as much done as you can before leaving for work in the morning

- Keep a daily journal of your experiences, feelings, thoughts

STRESS MANAGEMENT CONTRACT

Select five Desired Stress-Reduction Goals. Discuss the events or behavior which triggers the stressful situation, and define alternate strategies or behaviors. Set target dates for completion of desired behavior. List the reward(s) which you will receive for achieving the new, stress-reduced goal.

Desired Behavior	Triggers	Alternate Strategies	Target Dates	Rewards
(example) *Stop working 12 hr days*	*Too much paperwork*	*Delegate Prioritize*	*3/1/87*	*Go to a movie*

I make a commitment to manage the stress in my life.

_____   _____   _____
Signed   Dated   Partner

Exercise:

1. Do the above exercise on your own

2. Choose a partner and discuss your stress management contract with that person. Carefully listen to their stress management contract (offer any constructive assistance).

3. Sign your partner's contract. By doing so you are committing to supporting them in their stress management contract.

11 RULES FOR PEOPLE AND PROBLEM MANAGEMENT

These rules were developed as a tool to assist managers, upon completion of management development training, to transfer their learning to real life situations, such as formal and informal meetings (19). You can utilize these rules as a basis for management training discussions, as a guideline for more effective meetings, or as a tool for increasing interpersonal skills within your department or organization.

TWELVE RULES FOR PEOPLE MANAGEMENT	TWELVE RULES FOR PROBLEM MANAGEMENT
1. Treat people as equals; don't act superior and godlike to others.	1. Plan before doing; don't attack a complex problem blindly and foolishly.
2. Be genuine and spontaneous; don't be manipulative and sneaky.	2. Subdivide a complex problem into parts; don't lose sight of the forest because of all the trees.
3. Be empathic and feeling; don't be cold, impersonal, and uncaring.	3. Make assumptions explicit; don't let quicksand be the foundation for your arguments.
4. Be exploratory and open-minded; don't be so certain and dogmatic.	4. Test assumptions; don't assume that everyone sees the problem your way.
5. Be descriptive and specific; don't be evaluative and vague - you will make people defensive.	5. Debate assumptions and positions before any consensus is reached; don't be afraid of productive conflict.
6. Foster a problem management culture; don't try to control or blame others - they will become even more defensive.	6. Define the problem before solving it; don't implement a quick fix to the wrong problem.
7. Assume good intentions; don't assume that people are being devious or deceptive.	7. Collaborate on complex problems; don't stifle any available information - it may come back to haunt you.
8. Remember that you have blind sides; don't assume that your intentions are automatically understood.	8. Look to the deviant when the problem is complex; don't assume the majority is correct - it has common ignorance.
9. Listen carefully to what others say; don't assume that your reality is the only reality - perceptions are reality.	9. Foster trust and candor in gathering information; don't develop a CYA atmosphere.
10. Give everyone the opportunity to participate; don't dominate the meeting - don't keep talking on and on.	10. Consult/join on complex, important problems; don't force your simple solution on others, expecting them to accept it.
11. Be receptive, open, and responsive to others; don't let stereotypes and the past run your life.	11. Tell/sell on simple, unimportant problems; don't bother others - they have more important things to do.
12. Stop and examine the people management process at every meeting; don't assume it takes care of itself - it doesn't.	12. Stop and examine the problem management process at every meeting; don't assume it takes care of itself - it doesn't.

CHAPTER TWELVE
CAREER DEVELOPMENT

1   RECOGNIZING A NEED FOR CAREER COUNSELING

Employee Behavior. Employees first recognize that a problem exists with their current job or position, or that an opportunity for improvement is available, by the presence of any of the following symptoms.

- Lack of enthusiasm on current job, boredom, restlessness. Feeling of non-productiveness. Lack of challenge.

- Feeling that no matter how hard you try, you will not be recognized or rewarded for your efforts, talents, or skills.

- Living for the weekend, vacation time, retirement. Dreading Sunday evenings, dreading each morning.

- Physical and mental illness, symptoms of dis-ease or distress, depression, increased alcohol consumption, drug abuse, eating disorders.

- Spending more time on the phone, at lunch, coming in later and leaving earlier. Increased activities away from the job.

- Values and personality conflicts, feelings that people don't value you as they should, feelings that the people you work with aren't those you would chose to be with, difficulties with dealing with others around you.

Performance Behavior. These symptoms can be translated into performance behaviors, observable by the supervisor or manager of the troubled employee.

- Employee no longer seems to like their job. They appear restless and unmotivated. There is a decrease in their productivity, as observed by incomplete work or incorrect work, missing deadlines, etc.

- Lack of interest in receiving feedback, negative attitude towards and disagreement with the performance appraisal. Expectation of receiving praise for work which does not meet performance standards.

- Increased absences, especially on Fridays and Mondays. Increased tardiness.

- Overly inappropriate behavior such as engaging in horseplay, sabotage, or vandalism. Signs of hang-overs, change in speech or dress. Continued complaints about everything. Constant negative comments.

- Increased telephone usage for personal calls, longer lunch hours, increased tardiness and absenteeism.

- Increased difficulty with getting along with others, decreased team work.

Not all of these signs indicate a need for a change in career, however through discussions with the employee, the manager can better make that determination.

2 CHARACTERISTICS OF CAREER STAGES

It is also helpful for employees to understand the various characteristics of careers. When identifying a need for a change, one may well look at the stages listed below and determine where one fits currently and where one wants to go next.

STAGE I	STAGE II
Works under the supervision and direction of a more senior professional in the field.	Goes into depth in one problem or technical area.
Work is never entirely his or her own but assignments are given that are a portion of a larger project or activity being overseen by a senior professional.	Assumes responsibility for a definable portion of the project, process, or clients.
Lacks experience and status in organization.	Works independently and produces significant results.
Is expected to willingly accept supervision and direction.	Develops credibility and a reputation.
Is expected to do most of the detailed and routine work on a project.	Relies less on supervisor or mentor for answers, develops more of his or her own resources to solve problems.
Learns to perform well under pressure and accomplish a task within the time budgeted.	Increases in confidence and ability.

STAGE III	STAGE IV
Involved enough in his or her own work to make significant technical contributions but begins working in more than one area.	Provides direction for the organization by: a. "mapping" the organization's environment to highlight opportunities and dangers b. focusing activities in areas of "distinctive competence" c. managing the process by which decisions are made.
Greater breadth of technical skills and application of these skills.	Exercises formal and informal power to: a. initiate action and influence decisions b. obtain resources and approvals
Stimulates others through ideas and information.	Represents the organization: a. to individuals and groups at different levels inside the organization b. to individuals and institutions outside the organization.
Involved in developing people in one or more of the following ways: a. acts as an idea leader for a small group b. serves as a mentor to younger professionals c. assumes a formal supervisory position	Sponsors promising individuals to test and prepare them for key roles in the organization.
Deals with the outside to benefit others in organizations, i.e. working out relationships with client organizations, developing new business, etc.	

Figure 12-1 (20)

3 FACTORS FOR INCREASED INTEREST IN AN EFFECTIVE CAREER DEVELOPMENT SYSTEM

Today's organizations are increasingly interested in employee career development. This interest is in response to a diverse set of external and internal pressures such as:

External Factors	Internal Factors

1. Legal Restrictions
  - Affirmative Action or Balanced WorkForce regulations
  - Retirement regulations
  - Labor Union legislation
 	
2. Economic Pressures
  - Unstable economic conditions
  - Unemployment and underemployment
  - Availability and allocation of search resources
 	
3. Technological Changes
  - Computerization
  - Industry/occupational shifts
  - Availability of career development technology
 	
4. Social Transformations
  - Increased concern about quality of work life
  - Rising work force expectations
  - Dual career families
 	
5. Demographic Shifts
  - Increased educational level among workers
  - Decreased labor force mobility
  - Changing age and sex composition of labor force
	1. Financial
	  - Cash flow problems
	  - Competitive edge
	
	2. Technical
	  - Employee obsolescence
	  - Changing job requirements
	
	3. Organizational
	  - Increased desire to promote from within
	  - Reorganizations, mergers, acquisitions
	
	4. Political
	  - Pressure from employee expectations
	  - Increased role of human resource functions
	
	5. Human Resource Issues
	  - Excessive turnover and absenteeism
	  - Increased employee burnout
	  - Absence of promotable talent
	  - Need to increase workforce productivity

Table 12-1

While these issues will vary from company to company, and country to country, it is evident that most organizations are facing increased pressure to improve their career development practices.

4 CAREER COUNSELING FOR MANAGERS

One of the tasks of a manager is to provide career counseling to subordinates. This may come in the form of a formal annual Career Counseling Session, or throughout the year in informal settings, such as Review and Planning Sessions (RAPS). Unfortunately managers are not usually trained on how to conduct these sessions, and they tend to be incomplete, inadequate for the employee, and frustrating for both parties, and in many cases, non existent. They are seen by many managers as a waste of productive time, and by the subordinates as a waste of energy.

There are certain skills required to conduct an effective and productive Career Counseling Session. They range from understanding the roles and responsibilities of both parties in this process, to understanding all of the components required for a complete session. These skills are discussed below.

Career Counseling Process. Career Counseling is a highly motivating process with large dividends in productivity. The process is an active effort to match available jobs with the demonstrated skills and knowledge of employees, and their known work interests. When this matching works, it benefits all parties involved.

A signal for career counseling need is when an employee shows signs of boredom or lack of enthusiasm in his/her assigned job. This employee may still be functioning well, but is not as "into" the job as in the past. This may manifest itself in such obvious signs as increased tardiness, not contributing in meetings, volunteering to take on more responsibilities, perhaps in other areas. This could be caused to a lack of challenge on the job (they are performing at the highest level and have little to strive for), or by disinterest in the job (they are performing well below the expected level or what they are capable of).

Typically, one combines the annual performance appraisal with an opportunity to discuss future career aspirations. It fits into the process of reviewing performance over the past six months or year, and looking to the future in setting of goals for the next six months or year. If it is identified during the Performance Appraisal Session that the employee is interested in making a job change, you should schedule a Career Counseling Session in the near future.

The career counseling process is on-going. When an employee begins a new job, there will not (typically) be a need for a Career Counseling Session during the first, or perhaps second year. At the end of the second year certainly, it is helpful to take a look at how the employee is feeling about the job, and begin to look at future goals.

Career Counseling Roles and Responsibilities. An employee's career is his/her own responsibility. However, as a manager, you play an important role in this career counseling process. See Table 12-2.

Career Counseling Skills. Career counseling is one of the most tangible exhibitions of leadership. By seeking out individuals whose job skills have "outgrown" their work, counseling them about their career directions, and actively guiding them into more challenging and more rewarding assignments, you demonstrate you interest in your employees and your concern for their personal growth.

Some skills useful (and necessary) in the Career Counseling process are:

* Good listening skills
* Ability to empathize

Employee	Manager
Understand that your career is your responsibility	Make an active effort to develop people in your group
Know when it is time for a Career Counseling Session	Conduct the Career Counseling Session
Prepare for the Career Counseling Session	Provide honest feedback on the employee's self-assessment
Understand own strengths and weaknesses	Provide honest feedback on the employee's goals and aspirations
Look to the future	Assist employee in creating a Developmental Action Plan (if applicable)
Incorporate career goals with life goals	Assist employee in finding and obtaining a suitable job either within your work group or elsewhere within the organization
Take any actions outlined in the Developmental Action Plan (if applicable)	Document the Career Counseling Session
	Provide on-going support to the employee in reaching their goals

Table 12-2. Responsibilities in Career Development Process

* Understanding of the organization
* Knowledge of the Career Counseling process
* Ability to accurately assess skills
* Ability to provide honest feedback

Career Counseling Steps

There are five basic steps to conduct career counseling with your group. These actions are tasks to be performed by the manager or supervisor, however there are actions which the employee must take.

1. Identify a Candidate for Career Counseling

An employee is a likely prospect for career counseling when he/she 1) consistently meets or exceeds all job performance standards and output requirements, and 2) expresses a desire for more challenging work or a higher-level job.

Another candidate for Career Counseling is one who is performing below expected levels, well below what they are capable of. This employee may not recognize fully a need to move on to another job, hoping that "things will get better in this situation", which only causes frustration.

You may identify such a person through personal observation, prior feedback sessions, and during the performance appraisal session.

Not all employees whose performance is good wants or needs a job change. Your task is to interview and counsel likely candidates and find out what their job interests and capabilities are.

You should then arrange to meet with the employee for a formal Career Counseling Session. This should be in the form of a memo or letter to the individual, stating the date, time and place for the meeting. It should also provide a set of "thought-starters" for the employee to review, so that he/she comes to the session prepared. See Step 2 for a list.

2. Conduct the Career Counseling Session

The manager or supervisor and the employee meet with the purpose of discussing the employees career direction and aspirations or goals. During this Career Counseling Session, you as the manager will mostly listen, provide honest and sensitive feedback to the employee, and guide the discussion. The employee has the primary responsibility for leading the discussion.

The employee should answer the following questions during this session:

"What do I enjoy about my current position?"
"What do I dislike about my current position?"
"What kinds of tasks do I enjoy most?"
"What kinds of tasks do I least enjoy?"
"In what jobs have I experienced the most success?"
"In what jobs have I experienced the least success?"

"What are my strengths?"
"What are my weaknesses?"

"What are my life goals in two to three years?"
"What are my life goals in five to seven years?"

"What jobs do I know about which I think I'd like to try?"
"What areas do I want to explore and learn more about?"

As the manager, it is your responsibility to keep this discussion on track, to document the various areas of discussion, and to provide feedback in the areas of strengths/weaknesses and realistic career goals.

Depending on the discussion, you may identify an interest for more challenging work within your group, or you may identify an interest in moving to another group. Move to Step 3 if the employee is to remain in your work group. Move to Step 4 if the employee is to look outside your work group.

You finalize this Career Counseling Session with a document outlining the areas discussed, and the proposed actions.

3. Provide a More Challenging Assignment

If the employee's interest is more challenging work within your group, you should encourage him/her to offer ideas about possible new assignments, such as:

- training or coaching others
- more difficult, more skilled work (job enrichment)
- delegation of some supervisory duties

273

- job rotation
- other special assignments.

You should never knowingly give a subordinate an assignment which you feel is beyond his or her capabilities, or one in which the risk for failure is high.

The new assignment should be documented for all parties, including the personnel file.

Once the employee begins the new assignment, you should control the work carefully, especially at first. You should also provide a lot of feedback during the learning stages, to help ensure successful performance in the new assignment.

4. Help Place Qualified Employee in New Job

If the Career Counseling Session indicated that the employee is interested in a higher-level job outside of your work group, and you feel he/she is qualified, you have a responsibility to help the person find and obtain a suitable job within the organization.

During the Career Counseling Session, you should have identified some possible jobs which the employee is either interested in and/or qualified for. Your responsibility is to assist the employee in setting up "exploratory interviews" in areas of interest. You also have the responsibility of finding out which jobs are available which the employee expressed interest in.

Once the employee has found the job of interest, you need to identify the requirements of that job, and verify whether or not the individual has the qualifications for it. (You will want to work closely with your Personnel Department in this area.)

If the employee has the qualifications for open positions, you need to set up the interview process, and have discussions with the hiring manager. You also should "coach" the employee on interview techniques, to enhance their chances for getting the job, as well as showing your support.

If the employee does not have the qualifications for the desired position, move to Step 5.

5. Help the Employee Qualify for the New Job

If the employee does not have the qualifications for a job in which they are interested, you need to assist the employee in creating a "Developmental Action Plan", to guide the employee towards training, tasks, and experiences to help them acquire the qualifications.

You will work with the employee as well as the hiring manager in the development of these skills and knowledge.

This Developmental Action Plan should contain checkpoints for progress. Actual progress should be recorded, so the employee will know when the job qualifications are met.

Points to Remember About Career Counseling

- You have an obligation to help all members of your group find the work that will employ their skills and knowledge to the fullest - and will give each individual the greatest measure of job satisfaction and reward.

- Career counseling is a process of working together with individual employees to set realistic job goals, and then to guide them into jobs that best suit their skills and career aspirations.

- This activity should tend to be "upward directed". Your efforts should be to place the person in the highest level of work that fits his or her abilities and desires.

- An employee is a good prospect for career counseling when he or she consistently meets or exceeds all performance standards and output requirements of the job. This is particularly true when an employee shows signs of having "outgrown" the job; such as loss of enthusiasm and drive while at the same time performing well.

- An employee who is performing below expected levels, below the levels of which they are capable, may be a prospect for career counseling. This is particularly true of an employee who has a history of high performance. Their current job may simply not be of interest.

- When an employee's skills are well matched with the work, and fully employed, it benefits the person, the group, the supervisor, and the total organization.

- Career counseling is one of the most motivating of all managerial activities, because it demonstrates sincere interest in each employee's career goals, and actively helps the person to achieve them.

- Career counseling is an activity that requires advance preparation, sufficient time for a productive discussion between manager and employee, and conditions of privacy.

5   CAREER PLANNING - IN TODAY'S CHANGING ENVIRONMENT

Most of us are caught up in our day-to-day activities, and don't think about our career. Or we think about it, and decide to "do something about it tomorrow". However, when tomorrow comes, we are too busy to set aside the time to evaluate, assess or plan for our careers.

Some of us are simply not motivated anymore with our jobs, perhaps the job does not link to our lives in a meaningful way. We are coping with the day-to-day, but will we survive the feeling of being "boxed in". Or will we "give up", and become the "coaster", a prime candidate for removal in a takeover or reorganization.

Some of us feel that our careers are the company's responsibility. We are waiting for someone to take charge and lead us towards a career path. We experience frustration when this doesn't happen, feeling that our manager is insensitive to our needs, only interested in the bottom line, not in our personal development. We feel resentment when others, who are no more capable or qualified than us, move ahead into new and exciting jobs, while we just wait.

And then something happens which <u>makes</u> up <u>stop</u> and <u>act</u> - the organization is reorganized, or merged with another organization, or our middle management job is caught in the squeeze to "tighten up the ship". We find ourselves out, or at least potentially threatened with losing our job.

In these kinds of situations, the obvious "survivors" are those who are very good at career planning. These people are not as threatened by corporate changes because 1) they are in charge of their careers, 2) they have tied their career goals to their life goals, and 3) their current job is just that, not the only job they can do, or will have. These people know exactly where to look for the next job, have probably already been planning or developing for it.

Career Planning is an important aspect of our working experience. Without career planning we can just "drift" from job to job, perhaps never finding the "right job", therefore never really enjoying the experience of fulfillment and satisfaction within our work. Career planning is the process of examining and determining our life goals, tying these to our work goals, and developing a plan to achieve these goals. Career planning is a way of examining where you are now, where you want to be in the short- and long-term, and how you are going to go about getting there.

Your Life Goals. A life goal is usually expressed as something more personal which is beyond the framework of a job or career. The ideal life goal should provide inspiration over a lifespan. It should be your prime motivator, your daily booster. With life goals, one can better achieve and overcome challenges, one has more substance and direction to daily living. To help you develop your life goal, answer the following question:

> What do I want to accomplish with the talents and abilities I possess that will give me a sense of lasting fulfillment?

> > or

> What would have given my life more meaning?

Life goals can change, as one progresses through the stages of life. For example, when one is young, one may have a strong desire to make a lot of money; as one grows older, that desire for money may develop into a desire to contribute to society in some way, regardless of the pay you receive. Your life goals are not set in concrete, and should be examined from time to time, and kept current.

Tying your Career Goals to Your Life Goals. An important step in career planning is to incorporate your work within your overall life plan. You want to make sure that your work fits into the scheme of how you want your life to run. Too often we either 1) have no life goals or plan, or 2) have separate career goals and life goals. When this happens, one usually will be unmotivated in even the most glamorous of jobs, as it is not contributing to the way you want your life to run.

Alternate Career Paths. As mentioned before, survivors of corporate transitions usually have developed alternate career paths. When their job is gone, they move on to the next quickly, due to careful planning and preparation. Alternate Career Path planning is more than an idea in the back of your mind. It is fully researched, contacts are formulated, your plan is documented. Many successful people devote several hours each week over a period of months to develop and refine an Alternate Career Path. A well developed Alternate Career Plan, if necessary, can be executed within a few days or weeks.

Today it is imperative that such a plan be developed, with the constant changes taking place in the world of business, which could leave your job or your organization obsolete. Some of these changes are:

- **Restructuring** - streamlining to lower overhead and become more competitive. This creates the need to reorganize employees to new areas, or cutting headcount.

- **Mergers** - two organizations join forces to become more efficient or enter new markets. This creates an excess of resources, human and otherwise.

- **Dislocations** - driven by economic pressures, a company relocates its offices or plants, leaving behind those employees who cannot make the move.

- **Political** - political winds accelerate economic and social changes that can affect everyone.

- **Social** - double income families are more vulnerable to change; if one of the wage earners loses his or her job, it often means relocating to another area, creating the need for another job for both wage earners.

These needs demonstrate a need for everyone to have Alternate Career Paths, as anyone is subject to be affected by these changes.

Strategies for Career Planning. The following is a list of strategies to help you begin the Alternate Career Planning process. It is designed as a guideline, you will want to adjust to your personal situation. You are probably developing this plan while working in your current job, however these strategies will also work if you are beginning your initial Career Planning.

Step 1. Develop a Support System

We all need a little "push" to make changes in our lives. Our friends can sometimes offer that push. You will want to discuss your career plans with those friends and business acquaintances who will be supportive, and are willing to work with you in providing the motivation to move ahead in your planning process. You might try arranging a personal contract with someone who is willing to provide support and counseling on a regular basis. This could be with a spouse, close friend, or mentor. The contract could include meeting dates, progress checks, activities to be taken between meetings.

Make sure your support system is comprised of people who are supportive and willing to provide guidance and counseling. Planning for a career change is often scary, and you will want only those who are supportive to be a part of those plans.

Step 2. Streamline your Present Job

This may sound a little foolish, especially if you are thinking of leaving the job. But you are going to need time to plan your career, and by becoming more efficient in your current job, that time will be put to good use. This step is also useful in case you end up not moving to a new career or job, and keeping the one you have. Some ideas for streamlining are:

- Curtail excessive socialization on the job
- Concentrate on the controllables of the job
- Take on a more positive attitude
- Work hard to increase personal productivity
- Eliminate obvious time wasters
- If you are a manager, begin to delegate more
- Use lunchtime to work on your career planning
- Work to improve negative relationships
- Develop and foster relationships with those who can assist you in your career plans
- Dress and act more professionally

Step 3. Take Advantage of the Learning Opportunities in Your Current Job

Even while you are preparing your Alternate Career Plan, you can utilize opportunities on your current job to learn new skills, and gain new experiences which will be helpful in your new job or career. Search for new assignments which will provide you with these on-site learning experiences, develop new relationships with people who have skills you need to learn. Get into situations where you can practice some of the skills you will need to know in your next job. Your task in this step is to fully utilize all opportunities to grow and expand your knowledge.

You can find these experiences in the following areas:

- Ask your supervisor or manager for some new responsibilities where new learning possibilities exist. One area is to tackle a task no one else wants to do.

- Request the opportunity to learn how to operate a piece of equipment or software; it may be possible to learn this on your own time.

- Investigate the opportunities of company sponsored seminars or training that you can attend or take.

- Ask a colleague who is a specialist to help you develop some new skills.

- Identify accessible individuals whom you can learn from through informal meetings, interviews, and lunch meetings.

Step 4. Identify Your Skill Competencies

To qualify and prepare for your next career, you need to have a clear understanding of your current skills and competencies. These include both technical and human relations skills. The job market is moving so rapidly, and you want to make sure your skills are up-to-date before moving on.

To do this, you must look first at what you believe to be the present competencies required to keep you competitive in your job speciality. Include both technical and human skills. Verify this list by consulting with placement or human resource professionals. This will provide you with a skill analysis, alerting you to those skills or competencies you need to learn, and those no longer required. Finally, make a list of competencies you need to learn to make you more competitive.

Step 5. Decide How to Gain These New Competencies

You have two choices to increasing your skills. You can return to school, or undertake a self-instructional program at home. You may also be able to gain these competencies through educational programs within your organization.

While returning to school after many years can be pretty scary, it has some major advantages: 1) in some career fields, college is the best place to increase competency; 2) a college campus is an ideal place to network; 3) college professors make excellent mentors; 4) colleges offer many short non-credit courses so individuals can upgrade themselves at a modest cost; and 5) the college experience often helps improve self-esteem.

While self-instruction is not as widely acknowledged as a formal education, it can certainly provide several advantages: 1) the ability to study at your own pace, and study exactly what you want; 2) the ability to tailor your own course of study; 3) it is less expensive and therefore more available to many; and 4) the skills you learn can be easily applied to your current position as well as lend itself to you resume.

Step 6. Networking

Networking involves building relationships with those in your planned field, those who are knowledgeable professionals who are in a position to lead you to a new and better job opportunity. You can find these people within your organization, within professional organizations, at colleges, at your church, anywhere you come into contact with people!

It is important in networking to return something to the relationship, making it mutually rewarding for both parties. You must look for ways to repay them for their mentoring and assistance.

Here are some suggestions for beginning the networking process:

- Join a professional association in your career area. Attend meetings and actively participate. Talk to people, find out what is going on in the field.

- Attend conferences where you can meet other professionals in your area.

- Attend formal classes, seminars and workshops and talk to people, exchange career information with them.

- Arrange informational interviews with professionals to gain further indepth knowledge of the field.

Step 7. Market Your Career Plan

This step calls for you to discuss your new career plan with others in an attempt to gain entry into the new position you desire. Your plan is finalized and you are ready to make the move.

Include a summary of your career plans in your resume. This will include any educational courses, seminars, workshops, training you have attended or received, any significant steps you have taken to make this career move.

During your interviews, stress your past accomplishments. You do not want to appear to be making a move as a "loser". Then discuss what you have done in preparation for a new career. You will probably be asked why you want to make a career change, so be prepared to discuss this.

6 CAREER STRATEGIES

C. Brooklyn Derr (21) has developed a model for managing the 'New Careerists'. Managers must be aware of varied career orientations of the modern worker constantly as their worklife changes. Many people change orientations, others have mixed orientations. Effective managers must gather information to help their employees better understand that work, family and personal life stages interact quite extensively. By recognizing these career strategies the effective manager can work to improve employee job matches, increase productivity, minimize destructive political game playing and reduce turnover.

STRATEGIES	BENEFITS	COSTS
GETTING AHEAD STRATEGIES Know your organization Put your job first Have a career plan and move quickly Get a sponsor Punch the right tickets Thrive on challenge	Money; prestige/status; great self-esteem for those who succeed; high satisfaction with work; travel, comfort and luxury	Stress; health problems; neglect family and personal relationships; loss of autonomy; "is it worth it?"; constant moves and travel leading to limited roots in any community
GETTING SECURE STRATEGIES Find the right company Study the company culture and fit in Put the organization's needs first Try to become a member of the inner circle Decide which promotions to go after Build up your social debts Take your place for the long haul	Derive definition of success by the context of work rather than the content; personal and family relationships outside work can grow; derive pleasures from all work; often cordial and helpful coworker	Have all eggs in one basket (somebody elses); vulnerable to and often fear change; can become a "company person"; avoids deep relationships with others; feel unappreciated and betrayed when not highly rewarded or passed over for a promotion that goes to get-ahead types
GETTING FREE STRATEGIES Choose your work setting carefully Pay your dues through professional contributions Keep one step ahead of the game Hoard and control scare information Enlarge your peer group and network of allies Always come through when needed	Pleasures of autonomy; the creativity of freedom; the exuberance of independence; the ability to deepen and refine ones craft	Spotlight never leaves the one-person show; can become workaholic; can become anti-relationship and fail to build networks and contacts

Table 12-3. Career Strategies

STRATEGIES	BENEFITS	COSTS
GETTING HIGH STRATEGIES Pay your dues Seek out stimulating tasks Learn the skills of persuasion Develop patience and political skills Be ready to jump with the opportunities Choose the right organization	Great joy in the challenge of interesting and important work; often given a wide range of tasks because it is known that person can get the work done; positive rewards; some autonomy; good for self-esteem	Career can be disruptive of family and friendships; many temporary learning apprenticeships which also demand curbing ones creativity to absorb the mentors knowledge; individuals often more difficult to manage; can create obnoxious and self-preoccupied workers and careers
GETTING BALANCED STRATEGIES Look for the right organization/job Pay your dues Keep the rules Keep your strategy to yourself Get a sponsor Resist temptations to define success using a standard that doesn't meet your needs for balance Watch your timing	A high sense of happiness and energy when balancing is working; time for friends, family and other creative activity; strong sense of purpose; learning to make do with less money; new opportunities to rethink priorities	Takes much energy to balance and negotiates; hard to find companies that understand this orientation; need to wait until the right time and dues are paid; working relationships may suffer because person is on a tight schedule and doesn't have time to work on peer relations at work; need highly tuned political skills to anticipate problems; sometimes sacrifices self-development career development

Table 12-3 (cont'd)

282

7   THE MIDDLE MANAGEMENT CAREER PATH

The "typical" management career path moves individuals from an initial experience in a technical or specialist's role to the more general role of a middle manager. From that point career paths lead upward to new levels of specialization which demand a broader and more conceptual approach to decision-making and problem-solving (22).

The specialist's job is essentially one of applying particular kinds of technical knowledge and experience to the solution of primarily routine problems so as to ensure the completion of assigned tasks. Supervisory responsibilities at this level are closely related to task completion and to the proper use of techniques and skills.

The middle manager's job is much more one of coordination with counterparts in other functional areas to see that the work of his or her own group or department is related as effectively as possible to the immediate objectives and operations of the organization.

Senior managers are much less involved in seeing that work is actually done, or in meeting the day-to-day requirements of operational interdependence between and among functional areas. They are much more closely involved in setting long-term directions and developing policies for entire functional areas in order to give coherence to the operations of the corporation as a whole.

Career paths leading ultimately to the most senior levels of management inevitably and critically depend on the first important transition from technical or specialist supervision to the broader and much less precise role of middle management.

Transition from Supervision to Middle Management.

The transition from supervision to middle management demands an ability to deal competently with the following shifts in responsibility. Remember that this framework simplifies the complex tasks and responsibilities of supervisors and managers and for the organization these tasks may blur somewhat.

	SUPERVISION	MIDDLE MANAGEMENT
TECHNICAL EXPERTISE	Mastery of a specific function or area	Working knowledge of requirements of other functions/areas
GOAL-SETTING	Meeting goals set by superiors. Short-term	Breaking down broader and longer-term inter-departmental goals and setting subgoals for subordinates
PLANNING	Carrying out plans already decided on	Developing plans for the achievement of objectives
PROBLEM-SOLVING	Solving problems as they arise	Anticipating problems and preparing alternative solutions in advance
INTER-DEPARTMENT LIAISON	Usually not critical to job performance	Invariably of critical importance to job performance
LEARNING BASE	Formal and technically oriented; classes, courses, manuals, texts	Informal and behaviorally oriented; learning from others-peers, superiors and subordinates
THE INFORMAL SYSTEM	Incidental to getting the job done	Critical to getting the job done
SELF-RELIANCE VS. RELIANCE ON OTHERS	Where necessary, performance requirements can be met by relying on one's own skills	Must depend increasingly on the ability to delegate task performance to others

284

8   CAREER PLANNING WORKSHOP

The following is a model for a workshop which can be used within organizations to increase awareness of career planning. It should be conducted by a HRD or Career Counseling professional, who alternates between roles as instructor, group facilitator, and individual development counselor.

TOPICS IN A CAREER PLANNING WORKSHOP

INTRODUCTIONS OF PARTICIPANTS

MEETING EXPECTATIONS

OVERVIEW OF CAREER DEVELOPMENT
Overview of career development / career planning process
Discussion of why career planning is needed
Review of program content and objectives
Introduction to organization's career philosophy

INITIAL SELF-ASSESSMENT
Who am I? What Do I Want to Do?
    Self Concept
    Values clarification
    Personality characteristics / personal style
    Motivational patterns
    Occupational interests
    Personal preferences

Where Have I Been?
    Personal/educational background
    Work history/experience
    Key accomplishments/successes
    Peak experiences
    Significant life decisions
    Satisfying/dissatisfying experiences

COMPLETION OF SELF-ASSESSMENT
Where Am I Now? What Can I Do?
    Analysis of current job
        Behavioral demands
        Importance of various job elements
        Likes/dislikes
    Valued skills and abilities
        Professional / technical
        Managerial
        Personal

Figure 12-2. (23)

9 TRAINING SUPERVISORS AND MANAGERS TO BE CAREER COUNSELORS

Because the supervisor or manager is often the first person to observe problems with employees, and because many organizations no longer employ the services of a Career Counselor and require supervisors and managers to conduct career counseling sessions, there is a need to train them to be career counselors. The training is not as indepth as it would be for a professional HRD or Career Counselor, and is designed to be easily transferred to the workplace. It is assumed that a HRD or professional Career Counselor will conduct the training. The following model is suggested for designing such a training program.

1. **Needs Assessment.** Survey supervisors and managers about the kinds of individual problems they encounter and how much of each kind they see within their teams. Ask them what kinds of behaviors create the most challenge to them, and what they would like to receive training on. Pull together company statistics in problem behaviors.

2. **Course Design.** Structure the course as follows:

    a. Description of survey results from the Needs Assessment. Describe the kinds of behaviors which are causing the company money and lost productivity.

    b. Overview of issues affecting individual performance, such as motivation, personality, skills development, and career aspirations.

    c. Overview of problem diagnosis - how does a supervisor or manager decide when a problem or opportunity for improvement exists. This includes coaching skills, performance diagnosis models, counseling skills.

    d. Model of the company's career counseling process, overview of the program.

    e. Overview of career counseling terminology (see Figure 12-3).

    f. Skill practice. Show participants videotapes of good and bad examples of how counseling skills are used. Provide opportunity for role playing and case study review.

    g. Provide assistance and counsel to students as they begin to counsel their subordinates. Provide feedback on how well they used their new counseling skills.

    h. Be available on an on-going basis to provide support or answer specific questions on the career counseling process.

CAREER PLANNING TERMINOLOGY

Career. A career is a series of jobs that are related in some way. A career includes not only the work itself but also training, education, and development intended to improve how a job is done currently or to prepare for future advancement.

Career Development. Career development is a structured process of interaction between a representative of the organization and the individual, in which mutual expectations are discussed and negotiated.

Career Planning. Career planning is a subcomponent of career development and performed by individual employees. It is a conscious, deliberate process of identifying and exploring career opportunities, setting goals, establishing direction, and choosing the means by which to attain goals.

Career Management. Career management is another subcomponent of career development, performed by organizations. It is a systematic, ongoing process to facilitate individual career planning and help individuals attain career goals.

Career Path. Career paths are formal, detailed descriptions of interrelationships between jobs in an organization, expressed in terms of training, education, experience, and behaviors required for promotion or transfer from one to another.

Life Planning. Life planning is an individual process that encompasses career planning but transcends it. It is the process of establishing goals and direction for one's entire life, including such personal matters as when to establish a family, where to live and when to purchase a home, and retirement planning.

Career Counseling. Career Counseling is a process of helping individuals plan their careers.

Alternate Career Planning. Alternate Career Planning is a method utilized to move from an individual's current career to another. It is a subcomponent of career planning.

Figure 12-3

10   PREPARING FOR A JOB INTERVIEW

Learning about job interviews is a very effective career strategy. After all we need to be hired before we can beginour career. We may also get a good sense about the organizations support for the career development process as it relates to the organizational culture through this interview. We may be able to answer the question: "Do I really want to work here?"

A job interview is a sales presentation. A lot of us cringe when we hear the word "sales" and refuse to see ourselves as sales people. However, that is exactly what you are when you are being interviewed for a job. The following are a few tips for making this important sales call.

Preparation is extremely important to the interview process; the better prepared you are, the better your chances of being successful.

The preparation process includes the following:

- Developing or updating your resumé
- Researching information on the job
- Who is the interviewer?
- Knowing your competition
- Developing a list of your qualifications specific to the job
- What questions will you be asked?
- Developing a list of weaknesses
- Preparing questions you will ask
- Digging out "reference letters" which are applicable
- Developing a three month action plan for yourself once you get the job.

Sound like a lot of work? It's well worth it when you enter the interview knowing you are well prepared. Richard Bolles in 'What Color Is Your Parachute' (24) says:

> He or she who gets hired is not necessarily the one who can do that job best; but, the one who knows the most about how to get hired.

Resumé Update

When interviewing, you need to present a summary of your experiences and qualifications. You may have already completed an application; they may already have a copy of your resumé on hand. However, this package you are developing needs to include your resumé, as you will be referring to it in your interview (just as a salesperson uses a brochure). Make certain it is updated with your current position title and description. A list of some publications dealing in resumé development is listed in our Additional Readings Appendix. Research shows some items of importance as well as items of unimportance on a resumé (25):

Important:
- Neat and error-free

- Specific - high information content
- Succinct - single page if possible
- Marginally unique or unusual format

Not So Important:
- Positioning of information
- Color and quality of paper

Conclusions from other research states: "The generally preferred order of presentation of content items is personal data, education, work experience, awards and achievements, affiliations, and references" (26).

Job Information

Before your interview you will want to know as much about the job as possible. Some questions you will want to ask are:

- What are the duties and responsibilities? What will be expected of me?
- Who will I be reporting to? Who will be reporting to me?
- Who will I be interfacing with the most?
- Who currently has the position? Why is that person leaving?
- What specific qualifications are needed to do the job?

With a good understanding of the job, you will be much better prepared for the interview. You will impress the interviewer with the research you have completed. It will show definite interest in the job.

Where do you find this information? Try talking to someone who has held the position before. Use your mentor, hopefully someone with a broad knowledge of your industry or organization. Talk to the interviewer's administrative assistant or secretary. Talk to people in personnel. Research the Dictionary of Occupational Titles (27) at your local library. Talk to other employees within that department. Read an annual report on the organization. Ask questions of anyone who you know that has knowledge of the industry, organization or that position.

Research the Interviewer

You also need to gain understanding of the person or persons who will be interviewing you. Hopefully, this interview is with the hiring manager, perhaps the person you will be reporting to. You need to know if there will be a panel of interviewers, and, if possible, gather information on each person. Some questions you need to ask are:

- What is this person's "hot button" (sales, human resource development, research)?
- What is their general personality (loud, soft, strictly business, personable)?
- How long have they held this position?

- How well do they know the organization?
- Where do they fit in the organization?
- What are their hobbies?

Use the previously mentioned sources for getting the answers to these questions. Should you be outside of the organization, try to speak directly with this person when making the appointment for the interview. Here is a good opportunity to use your effective listening skills.

Some research in the field of job interviews along the areas of biases and psychological sets reports that, it is reasonably clear that certain personal characteristics establish a negative mindset in the majority of interviewers. Two such characteristics are:

- age (28) - interviewers tend to make negative decisions against the older worker because of the potentially shortened work life
- weight (29) - fat applicants are viewed as significantly less desirable employees than are average weight persons.

It is also thought the time of day in which the interview is conducted seems to be a determining factor as well as the quality of the person who preceded one in the interview room. There does appear to be certain advantageous times for interviewing (as in making sales calls):

- in the morning (people tend to become drowsy after lunch)
- being the first or last of the applicants

You obviously don't have direct control over these factors, however be aware of them.

Know Your Competition

Who is your competition? Having knowledge about the others being interviewed will give you a leading edge. You want to know such things as:

- What do they do now, how long have they done it?
- What are their likely strengths/weaknesses for this job?
- What is their political background within the organization?

Obviously, you are in a much better position to gather this information if you are interviewing within your current organization. Again, use those resources and contacts you've already developed. You can even "innocently" ask the question, "Who else is being considered for this job?" of the person you have made the appointment with. And you can make certain assumptions by just knowing their current position.

Your Qualifications

You need to develop a list of your strengths, or specific qualifications for this specific job. This list will compliment your resume. You now have data on what the job is all about, what the interviewer is looking for, and what strengths and weaknesses your competition holds, which will assist you in creating this list. The purpose is twofold. It shows the interviewer you have done research, again displaying definite interest and hard work. It is a tool for you to gain extra confidence by going through a period of self-analyzation. It also acts as a sales tool, a brochure to speak from as you are conducting the interview. Some of us become rather nervous in interviews, and feel uncomfortable talking about about ourselves: referring to this sheet will assist you in maintaining a very positive self-image.

Your list should be no more than one page, typed and double spaced. It should be easy to read from while resting on your lap or on the table. It should be sequenced in order of priority for the job. Let's assume the position you are interviewing for is a manager of trainers in a corporation. You might stress such qualifications as:

- any training you have conducted
- training programs you have developed
- supervision or management of support personnel
- your educational background

Be Prepared for Questions

You will be asked many questions by the interviewer, about you, your experience, your skills, your ability to assume specific responsibilities and follow through. The questions can generally be categorized in four areas:

Where have you been? Where are you now? Where are you going? How much money do you want?

You can prepare your answers to these questions in advance. Your previous preparation in the areas of resume development and listing your specific qualifications for this job can lead you to these answers. By researching the job, the company and the competition, you also know the salary range probably being offered. Think through these questions and formulate your strategy for answering them.

The Interview

Establish rapport with the interviewer immediately; perhaps commenting on something in his/her office. For example, she may have a picture of a sail boat on her wall, you might ask, "Do you sail?" This naturally could lead to a conversation which can act as a barrier-breaker, and introduction to the formal interview. Keep the small-talk short, the interviewer is operating on a time schedule and you want as much time as possible to present your real product - **you**.

Some feel that the interviewee should allow the interviewer to take control and begin the interview. Because you are viewing this as a sales call, our suggestion is that you try and take initial control. You might begin by saying, "thank you for the opportunity to talk about this position. I know you want to know about me, and I'd like to begin by reviewing my past experience, especially as it relates to this position." At this point you might want to hand the interviewer a copy of your resume, if they do not already have it in front of them.

There are some questions no longer allowed in the interview unless they are representative of occupational qualifications. Questions about your sex, age, marital status, children, criminal record and military involvement are not necessary data for making a hiring decision. It is stated in "What Color is Your Parachute?" that there are three courses of action, should you be asked questions in these areas:

1.   Answer the question and ignore the fact that it is not legal.

2. Answer the question with the statement: 'I think that is not relevant to the requirements of this position.'

3. Contact the nearest Equal Employment Opportunity Commission office.

Bolles also suggests that unless the violence is persistent, is demeaning, or you can prove it resulted in your not being employed, do not pursue the third choice, as it is too new of an area and unproductive to you. The second choice seems to be the best answer, and will gain respect from the manager interested in human relations.

Fader (30) reports the reason interviewers ask intimidating questions is that they really want to know:

1) will you do the job competently if hired?
2) will you get along well with other members of the staff?
3) do you have the temperament, stability, flexibility, and dependability required for the job?

She feels if you can convince the interviewer that you can respond "yes" to the above, that you will take the pressure off that person.

More than likely you will be asked to discuss your weaknesses. One example is: "Others have told me that I am into too many things. I am, but I feel in control". This response indicates to the interviewer that you are ambitious, willing to work and get involved, and remain in control.

Fader suggests "choosing an appropriate strength and reporting it as a weakness. An example she uses is: "I don't like to wait for people who take too much time completing their assignments". This shows the interviewer that you are a "doer", someone who will be valuable. Fader offers some other suggestions. You may be asked, "What can you do for us?" She says that today's companies, both large and small, want problem solvers. She also suggests researching the company before the interview, as you may be able to discuss a current problem intelligently at the interview.

One way to deal with questions about salary, is to _not_ deal with it if it is early in the interview. You might say you need to explore the dimensions of the job before considering salary. When you do discuss salary, try for the top salary possible, you can always accept less if necessary.

Be prepared with a list of questions you want to ask the interviewer. Jot them down so you won't forget to ask them. Some obvious questions are covering such issues as:

*   benefits

*   review periods

*   chances for advancement

However, you might try some strategic questions such as:

*   How do you see this organization is 5 years?

*   How do you see this position viewed within the organization?

*   What is this organization doing in the areas of flex time and job sharing?

Reference Letters

Dig out any letters referring to your "excellence" in areas relating to the job at hand. Include letters from professors or professional organizations to which you have contributed your time and effort. Just a few letters will get the point across. Do be sure they relate to the skills necessary to do this job.

Action Plan

The last item to be included in your package is your "Action Plan" for once you secure this position. Think about what kinds of activities would be expected of you in the beginning; such as meetings with your new staff, both group and individual meetings, planning sessions, training sessions and "setting up housekeeping" activities. List these out in a neat format. It will go a long way in showing your preparation and determination to get off to a good, fast start.

Helpful Hints

Here is a list of do's and don'ts (31):

- Arrive on time
- Cleanliness is next to godliness
- Respect business conventions and values
- Offer a firm handshake, look the interviewer in the eyes and smile warmly
- Be on guard for nervous mannerisms
- Be concise
- Remain calm - self-control is the key to professionalism
- Be yourself

Visualization

One very important thing to remember is the power of visualization. Just prior to going into the interview, close your eyes for a few quiet moments. See yourself conducting this interview in a positive, successful manner. Get a sense of the feeling you have of power and self-confidence. Imagine yourself at your very best. Hear your words, see your body language and remember to smile. This small exercise will pay off in allowing you to gain a sense of "centeredness" in what is typically a nerve-wracking experience.

Follow Up

Something we often forget to do is say "thank you". A follow-up thank you letter will serve two purposes: it will underline important messages, and set you apart from the majority. Thank you notes are a common courtesy most often ignored in business. An example of a follow up letter is shown in Figure 12-4:

The preparation for your interview will pay off with an added sense of self assurance and positive self-regard. The interviewer will see you as being committed, prepared and enthusiastic.

Dear Ms. Smith:

Thank you for the time spent with me on Tuesday. I learned a great deal about your organization, and I hope you learned about me. I would like to recap some of the major highlights of our conversation.

- The staff I would be managing are in need of training and development, having been neglected for some time. I have been responsible for the training and development of sales and sales support personnel for three years.

- Your department is in need of automation. I have worked with computers and office automation for ten years, and have set up systems in major organizations in the Southern California area.

- You said you would like to hire someone with a degree in Management. I received my Masters' Degree in Human Resource Management and Development earlier this year.

I feel I will bring to your organization the skills necessary to assist your staff in improving performance, production, and efficiency.

Thank you again. I look forward to hearing from you.

Figure 12-4. Sample Follow Up Letter

11 INTERNSHIPS

Field experience is a comprehensive term that applies to many diverse course offerings and programs. They are out-of-classroom learning activities sponsored by an organization or institution in which the learner has the primary responsibility for the educational endeavor; usually the student has responsibility for a specific task or work assignment, which is the major vehicle by which the student learns. There are at least seven broad educational goals that are frequently listed for field experience (32):

- Put theory into practice, develop higher cognitive skills
- Acquire knowledge
- Acquire and develop specific skills
- Increase personal growth and development
- Learn how to learn independently
- Explore careers
- Become responsible citizens

Field experience is a valuable supplement to classroom learning because it provides different and educationally important role development opportunities to students which are not available in the classroom. Additional roles in which the student engaged in field study may develop:

Initiator	Identifies, seeks finds, and secures the help and cooperation needed, often in an alien context
Problem Solver and Decision Maker	Functions in an open system, defining and solving the problems as they arise and making decisions in the course of carrying out the project that affect the student's life and the personal lives of others
Cultural Analyst and Strategist	Understands the cultural context well enough in which work is being done to function effectively in it
Interactor	Relates effectively with faculty supervisor, coworkers, clients, or customers, and is able to stay in touch with them and work through emotionally difficult relationships
Information Source and Network Developer	Develops personal information sources instead of relying on those provided by an instructor
Free Agent	Functions independently in a support system where rewards are given for workable solutions to particular and often unforeseen problems rather than for predetermined correct answers to set problems, and in an unstructured setting without the classroom support system assignment, syllabi, and tests

Value Clarifier	Makes value judgments in arriving at these workable (compromise) solutions or decisions that would not be expected in classroom work
Communicator	Is able to communicate effectively through the spoken and written word, through listening and reading nonverbal communication and to be emotionally involved in interpersonal interaction
Recipient	Is able to receive and utilize criticism constructively

Roles of Those Involved in Internships

The sponsor.
Significantly modified during a field experience/internship experience; shifts from one of the authoritative conveyor and interpreter of the knowledge and the methodological framework of an academic discipline to one of mentor. The sponsor must establish relationships with students that provide insight into their special abilities, interests, and needs as a basis for suggesting placement possibilities, and use. Must have the ability to help students identify and describe their own learning objectives for their field experience. This requires the ability to see the learning opportunities from the point of view of the students at their particular point of development. Additional skills are required in the documentation and reporting of learning, the development of reliable methods for reporting the students accomplishments. The sponsor must keep in touch with the student during the internship in a non-threatening, non-judgmental way to help them see and use the educational possibilities in their placements.

The project coordinator.
The work responsibilities and conditions of placement, such as the amount of compensation, if any, the time to report to work, and the place of work, the resources and the equipment to be made available, must be clearly spelled out. The project coordinator has an ongoing responsibility for interpretation, helping the student see the relationship of what they are doing and the work of others and the agency as a whole. The project coordinator is also responsible for the guidance and direction of the student in his or her work while on the site. Other responsibilities are evaluation of the students' work, the evaluation of the accomplishment of the students' learning objectives, serving as a model to the student for what it means to be a professional in that field.

The process of the internship or field experience

Identification of institutional and student goals:

    Cross-Cultural Experience
    Work Experience (Cooperative Education)
    Preprofessional Training
    Institutional Analysis
    Service-Learning Internship
    Social/political Action
    Personal Growth and Development

Field Research
Career Exploration
Academic Discipline/Career Integration
Career or Occupational Development

Development of learning objectives:

- Precise description of the end result desired, either knowledge to be attained or skill to be acquired
- Statement of the conditions under which the student will be expected to demonstrate the knowledge and/or skill
- Description of the minimum level of performance that will be accepted as evidence of the achievement of the objective
- Performance stability, how many times the behavior has to be demonstrated to be accepted as adequately learned

Arrangement of field placements, preparation for placement, placement, monitoring of student progress:

There are several important aspects of securing the placement for which the student should assume responsibility:

- Develop resume
- Correspond directly with firms or agencies
- Make appointments by telephone
- Be interviewed in person by someone at the agency.

Placing as much responsibility as possible on the student for securing the placement enhances the learning experience.

The sponsor will be continually lining up placement possibilities and making sure that previous ones are retained by developing close working relationships with supervisors and professionals in the field.

Criteria for accepting placements:

- Are the learning opportunities in the placement such that the student will have the chance to meet a significant number of the program learning objectives?
- Is the placement compatible with the student's resources? (financial, time)
- Can the student do the work expected in the placement?
- Is supervision adequate?
- Will the placement provide the student with sufficient opportunity to attain his personal learning objectives?

Assessment of student learning, and evaluation of program:

Assessment of learning is more difficult in this type of education as the faculty member does not have the same kind of control over the learning environment as in the classroom. Also the learning objectives in field experience education tend to be more complex than those of most classroom-taught courses. Some methods for assessment are:

* Written reports
* Oral presentations
* Diagrams/charts
* Simulations
* Performance tests

BIBLIOGRAPHY/REFERENCES

HUMAN RESOURCE DEVELOPMENT : INTEGRATING TRAINING, MANAGEMENT AND CAREER DEVELOPMENT

INTRODUCTION

(1)   Chalofsky, Neal and Reinhart, Carlene. **Effective Human Resource Development** (San Francisco: Jossey-Boss, 1988)

(2)   House, R. J. **Management Development: Design, evaluation, and implementation** (Ann Arbor, Mich: Burear of Industrial Relations, Graduate School of Business Administration, The University of Michigan, 1967:105)

(3)   Morgan, M.A. , Hall, D.T., & Martier, A. "Career development strategies in industry - where are we and where should we be?" **Personnel.**, 56(2), 13-30, 1979)

(5)   Fiedler, F.E. & Garcia, J.E. "Comparing organization development and management training" **Personnel Administrator**, 30(3), 35-47, 1985)

CHAPTER 10

(6)   Casner-Lotto, Jill, and Associates. **Successful Training Strategies: Twenty-Six Innovative Corporate Models** (San Francisco, Jossey-Bass, Inc. 1988)

(7)   Kolb, D.A. "On Management and the Learning Process" in **Organizational Psychology: A Book of Readings** end Edition (New York: Prentice-Hall, 1974)

(8)   Wlodknowski, Raymond . **Enhancing Adult Motivation to Learn** (San Francisco, CA: Jossey-Bass, 1985)

(9)   Tracey, William. R. **Designing Training and Development Systems** (New York: AMACOM, 1984)

CHAPTER 11

(10)   London, Manuel. **Developing Managers** (San Francisco: Jossey Bass, 1985)

(11)   Sinetar, M. "Entrepreneurs, Chaos, and Creativiey -- Can Creative People Really Survive Company Cultures?" **Sloan Management Review**, Vol. 26: 57-61, 1985

(12)   Osborne, Alex **Applied Imagination** (New York: Scribner, 1963)

(13)   Crawford, R. **Techniques of Creative Thinking** (New York: Hawthorn Books, Inc. 1954)

(14)   Gutknecht, Douglas B. and Miller, Janet R. **The Organizational and Human Resources Sourcebook** (Lanham, MD: University Press of America, 1986)

(15)   DeBono, E. **The Uses of Lateral Thinking** (New York: Basic Books, 1967)

(16)   Findley, Ben. "How Do You Spell Relief? D-E-L-E-G-A-T-E!" **Practical Supervision** (Round Rock, TX: Professional Training Associates, Inc. No 31, June 1, 1985)

(17)   Jenks, James and Kelly, John. **Don't Do. Delegate!** (Franklin Watts, Inc., 1985)

(18)   Lakein, Alan. **How to Get Control of Your Time and Your Life** (New York: Signet, 1973)

(19)   Kilmann, Ralth H. **Beyond the Quick Fix** (San Francisco, CA: Jossey-Bass Publishers, 1984)

CHAPTER 12

(20)   Dalton, Gene W., Thompson, Paul H. **Novations. Strategies for Career Management** (Glenview, Illinois, Scott, Foresman and Company, 1986)

(21)   Derr, C. Brooklyn. **Managing the New Careerists** (Jossey-Bass, 1986)

(22)   Hennig, Margaret and Jardim, Anne. **The Managerial Woman** (New York: Simon & Schuster, 1977)

(23)   Gutteridge, T., Otte, F. **Organizational Career Development: State of the Practice** (American Society for Training and Development, 1983)

(24)   Bolles, Richard Nelson. **What Color Is Your Parachute?** 1979 Edition (Berkely, California: Ten Speed Press, 1979)

(25)   Stephens, D.B. and Watt, J.T. and Hobbs, W.S. "Getting Through The Resume Preparation Maze: Some empiracally based guidelines for resumé format" **Vocational Guidance Quarterly** (28,1, 25-34, 1979)

(26)   "Resume Preparation: An empirical study of personnel managers' perceptions". **Vocational Guidance Quarterly**, (24, 229-237 1976)

(27)   **Dictionary of Occupational Titles**

(28)   Craft, J.A. and Doctors, S.I. and Shkop, Y.M. and Benecki, T.J. "Simulated Management Perceptions, Hiring Decisions and Age" **Aging and Work** (2, 2, 95-102, 1979)

(29) Larkin, J.C. and Pines, H.A. "No Fat Persons Need Apply: Experimental Studies of the Overweight Stereotype and Hiring Preference" **Sociology of Work and Occupations** (6, 1, 312-327, 1979)

(30) Fader, Shirley Sloan. "Those Intimidating Interview Questions" **Business Week's Guide to Careers**. (26-29.October 1984)

(31) Fox, Marcia. "Interview Do's and Don'ts" **Business Week's Guide to Careers**. Spring/Summer 1984 PP. 52-55

(32) Hulse, Lisa S. (Ed.) **1985 Internships** (Cincinnatti, OH: Writers Digest Books, 1984)

SECTION FOUR

ORGANIZATION DEVELOPMENT

INTRODUCTION TO ORGANIZATION DEVELOPMENT

Organizational Development is an emerging behavioral science discipline designed to improve organizational effectiveness. It is a systematic approach for improving the functioning of individuals, groups, and thereby, organizations. OD focuses primarily on developing the human, social and technical aspects of organizations.

Organizations are constantly changing; they are in continuous interaction with external forces (See Figure below). Changing customer requirements, new legislation, economic factors and new technology all act on the organization to cause change to it. OD provides methods and practices to help organizations adapt to these changes.

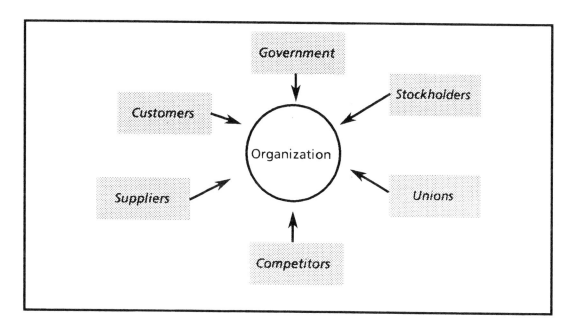

We see some of the goals of Organization Development as:

- Increased effectiveness of the individuals, workgroups and organization
- Increased profitability within the organization
- Increased worker satisfaction in the organizational setting
- Managed conflict
- Increased cultural sensitivity of workers, within the organizational setting.

Some definitions of OD are:

Organization Development is an effort which is planned, organization-wide, and managed from the top, to increase organizational effectiveness and health through

305

planned interventions in the organization's "processes", using behavioral science knowledge (1).

Organization Development can be defined as a planned and sustained effort to apply behavioral science for system improvement, using reflective, self-analytic methods (2).

Organization Development is a long-range effort to improve an organization's problem-solving and renewal processes, particularly through a more effective and collaborative management of organizational culture, with special emphasis on the culture of formal work teams, with the assistance of a change agent, or catalyst, and the use of the theory and technology of applied behavioral science, including action research (3).

Organization Development is a response to change, a complex educational strategy intended to change the beliefs, attitudes, values, and structure of organizations so that they can better adapt to new technologies, markets, and challenges, and the dizzying rate of change itself (4).

You can see from these definitions that OD is not just "anything" done to improve the effectiveness of an organization, rather a specific kind of change designed to produce a specific kind of end result.

As a manager, as a leader, as an Organizational Development practitioner, as a consultant, OD can introduce you to new methods and practices. The interventions set out in this part of our text have a direct application to the aspects of Organizational Theory and Organizational Behavior discussed in previous chapters. OD can provide the skills and knowledge necessary for establishing effective interpersonal relationships, diagnosing complex problems and devising appropriate solutions. In the move towards an information society, and the corresponding cultural and social changes, OD can help organizations remain viable and continue to survive.

CHARACTERISTICS OF ORGANIZATION DEVELOPMENT

- It involves a total organizational system.

- It views organizations from a systems approach, an interdependent set of integral component parts.

- It is supported by top management.

- It is intended to increase organization competence and health.

- OD is a planned effort. It entails a systematic diagnosis, detailed plan for improving the current state of affairs, and mobilization of the resources needed. Implementation, review, and reinforcement of the change activity is a part of the planning strategy.

- The services of a third-party change agent are often used. This agent may be a member of the organization, but should be external to the particular organizational subsystem initiating the OD effort.

- The effects and ramifications of change on tasks, structure, technology, and processes involving people and work groups are considered.

- It uses behavioral-science knowledge in the areas of leadership, communication, motivation, goal setting, learning, intergroup relations, small group behavior, conflict management, attitudes, organizational structure, interpersonal relations.

- It uses an action research intervention model, collecting research data, preliminary diagnosis, feedback, joint action planning, action, and re-diagnosis.

- It mainly focuses on changing the attitudes, behavior, and performance of groups or work teams rather than individuals.

- It relies primarily on experiential, action-oriented, as opposed to didactic, learning.

- It emphasizes the importance of goal setting and planning activities.

- It involves more of an emphasis on processes than content.

- It is a relatively long-term process.

- It is a dynamic, ongoing process.

ASSUMPTIONS OF ORGANIZATION DEVELOPMENT

Organization Development is based upon certain assumptions about individuals, groups and people within the organizational systems.

Individuals

- Most individuals desire personal growth and development when placed in a supportive and challenging work environment.

- Most individuals are capable of making a greater contribution to their organizations than those organizations are willing to permit.

Group Members

- One's work group is extremely important in determining feelings of competence and satisfaction.

- Most people want to be accepted by and get along well with their work group. These work groups can be made more effective if individuals work together more cooperatively.

- The formal leader of a work group cannot possibly perform all of his/her leadership functions at all times.

- Suppressed feelings adversely affect the functioning of groups and organizations. Group climate should be one of increased openness.

- The level of interpersonal trust and support is much lower in most groups and organizations than is desirable.

- The solutions to most attitudinal and motivation problems in groups are transactional. All individuals in the system or subsystem must modify their mutual relationships.

PEOPLE IN ORGANIZATIONAL SYSTEMS

- Most managers in organizations are members of overlapping work groups. The manager functions as a "linking pin", serving as the superior of one group and as a subordinate and peer in another. The leadership style and climate of the higher-level group gets transmitted downward to the lower-level group via the manager.

- Resolving conflict in such a way that one party wins triumphantly and the other loses severely may be realistic and appropriate in some situations, but in the long run it is not healthy for the organization to solve most organizational problems in this way.

- Improved performance due to OD efforts needs to be supported and maintained by appropriate managerial changes in other subsystems of the organization, such as performance appraisal, training, personnel selection and placement, and communication.

- Because organizational change takes time and patience, OD people need to keep a relatively long-term perspective.

We have broken down Organization Development into three chapters in this text:

- First, we discuss the nature of planned change, a most important component of OD. We describe different techniques found in OD programs, as well as discuss the natural resistance humans have to change.

- Second, we discuss interventions most typically utilized in the organizational setting. This is not a discussion of all of the interventions found, that would take an entire text. However, we have selected ones we believe are most effective and practical. You will find other sprinkled throughout this text, including: career-life planning, stress management, power, conflict, intergroup models, goal-setting, job design models, Likert's System 4 Management, and corporate culture.

- Third, we discuss the role of the change agent, consultant, or facilitator in the OD process. We have added some information for those of you who will be either acting in the role of consultant or hiring a consultant.

CHAPTER THIRTEEN
THE NATURE OF PLANNED CHANGE

1   CHANGE...Introduction

Companies today are facing a wide range of social, economic, political and technological changes. On the **social side**, there is a greater concern with the public image of the organization's behavior. For example how an organization deals with toxic waste. While it has always been a problem, environmentalists are causing greater strain on the organization to feel the impact it has on society. Another social issue is the change in employment, more dual family careers, more women in the workplace, an increase in part-time work. This is evidenced by the need for flex hours, the consideration of child care, the inability of some executives to be as mobile as before. Some companies are moving more towards the employment of part-time or temporary workers, to cut down on the costs of benefits.

Today's workers are different from even a decade ago. There is more demand for employer's to give workers a say in decisions concerning the goals and objectives of their jobs. In the case of "knowledge workers", there exists a great degree of autonomy in the method and form of their working. Companies fail to keep certain types of workers due to the nature of the work or work environment. More workers are demanding more "balance" in their lives, are not as easily swayed to "working harder and moving up the ladder", especially if the move up requires moving away from a desired location. People are more concerned with the quality of life.

Economic pressures on organizations are requiring change. Takeovers, mergers, reorganizations usually require a different method of operation. Government imposed funding on public organizations is demanding new disciplines and new approaches. Dramatic changes in overseas markets affect change. Retaining one's competitive edge often requires change.

Technology has moved us from manufacturing to assembly-type operation. Often it is more cost effective to bring pieces together which have been manufactured elsewhere. This calls for a shift in focus on an organization, as well as a shift in location. At the high-tech end, smaller companies have to work harder to compete with the giants. With such technologies as word processing, computing and telecommunications, workers are requiring retraining just to keep their jobs. The changes in this area are many.

Organization Development efforts are directed at bringing about planned change within an organization to increase the effectiveness of that organization. Organizations can use planned change to more readily solve problems, to learn from experience, to adapt to changes, and to influence future changes. Kurt Lewins' change model, the planning model, and the action research model offer different concepts of the phases through which planned change occurs in organizations (5).

MANAGING CHANGE

In times of increasing international competition and change, many organizational leaders are searching for more relevant and effective ways of accomplishing their work with a sense of quality, clear mission, and productive, long-term results. At the same time individuals are seeking increased responsibility, creative challenge, higher levels of performance and purpose in their work. Today, more than ever before, leaders, managers and employees are questioning how best to integrate their skills for enhancing the effectiveness of people, organizations, communities and world.

THE PROACTIVE CHALLENGE?

The old reactive behavioral policies and programs that describe how people and systems work are of less relevance today than ever before. These reactive approaches harbor assumptions that stifle the potential for innovation and creativity. And as Douglas McGregor (6) taught us many years ago, managers and organizations always base their actions on implicit or latent theories and assumptions.

Organizational students, consultants and managers sometimes miss the essence of McGregor's view of the polarity in management styles because they fail to see that his terms are metaphorical and their usage reflects the tensions inherent in each of us as managers, leaders and employees. McGregor was not writing a 'how to' book for Theory Y managers or a book to lay blame only at Theory X style, but exploring how faulty assumptions often lead to ineffective leadership and management practices. Theory Y only implies our potential to manage well, if we can become more self-aware and examine those narrow personal assumptions which support our ineffective management practices.

McGregor built his theories upon the research of Lewin, Maslow, and Herzberg which emphasized the following ideas: redesigning work systems to make quality everyone's business; making staff work as coaches not cops; initiating the principles of effective teamwork; fitting people to jobs; giving workers more control over their own development; and emphasizing the importance of a system of management, not just technical mastery. However, he did place the burden of change upon each manager, and urged them to examine their own management assumptions (7).

Each of us has probably found times in our lives when we were acting upon our own Theory X assumptions as a complement to our Theory Y assumptions. In addition, each component, Theory X or Theory Y, has both positive and negative aspects. If we wish to become effective leaders, managers, workers and individuals, we must accept our limitations, our very human nature, and always begin with our own values and perceptions. This personal self-assessment or assumption analysis is essential for building both individual and organizational productivity, performance and health. We need to examine our faulty assumptions, while avoiding destructive win-lose thinking and dead-end self-fulfilling prophecies.

Whether conscious or not, many of these negative/reactive assumptions guide our expectations and eventually our behavior, reinforcing the results that we planted in our minds earlier in the cycle. This observation has many parallels in organizational thinking and practice. Managers who think workers are ignorant or lazy, will then act upon this assumption and get the results they expect -- like passive workers or shoddy, marginal products. Here are some additional harmful assumptions for all of us to think about:

- You don't need to respond to issues until they become major problems or someone in charge becomes aware that something is wrong -- 'if it's not broken, don't fix it'.

- All problems can be broken down into logically arranged, component pieces and solved independent of each other, as long as we use rational and logical problem-solving methods.

- It's all right to blame our failures on other individuals and trends beyond our control. Let's think of ourselves as the property of those we work for and find some way to shift responsibility.

- Adopt a philosophy which views innovation as abrupt and drastic change in the normal mode of operations which requires us to make large investments in new technology and equipment. This assumption is one that supports the need for a giant leap forward and is geared to seeking our evaluation in the one big breakthrough.

In contrast, proactive assumptions suggest more healthy and dynamic possibilities that are applicable at any level of personal behavior or system effectiveness:

- Anticipate and sense issues before they become problems, erupt into crisis, or overwhelm our abilities to respond effectively -- 'attend to it constantly, even before it breaks down'.

- All problems can't be reduced to logical pieces of a puzzle and solved independently of each other. Complement rational problem solving methods with creative and innovative thinking.

- Take responsibility for your own destiny, anticipate and examine behaviors, values and trends which might negatively impact you or your company in the future.

- Keep ahead of change by managing it -- become a student of change. Don't let yourself ignore the signals which indicate that something is even slightly wrong, even when it appears to most people that everything is perfect.

- Adopt a philosophy which views success, wellness and productive living as an integrated, and gradual process of improvement. Practical and effective outcomes will emerge from your efforts at building a solid foundation of continuous learning.

The signals are becoming clearer everyday that the old world is dramatically different and new assumptions and creative responses are now demanded. Today, a more comprehensive model is needed, one that includes concern with the most unique dimensions of the individual and a vision of system possibilities. This is why creativity is so important today. We need to understand what we are up against in the competitive marketplace that we are now encountering locally, nationally, and internationally.

Conventional ideas about how organizations manage change, new workers, and competitive markets are under siege. Most voices are being raised to challenge narrow and short-sighted organizational models and perspectives. The challenge ahead is that we involve our entire system in order to utilize our most innovative capabilities for constant learning and innovation.

New learning possibilities point the way to a more humane and productive future. Well-worn formalities provide no certainty under the onslaught of rapid change and competition.

CHANGE: A PRIMER

The challenges of change are upon us: the volatility of changes in new technologies, information and international events are enough to make any leader or manager feel dizzy exhilaration and even apprehension over the rapidly changing local and global landscape. As Bucky Fuller reminded us several years ago, think globally and act or participate locally, but do them together anyway because that is the future!

Change is the name of the game today. Our world can only rejoice because its deepest problems are not static. Everyone will become impacted by the nature and rate of change. No one will avoid the effects entirely. Many of us will have some input into how these changes will be implemented, and others will be able to capitalize on the positive effects and lessen the negative impacts. None of this will be simple: everyone, however is responsible for the results.

These facts call for more aware and information and knowledge rich organizations and personnel. Johnston (8) persuasively documents the need and effectiveness of more liberally educated managers:

> Briefly, we, too, are struck by the pervasiveness and increasing rapidity of change and the need for adaptability. But, we see in all this a strong case not so much for job-specific skills training as for educational breadth ... But, largely because it fosters adaptability, we regard broad or liberal education as the best possible foundation for sustained management productivity.

MANAGING CHANGE: A GENERIC APPROACH

The key is to recognize that change like learning is continuous. It is impossible to precisely predict or easily adjust to it. Change is now such a riddle because we try too hard to think in old terminology and categories. What we really need to do is become more proactive in our general thinking and try to manage, not master change. This strategy is practical and focuses upon the nature and impacts of change wherever we find them.

LEVELS OF REACTION AND RESPONSE TO CHANGE

When faced with the realities of unpredictable events, we often rely upon one of several strategies. First, we can ignore or deny the realities of what is happening around us. Second, we might reactively adjust to changes after the impacts have devastated our ability to adequately cope. Third, we can profitably anticipate some of the negative impacts and focus upon using our knowledge of the positive dimensions of change to devise practical strategies to profit from them. The goal of strategic management is to move as quickly as possible from denial to the utilization of change management as a business strategy.

CHANGE PRINCIPLES

Let's explore some research on change that will indicate several principles helping us to take advantage of positive change opportunities. We must always recognize that we will not be an effective change manager unless we consider the issue of timing. We often satisfice rather than optimize because of the constraints of time, and the impossibility of deciding the best alternative. And time itself is only meaningful when we measure it through changes; the before and after pictures of the changing impacts of real events.

Change is only meaningful because it is subjectively determined and felt. People perceive the impacts of change in their own emotional way. This ability is limited by our fears, low self-esteem, lack of education, inability to distinguish good from bad information, and our failure to understand the perversity of human nature. Thus, we need to understand the human dimensions of change. We must learn more about how people emotionally interpret proposed changes to determine whether they will embrace them or resist them. To do this, managers must begin by becoming more empathetic towards their workers when changes are proposed.

Kirkpatrick (9) suggests that three things are needed for making change more effective. Empathy, along with good communication, and participation are the three keys to successful change. The way to become empathetic is to learn more about your employees, and also try to understand some of the barriers that will prevent leaders and managers from reaching rapport with employees: being preoccupied with something more important; not interested in the message; don't respect the sender; think you know what the message will be before it is sent; don't want to understand; being physically tired; thinking about other things than the message; being distracted; pretending to listen or understand.

Change is often difficult to categorize and measure because it defies any complex modeling of cause and effect. Change is often seen as both cause and effect; separating them isn't easy. Change effects are often not perceived immediately because the time lag between the initiation of change (cause) and perception of impacts (feeling or seeing) the effects. When anticipating a new event or action and the expected effect is delayed, we are feeling the impact of this time lag.

Change is also value-based because it impacts and even expresses our most important priorities. It is very hard to quantify this value precisely because it depends upon our perception and other experiential skills, including maturity, length of time at the job, and degree of responsibility working at numerous aspects of the business.

and customer needs; finally, becoming friendly with computer spreadsheets because they provide opportunities to make comparisons (10).

Let's explore some additional features of change. We must more astutely use the power of change expectations and anticipation. Before change can be profitable, people must know about it; this will also reduce resistance. We are limited by our fear of change and other barriers; the same barriers that constrain our creativity. Managing change requires us to remove these barriers. We must also learn not just to measure it, but sense it and touch it in our gut. Good leaders know the value of hunches, seat-of-the-pants experience, and timing.

At some point in time we must stop trying to simplify change and begin to use it to our advantage. What we really need to do is recognize that change is complex; so our models must try to focus on specific areas that make a difference: that balance simplicity with cost, accuracy and benefits. We must empathize, communicate and empower our employees because they are the ones who see and respond to change; yet, they often don't have the power to act. When we try to use old models that optimize reactive viewpoints for the short-run, we focus to narrowly upon variables which ignore the major influences just beyond the reach of our methods.

Liberally educated leaders and manager generalists know how to move beyond a narrow focus, with expanded information outside our traditional areas of concern.

Because we all sometimes suffer from information overload and a limited threshold for tolerating things unique or different, we then reduce the number of things that we pay attention to. The value of any well designed information system is that it can provide us with the relevant information that we need to manage change and face the competitive challenges ahead.

Before introducing a change to subordinates, the manager should (11:183):

1) Be clear about the objectives of the change.

2) Determine the likely impact of the change on the organizational unit.

3) Determine who in the organizational unit will be affected by the change, how, and to what degree.

4) Try to predict the reactions of persons who will be affected by or called on to implement the change.

Innovation is the generation, acceptance, and implementation of new ideas, processes, products, or services. People are the innovators. They are the main ingredient in the success of a corporation. Kanter speaks about two different styles of thought shown in Table 13-1 (12): Integrative and Segmentalism. It is obvious that integrative thought patterns are more beneficial to the organizational system. Table 13-2 shows integrative devices which build support and cooperation within corporations.

INTEGRATIVE	SEGMENTALISM
Change seen as an opportunity to test limits	Compartmentalized actions, events and problems
Combine ideas from unconnected sources	Anti-change
View problems as wholes, related to larger wholes	See problems narrowly with no connection to other problems
Invisible organization boundaries to ensure shared information	Guided by the past rather than the future
Disregard failures of the past and move on to the future	Maintain the status quo
Actively embrace change	Inhibits innovation
Team oriented	Discourages people from seeing or revealing problems
Improve upon existing things or conditions	Difficult to transmit innovative ideas
Rely on company people for innovations	System trusted more than individuals
Feeling of belonging	Rewards after the achievement
Rewards before not after the fact	Extremely tight control
Incentives for defining new problems to work on or pet projects	No power given to potential innovators

Table 13-1. Styles of Thought

Device	Result
Frequent mobility (including lateral moves) = circulation of people	• Movement of information to different areas of the organization • Retaining contact with people in neighboring areas in order to gain needed information or support • Making new contacts (creating links) and getting fresh ideas • Exchanging favors with old and new contacts
Employment security	• Increases output • Creates innovation • Eliminates fear
Team Mechanisms	• Immediate exchange of support and information at middle and upper levels • Successful problem solving and innovation • Diversity of sources and variety of ideas • Carrying out of major tasks which are spread evenly throughout team • Understanding of what is happening at different levels
Complex ties permitting crosscutting access: ex: manager and a connected department ex: manager to upper level	• Creates inter-unit contact between managers • Working relationships (both formal and informal) with persons from other functions or disciplines • Mobilization of support or resources in order to facilitate a desired result • No fear of violating protocol because it is understood by all that there is no specific boss to anger • Alternative sources of power

Table 13-2. Integrative Devices that Aid Network formation - Building Support and Cooperation (12)

CONCLUSION, IMPLICATIONS AND THE TASK AHEAD

Today, our approach to organizational life in uncertain times requires more than one narrow approach. It is necessary to look at a strategic perspective for integrating ideas regarding quality of work life, technology, structure, leadership, and ways of motivating and rewarding employees. We must find new opportunities for developing all our productive assets. More important, our organizations need effective, proactive programs for employee health promotion and human resource development: We need strategies that foster creative problem solving, strategic thinking, experimentation, good communication, risk taking, realistic planning and empowerment through collaboration. In addition, our organization must develop improved awareness of the forces that operate to limit their true potential: old metaphors, models, frozen attitudes and incompetent systems.

The task is no less than stimulating the organizational imagination, thinking, and critical concern with the complex and interdependent nature of organizational life. We need to devise ways of supporting participation, forms of collaborative work relations, goal-directed feedback, and opportunities for enhancing organizational traditions and values, ways of fostering care, compassion, service, spirit, commitment, excellence and productivity.

2   FORCE FIELD ANALYSIS

Lewin suggests that in problem solving, or in the development of change strategies, one should view the present situation -- the status quo -- as being maintained by certain conditions or forces. There are **driving forces** (those forces which aid in changing the situation), and **hindering forces** (those forces which are obstacles to changing the situation). A group or organization stabilizes its behavior where the forces pushing for change are equal to the forces resisting change (see Figure 13-1). Increasing or decreasing either forces or a combination of both will allow change to occur.

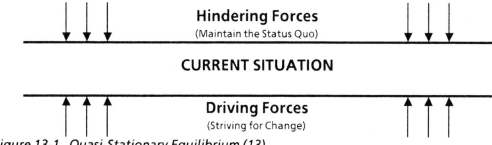

Hindering Forces
(Maintain the Status Quo)

CURRENT SITUATION

Driving Forces
(Striving for Change)

Figure 13-1. Quasi-Stationary Equilibrium (13)

Lewin viewed the change process to include three aspects (14). See Figure 13-2.

1) Unfreezing the present level L^1 -

> *reducing those forces maintaining behavior at the present level (example: introduce information that shows discrepancies between behavior desired by organizational members and those behaviors they currently exhibit)*

2) Moving to a new level L^2 -

> *shift behavior to a new level (example: developing new behaviors, values, and attitudes through changes in organizational structures and processes)*

3) Freezing at the new level -

> *stabilizing behavior at the new level (example: use of supporting mechanisms that reinforce the new organizational state, such as organizational culture, norms, policies, and structures)*

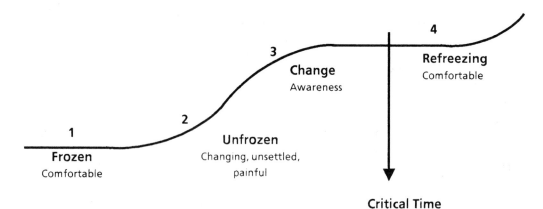

Figure 13-2. Lewin's Change Process

316

3 CHANGE PLANNING MODEL

The two principles underlying this model are that all information must be freely and openly shared between the organization and the change agent, and that information is helpful only if and when it can be directly translated into action (15). The basic concept is a seven-step process, shown in Figure 13-3:

Figure 13-3. The Planning Model

4   CHANGE PROCESS MODEL

This model represents the stages one must pass through to change any habitual behavior. It supports Lewin's model.

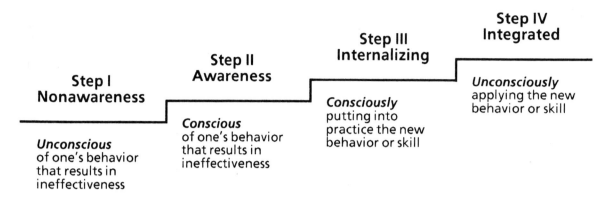

Figure 13-4 Change Process Model

Step I. Nonawareness

Most of us have habits that make us somewhat less effective than we might otherwise be. Many of these habits are of no concern to us because we don't know we have them or we aren't aware that they are interfering with our effectiveness.

Think about the behavior of some of your work associates. You are probably aware of habits that lessen their effectiveness in certain situations. As long as your colleagues are unconscious of what you know, they are unlikely to make any effort to change their behavior.

Step II.Awareness

In Step II, something happens to raise one's awareness of an ineffective habit. This may happen if someone views a video made of them in a work situation, or hears a tape recording of a meeting, or the particular behavior may be pointed out to them by someone else.

This awareness might create the desire to change the habit, especially if there is some support system to help in making the change. If the desire to change the habit is strong enough, the person then moves to Step III. Often, however, individuals get "stuck" in Step II, either by rationalizing the bad habit as being "not so bad", or by believing that simply wanting to change the habit will in fact effect the change.

Step III. Internalizing

In Step III, one must consciously practice the desired behavior. This means taking part of the attention that one normally places on the content of actions, and focusing on processes. The greater support one receives for changing to the new behavior, the easier it will be, in fact it is critical to get positive feedback to the new behavior. There could be a tendency to fall back to the old, familiar habit if one finds oneself under a stressful situation.

Step IV. Integrated

In this final stage, the individual is applying the new behavior without having to consciously think about it. It now comes as naturally as the old habit once did. There are some natural stages one progress through when integrating new behavior:

Resistance - a natural tendency to stay with what is familiar

Being unsure - uneasy feeling as one starts to apply the new skills

Comfort - less uneasy feeling and being comfortable with the new behavior

Expansiveness - trying out the behavior in other settings

Success - automatically and unconsciously using the new behavior as part of one's natural style.

5 ACTION RESEARCH MODEL

This model focuses on planned change as a cyclical process (see Figure 13-5) involving collaboration between organizational members and organizational development practitioners. It is aimed at both helping a specific organization increase its effectiveness and at developing new knowledge that can be applied to other settings (16).

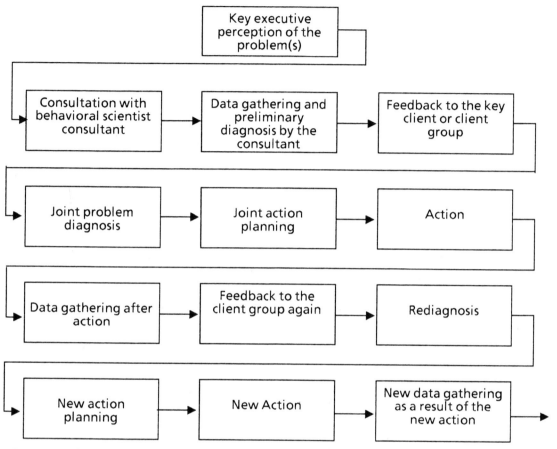

Figure 13-5. Specific Steps of Action Research Model (16:307)

1) **Problem perception** - the process begins when a powerful key executive realizes that the organization has one or more problems and persuades others in the organization that a behavioral-scientist consultant should be contacted.

2) **Collection of data and preliminary diagnosis** - consultant gathers information about the on-going system and arrives at certain hypotheses or hunches about possible courses of action that should be followed.

3) **Feedback and joint diagnosis** - all relevant information obtained by the consultant is shared with the client group. The consultant is careful to protect all sources of information. The practitioner and the client group then jointly diagnose the situation and discuss whether there exists any real problems worth alleviating.

4) **Data gathering, feedback, and rediagnosis** - data is gathered after action has been taken and fed back to the client group by the consultant. This usually leads to a rediagnosis, the taking of new action, and so on.

6   CHANGE METHODS

One change method is based on French and Bell's (17) research. It offers three topologies of change methods.

Individual group and task process topology. The first topology is based on two questions which constitute dimensions. Who or what is the target of the intervention, individual or group? Is the focus of the technique on the task, or process? See Figure 13-6.

	Focus on the Individual	Focus on the Group
Focus on task issues	Role analysis technique Education: technical skills; also decision-making, problem-solving, goal setting and planning Career planning Possibly job enrichment and MBO	Technostructural changes Survey feedback Confrontation meeting Team-building sessions Intergroup activities
Focus on process issues	Life planning Process consultation with coaching and counseling of individuals Education: group dynamics, planned change Third party peacemaking	Survey feedback Team-building sessions Intergroup activities Process consultation

Task vs. Process dimension (row label spanning both rows)

Figure 13-6. Individual vs. Group Dimension

Target group topology. The second topology is based on the identification of the organizational unit which is the target of the change intervention. See Figure 13-7.

Change mechanism topology. This third topology uses as a basis for its division the underlying dynamics of the technique, which are the probable causes of its effectiveness. See Figure 13-8.

Target Group	Types in Intervention
Interventions designed to improve the effectiveness of **INDIVIDUALS**	Life- and career-planning activities Role analysis technique Coaching and counseling Education and training to increase skills knowledge in the areas of technical task needs, relationship skills, process skills, decision-making, problem-solving, planning, goal setting skills
Interventions designed to improve the effectiveness of **DYADS/TRIADS**	Process consultation Third-party peacemaking
Interventions designed to improve the effectiveness of **TEAMS & GROUPS**	Team building -- task directed, process-directed Family T-group Survey feedback Process consultation Role analysis technique 'Start-up' team-building activities Education in decision-making, problem-solving, planning, goal-setting in group settings
Interventions designed to improve the effectiveness of **INTERGROUP RELATIONS**	Intergroup activities -- process-directed, task-directed Technostructural interventions Process consultation Third-party peacemaking at group level Survey feedback
Interventions designed to improve the effectiveness of the **TOTAL ORGANIZATION**	Technostructural activities Confrontation meetings Strategic planning activities Survey feedback

Figure 13-7. Target Group and Types of Interventions

Hypothesized change mechanism	Interventions based primarily on the change mechanism
Feedback	Survey feedback Process consultation Organizational mirroring T-group
Awareness of changing socio-cultural norms	Team building T-group Intergroup interface sessions
Increased interaction and communication	Survey feedback Intergroup interface sessions Third-party peacemaking Organizational mirroring Management by Objectives Team Building Technostructural changes
Confrontation and working for resolution of differences	Third-party peacemaking Intergroup interface sessions Coaching and counseling individuals Confrontation meetings Organizational mirroring
Education through: (1) New knowledge (2) Skill practice	Career and life planning Team building Goal setting, decision making, problem-solving, planning activities T-group Process consultation

Figure 13-8. Emphasis of Intervention in relation to Different Change Mechanisms

7   PLANNING FOR CHANGE

The following discussion is one that surrounds the entire area of managing people. For managing change within an organization, is to optimize people management skills, techniques and practices.

Involve All Employees in Planning For Change. This helps employees understand the change, gives them the confidence that management is not going to do wrong by them, and makes use of the ideas of those most intimately acquainted with the people. It is well known that when people are part of the planning or decision making stages, they will adapt to the changes more readily.

Communicate and Use Feedback. Providing opportunity for employees to voice their own opinions and raise their objections can 1) reduce the objection, 2) raise some valid points which would have otherwise gone unnoticed, and 3) reveal the underlying reasons for negativity, which can then be handled.

Consider Effects on Working Environment and Group Habits. Consider such issues as breaking up congenial work groups, disrupting commuting schedules and car pools, preferences in age group assignment, or educational level of the group assignment, or the assignment of someone to a group with incompatible standards of conduct.

Inform Employees About the Change Effort Before It Begins. Make them aware of the changes which are to take place and the expected outcome, in terms of benefits to them.

Build a Trusting Work Climate. Try to eliminate rumors and mistrust by keeping the lines of communication open. People can better handle "bad news" than being kept in the dark. Try to alleviate their fears about the proposed changes.

Use Problem-Solving Techniques. Get the problems to the level of those most familiar with it. Allow those employees to use problem-solving techniques to work on those issues, and make recommended changes. Again, by having some hand in the decision making process, they will more likely embrace the changes.

Involve Employees in the Implementation of Change. Allow the employees to have some say in how the change is to be implemented, for they often will have the best ideas creating the least amount of disruption.

Ensure an Early Experience of Successful Change. When implementing the change, praise those who have had immediate successes, those who have helped the situation.

Quickly Stabilize and Spread Successful Change. Support and timely assembly of a human support system dedicated to maintaining the new and different, the people who are interested in its success. Make sure that the change affecting one group has a positive effect on other groups or allied systems.

8   RESISTANCE TO CHANGE

Rosabeth Moss Kanter and Goodmeasure, a consulting firm, have developed a list of the ten most common reasons managers encounter resistance to change, and tactics for dealing with each (18).

- **Loss Of Control.** Most people want and need to feel in control of the events around them. Change is exciting when it is done by us, threatening when it is done to us.

  Allow room for participation in the planning of the change. Leave choices within the overall decision to change. Ownership counts in getting commitment to actions.

- **Excess Uncertainty.** People need to know what the next step is going to be, where they will be as a result of the change, to have a comfort level with the change. Managers who do not share information face a great deal of resistance to change.

  Provide a clear picture of the change, a "vision" with details about the new state. Share information about change plans to the fullest extent possible. Divide a big change into more manageable and familiar steps; let people take a small step first.

- **Surprise, Surprise!.** Resistance occurs when changes are sprung on people without proper groundwork or preparation.

  Minimize surprises; give people advance warning about new requirements. Allow for digestion of change requests, a chance to become accustomed to the idea of change before making a commitment.

- **The "Difference" Effect.** Change requires people to become conscious of, and to question, familiar routines and habits. Commitment to change is more likely to occur when the change is not presented as a wild difference but rather as continuous with tradition.

  Minimize or reduce the number of "differences" introduced by the change, leaving as many habits and routines as possible in place.

- **Loss of Face.** People are certain to resist, if accepting a change means admitting that the way things were done in the past were wrong. Commitment to change is ensured when past actions are put in perspective as the apparently right way to do it then, but now times are different.

  Repeatedly demonstrate your own commitment to the change.

- **Concerns About Future Competence.** Sometimes people resist change because of personal concerns about their future ability to be effective after the change.

  Offer positive reinforcement for competence; let people know they can do it. Look for and reward pioneers, innovators, and early successes to serve as models.

Provide sufficient training and education, as well as a chance to practice the new skills or actions. Make standards and requirements clear -- tell exactly what is expected of people in the change.

- **Ripple Effects.** People may resist change for reasons connected to their own activities. The change may disrupt other kinds of plans or projects. The change may also negate promises the organization has made.

  Introduce change with flexibility and sensitivity. If possible allow people who have children to finish out the school year before relocating, or managers to finish a pet project, or departments to go through a transition period before facing an abrupt change.

- **More Work.** Change means more work, requires more energy, more time, and greater mental preoccupation. There is ample reason to resist change, if people do not want to put out the effort.

  Help people find or feel compensated for the extra time and energy that change requires.

- **Past Resentments.** Anyone who has ever had a gripe against the organization is likely to resist the organization introducing change.

  Listen to and respond to old grievances that have been left unresolved.

- **Sometimes the Threat is Real.** Sometimes the change does create winners and losers. Managing change well means recognizing its political realities.

  Avoid creating obvious "losers" from the change. But if there are some, be honest with them - early on.

  Allow expressions of nostalgia and grief for the past -- then create excitement about the future.

9 IMPLEMENTING A CHANGE OR OD PROGRAM

A successful, long-term, change or organizational development project begins with and is guided by a conscientiously and deliberately planned strategy. An organizational-change strategy is a comprehensive plan based on a thorough analysis of organizational needs and goals. It is designed to bring about specific changes and to ensure that appropriate steps are taken to maintain those changes. Included in it are definitions of end objectives, outlines of specific actions designed to produce the desired outcomes, time frames, and an evaluation or monitoring system. The strategy must specify alternative as well as primary interventions and take into consideration the power and influence dynamics of the organization.

While individual requirements within an organization may change these, there are certain general steps in the process of **building a strategy:**

1) **Defining the Change Problem.** Information is gathered regarding the performance of the organization and deterrents to desired performance levels. Care must be taken not to confuse symptoms with causes in this stage.

2) **Determining Appropriate Change Objectives.** Change objectives are clearly and specifically defined, in both behavioral and quantitative terms, so that they are appropriate to and consistent with the particular organization.

3) **Determining the Systems' and Subsystems' Readiness and Capacity to Change.** Analyzing readiness, willingness, and capacity to change can help determine where to start the change and which interventions to use.

4) **Determining Key Subsystems.** The total organization is reviewed to determine its key parts and its key personnel. Focus on those groups who will exert the greatest impact on organizational performance and those managers who influence the direction of the organization.

5) **Selecting an Approach and Developing an Action Plan for Reaching Objectives.** Determine which intervention to use, where to start within the organization, who will be involved in the effort, how much time is required, and how the effort will be monitored.

When building a strategy, certain **organizational dynamics or change requirements** should be kept in mind:

- **Unmet Needs or Goals** - select interventions based on unsolved problems or goals that are not being reached.

- **Support System** - identify supportive forces in the organization and work with those forces.

- **Chance for Success** - the entire OD effort and each related activity should represent some chance for success.

- **Multiple Entry** - within a large organization, which has a tremendous capacity to withstand change, apply pressure to several different facets of the organization.

- **Critical Mass** - develop a strong and building thrust within the organization.
- **Organizational Control** - success is more likely when the affected group has some autonomy or control over its own operations.

- **Appropriate Levels of Involvement** - involve those who will be affected by the proposed change; know who will need to be active in decision making, who will need to be given information, and who will need to provide input for evaluation.

- **Communication to All Levels** - develop plans for communicating intentions, goals, and progress to the entire organization.

- **Determination of Feasibility** - enlist the aid of people in determining the feasibility of plans.

- **Linking with Internal Change Agents** - link change teams from several disciplines or functions within the organization

After building a strategy, **initiation** of the change effort is ready. There are several alternatives and approaches the organizational development specialist can use:

- **Selection of a Winner.** Selection of a project that is associated with a high probability of success and little chance of failure. This provides a potentially high, quick return, and opens doors to other opportunities as a result of early success.

- **Use of a Power Play.** Start with the most influential and powerful group in the organization (perhaps team building with the manager of this group and his staff). This can provide a high potential for change because of the group's power to implement the change as well as a high return or impact attributable to the group's control over numerous variables.

- **Limitation Through a Pilot Project.** Initiate the change within a limited area of the organization. This is usually more accepted by key managers, and affords greater manageability.

- **Concentration on a Business Problem.** Attempt to concentrate on attacking an acknowledged business problem such as turnover, absenteeism, poor quality, high scrap, or deteriorating relationships. The approach is perceived as legitimate, and the chance for success is enhanced because the effort is limited in scope.

- **Control Through Action Research.** A controlled experiment in which some aspect of the organization is changed and the impact is then monitored and evaluated. This is similar to the pilot-project approach, but is generally more tightly controlled and limited in scope.

- **Reduction of Organizational Pain.** This approach is similar to the business problem approach, except that "pain" is defined more broadly than is "problem". This might include poor decision making or problem solving, the inability to obtain valid information from subordinates, the unwillingness of subordinates to take the initiative in directing their own activities.

- **Involvement in an Imposed Change.** The change agent becomes involved in a project or change that the organization has already mandated. The need for change is already established, the change itself is the natural process employed in the intervention.

- **Association with the Influence Leader.** Similar to power play, except the focus is on an individual, rather than a group.

- **Association with OD Support.** Initiate change in parts of the organization already supportive of OD values and activity. Projects can be initiated quickly and the potential for success is high.

- **Total-System Intervention.** Affect all parts of the organization simultaneously. Few managers consider this approach to be a viable starting point for OD.

CHAPTER FOURTEEN
ORGANIZATION DEVELOPMENT INTERVENTIONS

1   INTERVENTIONS... Introduction

Organization Development interventions are those actions intended to help organizations improve their effectiveness, including increased quality of work life and productivity.   Interventions derive from careful diagnosis and are meant to resolve specific problems and improve particular areas of organizational functioning identified in the diagnosis. Interventions vary from standardized programs that have been developed and used in many organizations to relatively unique and custom designed programs that are tailored to a specific organization or department.

The term intervention here refers to any planned change activities that are intended to help an organization become more effective in solving its problems. There are usually three characteristics of O.D. interventions:

1.   They must be based on valid information about the organization's functioning -- as a result of accurate assessment or diagnosis;

2.   They must derive from organizational members' free, informed choices -- where members are actively involved in making decisions about change, rather than having an intervention imposed upon them;

3.   They must gain members' internal commitment to these choices -- the organization accepts ownership of the intervention and takes responsibility for implementing it.

Types of O.D. Interventions. The types of O.D. Interventions can be classified according to the primary targets of the change programs.

● People and organizational processes - such as communication, conflict management, problem solving, leadership, and group dynamics

● Technology and organizational structures - including work method and work flow, division of labor, hierarchy and work design, and quality of work life

● Human resource systems - focusing on mechanisms for integrating people into organizations, including performance/reward systems, and career planning and development

- Strategy and environment - including strategic choice, environmental assessment, and corporate culture.

Our discussion of interventions certainly does not include all the interventions available and in use today. However, we have tried to discuss those most frequently in use in organizations today.

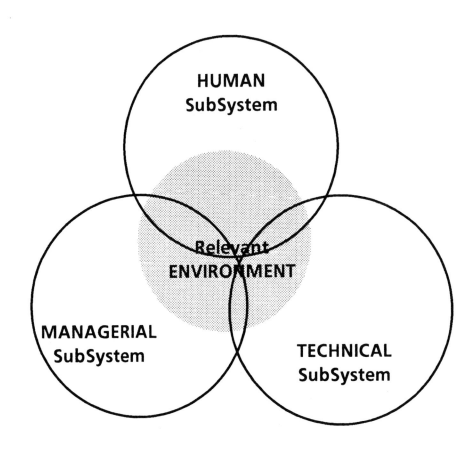

Figure 14-1 Systems Approach to Organizational Development

2 SURVEY FEEDBACK

Survey feedback is a systematic method of collecting data about a total organization, feeding back these data to groups at all levels within the organization, and asking these groups to use the information as a basis for planning and taking corrective action. This approach is closely related to the System 4 Theory of management.

There are several steps involved in survey feedback:

1) Top-level management must be involved in the initial planning.

2) A questionnaire (standard or customized) is administered anonymously to all organization members. See sample of measures below.

3) A computer analysis of the results. Separate tabulations are provided for each group and for each higher level of responsibility within the organization.

4) A consultant feeds back the information to the top executive team and then down through the hierarchy in functional teams.

5) Each manager meets with subordinates to interpret the data and make corrective action plans. The consultant attends all the meetings to help the group relate the data to its own specific situation and set action goals.

Sample Of Measures

Organizational climate
    Organization at work
    Communication flow
    Emphasis on human resources
    Decision-making practices
    Influence and control
    Absence of bureaucracy
    Coordination
    Job challenge
    Job reward
    Job clarity
    Work interdependence
    Emphasis of cooperation

Supervisory leadership
    Managerial support
    Managerial goal emphasis
    Managerial work facilitation
    Managerial team building

Peer relationships
    Peer support
    Peer goal emphasis
    Peer work facilitation
    Peer team building

End Results
    Group functioning
    Satisfaction
    Goal integration

3   ORGANIZATIONAL DIAGNOSIS

The model shown in Figure 14-2 expands a diagnostic framework from interpersonal and group issues to the more complicated contexts in which organizations are managed (19). It provides six labels, under which can be sorted much of the activity, formal and informal, that takes place in organizations. The labels allow consultants to apply whatever theories they know when doing a diagnosis and to discover new connections between apparently unrelated events. The circle describes the boundaries of an organization to be diagnosed. Environment needs forces difficult control from inside the organization.

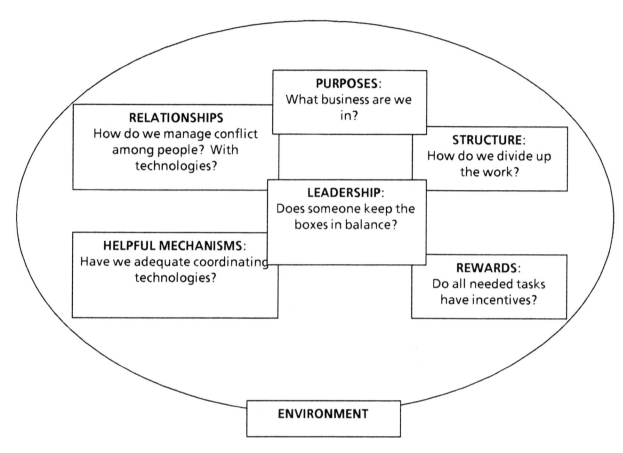

Figure 14-2. The Six-Box Organizational Model (19)

How To Collect Data :

1) Observation - watch what people do

2) Reading - follow the written record - speeches, reports, charts, graphs

3) Interviews - question those involved with a particular project

4) Survey - questionnaires - standard or customized to fit the situation (most useful method when data is not obtainable in other ways)

All four methods can be used to isolate the two major kinds of discrepancies - between what people say (formal) and what they do (informal), and between what is (the organization as it exists) and what ought to be (appropriate environmental fit).

4 TEAM BUILDING...BUILDING A HIGH PERFORMING TEAM

The traditional model of management found in most companies fosters organizational blindness to traditional problems. This occurs because at the lower levels of management or supervision, the person is still is a "doer", in addition to having some managerial tasks. As a manager progresses through the management ranks, he/she moves farther away from the "doers", until they loose touch with bottom-line people. However, this model fosters a divided system, of doers and managers; the two levels loose the chance for interacting on a regular basis. This prevents the manager from experiencing first hand the day-to-day problems and issues occurring at lower levels of the organization or department over which he/she is head! And it prevents the lower levels from learning about and identifying with some of the concerns they will be exposed to as higher level managers.

In addition, the "doers" on the line do not have a chance to interact with each other, as this model typically consists of individual workers performing individual tasks. There is no chance for synergism or teamwork in this model.

Benefits of Team Building. In Team Building, one looks at ways of effectively combining the individual doers into a unit, a proactive team. The modern manager is today moving from managing a one-to-one situation to managing one-to-group. Some benefits of this change are:

• The doers have a chance to provide input into issues concerning the team

• Everyone is responsible for the effective performance of the team

• The doers begin to think like higher-level managers

• Higher-level managers do not forget what it is like to be at lower levels

• Management is not solely responsible for solving the problems of the team

• Workers learn not to pass problems up or down stream in the organization.

There is, thus, an excellent opportunity to build upon the synergism of the team. Let's define synergism:

> *Synergism is the simultaneous actions of separate entities which together have greater total effect or parts than the sum of their individual effects or parts.*

The team represents a unit similar to a family group. "Family group members" interact regularly with each other to work on problem solving, improving the performance of the work unit, addressing issues which involve the team. Why can't work teams function in much the same way? They can with training.

There are certain rewards in working within a family type work environment. Members of a family team are usually more supportive toward one another than in the usual work group which is comprised of unrelated individuals. However in an effective or high performing team, members have a high trust and respect for one another. Communications in a team are more open than outside, as it is imperative for the high functioning level of the team to be based on honest and open feedback. A team is a more friendly place to work, meeting some of the higher levels of motivations within the team members. Overall, teams tend to accomplish more than work groups of disparate individuals.

Higher level managers are also family group members of a higher level group (see Linking Pin). This is the connection of each unit to the entire organization.

Some family groups are also inter-departmental, teams formed to solve particular problems which affect more than one functional team or department.

Wilson Research (20) has identified eight attributes typically present in high performing teams:

- **Participative leadership** - creating an interdependency by empowering, freeing up, and serving others

- **Shared responsibility** - establishing an environment in which all team members feel as responsible as the manager for the performance of the work unit

- **Aligned on purpose** - having a sense of common purpose about why the team exists and the function it serves

- **High communication** - creating a climate of trust and open, honest communication

- **Future focused** - seeing change as an opportunity for growth

- **Focused on task** - keeping meetings focused on results

- **Creative talents** - applying individual talents and creativity

- **Rapid response** - identifying and acting on opportunities.

Phased Approach. Team Building requires a phased approach. You cannot expect a group of individuals to immediately take on group goals and perform as a team, especially those who have achieved individual success and excellence. There are three basic phases to establishing a family group, or team:

- **Phase 1. Collection of Individuals.** In this phase, individuals are given the opportunity to form identities within the team. Teams at this stage typically have individual goals rather than group goals, do not share responsibility, avoid changes, and do not deal well with conflict. Phase 1 allows for members to begin to define their purpose and responsibility on the team, identify the skills of others, and develop "norms" for working with others.

- **Phase 2. Groups.** In this developmental stage, individuals begin to form groups. Members begin to develop a group identity, define roles, and clarify their purpose. The group at this stage is centered around a leader who provides direction, assigns tasks, reviews performance, and is the primary focus of communication.

- **Phase 3. Team.** In this final stage, one able to focus energy, respond rapidly to opportunities, and share both responsibilities and rewards. Teams are purpose-centered, members not only understand the purpose of the team, but are committed to it and use the purpose to guide actions and decisions.

Management or Leadership Style. Traditional management (authoritative) is unable to move a group of individuals towards a high performing team. The traditional manager "tells" employees what to do, "directs" the actions of workers in the performance of their tasks. This creates a dependent relationship between doer and manager.

A **Participative Manager** allows for employees' growth, gives more responsibility, more freedom, asks for input and suggestions, engages in mutual goal-setting, and makes feedback more of a two-way communication. This fosters an "independent" relationship.

Team Building requires a further step towards **Participative Leadership**. The move here is towards "interdependence", allowing team members to relate to each other in a way that recognizes and uses each member's strengths. By creating interdependence, the group shares the responsibility for what is occurring in the work unit.

Shared Responsibility. A manager (or leader) can encourage a sense of shared responsibility and true teamwork among team members by doing some of the following:

- Give assignments which require unit members to work together in cooperation to complete a task.

It is very important to share information and establish a climate which encourages this. This includes both upward and downward communication between manager and team members, and among team members.

- Create opportunities for unit members to assist each other in completing tasks.

Inform the team members of the whole-group task and how their part fits into this whole task. Encourage team members to help each other in attaining this task.

- Help unit members to see the unique abilities in each other and to recognize each other's limitations.

Provide cross-training among team members, increasing each team members ability to better serve the team.

- Create a reward system which gives members a greater stake in what the work unit as a whole achieves rather than in what they achieve individually.

Purpose, or Mission. Development of a team mission statement is a tool to increase a "bonding" among team members. A statement of the team's mission or purpose is a general description of what it is that the team does. To develop a mission statement, answer each of the following questions:

- Who are we?
- What do we do?
- For whom?
- Why?

The mission statement should be developed by team members, utilizing brainstorming. Each team member answers the above questions, a scribe captures these answers / thoughts on a board or flip chart, and brainstorming is used to edit the individual statements into one statement for the team. It is also helpful to have a team name, again to increase identity and ownership for the team's progress, as well as provide a sense of a family group.

Team building is one of the most popular Organization Development interventions. Research shows that team work is much more efficient than individual contribution, the whole being greater than the sum of its parts. This technique is generally one of the first used by an OD specialist or consultant, and usually leads to other interventions, such as Quality Circles.

There are certain components of a good team, some of which are:

- Mutual trust and support
- Open communications
- Clear objectives and mission
- Everyone values the team and has input
- Conflict is open
- Each person accepts responsibility for the group

NOTE: Team building must have top management support and participation.

Basic Steps to Team Building

- Develop a mission - a statement of purpose and standards of excellence

- Set goals - what needs to be done to accomplish the mission (departmental and organizational)

- Establish roles and relationships - interdependencies among groups and departments

- Set objectives - areas of improvement

- Develop an action plan - assignments to be completed (who, what, when, follow-up, evaluation)

Some of the benefits to managers are:

- More control
- Group direction
- Awareness of group's activities
- Sense of commitment from group
- Each member held accountable

5 EFFECTIVE TEAM MEETINGS

Probably the best place to begin team building is in meetings. Meetings are a microcosm of the work scene. How people conduct themselves in meetings very often resembles how they are outside the conference room. How people interact with others in a meeting is usually a carryover from outside. The task of the family group leader, or manager, is to facilitate productive, well-planned and executed team meetings. Managers spend from one-third to one-half of their time in meetings, however, most are not necessarily skilled in running them.

Symptoms of Ineffective and Inefficient Meetings:

- People complain that they spend too much time in meetings
- People drift in late so that meetings don't start on time
- It is difficult to get agreement on the agenda
- One person or a small group dominates meetings from the outset
- It is hard to get a hearing on new ideas because of negativism and resistance
- People seem to devote more energy to finding out what is wrong with an idea than what is good
- It is difficult to get most participants to open up and offer their ideas or possible solutions
- Sessions do not produce all of the options that are available
- Meetings seem to drift and people reach decisions only in the last few minutes
- Decisions are the product of frustration and time pressure, or of a desire to end the meeting
- Decisions are arrived at by majority vote
- Meetings tend to run on longer than anyone wants
- There is more competitiveness than cooperation in the group
- After meetings, participants spend much time rehashing what went on in the meeting
- After decisions are made, participants seem confused about what exactly was decided
- The same issues are hashed over from one meeting to the next
- Participants leave with unclear ideas as to how decisions are to be implemented
- Much talking in meetings has little or nothing to do with the agenda
- Some people complain that their contributions are not taken seriously by the rest of the group
- People seem to be quick to disagree with a contribution even before they have enough information to evaluate it properly
- People do a lot of interrupting of others
- People offer ideas and suggestions that are ignored by everyone else
- People put others down in meetings
- It is generally felt that meetings are a huge waste of time

Obstructive Roles in Groups:

There are certain behaviors which tend to keep a group from functioning effectively. These behaviors get in the way of proper functioning of the group.

- **Shutting out:** Silencing a member by interrupting, changing the subject, or putting down. The person who has been silenced will often react by remaining silent, thus depriving the group of his or her thinking. This can also discourage others from contributing.

- **Analyzing:** Putting labels on or suggesting motives for another's behavior. This does not help the group move towards achievement of its goals.

339

- **Dominating**: Taking over a meeting and preventing others from contributing. This prevents contributions from all group members. While this person may have leadership qualities which can be useful to the group, you will want to confront the situation and bring others into the discussion.

- **Yes-butting**: Seeming to agree or respect another's position before arguing against its validity. This tends to add confusion to discussions, and is a form of put down.

- **Naysaying**: Being negative about ideas or suggestions before they are really considered. While the "devil's advocate" role is useful to group discussions, constant negativity is restrictive to the functioning of the group. It discourages all ideas being opened up for discussion.

Group-Building Behaviors:

These behaviors can eliminate some of the items listed above and move meetings toward a more effective / efficient state.

- **Confronting**: Insisting that the group deal with issues that it appears to want to avoid. This could involve the group sidestepping an issue, or dealing with destructive and offensive behavior among group members.

- **Gatekeeping**: Providing opportunities for all members of the group to contribute. This avoids a few members of the group monopolizing the discussion.

- **Mediating**: Intervening to clarify the respective positions of two or more disputants. Mediating is not arbitrating, the leader does not take a position. Mediating can restore some forward movement to the group when it is stuck.

- **Harmonizing**: Finding areas of agreement in the arguments of two or more members of the group. Often, people in a debating situation use different words for the same meanings, and harmonizing allows group members to see more clearly the positive aspects to the debate.

- **Supporting**: Reinforcing the right of a group member to speak or to have his or her opinion discussed. This avoids shut-outs of group members, and allows for healthy discussion of all ideas.

- **Summarizing**: Summing up various or even divergent contributions. This avoids ideas getting "lost", keeps all ideas on the board, helps to avoid confusion.

- **Processing-observing**: Commenting on what goes on in the group. This keeps the group discussion on target, minimizes destructive behavior, discourages side conversations among subgroups, and forces the group to look at itself while it is functioning.

Suggestions for Generating Participation:

- Ask open-ended questions
- Call on people directly
- Ask people to come prepared
- Ask members of the group to acknowledge each other
- Use appropriate silence - wait for answers
- Redirect questions back to other group members
- Use ice breakers and warm-up exercises

- Avoid win/lose situations
- Self-disclose - share personal examples
- Write key statements on flipchart and post
- Make eye contact
- Move close to the person you want to reinforce
- Use humor
- Stay open to the viewpoints of others

Consensus :

Most organizations utilize "majority vote" as the method for decision making. Consensus is a more effective method because more options are offered, and the decision is "bought into" by all members of the team. This leads to more commitment to the successful implementation of the decision. A group should follow these steps in arriving at a consensus decision.

1 Encourage all participants to have a full say. Create an atmosphere where all members can voice their opinions, even their smallest concerns.

2 Emphasize positives. People find it easier to discuss negatives, encourage members to keep opinions equal.

3 Find out how serious the negatives are. Let others in the group discuss the negative concerns of others. The seriousness of the concern may loose its impact if the group is able to offer suggestions on how to turn it into a positive.

4 Keep summing up the areas of agreement. As deliberation goes on, people will often qualify their negative positions or give them up entirely. Eventually, problems and disagreements almost seem to melt away.

There may be times when group consensus cannot be reached. At that point, the key is to find a solution which all can "live with", even if it would not be their choice.

MEETING CHECKLIST

BEFORE THE MEETING

Check items applicable:

_____ 1. Plan the meeting carefully; Who, What, When, Where, Why, and How many.

_____ 2. Prepare and send out an agenda in <u>advance</u> and allow for group input.

_____ 3. Come early and set up the meeting room.

AT THE BEGINNING OF THE MEETING

_____ 4. Start on time.

_____ 5. Get participants to introduce themselves and state their expectations for the meeting.

_____ 6. Clearly define roles, i.e. scribe, gatekeeper, etc.

_____ 7. Set time limits, review agenda order, assign someone as timekeeper.

_____ 8. Review action items from the previous meeting.

DURING THE MEETING

_____ 9. Focus on the same problem in the same way at the same time.

_____ 10. Clearly state any decisions reached at the end of each agenda.

AT THE END OF THE MEETING

_____ 11. Establish action items: Who, What, When, Where.

_____ 12. Review any minutes taken.

_____ 13. Set the date and place of the next meeting and develop a preliminary agenda.

_____ 14. Ask for feedback on the effectiveness of the meeting.

_____ 15. Thank all participants for their contributions.

_____ 16. Close the meeting crisply and positively.

AFTER THE MEETING

_____ 17. Prepare the group minutes and distribute.

_____ 18. Follow-up on action items, prepare preliminary agenda and distribute

Figure 14-6. Meeting Checklist

6 FACTORS CONTRIBUTING TO TEAM DEVELOPMENT AND EFFECTIVENESS

The mere existence of a group does not ensure that it will operate effectively; a group is more effective only to the degree to which it is able to use its individual and collective resources. The measure of the group's effectiveness is its ability to achieve its objectives and satisfy the needs of the individuals in the group.

The success of an organization depends on the ability of the groups within it to work together to attain jointly determined objectives. Today's leaders must be concerned with developing more cohesive and cooperative relationships between individuals and groups. Similarly, the development of effective groups or teams within the organization will determine, to a large extent, the ability of the organization to attain its strategic goals.

Team development is based on the assumption that any group is able to work more effectively if its members understand and embrace the following factors (21).

Shared Goals and Objectives. Beyond a simple understanding of the immediate task, members of the team must understand the overall role of the team within the total organization, its responsibilities, and the task the team wants to accomplish. In addition, each team member must be committed to these goals and objectives. One way to insure this commitment is to involve all team members in defining the goals and relating these goals to specific problems that are relevant to team members.

Utilization of Resources. Team effectiveness is enhanced when all members are given the opportunity to be heard and contribute. It is the team's responsibility to utilize all of the individual resources available.

Trust and Conflict Resolution. The ability to openly recognize conflict and seek to resolve it through discussion is critical to the team's success. For a team to become effective, it must deal with the emotional problems and needs of its members and the interpersonal problems that arise in order to build working relationships that are characterized by openness and trust.

Shared Leadership. Teams are not effective if only established to implement decisions made by their leader or others not in the group. The development and cohesion of a team occurs when there is a feeling of shared leadership and responsibility among all team members. Each member is responsible for both task functions and maintenance functions, which are necessary to keep the group interacting effectively. Task functions include: initiating discussions or actions, clarifying issues and goals, summarizing points, testing for consensus or agreement, and seeking or giving information. Maintenance functions include: encouraging involvement and participation, sensing and expressing group feelings, harmonizing and facilitating reconciliation of disagreements, setting standards for the group, and "gatekeeping" or bringing people into discussions. Groups perform better when all members perform these functions.

Control and Procedures. A team needs to establish procedures that can be used to guide or regulate its activities, such as meeting agendas and time schedules. The group should determine which control methods to use, such as a facilitator in meetings.

Effective Interpersonal Communications. Effective team development depends on the ability of team members to communicate with one another in an open and honest manner. This is apparent when team members listen to each other, and attempt to build on one another's contributions.

Approach to Problem Solving and Decision Making. The team must adapt a method for accomplishing these two important tasks. The lack of agreed-upon approaches to these functions can result in wasted time, misunderstandings, frustration, and often, bad decisions.

Experimentation / Creativity. The team must occasionally move beyond the controlled environment into new areas and experiment with new ways of doing things. This allows creativity to surface among team members, allowing the team greater flexibility in dealing with problems.

Evaluation. The team periodically should examine its group processes, and evaluate how effectively it is working. Any problems with procedures or methods, or even team members, must be dealt with openly and honestly among the team members.

7 CONDITIONS WHICH SUPPORT EFFECTIVE TEAM PROBLEM SOLVING

1. Team members readily contribute from their experience and listen to contributions of others.
   Every member brings a certain expertise to the team - utilize this expertise in the problem solving efforts.

2. Conflicts arising from different points of view are considered helpful and are resolved constructively by the team.
   Team members should feel free to express their opinions and thoughts towards the problem at hand.

3. Team members challenge suggestions they believe are unsupported by facts or logic, but avoid arguing just to have their way.
   Encourage critical thinking, avoid senseless arguments.

4. Poor solutions are not supported just for the sake of harmony or agreement.
   Encourage all team members to feel free to disagree.

5. Differences of opinion are discussed and resolved. Coin tossing, averaging, majority vote and similar cop-outs are avoided when making a decision, reaching consensus is the desired state.
   Through consensus, each team member agrees to support the decision.

6. Every team member strives to make the problem solving process efficient and is careful to facilitate rather than hinder discussion.
   Careful planning and training on a problem-solving method enables all team members to act as facilitators.

7. Team members encourage and support co-workers who may be reluctant to offer ideas.
   Encourage every team member to feel responsible for the outcome of the problem.

8. Team members understand the value of time, and work at eliminating extraneous and/or repetitious discussion.
   Set gatekeeping rules at the beginning of the problem-solving discussion. Avoid 'war stories'.

9. Team decisions are not arbitrarily over-ruled by the leader simply because he/she does not agree with them.
   Encourage the 'leaderless team' idea, gain better support for implementation of decisions.

10. The team understands that the leader will make the best decision he or she can, if a satisfactory team solution is not forthcoming.
    When the team cannot provide the solution, support for the decision of the leader is given by team members.

8 COLLABORATION AS A SOURCE OF POWER IN TEAM BUILDING

Collaboration, defined as "the act of working together", has many benefits when used properly in a team building situation. Listed below are a few.

- Collaboration builds an awareness of interdependence. When people recognize the benefits of helping one another, and realize it is expected, they will work together to achieve common goals. The effort is non-threatening.

- When people work together to achieve common goals they stimulate each other to higher levels of accomplishment. Fresh ideas are generated and tested, and the team's productivity exceeds any combined efforts of employees working individually.

- Collaboration builds and reinforces recognition and mutual support within a team. People have an opportunity to see the effect of their effort and the efforts of others on achievement.

- Collaboration leads to commitment to support and accomplish organizational goals. People gain personal power in the form of confidence when they know others share their views and are acting in concert with them.

Collaboration can be encouraged and supported in the following ways.

1. Identify areas of interdependence that make collaboration appropriate. Involve team members in planning and problem solving to help them identify where collaboration is needed.

2. Keep lines of communication open between everyone involved in a problem, project or course of action.

3. Let the team know in advance that teamwork will positively influence individual recognition.

9   MANAGEMENT BY OBJECTIVES

Management by Objectives (MBO) was formulated in 1954 by Peter F. Drucker, who suggested that through discussions and involvement, a subordinate will be motivated to work harder and consequently improve performance. There are many different MBO systems; or, some rather formal and elaborate, others more informal and simplified. An example of MBO is shown in Figure 14-3:

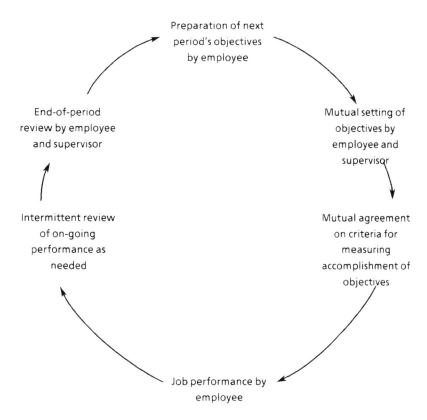

Figure 14-3. Circular Process of Management By Objectives

MBO has evolved in many organizations because it addresses certain factors inherent in a person's job:

1. Employees can perform better when it is clear to them not only what is expected of them, but how their individual efforts contribute to the overall performance of the organization.

2. Employees usually want to have some say in the particular results that are expected of them.

3. While performing, employees have a need to know how well they are doing.

4. Employees want to be rewarded in line with their levels of performance.

10   COLLABORATIVE MANAGEMENT BY OBJECTIVES

French and Hollmann in their article "Management by Objectives: The Team Approach"(22) suggest that Management By Objectives (MBO) could be strengthened considerably by increasing the opportunities for systematic collaboration among managers. Peter Drucker originally described MBO as an emphasis on teamwork and team results, however most MBO programs have taken a one-to-one approach.

Collaborative Management by Objectives (CMBO), suggests a process of overlapping work units interacting with higher and lower units on overall organizational goals and objectives, unit goals and objectives, and individuals interacting with peers and superiors on role definition and individual goals and objectives.

French and Holliman suggest some contingencies for successfully implementing CMBO are:

- A strong desire on the part of the top management team to cooperate with and help each other.

- Some modicum of skill in interpersonal relations and group dynamics.

- Proper timing in the introduction - it should be introduced only when diagnosis suggests its applicability and usefulness as well as organizational readiness.

- Commitment to and skills in participative management, as well as a willingness and ability to diagnose the impact of the goal-setting and review processes on organization members and organizational functioning.

- Commitment to adequate time to develop effective group dynamics, communication and interaction skills.

An example of CMBO is (23):

> A sales organization holds group meetings at regular intervals in which salespeople set goals, discuss priorities, and identify results to be achieved before the next meeting. The group holds each member responsible and accountable for meeting their goals. The superior acts as a chairman, stresses a constructive, problem-solving approach, encourages high performance and provides technical advice when necessary.

> The salespeople in this situation held more positive attitudes toward their jobs and sold more on the average then sales people in a traditional MBO situation.

CMBO is closest to the Organizational Development approach, diagnosing and affecting the entire organizational structure.

11 THE MANAGERIAL GRID

The Managerial Grid is a framework developed by Blake and Mouton, in which a variety of findings about managerial behavior can be fitted. It is a behavioral road map.

The model proposes two assumptions about managerial behavior:
1) Concern for production, and
2) Concern for people.

In the grid framework, the manager who shows a high concern for both production and people is the most effective manager in an organizational setting .

The model discusses five basic managerial styles:

1) *1,1 style*, **impoverished management** displays little concern for either production or people.

2) *1,9 style*, **country club management** displays high regard for people, little for production.

3) *9,1 style*, **authority-obedience**, completion of tasks within constraints, with little concern for people.

4) *5,5 style*, **organization man management**, moderate concern for both production and people.

5) *9,9 style*, **team management**, ideal style, high regard for both production and people.

Figure 14-4 shows the managerial grid. There are six phases in the managerial grid program, which if followed systematically, allegedly can bring a manager from his/her current style to the 9,9 ideal style.

- The grid seminar
- Intergroup development
- Developing an ideal model
- Implementing the model
- Monitoring the ideal model

Some conclusions about 9,9 style are (24):

- Productivity and sales are significantly advanced by 9,9 oriented team management.

- Career progress for persons who manage in the 9,9 style is accelerated in comparison with other methods of supervision.

- A 9,9 approach increases satisfaction from work.

- Physical health is greater for those who manage in the 9,9 way.

A 9,9 manager places high value on sound, creative decisions that result in understanding and agreement. He listens for and seeks out ideas, opinions, and attitudes different from his own. He has strong convictions but responds to sounder ideas than his own by changing his mind. When conflict arises, he tries to identify reasons for it, and seeks to resolve the underlying causes. When aroused, he contains himself even though his impatience is visible. His humor fits the situation and gives perspective; he retains a sense of humor even under pressure. He exerts vigorous effort and others join in (25).

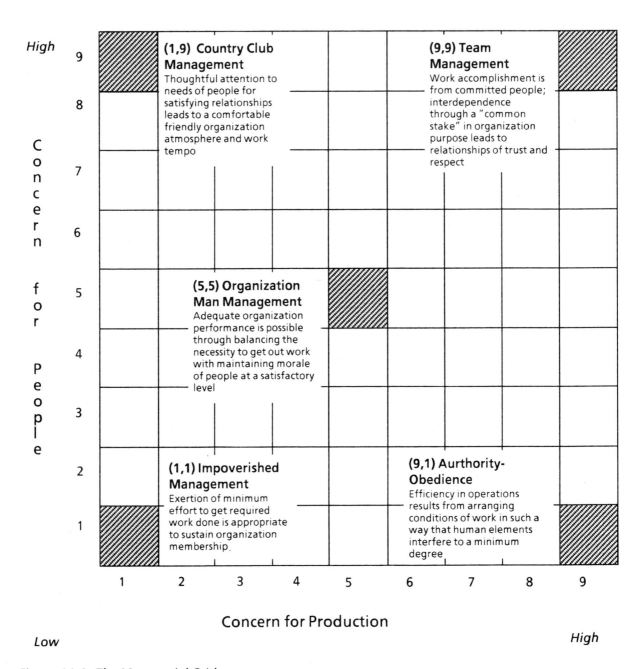

Figure 14-4. The Managerial Grid.

12   THE SCANLON PLAN

The Scanlon Plan is a way of industrial life -- a philosophy of management -- which rests on theoretical assumptions entirely consistent with Theory Y. The plan embodies two central features, which in their operation, bring about profound changes in organizational relationships, attitudes, and practices (26):

Cost Reduction Sharing, a means of sharing the economic gains from improvements in organizational performance. Utilizes a ratio between the total manpower costs of the organization and a measure of output such as total sales or value added by manufacture.

- It is directly related to the success of the members in improving the over-all economic success of the organization.

- When properly developed, cost reduction sharing gains genuine acceptance (it is perceived to be equitable) and provides true motivation.

- It is reasonably well related temporally to the behavior which produced it (cause and effect).

Effective Participation, a formal method providing an opportunity for every member of the organization to contribute his brains and ingenuity, as well as his physical effort, to the improvement of organizational effectiveness. It encourages and rewards the distinctively human contribution.

- It is the means of providing every member of the organization the opportunity to satisfy his higher- level needs, achieve recognition and other important social and ego satisfactions.

- Committees are formed to receive, discuss, and evaluate every means that anyone can think of for improving organizational effectiveness, and put into effect those that are considered workable.

The Scanlon Plan lies on a Theory Y assumption that all workers are capable of self-directed effort toward organizational goals provided their work gives them opportunity for taking responsibility for their actions and using their abilities.

13   QUALITY OF WORK LIFE

Quality of Work Life (QWL) has been described as a process of joint decision making, collaboration and building mutual respect between management and employees. It could be defined as the degree to which members of work organizations are able to satisfy important personal needs through their experience in those organizations. When quality of work life is in existence, workers share fully in making decisions that design their lives at work.

The quality of work environment is a human perception, dependent on each workers personal sense of what makes a good working life.

QWL is not an exact science or approach, and has many faces, some of which are:

- Reasonable compensation and fringe benefits
- Job security
- A safe and healthful work environment
- Recognition for achievement through promotion and pay
- Participation in decision making
- Less rigid work habits, production permitting

More recently QWL programs have grown to include:

- Some responsibility for work process
- Consideration of social aspects of life on the job
- Work teams with group projects and shared tasks
- Quality circles
- Full information sharing
- Flexible work hours
- Team supervision
- Training and development courses
- Education tuition
- Promotions from within
- Profit sharing

Figure 14-5 shows the elements of a quality of work life program.

Direct people managers can improve opportunity and power by following these steps:

- Support learning: help people to be effective by supporting and enhancing their learning on the job, and their knowledge of their jobs' importance and relevance.

- Hold career conversations: counsel subordinates on career and growth opportunities, help them see what they need to do to take advantage of them.

- Form problem-solving groups: create groups or task forces to work on key problems that impact the work of members of the groups, and the organization.

- Make contacts/add visibility: make people more visible to senior managers and more recognized for their own particular contributions.

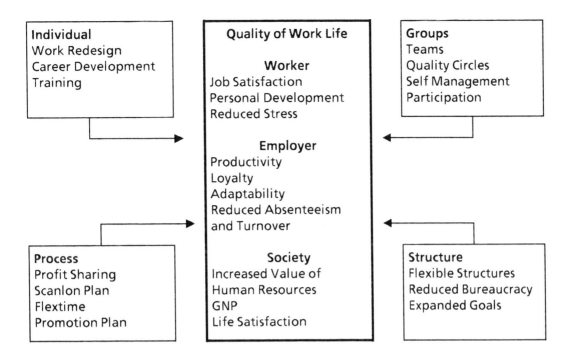

Individual Work Redesign Career Development Training	Quality of Work Life **Worker** Job Satisfaction Personal Development Reduced Stress **Employer** Productivity Loyalty Adaptability Reduced Absenteeism and Turnover **Society** Increased Value of Human Resources GNP Life Satisfaction	Groups Teams Quality Circles Self Management Participation
Process Profit Sharing Scanlon Plan Flextime Promotion Plan		Structure Flexible Structures Reduced Bureaucracy Expanded Goals

Figure 14-5. Quality of Work Life Elements

- Share information: find out what information is needed, and see that the people who need it get it when they need it.

- Open access to resources: give people the control and flexibility over supplies, resources, and actions that are needed to get their work done more effectively, without having to go through unnecessary and wasteful steps.

- Add discretion: enhance people's power by giving them more discretion to make decisions, and more chances to learn to do it better.

The younger worker has a new idea of work, a "giving-getting" perspective, what he gives in return for what he gets as an exchange relationship. Daniel Yankelovich (27) states that college educated people "believe that if they are willing to work hard by the old rules they can win the traditional rewards -- the car, the TV set, the house in the suburbs, respectability. What they question is not whether the old rules work, but whether they are worth the bother: they question both the kind of work the society demands and the 'payoff' it provides".

The more educated and aware worker is seeking more self- fulfillment in all dimensions of their lives. They resent sharp social class distinctions between employee and employer. They do not automatically accept the authority of the boss. They want to participate in decisions that affect their work. They prefer variety to routine and informality to formalism. They want their work to be interesting as well as to pay well and to give them an outlet for creativity. They seek responsibility and they like to set their own goals. They enjoy working in small groups in a relationship of collegiality rather then rigid hierarchy. They desire constant feedback: a running connection on how they are doing on the job (27). Quality of life issues for such workers cannot be separated from quality of work issues.

There are three major approaches to expanding opportunity and power for improved productivity and quality of work life:

1) **Multidirectional career options** - creating and developing a variety of possibilities for movement from every job so that no job is an automatic dead-end.

2) **Task redistribution within work units** - each person's or group's tasks make best use of the people involved, and provide adequate challenge.

3) **Worker-management problem-solving structures** - allow people to attack problems in flexible temporary teams, coordinated and managed systematically.

How QWL Ties in With Job Satisfaction and Productivity (28):

At their best, QWL programs increase both job satisfaction and productivity. It is easier to make employees happy then to elevate their performance. When QWL programs do improve productivity, the improvement often comes about because of improved satisfaction. Productivity improvement is a likely fallout from worker involvement.

There are certain conditions associated with successful programs. When these conditions are met, both job satisfaction and productivity are likely to increase. Nine of these are (29):

- Clearly define the QWL program
- Acquire commitment from both labor and management
- Involve employees from many levels in the program
- Learn from mistakes made early in the program
- Do not bypass middle management in the planning of the program
- Choose leaders for the program with the appropriate leadership style
- Identify program goals
- Use outside consulting help when needed
- Select workers who can be motivated to achieve excellent performance.

Technology has been powerful in its effects on quality of work environments. An example of how technological change can effect the working environment follows:

Equipment and process
technology

effects

Operating policies and
practices

which create a

Working environment

to which workers react with

Particular perceptions
and expectations

resulting in

Perceived quality of
working life

----

14 PARTICIPATIVE MANAGEMENT

Participative management is not a specific technique but rather a concept of applied management that involves employee participation in developing and implementing decisions that directly affect their jobs. It is based on the philosophy of trust, respect, and supportiveness between managers and subordinates.

Participation can be forced by law, or it can be voluntary by consensus between management and employees. Participation can be formal (for example a union), or informal (verbal agreement). Participation may be direct, when each employee is involved with the discussion and decision, or indirect, when an elected representative speaks for employees to a higher level group. Participation can vary in degree from no participation, where all direction comes from above, to full participation, in which managers and subordinates jointly reach decisions.

There are four broad categories which seem to be compatible with participative management (30):

1) Routine Personnel Matters - hiring, discipline, training, method of payment to be used

2) Job Itself - work methods, job design, goal setting, speed of work

3) Working Conditions - hours of work, plant or office layout, interior decorating

4) Company policies - layoffs, profit sharing, benefits, capital investments, dividends

Within these categories, at least four major varieties of participation can be identified (31):

1) Participation in setting goals (Management by Objectives)

2) Participation in making decisions

3) Participation in solving problems

4) Participation in developing and implementing change.

In addition, there are different ways to use Participative Management:

a) with respect to individual subordinates

b) in the context of the superior-subordinate relationship

c) in a group context.

An example of participative management is the Hawthorne Studies, in which the primary factor was simply special attention, a small element of the participative management approach. Roethlisberger said (31):

> People like to feel important and have their work recognized as important...They like to work in an atmosphere of approval. They like to be praised rather than blamed...They like to feel independent in their relations to their supervisors...They like to be consulted about and participate in actions that will personally affect them.

From the Hawthorne Studies we find a variety of factors other than special attention which impacted the situation. The Hawthorne workers were specially treated and were subject to special attention, good supervision, participative-management practices, and self-fulfilling prophecy.

Organizations should not move to more participatory forms of management without being aware of some of the central questions, concerns, issues, and tensions around participation (32).

- **The paradox of paternalism**. Democracy may be imposed on the employees by leaders who then expect gratitude. Participation under these circumstances can be seen as a gift rather than a right, arousing resentment, or concern that it can easily be taken away.

- **The need for visible results**. Without results indicating that the process of participation made a difference, it can be considered worthless. People who participate need some indication that their involvement was meaningful, that some decisions would be different were they not involved. People need to feel that they benefit from contributing more to an organization's effective functioning.

- **The problem of power**. Managers do not want to give up power, especially when in so many organizations supervisors and middle managers feel sufficiently powerless anyway. Participative management can create fear among this group as organizations discover how participation in the form of "self-management" can cut down the number of supervisors required. Unions may also resist participatory proposals out of concern about encroachments into their prerogatives if they cooperate with management.

- **Time**. Participative management and involvement in decision making is time consuming, and there is no guarantee that the decisions made democratically will be of higher quality than those made autocratically. Participative management also requires extra time for workers to invest in meetings. The workers may display apathy and shirk responsibility. Not all workers demonstrate a need for participation in decision making.

- **Participate or else: the question of voluntariness**. As mentioned earlier, people differ in their interest in participation. Also people care more about some issues than about others. Therefore, it is unrealistic to assume that everyone will contribute or involve themselves in the same way. It is also unreasonable to hold off making decisions or taking action unless everyone is involved.

- **The knowledge gap; or participators are made, not born.** Not all people in organizations know how to exercise power once they have it. Also, the information gap between workers and managers may be difficult to overcome, and the better informed (managers) may still have a greater voice in decisions. There are three kinds of knowledge essential for effective participation, all of which are unevenly distributed among organization members:

  1) The ability to contribute to discussion and decision making as general processes
  2) Understanding of the relevance of decisions or issues to larger organizational contexts
  3) Substantive knowledge of the matters at hand.

357

The knowledge gap may eventually undermine the goals of participation. People with lower skills, with less autonomous, more routinized jobs might lose interest in participation.

- **The "big decision" trap.** Employees become frustrated when they are one of many voicing an opinion about large decisions, while having no control over local ones, such as arrangement of equipment or timing of coffee breaks, which make a significant difference in work life quality. Many employees feel uninformed about macro issues and thus threatened by having their opinion solicited. However, employees can easily offer their opinion about local issues.

- **The non-democratic nature of innovation.** Creative ideas do not always spring from participatory processes, innovation may derive from the single-minded determination of autocratic geniuses. Participation of large numbers of people might interfere with the decision to take a risk or adopt a new direction, for which strong leadership could be required. However, participative management can guarantee that creative new ideas from unexpected sources will have an outlet for expression.

- **The fixed decision problem.** Certain constraints may fall upon decisions made through participatory methods, calling for either a fixed decision or constant negotiation. The latter is disruptive and dysfunctional, however the former cuts down on the use of participative decision making. `

- **Escape from freedom.** Turning over a task or an issue to a group of organization members with no guidelines, objectives, constraints, or limits can be extremely ineffective, due to the frustration of having too many choices. Delegation does not mean abdication. Responsible parties (managers or leaders) do not give up all of their control or responsibility for results just because they are involving a wider circle of people, nor should they leave the participating members to flounder without help.

- **The internal politics of teams.** Declaring people to be a group does not automatically make them one, nor does requesting decisions in which everyone has a voice ensure that democratic procedures will always be followed.

- **Social and emotional pressures: "It's hard to fire your friend".** Participatory organizations that stress cooperation and overlay a feeling of community on a business can make it hard to get rid of troublesome people, if a loose working relationship has developed. Sometimes more impersonal decisions from the top can save everyone's face. This underscores the importance of differentiating issues: those which should be delegated to a group, and those which people would prefer to have decided by some more centralized process.

- **Great expectations.** Organizations that appear to promise a great deal can disappoint its employees, causing frustration and cynicism if expectations that are aroused are not fulfilled. Manage expectations by setting realistic and attainable goals.

- **Not all organizational problems disappear.** Participatory systems are not organizational utopias that solve everything. It is good for some things, in some areas; it is not addressed to every management problem.

There are nine basic "lessons" about implementing participatory management (32):

1) Start small and with local issues.

2) Neither promise nor expect too much.

3) Allow people to define for themselves the issues they want to discuss (including managers as team members) and to opt out of those they wish to avoid.

4) Involve parties whose power might be at stake (middle managers, union, etc.) and give them important, rewarded roles in the new system.

5) Provide education on both the skills of participation/ decision making and the issues to be discussed.

6) Maintain leadership. Be explicit about the "fixed" items and the constraints on decisions.

7) Make sure minority views are heard; be wary of group pressure.

8) Keep time bounded and manageable.

9) Provide rewards and feedback, tangible signs that the participation mattered.

15 QUALITY CIRCLES

A quality circle is a group of five to ten specially trained employees that meet once a week for an hour for the purpose of spotting and solving problems in their work area. The circle is usually composed of a normal work group, a group of people who work together to produce a specific component or service (33).

Some objectives of quality circles are:

- to improve quality
- to improve productivity
- to improve employee morale and motivation
- to instill awareness of cost containment
- to improve and utilize employee creativity
- to develop employees into managers
- to help employees grow professionally and personally

The following characteristics must be present for a quality circle program to have success:

- Participation must be voluntary
- Management must be supportive by allowing circles to meet on company time, by officially recognizing the activities and results of circles, and by allocating resources to support the program
- Training in problem solving methods, group process techniques, and data gathering and analysis must be a fundamental part of the program
- Quality circle members work together as a team
- Quality circle program needs a people-building rather than a people-exploiting orientation
- Team members work to solve problems, not just identify them
- Each circle has the right to select its own problem for study and solution

In setting up a quality circle, a plant steering committee composed of labor and management usually decides which area of a company could benefit from a circle. Then five to ten workers are asked to serve on a circle and to meet once a week on company time. In addition to the employees, those attending circle meetings include the immediate supervisor and a person trained in personnel or industrial relations; the latter instructs the workers in elementary data gathering and statistics. Many organizations use an outside consultant to start up their circles. The circle selects and analyzes a problem, develops a solution, and presents their findings to management, which generally accepts the group's recommendations.

It usually takes a few weeks to get a circle moving because the success of the circle derives from the education its members receive in analyzing and solving problems. Workers are instructed in the techniques of brainstorming and are shown how to collect data and plot them on a graph. Circle leaders, usually the immediate supervisors, need training in leadership skills, principles of learning, and motivation, participation, and communication techniques. The leader must also be trained in data collection and problem solving.

It is important to stress that a quality circle consists of specially trained employees -- trained in the areas of identifying problems, collection of data, charting and analysis of data, and group dynamics.

Planning a circle - typically begins with a top level executive making the decision to implement the quality circle technique. This usually leads to identifying and selecting a consultant who will assist top management in implementing the quality circles in the organization, although in some cases, an in-house facilitator will be identified and trained in special circle methods training.

One of the most important steps in this phase involves selecting the quality circle steering committee, which becomes the group that directs quality circle activities in the organization. The steering committee has several responsibilities: establishing circle objectives in terms of the kinds of bottom-line improvements, determining actions that are considered outside the charter of the circles, choosing the in-house facilitator, the person who will be responsible for daily coordination of the quality circle activities, selecting leaders for the pilot project.

Initial Training Requirements - the facilitator and pilot project leaders, usually with the consultant, are trained in basic QC philosophy, implementation, and operation.

The group leader needs certain discussion leader techniques to ensure success of the quality circle:

1) Makes sure everyone agrees on how to define the problem.
2) Sees that all group members participate.
3) Distinguishes between idea getting and idea evaluation.
4) Does not respond to each participant or dominate the discussion.
5) Sees that effort is directed toward overcoming surmountable obstacles.

Initiating the Circles - this usually begins with department managers conducting QC familiarization meetings with employees, with the facilitator, circle leaders and an executive participating as speakers. During this overview session, employees are told they will be asked if they want to participate. Circle leaders contact each employee to determine circle membership and the circles are constituted.

The Circle in Operation - each circle begins its job of problem solving and analysis.

- **Problem Identification** - the problems identified by circle members are usually mundane ones that are not of particular interest to anyone outside the circle's work area. The circle members are resident experts in solving these work group problems.

  Brainstorming is the technique most often used to uncover and identify problems and their solutions. Brainstorming involves having circle members volunteer ideas as they come to mind, without fear of being criticized by other circle members.

- **Problem Selection** - the members select the number one problem they wish to focus on.

- **Problem Analysis** - the circle members collect and collate data relating to the problem and analyze them using data collection, statistical analysis and problem solving techniques. Perhaps the biggest benefit derived from quality circles is the sense of satisfaction members get from being involved in the actual problem analysis process.

- **Recommend Solution** - the group's solution is then presented to management orally by group members with the aid of charts and graphs.

- **Solution Review and Decision by Management** - the presentation is made to the individual to whom the supervisor reports, and in most cases, the circle suggestions are approved by the manager.

  The bottom line of a well-implemented quality circle program is that it creates a thinking, caring work force of people who take pride in their work because their needs are harmoniously meshed with company goals. It's truly a win-win situation(34).

There are several reasons quality circles can fail, some of the most commonly cited include (35):

- Union objections. Unions have traditionally viewed attempts by management to improve productivity with suspicion

- Takes time from the job. A management that still emphasizes that higher productivity is a result of high technology and management guidance may resent time away from the job and even the possibility of overtime pay

- Hostility of middle managers and supervisors. The fear from this group usually stems from a perceived loss of authority and a change in the way things are done

- Lack of credibility on the part of workers due to past management practices. Without credibility, any attempt by management to improve productivity will be viewed as another manipulative ploy

- Past experience with a suggestion program. Workers may have had poor experience with this type of program in that suggestions may have been ignored or not acted upon. Quality circles may be viewed as another step in this direction

- Quality circles mean change. Simply stated, many people simply resist change

- Inadequate training. An inadequately trained circle leader who is unable to give a sense of direction and leadership to the group can negatively affect the circle's ability to perform constructively

- Poor management response to the circle. This includes management support of the group as it develops into a working entity, as well as timely response to circle suggestions

- Unrealistic expectations. This can include too much push too soon, for financial review or increase in productivity

- Vague measures. Lack of skills in measures, problem definition and analysis, and problem solution may result in a project or proposal that is vague and disorganized

- Facilitator dependency. The leader becomes trapped in a role as the group's decision maker, rather than its facilitator.

Some Alternatives to Quality Circles:

- Group Suggestion Program. This approach relies on the initial enthusiasm and knowledge of the workers. Good ideas and suggestions produced by quality circles are captured without having to continue the training required by circles. Communication upward is improved and management is able to more easily identify workers with potential. Those who are closest to the actual work get an opportunity to share their thoughts on quality and productivity issues while management benefits from their suggestions.

  There are some disadvantages to this approach. Workers can feel manipulated. Workers see their suggestions saving the company money, yet they get no further opportunity to contribute or to enhance their daily working lives through ownership of issues.

- Special Projects. Implement quality circles only as necessary for special projects (for example in a time of change). Employees get an opportunity to influence the change as well as work out the flaws of the new system. The organization benefits by easing the employees painlessly into the new system as well as by gathering information. The problem or project at hand defines the circle's lifetime.

  The biggest danger with this approach is that it raises expectations and then brings them to a halt on a regular basis. After a given length of time, employees who have been through the start up cycle several times will be extremely critical, if not hostile, towards the system.

- Transitional Vehicle. Use quality circles as a transitional vehicle for a permanent move towards a more participative management style. With this alternative, quality circles are transformed into teams within the work group. Within a team, workers are given responsibility for implementing their own suggestions and taking over some supervisory duties. Teams allow work groups to have responsibility for day-to-day decision making concerning their work area. Quality circles help to prepare workers for participative management by developing problem-solving skills.

  This process can be a long and inefficient road to participative management. Circles can die out before the change is completed.

16 MODELING

The general purpose of modeling is to demonstrate an appropriate integration of theory and practice -- to prove that theory is livable and viable by involving the learner cognitively, affectively, and behaviorally (36).

This application of modeling allows the learner to observe the behavior of appropriate models as well as the consequences of his behavior. Subsequently, the learner practices the observed activities until they are performed skillfully.

As a training approach, modeling offers the following benefits:

- Provides motivation - learner is motivated to become aware of beneficial alternatives to present behavior

- Fosters self-acceptance - learner is encouraged to accept his present identity and to continue personal development

- Promotes change - learner makes a conscious decision to try behavioral alternatives
- Reduces the tension of learning - learner is allowed to practice the components of a skill one at a time; consequently each learning task is simplified and less stressful

- Allows for reinforcement - skills are practiced over time until they become refined and ultimately integrated into the learner's own style

- Creates a positive learning environment - modeling reduces the distance between trainer and learner, creating an atmosphere in which each learner is permitted to progress at his or her own rate.

```
                                                    Transfer
                                         Behavioral
                                         --------------
                                         Integrative
                              Behavioral
                              Affective
                              -------------
                              Refinement
                    Behavioral
                    Cognitive
                    -------------
                    Practice
           Cognitive
           Affective
           --------------
           Choice
      Affective
      --------------
      Acceptance
Cognitive
--------------
Awareness
```

Figure 14-8. The Modeling Process

364

Awareness - learner pays attention to present behavior and is introduced to the existence of options for behaving differently.

Acceptance - learner is allowed to acknowledge that his or her present behavior is no longer beneficial.

Choice - the trainer spontaneously models a more beneficial behavior, the learner commits to change and adopting the new behavior.

Practice - learner has the opportunity to practice the new behavior in a structured activity.

Refinement - learner modifies the behavior to fit his or her particular personal style. Learner receives feedback on the new skill from the trainer and reinforcement to continue the learning/refining stage.

Integration - learner uses the new behavior unconsciously and effortlessly.
Transfer - the learner uses the new skill as part of his normal behavior pattern in situations other than the learning environment.

Interpersonal Behaviors and Skills That Can Be Modeled

The specific behaviors or skills that can be modeled are numerous. Modeling is well used in training on technical skills, such as machine operation, drawing a blueprint, presenting a sales talk. Certain interpersonal skills can also be modeled effectively.

Some skills and examples of modeling are listed below (36):

Focus on Self
Disclosure - trainer discloses facts about self, feelings, beliefs, values, desires, needs, expectations.

Assertion - trainer uses the "broken record" technique, perhaps to combat against resistance from learners.

Focus on Other
Acceptance - trainer gives a non-evaluative response to a learner who is disagreeing with him.

Confrontation - trainer informs a learner that a particular behavior manifested by that learner affects the trainer negatively; in addition, the trainer clarifies preferences and consequences.

Feedback - trainer tells a learner how the learner is perceived

Support - trainer expresses appreciation for something that a learner has said or done.

Mutual Focus

Conflict management - trainer identifies an issue of conflict between learner and himself; the two parties generate alternatives and agree on an appropriate action.

Immediacy - trainer tells learner how he is reacting to the learner at that moment.

Mutuality - trainer cooperates with a learner for reciprocal achievement of goals.

Flexibility - trainer abandons his original plan and accepts a new approach suggested by learner.

Determining When and How to Use Modeling

The following factors should be considered before using modeling:

1) The degree to which the group is attached to traditional sources of power

2) The extent of the trainer's credibility

3) The degree to which the group is open to consideration of new ideas
4) The group's current stage of development

5) Technical considerations, such as number of learners and time frames

6) The learners' degree of psychological sophistication and psychological level of functioning

7) The degree of distance that the trainer wants to establish at the time

In addition, the trainer might ask the following questions:

- How much am I willing to risk?

- How can I legitimate my choice of a type or level of modeling?

- How might my choice of the type of modeling I employ coordinate with or expand my style?

- How competent do I feel in my understanding of an integration of the skill to be modeled?

- What is the nature of my contract with the learners (purpose, goals, time frame)?

17   PROBLEM SOLVING: DEFINITIONS, ISSUES AND STRATEGIES

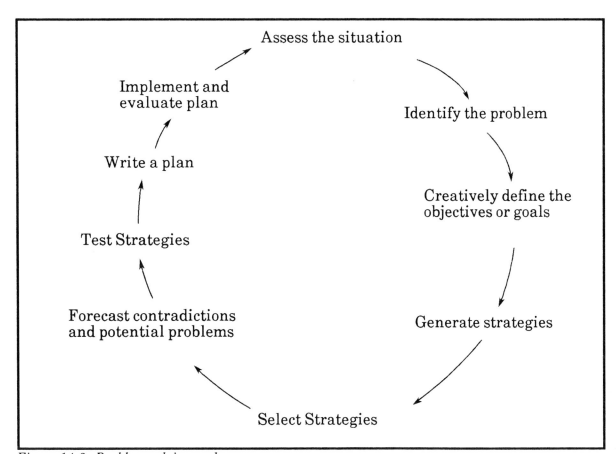

Figure 14-9. Problem solving cycle

Definitions

A problem is a discrepancy between current conditions and desired outcomes. Problems are solved by developing goals or objectives which, when achieved, reduce the discrepancy or gap between ideal and reality. Problem solving strategies utilize a wide variety of information to both set and achieve goals.

The problem solving process includes two dimensions of problem analysis and decision making. Problem analysis is the identification of those factors or forces that prevent goal attainment. Decision making is the process of determining goals and action strategies for reaching those goals. Organizational and strategic planning depend upon the processes of identifying significant problems, setting realistic goals and objectives, diagnosing the forces and influences that impact the problem, and suggesting how a specific set of interventions can solve or lessen the problem.

Problem solving is a strategic process when it includes rethinking old ideas, recognizing the reality of constant surprise and focusing upon the premise of trying to do the right things, not just doing things right.

Problem Solving Stage	Characteristics
Assess the Situation	* What is occurring that requires changes? * How can we promote significant change? * What information do we need? * How does this situation relate to our other priorities? * Where should we begin in the problem solving model? * Do we need to go through all steps or merely improve or test a strategy or implement a plan that has not yet been put into practice?
Identify the Problem	* What is actual problem or deficit condition? * What is desired that is not happening? * What is happening in terms of who is involved, where, when, what, and how much? * What objective measures, variables or indicators can we use to identify the extent of the problem?
Define Goals and Objectives	* Outcomes or results expected * Criteria or measures for judging when we are falling short of goals and objectives * What resources are available to assist us * Focus here on ends, not means or strategies
Analyze Focus	* Document past and present forces or influences that created the problem situation * Analyze the context and payoffs or benefits of past decisions impacting problem * Do a force field analysis
Generate Alternative Strategies	* Fantasize freely about a solution to the problem. Share fantasies and compare solution patterns * Brainstorm about supporting or hindering forces and brainstorm actions to support the former and remove the latter * Synthesize a list of items that appear to have some organic or logical connection. Each combination should be defined by a description of the strategy to be used
Select the Best Strategy	* Select a strategy by selecting the criteria of most benefit and least cost. Assign a value to items on list with highest benefit and least cost * Are strategies meeting goals or wants
Forecast Potential Conflicts and Problems	* Brainstorm a list of things that could go wrong * Rate potential problems in terms of probability (1 - 10) of happening or having a high potential as a threat * For items listed 5 or higher, list possible preventive measures
Test Strategies	* Test strategy in order to reveal more potential problems or clarify commitment to carry out the strategy
Write a Plan	* List all the tasks necessary to carry out strategy * Order tasks * Write a plan with primary responsibilities and deadlines
Implement and Evaluate a Plan	* Act as if your strategy or plan can be implemented * Be persistent in carrying out the strategy - errors and failures are normal * Evaluate and revise your plan according to data gathered regarding its successes and failures

Table 14-1. Characteristics of Problem Solving Cycle

Creative Problem Solving

Creative problem solving requires that we utilize both critical (evaluative, analytical, linear thinking) and imaginative (generalizing, visualizing, abstracting, intuiting) functions. Creative problem solving can be defined as the generation (creation) and evaluation (judgment) of information; thus both tasks must be synthesized in a mutually reinforcing manner during creative problem solving. However, excessive judgment during times of idea generation can hinder creative ideas, information and goal setting.

During the process of creative problem solving, the critical function must be suspended and the imaginative function stimulated; premature judgment must be avoided before numerous ideas are explored. However during latter stages of the problem solving process, evaluation and judgment are certainly needed: critical and creative functions must be made to complement and support each other.

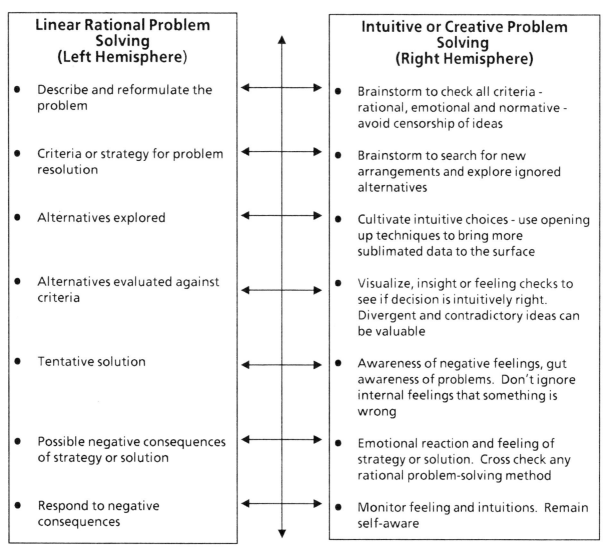

Figure 14-10. A Model of Integrated Problem Solving

369

Problem Solving Challenge	Intervention Strategies	Traps
1.Maintaining or renewing a given level of performance	*Train workers to be an active support system to motivate and ensure constant innovation *Periodic review of procedures by trusted outside consultants *Feedback from clients *Create a monitoring role *Rotate personnel to prevent burnout	* Do not rely solely upon the support and energy of the consultant. Get ownership of new practices to reduce dependency * Lack of skills training must be addressed early ÷ in order reduce frustration and discouragement
2. Creative downsizing and simplification	*Promote proactive initiatives *Study procedures used in successful cutback experiences in other systems, divisions, companies of similar industries *Brainstorm potential positive outcomes and involve everyone in creating and implementing ideas for saving money, sharing resources, providing alternative sources of support, retraining, exploring new markets, and scanning for innovative models and utilizing part-time resources *Develop a better historical understanding of previous down cycles *Make sure training and retraining programs are utilized *Explore outplacement and early retirement options	* Do not accept the reactive fatalistic position of the client * Do not support the assumption that only a few at the top should be involved in cutback decisions without getting those most affected involved
3. Helping client comply effectively with regulations and mandates	*Collect enough data on who decided regulations, and why, so that a simulation and role play can be developed *Brainstorm positive and negative consequences of regulations *Identify and explore both high and low quality ways of complying with regulations and consequences of each compliance *Explore effect of degree of compliance upon productivity and quality *Draft a memo to regulators based upon this assessment	* Help parties avoid polarization by role playing and taking the role of the other party (either regulator or regulated) in order to better understand the rationale and the impact of the regulations

Table 14-2. Problem Solving Contexts for Intervention Decision Making (37)

Problem Solving Challenge	Intervention Strategies	Traps
4. Implementing improvements	* Overcome disincentives to make improvements (eg. pain caused by drop in profits, complaints from clients, low morale, drop in quality of product, service or productivity) * Group brainstorm the positives and negatives about current operations and work life - prioritize the areas of excellence * Visualize the medium to long term future (1 to 5 years) and make concrete observations of the good things going on in the system * Form temporary task forces to define and work on planning for action on the priority images * Help organization use internal resources, HRMD department, and/or consultants to formulate concrete goals and do stepwise planning	* Be aware of organization's tendency to focus upon problem/pain instead of stimulating work with positive images of potential * Don't assume the organization or client has the skills and experience to see their future in positive times, much less plan for a new day
5. Creating conditions for innovation	* Develop a "who is good at what" task bank - put the right task or planning teams together once the problem-solving task has been analyzed * Exchange successful practice procedures, interventions, tools and ideas for innovation * Establish recognition and reward procedures which acknowledge innovations * Meet with managers to discuss providing flexible time assignments for innovation development	* Don't fall into the trap of trying to get innovator to describe their innovations * Don't give low priority to setting up innovative techniques and systems for documenting and rewarding innovation
6. Facilitating and disseminating of innovations	* Establish procedures for selecting, training and supporting the innovation documentation team who take pride in the written, visual or audio records of innovation and the importance these records might have for stimulating morale, work pride and the values of work excellence and commitment * Establish pilot projects but don't expect innovations to spread evenly throughout an organization - many pilot projects won't serve as demonstrations because innovators often won't spend time communicating what they are doing to interested visitors. Rely upon a consultant facilitator or member of documentation team who has the strategic skills essential for making linkages for potential adapters * Spend time at the demonstration site observing and probing those using the innovative procedure and then spend time with consultants exploring how the demonstration hosts achieved the change	* Don't assume that by mandating participation that everyone will then get involved in the change process at the same time * Don't assign documentation to a low priority, unskilled role * Don't assume that productive visits for demonstrating innovation just happen - plan them

Table 14-2 (cont'd)

19   SOCIO TECHNICAL SYSTEMS

Sociotechnical Systems (STS) is most often associated with Eric Trist and the Tavistock Institute of Human Relations in Great Britain. It was one of the first theories to view workgroups, organizations and society in an integrated manner. Trist discovered (38) in his studies that self-regulating work teams sharing jobs, safety and responsibilities were more effective. The key variables explaining effectiveness combine both technological and social factors. For example, at one coal plant in South Yorkshire, new technological methods of "short wall" mining, in contrast to old "long wall" methods, broadened the task structure of work to include more teamwork and less close supervision. This team responsibility, in turn, promoted even more group cohesion, self-regulating standards, and increased participation, leading to reduced absenteeism, turnover and fewer accidents.

The sociotechnical framework is a response to Taylors' techno-economic and rigidly specialized view of work design. Taylor had no concept of social systems in his model, so he used only narrow, technical measurements for work tasks. Unfortunately, he removed most of the involvement and discretion from jobs. Trist, unlike Taylor, did not ignore the fact that the relationships of appropriate technological and structural settings help create the social cultural climate for either positive or negative interpersonal relations and ultimately productivity, and effective goal attainment. Taylor ignored, unlike Trist, how the technical and social systems reinforced each other by providing the worker with more motivational involvement through a whole view of what was being done. The STS framework, thus, requires simultaneous scanning, monitoring and recognition of these mutual dependencies in order to achieve long-term results (see Figure 14-11).

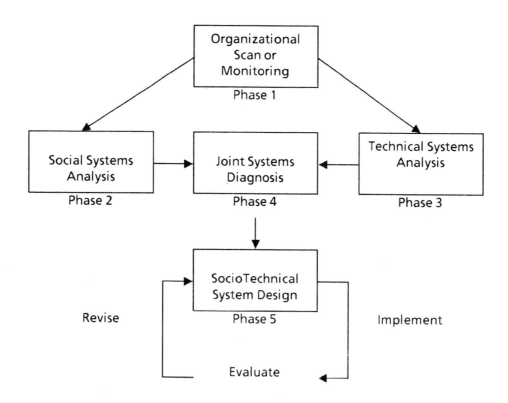

Figure 14-11 Sociotechnical System Design Processes

372

Phase 1- The Organizational Scan.

The STS Scan is used to identify the various components of the organizational system -- culture, mission, philosophy, environment, products, boundaries, problems, issues, units of operation. The scan phase views all the interrelated element that allow the organization to convert or transform inputs into outputs.

Phase 2 - Social System Analysis

The social system is the coordinating and integrating component between the technical aspects of task work and the constraint of the environment.

The social system can be diagnosed or analyzed by focusing upon describing the following dimensions:

- Roles that contribute to transformation of inputs into outputs;

- Focal or important roles that are the most crucial in the above transformation process

- The role network or the relationship between organizational roles and social roles and when, why and how the roles interact. Each role can then be evaluated (high-medium-low) in regards to the following design dimensions: skill variety, autonomy, significance, task identity, feedback and future opportunities.

Phase 3 - Technical System Analysis

The units of production operation and tasks are examined to determine the specific steps necessary to convert input to output. Within the task structure, situations are listed that could create disruptions in the transformation process -- these are called variances. The most disastrous can be labeled key variances. All variances should be controlled as close to the problem source as possible.

Phase 4 - Joint System Diagnosis

This task requires representative data collection, checking the variance problems and specific job task analysis (see Table 14-3). The data must be gathered by a cross-section of the total system through task forces, planning committees, and internal and external consultants. The executive level and strategic planning groups can review the data and offer guidance regarding design considerations.

Phase 5 - Process Evaluation and STS design

Organizational design based upon STS principles should not derive from technique or form alone. It should derive from the culture, environmental issues, problems and goals of the organization. Technique must be aligned with the cultural values that promote organizational learning, risk-taking, experimentation, entrepreneurism, flexibility in procedures, self-regulating processes and the opportunity for discretion and involvement in the job.

People work better when the organization gets out of the way and allows the worker many opportunities to satisfy their own needs and goals through autonomy, feedback task significance, skill variety and the opportunity to risk failure and still receive support.

Tasks are performed better when each worker is relatively multi-skilled, knows how to diagnose problems, and able to tolerate ambiguity and complexity.

373

The **organization** performs better when it is able to scan, diagnose, monitor and respond to threats and opportunities in its environment, creates the best fit between social-cultural and technical systems, and policies, structures and leadership support STS .

Variances	Where Occurs	How to Control	By Whom (Role)	Activities Essential to Control

Table 14-3.Joint Systems Diagnosis for Variances

Information Essential to Control	Suggestions for Job or Organization Redesign	Suggestions for Social System Design and Issues	Suggestions for Changes in Technology or Social Systems

Table 14-3. Joint Systems Diagnosis for Variances(cont'd)

Compatibility	The design must be compatible with the objectives
Minimum Critical Specificity	no more should be specified about a job than is absolutely essential
Variance Control	In programmed events or deviations from standard should be dealt with as near the point of origin as possible
Multi-Functional Principle	Design the organization so that it can achieve its objectives in more than one way
Boundary Location	Roles that require shared access to knowledge or experience should be within the same departmental boundaries
Information Flow	Information systems should be designed to provide information to the organizational unit that will take action on the basis of the information
Support Congruence	The system or social support should be designed to reinforce the behaviors that the organization structure is designed to elicit
Human Values	An objective of organization design should be to provide a high quality of work life
Completion	As a design is implemented, its consequences indicate the need for redesign

Table 14-4. STS Design Principles (39)

374

INTRODUCTION

Health promotion is one of the newest interventions that can assist the organization in its development and renewal process. This unit will explore what kind of benefits you and your organization can expect; the costs associated with ignoring personal and organizational health issues; how to develop an integrated and effective organizational health promotion effort; and finally, some things any organization should know before beginning a heath promotion effort.

ORGANIZATIONAL HEALTH PROMOTION ISSUES

Organizational health promotion is the term most often used when discussing the application of health and wellness strategies and principles, including the behavioral changes, to institutions and organizations. Health promotion can be defined as the systematic efforts by institutions and organizations to prevent illness, disease or premature death of its employees through education, behavior change, and cultural and organizational supports. Organizational health promotion is a strategic effort to reduce the health and lifestyle risks of employees through planned changes in individual behaviors and other predisposing conditions in the organization. The concern is with facilitating the process of good interaction and communication, as well as building more effective and productive organizations. Let us reduce this definition to more manageable ideas.

A health promotion program is a process set up in your organization to help your employees to achieve a healthier, more effective lifestyle. Each employee must be made aware that their everyday habits and choices (whether eating, sleeping, working, smoking, exercise) and their current physical condition (blood pressure, HDL and Cholesterol levels) will put them at risk for certain diseases. This means that lifestyle choices and action habits may increase the chances of our dying early or experiencing a lessened quality of life as we age. The three most prominent risk factors are hypertension, high cholesterol (low HDL) and smoking. Other prominent factors are diabetes, obesity, physical inactivity, poor diet, excessive alcohol consumption, and high stress. Remember that health promotion is more than risk reduction; it is a means of optimally improving the quality of your life. If we use this definition, we may also guardedly use the wellness concept. The key principle is that people, as well as all work systems, regardless of current condition, are capable of making significant improvements by using proper assessment, planning, thoughtful implementation strategies, feedback, marketing and evaluation. Wellness and health promotion efforts, therefore, are not final achievements that once reached are then self-perpetuating, but are rather part of an ongoing process that requires a resourceful, disciplined, sustained and organizationally relevant commitment. Thus, health promotion must focus upon new approaches that not only stimulate, motivate and inspire workers, but also help organizations and workers to recognize their mutual interests and the productive potential of working together.

THE BACKGROUND: LIFESTYLES, HEALTH, AND WELLNESS

The U.S. Center for Disease Control estimates that about 50% of all deaths under 65 years old are related to lifestyle excesses. This finding is supported by the 1975 Framingham Study which identified the the proportional impact of the four leading contributors to early death and diseases. The four primary contributors are (40):

1. Lifestyle   53%
2. Environment   21%
3. Heredity   16%
4. Medical care   10%

Researchers now believe that preventive, active, and integrated approaches to health promotion can have a positive influence on at least the first and last categories. Other research on accidents, suicides and homicides generally confirms the estimation of mortality for factors of social and life-style influences.

Let us not take anything for granted, but it seems fairly obvious that the place where we work, spend so much of out time and derive so much of our self-esteem, should become the primary focus of our attack. I guess a more appropriate question might be: Why has this approach not taken hold sooner and without the obvious starts and stops that we have historically observed?

The most common, traditional definition of "health" is the dictionary definition: "free from sickness." Many still harbor the inaccurate belief that if we are not sick, then we must be healthy. Personal health care is defined through formal visits to the doctor when we are sick. Virtually all health benefits are designed to reward sickness and disease, not productive health and living. Our health care system might be more accurately labeled a "disease care" system. In contrast, promoting health as wellness simply means taking an active interest in our total life and effectiveness while we are healthy. The wellness attitude requires us to identify and change lifestyle habits that place us at risk for contracting certain degenerative diseases as we age.

Since our definition of active health and wellness indicates a long-term process of learning to take personal control of one's health and well-being, slow but steady progress should not be confused with promised results of short-term fads or even with your current state of health. You may also be in excellent health without actively knowing that you are practicing a wellness lifestyle. Conversely, you may become vigorous in your pursuit of a healthy life, yet still have some health problems as a result of your heredity, poor health behaviors in early life, or lack of knowledge concerning strategies for reducing health risk factors and maintaining positive behavioral changes. For this reason, awareness through education and health assessment is only the first important step.

The goal of effective health promotion programs is to maximize flexibility, choice and personal responsibility throughout the organization. This process requires a comprehensive approach to optimal functioning, including health choices and work performance. When employees feel the negative health effects of inconsistent and unclear work policies, poorly-designed jobs and rapidly increasing stress levels, disability claims increase dramatically. In such situations, organizations should not assume that simply providing adequate insurance benefits, or adding copayments, will solve the problems of excessive health care utilization, increased health care costs, absenteeism, and turnover.

These problems are often inherent in the design of the organizational culture, policies and structures. Such problems must be addressed as leadership, management and human resources or training issues that are intimately related to other issues such as low productivity and poor work quality. This total organizational approach demands a long-range approach. Let us become proactive and not wait for a crisis that requires us to react with half-hearted and half-planned efforts and programs.

376

THE WORKPLACE HEALTH PROMOTION IMPERATIVE

The positive impact of increasing personal accountability and involvement on the overall American workforce has a long ways to go before we can let up the pressure. In fact, the momentum for a revolution in wellness is now substantial. Some of the negative statistics have motivated companies of all sizes to show an increasing interest in workplace health promotion and employee development:

> Twenty-nine million workdays are lost annually due to hypertension, stroke, and coronary heart disease; thirty percent of the 100 million U.S. workers suffer from high blood pres- sure and are risk for developing strokes, heart and/or kidney disease; over 30% of the U.S. population still smokes, and smokers have a much higher risk for many diseases; about 10% of the workforce can be classified as problem employees (40).

Health care now consumes more than one out of every nine dollars earned by the average worker, meaning that they must work over one month each year to pay these costs. Employers now pay half of the nation's health bill which accounts for 10% of the total compensation to employees. General Motors revealed that over $400 of the cost of a 1984 GM car was the result of health care costs for employees. Companies are spending over $700 million annually to replace the more than 200,000 men between the ages of 45 and 65 who are killed or disabled by coronary heart disease.

Most chief executive officers (CEOs) are concerned about upward national trends in health care costs, particularly those that impact their own company. Reports, similar to the following one from the Harvard Business Review, are difficult to ignore and are very disturbing to progressive companies.

Company expenses for health care are rising at such a fast rate that if unchecked, within eight years will eliminate all profits for the average "Fortune 500" company and the largest 250 industrials. From 1981 to 1983, the average rate of increase of health insurance premiums for these companies was a staggering 20%, and health care costs amounted to 24% of average corporate profits after taxes. Although the rates of cost increase moderated in 1984, their growth was still much higher than that of the Consumer Price Index (41).

THE COSTS OF IGNORING INVESTMENT IN PEOPLE

Let us document some of costs that result from ignoring this investment in people: costs related to salary, medical treatment, rehabilitation, survivor benefits, workers compensation, distress, pay for temporary workers, overtime for others, training, retraining, rehabilitation for workers who resume work after long absences, turnover, recruitment, selection, hiring replacements and administrative overhead. By investing in human resources and health promotion activities, organizations can better control their risk factors associated with disease and productivity sapping costs.

The following factors reduce personal life expectancy, worker morale, organizational productivity, and the quality of life for all workers: eating, smoking or drinking excessively; failing to adequately communicate or to resolve work conflicts; designing jobs poorly or giving poor performance. We cannot continue to ignore the consequences of our limited investments in people's health and well-being without creating such unwanted products as troubled employees and lowered productivity.

377

Two conservative estimates of the overall financial impact of troubled employees on the average company are that:

1. 18% of any workforce causes 25% loss of productivity.
2. 10% of any workforce is causes 37.5% loss of productivity.

These productivity percentage estimates are based on such measurable factors as absenteeism, sick leave, accidents, and rising health benefits claims. The estimates do not include the hidden costs of poor decisions, corporate theft, decrease in quality of work produced, early retirement, and workers' compensation claims.

THE BENEFITS OF INVESTING IN PEOPLE

The organizational benefits are: creating a more satisfied and productive workforce; reducing health care costs, disability and worker's compensation claims that are associated with life-style related behavior; and reductions in employee turnover, absenteeism, poor morale, negative worker attitudes, and dysfunctional group norms. In the final analysis the cultural norms of the work environment and the standards of acceptable managerial behavior will support or detract from a more healthy, effective, and productive orientation. This organizational support will then help sustain positive lifestyle changes.

By building a strong health promotion effort, human resources, and an employee assistance programs can begin to work together to reduce the many costs associated with poor productivity, health/life-style excesses, and employee problems. The savings from reducing poor health, ineffective performance, lost productivity and personal distress can never be measured precisely. But we can measure and evaluate some of the savings that will have a positive effect on work group and overall productivity .

THREE LEVELS OF ORGANIZATION HEALTH PROMOTION

There are three levels of organizational health promotion. Let us briefly review these stages.

The first level is focused upon awareness and information contained in introductory talks about health promotion or payroll stuffers on changing negative health behaviors.

The second level is general health information, along with structured programs, i.e., hypertension control screenings and Health Risk Appraisals (HRA) that serve to determine risk factors or predisposition to disease. This motivational level begins to help the individual to consolidate some of the information gained through awareness and attempts to provide a foundation for successful behavior change at a later time.

The third level is composed of fairly comprehensive health promotion programs that focus upon intervention systems for ongoing behavioral change. These include enlarged opportunities for promoting change through human resource incentives, rewards and supporting policies. This level is also concerned with organizational change, organizational work redesign, cultural change, organizational philosophy, values, norms, and management styles.

We must learn how to make our organizational cultures promote positive values, health promotion and life-long personal, organizational and community wellness. We must become more aware of the destructive trends that impact society, organizations and individual lives. We can accomplish these productivity enhancing goals only by viewing the organization as an interdependent, open system that has structural, policy and behavioral health components.

COMPONENTS OF HEALTH PROMOTION

Health promotion planners often develop too narrow a focus for organizational wellness system activities. To fully understand a comprehensive perspective, we have listed below the main categories and programs that any health promotion system should provide. Please feel free to expand upon any of the following topics and continue to supplement them throughout the course (40):

1. Self-Care Practices
   A. Breast Self-Exam.
   B. Blood pressure self-monitoring.
   C. Healthy Back Care.

2. Reduced Use of Harmful Substances
   A. Alcohol education.
   B. Drug Abuse Awareness.
   C. Smoking Cessation.

3. Individual Safety Practices
   A. Workplace Safety Practices.
   B. First Aid and CPR.
   C. Safe Driving Practices.

4. Coping Skills
   A. Stress Management.
   B. Time Management.
   C. Positive Self-Image.

5. Fitness
   A. Aerobic Exercise.
   B. Fitness Testing.
   C. Weight Reduction.

6. Nutrition
   A. Diet Analysis.
   B. Nutrition Education and Modification.

7. Appropriate Use of the Health System Benefits
   A. Health Insurance Utilization Education.
   B. Benefits Review.

8. Patient Compliance
   A. Diabetes Control.
   B. Hypertension Control.
   C. Heart Disease Education.

9. Consumer Education
   A. Food Label Reading.
   B. Seat Belt Safety.
   C. Athletic Equipment Education (i.e., shoes).

10. Medical Screenings
   A. Health Risk Appraisals.
   B. Multiphasic Screenings.

379

C. Cholesterol Testing.

11. Workplace Policies
    A. Smoke-free Workplace.
    B. Personnel Policies (i.e., sick leave).
    C. Healthy Foods Program.
    D. Reward Systems.

CAN HEALTH PROMOTION AT WORK REALLY WORK?

As an environment for promoting health lifestyle changes, the workplace represents advantages not found in other settings. Some of the advantages detailed by one research team are included in the following:

1. The employees represent a captive audience. They can be contacted and recruited at little cost to the employer.

2. Workplace populations include individuals normally unlikely to seek professional help for personal problems.

3. Work settings are most often more convenient for participants than community- based facilities.

4. The social and organizational characteristics of the workplace may increase treatment effectiveness.

5. Workplace programs, done well, can reduce health care costs. This can benefit both employer and employee.

6. Health promotion programs are inexpensive, yet often viewed as an employee benefit (40).

ASSESSING HP NEEDS AND INTERESTS

The primary purpose of this first step is to gather data describing employee health, health care costs, absenteeism, and turnover. These utilization and expenditure patterns are examined along with employee attitudes toward their work and proposed health promotion activities. Management involvement is essential during this early developmental phase.

ESTABLISHING GOALS FOR HP EFFORTS

Clearly written goals are essential for effective implementation and long-term evaluation of company health promotion efforts. These goals can be expressed in numerous ways. One goal might be to decrease the utilization of health care resources by X% over the next several years. Another might be to involve a certain percentage of the workforce in one or more activities during a given year. If the company wants to implement a smoke-free workplace, the goal might be to reduce the number of total smokers through smoking cessation activities prior to the new policy taking effect. Goals of the program must reflect some of the reasons why the company originally began a health promotion program. Five of the most often cited reasons are:

1. To help contain health care costs,
2. To increase productivity and morale,
3. To better manage human resources,
4. To comply with health and safety regulations, and

5. To foster a better public and organizational image.

PLANNING THE HP EFFORT

Preparatory activities will center on a variety of critical details and questions: How much money, time, and human resources will be allotted to health promotion? What programs will be conducted? When and where will they be held? Who will deliver them? How will employees be attracted to these activities? How can quality be assured? What evaluation criteria will be used to measure effectiveness? How can community resources be utilized?

IMPLEMENTATION OF HP ACTIVITIES

If the groundwork has been properly laid, the program director will be able to concentrate on logistical details and intercompany marketing efforts to maximize program involvement. The range of interventions coming under a broad definition of health promotion or wellness include: employee assistance programs, health promotion newsletters, back injury prevention, first aid, CPR, weight reduction, nutrition, smoking cessation, implementation of a smoke-free workplace, safety programs, cancer screenings, high blood pressure programs, stress management, physical fitness, health risk appraisals, and many more that meet the criteria specified.

EVALUATING YOUR HP PROGRAM

Evaluation actually begins during the planning phase because decisions made at that time will determine how later measurements of success or failure are applied.

Voluntary Health Risk Appraisals (HRA) are commonly given to all interested employees at the beginning of a program. At the end of the first year, another HRA is given and the two are compared. The results answer the question, "Have participants significantly reduced one or more risk factors as a result of health promotion activities"? Is there a difference between those who participated in health promotion activities and those who only took the HRAs? Is the HRA itself an intervention? Do participants' risk factor reduction scores correlate with reduced utilization of health care resources? This last question may take several years to answer.

Pen and Pencil Questionnaires are also frequently used, often concurrently with HRAs, to evaluate attitudes and behaviors of participating and non-participating employees. Questions may include, "How did you like this activity?" "How much has this intervention effected your behavior?" "Was it long enough?" "How effective were the communications announcing the program?"

The two questions that each program director must ask to evaluate health promotion efforts are, "Is this Program effective?" and "What is (or will be) its cost-benefit?" The question of effectiveness will involve a broad evaluation of program factors, including improved, long-term organizational functioning, increased morale, reduced absenteeism, and turnover. These factors do influence the bottom line, but cost influences are seen over a longer time frame. The keys to successful cost effectiveness are diligence, patience, monitoring and feedback.

CONTRIBUTING CAUSES OF HEALTH CARE COST INCREASES

Health care costs have outgained the annual inflation rate for at least the last five years. Health care amounted to 4.4% of the GNP in 1950, and by 1984 this figure had risen to almost 11% or $388 billion. If this trend continues at 10% annually, (a figure well below the recent rate of increase), the U.S. will be spending $1.7 trillion per year on health care at the end of the century, or almost $5,500 per person (41). The following are among the factors contributing to the upward trend in health care costs and have led us to where we are today.

1. An increasing proportion of the American workforce now has medical coverage.

2. Benefit and reimbursement levels have increased for most employees in the last decade due to collective bargaining and the need to attract and retain good employees.

3. The traditional third party payer process (i.e., insurance carriers) does not hold the consumers of health care resources directly accountable, resulting in over-utilization.

4. A portion of the cost for Medicare and Medicaid patients has been shifted to the private sector. In hospitals, prospective payment (a predetermined amount based on the diagnosis) for Medicare patients has generally led to more costly hospital stays for regular insurance patients (often called "cost-shifting").

5. Medical malpractice litigation against physicians and medical institutions has tended to produce a defensive style of medical practice often characterized by over- utilization of laboratory and other services to prevent lawsuits.

6. Technology-intensive health services keep people alive longer at a higher cost, and with technology, equipment, and facilities that quickly become obsolete.

HEALTH PROMOTION AS COST-CONTAINMENT

Health promotion as a health care cost containment tool can best be viewed as a company investment paying long-term dividends. One researcher states that "organizations seeking only short-term solutions to the health care cost crisis, and failing to invest some of those savings in long-range programs such as health promotion, will find themselves on a gradient of escalating health care costs equal to that preceding the cost containment effort" (41). The cost containment curve will abate only when a company reinvests wisely in health promotion.

The research evidence is now accumulating to support the belief that work- place health promotion can produce economic savings for employers. Two recent literature reviews, have found evidence that a number of programs can save employers money by reducing health care, disability, or absenteeism costs. Some of these type programs include the following: stress management, alcohol and drug abuse control, hypertension control, colorectal and breast cancer screening, smoking cessation, physical fitness, weight management, nutrition, and back injury prevention. However, other researchers are quick to point out that most of the data relating to cost are descriptive in nature and are not derived from long-term, controlled studies. This is a common weakness of work place change efforts in that program implementers are more concerned with obtaining results rather than using scientific methods

HEALTH PROMOTION TRENDS IN THE WORKPLACE

Most of the comprehensive programs for health promotion occur in large companies where resources are available. Proportionally, small companies have been hit just as hard, or harder by skyrocketing health care costs. A great need exists to apply the lessons learned by large companies to companies with less than 200 employees, which make up over 90% of all corporations in the U.S.

Another trend will be a greater diagnosis of organizational systems and cultural issues for evaluating the needs and readiness of a company for health promotion. Some health promotion programs have failed because of negative or adversarial relations between labor and management. Better knowledge and measurement of the cultural factors affecting health promotion is imperative. The near future also indicates a closer link between long-term cost management efforts and health promotion. Employers are beginning to realize that for any cost management effort to work in the long run, employees must ultimately play a more responsible and enlarged role in their own lifestyle decisions and in health care.

A FINAL WORD

The premise that guides this section and this book is that we must learn to strategically identify potential problems and intervene to insure personal and organizational productivity. Effectively managed organizations must recognize that the growing health promotion movement is neither a fad nor an extravagance. Health promotion is here to stay as an important component of any optimally-functioning organization. The insurance industry is one that is taking a particularly strong leadership role in this area.

Not many years ago, workplace health promotion programs were begun because they seemed like a nice benefit to provide, or were "a good idea at the time." No good data or proven formulas existed to draw from or model after. Now, employers as well as health promotion professionals know that the evidence of investing in comprehensive health promotion adds up to increased productivity through reduced costs and improved performance. We will explore some of this data in future chapters. Subsequent follow-ups of these early efforts reveal that a "win-win" outcome for organizational health promotion is possible, even predictable, when done correctly. Health promotion in the workplace can be a valuable employee benefit as well as a crucial cost containment strategy.

CHAPTER FIFTEEN
ORGANIZATIONAL DEVELOPMENT CONSULTANTS

1   BUSINESS MANAGEMENT CONSULTANTS... Introduction

The world of modern business has grown increasingly complex and the challenges facing today's manager is quite different from even a few years ago. This has led to a growth in the use of the business consultant, someone who brings unique expertise and skills into the contemporary business organization to help it solve problems and plan for an uncertain future. A skilled and knowledgeable consultant can significantly aid management in making better decisions to meet the future.

SOME OF THE REASONS BUSINESSES FAIL ARE:

- While their founders have entrepreneurial drive and vision, they do not have the skills necessary to manage a modern business;

- The businesses are underfunded and their owners do not know how to raise additional capital;

- The business environment presents unforeseen problems (such as market competition or rapidly changing economic factors) that demand a quick and correct response.

A business consultant can be helpful in assisting management in overcoming these failures by providing skills and knowledge in areas which the modern generalist manager is lacking. A basic and practical definition of consultant is,

"anyone who possesses skills, abilities, or knowledge you need but do not have".

You might think of a consultant as a "tool", the purpose of which is to help you accomplish a specific task. Another role of the consultant is a "problem-solver", also a "teacher". A consultant can not only solve your immediate problems, but also teach you how to manage these problems in the future.

BENEFITS OF HIRING A CONSULTANT

Aside from helping solve specific problems which confront a business, consultants also offer several other benefits:

- A consultant brings a measure of objectivity to an organization and its problems. Most often there is no "hidden agenda", and the consultant can render impartial judgment. This is particularly important if, in solving the problem, reorganization is likely to occur, or people will loose their jobs.

- A consultant (hopefully) will have the most current, "state-of-the-art" knowledge of the field, and oftentimes, it is more cost effective to "rent" this knowledge for a particular problem.

- A consultant may bring a nontraditional creativity to the problem, one which may not automatically surface in a traditional setting.

- A consultant can also offer "anticipatory consulting" in addition to solving a particular issue or problem. This form of consulting allows management to utilize the services of a consultant to chart future directions, anticipate problems before they emerge, and plan more effectively for the future.

Hiring a consultant is not without risks. You may find resistance among workers in dealing with an "outsider" who is reported to be an "expert" in their line of work. Consultants are costly, and can waste funds if the end results are not achieved. Consultants may select a solution to the problem which is not feasible, or may not be practical to implement. Consultants are not apt to have as much invested in maintaining the "status quo" as an insider, and this may be perceived as a threat. Consultants are almost surely to introduce change to the existing environment, and this may increase the natural resistance to any proposed changes.

The selection process is as important, or even more so, as the actual work completed by the consultant. Please see the discussions on consultant selection.

2 ORGANIZATION DEVELOPMENT CONSULTANTS - WHAT THEY DO

OD consultants act as change agents in the Organization Development process within organizations. They do so to help these organizations increase effectiveness and profitability. They strive to anticipate, prevent and identify problems, reduce conflict, and impact the overall culture and process of the workplace.

OD consultants concentrate on the process of changing systems within companies. However, in addition, OD consultants must work with people to influence decisions which aid in making things happen and getting them done. They must act as intermediaries between groups in conflict, bargaining and negotiating to find mutually beneficial solutions to problems that prevent people from working together cooperatively.

OD consultants create, plan, initiate, promote and support the change process; implement or institutionalize programs; advise and sell top management on programs; and aid groups in working together as a team to implement approved plans.

An OD consultant applies a systematic, analytical approach to problems, and presents his findings from a senior management perspective. Consultants concentrate on a cost/benefit perspective, following a flexible format of presenting their final analysis:

- Define the problem; quantify the problem's size and scope; quantify its future magnitude

- Select objectives and measurement criteria

- Describe all worthwhile alternative approaches

- Evaluate benefits; quantify where possible

- Identify "political" and other constraints on alternatives

- Divide recommendations into "actions" and "further study" classifications and summarize

NECESSARY SKILLS TO BE A CONSULTANT

- Judgment
- Sensitivity, a caring humanistic attitude
- Diplomacy, communications skills with different types of people
- Pro-activity
- Problem solving/analytical skills
- Personally be a good manager
- Organization savvy - seeing the large picture
- Time management
- Patience and persistence
- Sales and marketing skills

3 ROLES OF ORGANIZATION DEVELOPMENT CONSULTANTS

As change agents, OD consultants have many roles: interventionists, planner, teacher, trainer, facilitator, mediator, clinical sociologist, OD specialist, priest, conflict negotiator, process helper, diagnostician, problem solver, idea generator, devil's advocate, counselor, psychologist, catalyst.

There are two types of consultants -- inside and outside. Inside consultants are employees of the organization; outside consultants are affiliated with consulting firms or are independently employed. Both types are used as change agents in the Organization Development process, called into an organization or specific department of an organization to assist in this process.

Inside Consultant

An inside consultant is an employee of the organization, works within the framework of the organization to affect change. As such this person enjoys certain advantages over an outside consultant:

+ Knows the company practices, culture and systems
+ Knows where to solicit support; whom to enlist as proponents of a program; where the power lies
+ Knows where those with similar interests can work effectively together, or who will present resistance
+ More apt to be trusted; already has established a rapport with fellow employees
+ Represents a 'company team member' who shares common goals and objectives, and is viewed as 'being in the same boat'

However, an inside consultant does face certain adversities:

- May lack experience in dealing with difficult organizational problems
- Background may be exclusive to one area; may not posses the scope of understanding and available resources to effectively solve any problem
- May be perceived unfavorably by his colleagues; if so, his judgment will not be valued or accepted
- If he has an image of incompetence, is mistrusted, or appears to exhibit a lackadaisical attitude within the organization, the managers, supervisors and peers affected will never agree to his programs for change and his credence as a consultant will be nil

Outside Consultant

An outside consultant either works for a consulting firm or is independently employed. An outside consultant is hired by the organization to perform any number of activities. There are a set of advantages and disadvantages associated with this position also:

+ Brings objectivity to the problems within the company
+ Has a fresh perspective, is uninfluenced by politics or other elements which prevail within the organization
+ May be more well-versed in adverse situations
+ May be seen within the organization as more credible when being confronted with embedded cultural attitudes such as groupthink
+ Being independent from the organization, the outside consultant owes no allegiance to any party

+ An outside consultant's reputation is not at stake
+ An outside consultant can demonstrate his expertise without suffering the adverse ramifications of failure that may impede his progression within the organization
+ An outside consultant's speciality lies in handling difficult problems, and he is knowledgeable in this area

- May not be privy to the 'undercurrents' or ulterior motives that an insider would know about
- Does not generally have an understanding of the company's culture, systems and inner workings
- Does not have to be committed to the changes that may be implemented; does not have to work through the difficulties that result or suffer the negative consequences

4 SELECTING A BUSINESS CONSULTANT

As mentioned in the introduction, the selection of a consultant is as important as the actual work performed by the consultant. In some cases even more so. Selecting the proper skills and knowledge is key to correcting and overcoming the problem or issue. We will attempt to provide you with some helpful hints for hiring a business consultant.

Needs Assessment: The first step in determining if you really need a consultant is to conduct a needs assessment. This process forces you to follow a formal procedure in determining your requirements, rather than following intuition (which may or may not be correct).

In performing a needs assessment, you first examine the situation currently confronting the business:

1 **Describe the current situation, or "what is".**

   The current situation is determined from an examination of data, consisting of present and past performance statistics. This will show trends, history, and allow you to evaluate statistically where you are now.

2 **Determine the goal, or "what should be".**

   By examining past historical data, you can better determine and set realistic goals for the future. You can also perform "benchmarking", or a review of performance data from other companies in your industry.

   Now you can determine if there is a "gap" between "what is" and "what should be". If a gap does exist, a **need** has been determined.

3 **Define the performance standards which, when met, will signal that you achieved the "what should be".**

   When examining 1)current situation and 2) organizational goals, you will define performance standards which bring you to the desired state. These standards should be realistic, observable, and quantifiable. These performance standards will be helpful in determining the success of your business consultant.

You have now uncovered a "need" within your organization. If you do not have the managerial, financial, technical, or human resources to achieve the goals, you may "rent" these resources in the form of a business consultant.

Defining the kind of services you need to have performed will determine the kind of relationship you establish with a consultant. A short term relationship will be required if your problem is an unusual one which will not likely recur. A long term relationship will be required if your problem is more complex. In a short term relationship, all you need be concerned with is determining whether the consultant has the required skills, knowledge and abilities to fix your problem. However, in building a long term relationship, you must be concerned with much more, such as the possession of technical skills, personality, ability to work with the employees and you, and your comfort level with and trust of the consultant.

Sources for Finding Consultants: Depending on the type of service you require, you can find consultants through the Yellow Pages, newspaper ads, friends, and professional associations. Through the Yellow Pages and newspaper you can find such services as building maintenance or lawn care. You may try friends and professional acquaintances who have similar business requirements as you and have utilized the professional services of a business consultant. (Remember, however, that what worked for them is not guaranteed to work in your situation.) Many professional associations provide referral services for consultants with specific skills and abilities. (In this case, remember that membership to a professional association does not always indicate professional accomplishment.) It will be important to interview several consultants prior to hiring.

Initial Contact: When you initially call a consultant, you might want to mention any referrals (friend, associate, professional association). This will convey to the potential consultant that you are not just "shopping around", and lend a sense of seriousness to the conversation. You will also want to convey that you are not looking for "free advice", and are seeking an information interview with him/her in order to ascertain their suitability to help you. This interview will serve both parties to determine a "fit" between what is needed and what is available.

Prior to meeting with the consultant, you will want to check his/her references and review a current resume. If the individual is licensed or is a member of a professional association, check with the licensing authority or the executive director of the professional association to determine if any complaints have been lodged against him or her. You may also ask the consultant to provide you with a list of previous clients, and contact them (unless asked specifically not to by the consultant).

Initial Interview: This is extremely important in the selection process. No matter how good the individual sounds over the phone, or how good the references turned out, it is imperative to have a "personal interview" with an individual with whom you are going to trust a business problem, inside information about your company, and establish a business relationship which will affect your business. You may use any of the interview formats discussed below, structured, unstructured interview, or stress interview.

> **Structured Interview** makes use of predetermined questions. This allows for standardization of all interviews, allowing comparable data to be reviewed. It is helpful to keep the interviewer on track, and useful if more than one person is doing the interviewing. Some questions you might want to ask are:
>
> Professional expertise questions - does the candidate possess the essential knowledge to solve your problem?
>
> Task-simulation questions - does the candidate possess the theoretical and practical knowledge necessary?
>
> Work willingness questions - is the candidate available?
>
> **Unstructured Interview** consists of open-ended general questions, which get the candidate to discuss how he/she may be helpful to your company. Some questions are:
>
> What sort of things has he/she accomplished for other companies?
>
> Describe your goals as a consultant, tell me a little about yourself.

It is helpful to combine structured and unstructured interviews, to ensure comparability among the candidates.

Stress Interview places the consultant deliberately under a great deal of stress. This lessens the chances of the candidate presenting a facade, increasing the chances of presenting the real person. This is particularly helpful if the project will be one of high stress. Some ways to create stress are:

Conduct the interview in your office, not the consultants.

Have inadequate lighting in the office.

Have two or more interviewers.

Use of argumentative and provocative questions.

There is some risk with utilizing the stress interview, you might "turn off" the candidate, one who would have been useful to the project, or the data received is not always related to the project at hand.

Whatever method, or combination of interview formats, you still run into the situation where both parties "put forth their best foot". This personal interview does not guarantee a proper selection, however it does give you more data to work with in the selection process.

There is no real determination as to how many candidates you should interview. Interviewing is costly and time-consuming, and the following guidelines may help:

- Schedule as many interviews as possible in your given time and money constraints. Schedule a representative number of interviews for those available.

- Do not stop the interviewing process with the first candidate, even if the fit appears to be perfect. The remaining consultants you interview can serve as backup, in case your first choice is unavailable. Do not make a hasty decision.

- Keep interviewing until you find the right consultant. If you do not find a suitable candidate within a reasonable time, examine the situation to determine if your goals and problems are well defined and are being presented accurately.

It is usually best to meet at the candidate's office. This allows you to observe the individual in their setting, noting such things as:

- The general feel of the office, tensed or relaxed

- Is the office busy - this could indicate a successful business, or the inability to take on more work

- Does the candidate keep you waiting beyond the time scheduled for the interview

- Does the candidate interrupt your interview to take routine calls - this could indicate an inability to prioritize tasks, or a lack of commitment.

While these things are not related to the project or task, they add to your overall initial impressions of each candidate, adding to the data for selection criteria.

The following areas should be covered in the initial interview. Remember that the purpose of this is to get as much information as you can about this consultant and his/her ability to help you solve your business problems.

Problem Description: You will want to begin by describing your company and its current situation. Give a thorough description of the needs assessment process and the resulting needs / problem statement. You will want to give the consultant as much information as required to make a judgment about his/her ability to solve your problem. Of course the risk here is giving too much information, which could end up in the hands of competitors, on the other hand not giving enough information may prevent the consultant from realistically assessing the situation in order to be successful.

Education: Consultants are likely to point out their official certifications or past education/achievements as proof of being a legitimate consultant. However, anyone can be a consultant provided they have acquired, from whatever source, skills, abilities, or knowledge that someone else needs. The issue of education is important, but if the consultant does not possess the skills, knowledge and abilities you need, advanced degrees will be of little value. Of even greater value than advanced degrees is continuing education or professional development involvement, indicating a current knowledge of the field.

Past Consulting Projects: You will want the candidate to describe past consulting projects which are similar to yours. You should note that you understand the confidentiality issue, and that you expect full confidentiality with your situation. A consultant may not be able to discuss many projects, perhaps being new to the field and few previous consulting experiences, or for ethical reasons unable to discuss previous projects.

Computers: Consultants may or may not have the resources of a computer. This is only important in relation to the problem to be solved. While modern computer technology can promote increased productivity, it may not be necessary for your project. A computer can be helpful in making a consultant maximally productive in such functions as word processing, project planning and management, and economic forecasting. It could perhaps reduce the overall cost of the project, if a "canned" proposal already resides on the computer, allowing the consultant to "customize" to your own project, without "recreating the wheel".

Negotiating the Fee: Having determined that both parties feel there is a "fit", the matter of fees must be dealt with. You will want to determine the following information:

- What is the consultant's usual billing structure? If billing is by the hour, what is the standard hourly fee? Are there any variations in billing methods? How are the hours counted?

- What, if any, is the expected retainer? How often will you be billed?

- To what extent will the fee be based on your level of satisfaction?

- Will there be any penalties for late project completion?

- What, in the consultant's best estimate, will the total project cost? The initial cost estimate should be used only as a guideline to provide comparative data with all candidates.

393

Letter of Agreement: Once you have selected the consultant you are going to hire, you will want to firm up your agreement in the form of a written letter. This letter will outline the agreement between your company and the consultant, and include the following areas:

- General problem statement
- Description of tasks you want the consultant to accomplish
- Time frames for task and project completion
- General description of the performance standard
- Penalty date and description
- Data confidentiality clause
- Fees, and fee schedule, description for handling any unforeseen expenses, and total estimated fee
- Termination clause

Hiring a consultant is not an easy matter, nor is it guaranteed to solve your organizational problems. However, the more systematic and careful you are in the selection process, the more successful the encounter may be.

HELPFUL HINTS WHEN HIRING AN OUTSIDE CONSULTANT

- Never allow consultants to make decisions for you

- Do not use consultants to arbitrate disputes between staff members of your organization

- Do not assign the consultant to make personnel evaluations

- Do not use the consultant to perform direct labor

- Use the consultant to help you define, outline and routinize the tasks to be done

- Use the consultant as an idea generator and devil's advocate

- Teach the consultant as much about your business as you can

- Continually ask questions of your consultant

- Make clear your expectations and what you hope will be done

- Do not be afraid to discuss how much time and money is involved

- Remember that without your cooperation, the consultant can not do his job

5   WORKING WITH THE ORGANIZATIONAL DEVELOPMENT CONSULTANT

Organizational Orientation: It is now determined what the consultant is going to do for your company and when. Now is the time to orient the employees with whom the consultant will be interacting. You may want to schedule orientation meetings with the consultant and each group with whom he/she is going to work. Some concerns in this area are:

● You don't need to tell your employees everything, just enough to provide a general overview of the project and why you have selected a consultant to work on the project.

● Do not promise any changes to be made after project completion, this may lead to the creation of expectations which cannot be met. It can also create unnecessary fear.

● Understand the "grapevine", or informal form of organizational communication, and how word of the consultants involvement will spread throughout the organization.

Monitoring the Consultant's Performance: During the hiring process (see Selecting a Consultant), you reached certain agreements with the consultant, as outlined in the Letter of Agreement. The areas of monitoring are timeframes, costs, and quality of activities. The consultant should be submitting reports on a regular basic outlining the services which are being performed, the costs and timeframes, and the outcomes (if applicable at this time). You should be meeting with the consultant regularly to review these items. By doing so, if there are areas which are not meeting the agreed upon performance standards, action can be taken <u>during the project</u> to correct. This is far more advantageous than waiting until project end to find 1)the project is not complete at the required time, 2) unforseen expenses drove the estimated cost of the project much higher, or 3) the quality of the consultant's work was not as expected.

While quality of the consultant may be difficult to judge (as you did hire him/her because you did not have the set of skills, abilities, or knowledge to solve a particular problem), you should concentrate on the process involved and on the nature of the output. Are the agreed upon tasks being undertaken and reported? Is the output something which you will be able to implement? Will you be able to use the output in the future without the aid of the consultant?

Evaluating Proposed Solutions: The consultant can offer at least two courses of action: to do something, or to do nothing. While the latter is unlikely, it may be the best solution. However, typically, there will be a recommendation to do something. With this, there are two recommendations the consultant may make: a single course of action, or a choice of alternative solutions. The original problem statement will usually dictate the choice here.

In evaluating each proposed solution, you must understand that each will have a set of pros and cons. You will need to utilize the consultant's expertise and past experiences to help you see both sides of each solution. You will select a solution, based upon the determination that it will offer the best possible consequence or outcome. For each proposed solution, ask the following:

1) Does this proposed course of action really solve the problem?

2) Can we implement this proposed course of action with a minimal of undesirable consequences or side effects?

3) Can the company afford this solution? Do we have the financial and human resources as well as the time to successfully implement it?

If the answer to any of these questions is no, reject that possible solution and move on to another. Select the solution to which the answers are yes.

Pilot Test: You may consider a pilot test of the selected solution. This will allow you to study the feasibility of the solution throughout the entire organization. The objective is to observe the program on a smaller scale, and to introduce changes as needed to fine-tune the procedures before investing the larger sums of money necessary for full implementation.

Final Report: The consultant should provide you with a final report outlining the project and all of its components. This should include the activities / services performed, the results or outcomes, the proposed solutions, and a detailed description of the selected solution. It should also include an implementation plan for you to follow.

Your final evaluation of the consultant should be in the areas of the Consulting Process and the Final Report. In evaluating the Consulting Process, you may ask some of the following questions:

- If the consultant did research, was it rushed? Did it show a familiarity with the research literature? Did the consultant seem to know what he/she was talking about? Did he/she explain it to you in language you could understand?

- Was each step of the consulting process documented? Did the consultant appear to cut corners and take shortcuts?

- Did the number of options generated by the consultant seem appropriate for the problem?

- Did the consultant appear open to your suggestions and input, or was there resistance to input from other sources?

In the evaluation of the Final Report, you may ask:

- Did the solution or options suggested in the consultant's final report actually solve the problem?

- Were the solutions feasible, or were some of them unrealistic in terms of your organization's resources?

- Did the consultant's final report address your needs, or seem to be an advertisement for future services?

- Does the final report seem to represent fair value for the dollars spent?

And finally,

- Consider your original need and the problem that emerged. Do you feel that the consultant has effectively helped you to deal with the problem? **Is your business better off now than before?**

6 FAILURE PATTERNS FOR OD CONSULTANTS

Organization Development consultants do fail from time to time in their role within organizations. Here are a few patterns generally found when an OD consultant, both inside and outside, fail.

- Failure to obtain and work through a contract (applicable to both external and internal consultants)

- Failure to establish specific goals for efforts and interventions

- Failure to demonstrate sufficient courage to confront the organization and key managers in particular

- Failure to be willing to try something new

- Failure to determine the identity of the real client

- Failure to work with real organizational needs

- Failure to implement genuine Organization Development (by becoming involved in marketing rather than OD, for example)

- Failure to develop viable options

- Failure to coordinate with the organization (by circumventing the thinking and readiness of the personnel)

- Failure to work with the organization as it is rather than as the consultant would like it to be

- Failure to measure or evaluate OD activities

- Failure to plan for and avoid managerial abdication

- Failure to solve problems (by becoming involved in "quick fixes")

- Failure to specify both short- and long-term goals for the intervention

- Failure to be honest about what needs to be done and why

- Failure to determine whose needs are being met

- Failure to plan for and build toward the client managers' ownership for the OD effort

- Failure to escape entrapment in the "mystique" of OD, which leads to a distorted interpretation of the OD process

- Failure to tailor the effort to the jointly analyzed needs of the specific organization.

Combating Failure Patterns

The consultant who conscientiously attends to the following activities may have greater success in overcoming failure patterns:

- Building a strategy -- systematically outlining the specific activities and project time-lines

- Establishing a project management and modeling skills -- this provides an illustration of the ways in which the various interventions tie together and build on each other

- Engaging in joint planning with prospective clients -- during the proposal development and prior to the launch of a long-term effort

- Incorporating review and evaluation sessions -- provides for periodic review and evaluation sessions in which activities are examined

- Using consulting teams -- directly or indirectly involve one or more fellow professionals to allow more awareness of and sensitivity to potential failure patterns

- Participating in OD activities -- participate in the application of the interventions used

- Ensuring professional development -- continually update skills and conceptual framework

- Resting and Relaxing -- be familiar with different approaches to stress and peak periods away from OD activity

BIBLIOGRAPHY/REFERENCES

ORGANIZATIONAL DEVELOPMENT

INTRODUCTION

(1)   Beckhard, Richard. **Organization Development: Strategies and Models** (Reading, MA: Addison-Wesley Publishing, 1969)

(2)   Schmuck, Richard and Miles, Matthey. **Organization Development in Schools** (Palo Alto, CA: National Press Books, 1971)

(3)   French, Wendell and Bell, Cecil, Jr. **Organization Development** (Englewood Cliffs, NJ: Prentice-Hall, 1978)

(4)   Bennis, Warren G. **Organization Development: Its Nature, Origins, and Prospects** (Reading, MA: Addison-Wesley Publishing, 1969)

CHAPTER 13

(5)   Huse, Edgar F. and Cummings, Thomas G. **Organization Development and Change** Third Edition (St. Paul, MN: West Publishing Co., 1985)

(6)   McGregor, Douglas. **The Human Side of Enterprise** (New York: McGraw-Hill, 1960)

(7)   Gutknecht, Douglas B. and Miller, Janet R **The Organizational and Human Resources Sourcebook** (Lanham, MD: University Press of America, 1986:36-37; 110-115)

(8)   Johnston, Joseph S. and Associated. **Educating Managers: Executive Effectiveness Through Liberal Learning** (San Francisco: Jossey-Bass Publishers, 1986)

(9)   Kirkpatrick, Donald L. **How to Manage Change Effectively** (San Francisco: Jossey-Bass, 1988:)

(10)   Waterman, Robert **The Renewal Factor** (New York: Banham Books, 1988: 132-135)

(11)   Doyle, Patrick. "Considerations for Managers in Implementing Change" **The 1985 Annual: Developing Human Resources** (San Diego, CA: University Associates, 1985)

(12)   Kanter, Rosabeth Moss. **The Change Masters: Innovation for Productivity in the American Corporation** (New York: Simon & Schuster, 1983)

(13)   Huse, Edgar F. and Cummings, Thomas G. **Organization Development and Change** Third Edition

(14)   Lewin, Kurt. **Field Theory in Social Sciences** (New York: Harper & Row, 1951)

(15)   Huse, Edgar F. and Cummings, Thomas G. **Organization Development and Change** Third Edition

(16)   **Ibid**

(17)   French, W.L. and Bell, C.H. **Organization Development: Behavioral Science Interventions for Organization Improvement** (Englewood Cliffs, NJ: Prentice-Hall, 1984)

(18)   Kanter, Rosabeth Moss. "Managing the Human Side of Change" **Management Review** (April, 1985)

CHAPTER 14

(19)   Weisbord, Marvin R. "Organizational Diagnosis: Six Places to Look for Trouble With or Without a Theory", in French, Wendell, Bell, Cecil, Jr. and Zawacki, Robert. **Organization Development. Theory, Practice and Research** (Texas: Business Publications, 1983)

(20)   Buchholz, Steve and Roth, Thomas. **Creating the High-Performance Team** (New York: John Wiley & Sons, Inc, 1987)

(21)   Alexander, Mark. "The Team Effectiveness Critique" **The 1985 Annual: Developing Human Resources** (San Diego, CA: University Associates, 1985)

(22)   French, Wendell L. and Hollman, Robert W. "Management by Objectives: The Team Approach" in French, Wendell and Bell, Cecil, Jr. and Zawacki, Robert. **Organization Development. Theory, Practice and Research**

(23)   Likert, Rensis. **The Human Organization: Its Management and Value** (New York: McGraw-Hill, 1967)

(24)   Blake, Robert R. and Mouton, Jane S. "What's New With The Grid" in French, Wendell and Bell, Cecil, Jr. and Zawacki, Robert. **Organization Development. Theory, Practice and Research**

(25)   Blake, Robert R. and Mouton, Jane S. **The New Managerial Grid** (Houston: Gulf Publishing Co., 1978)

(26)   McGregor, Douglas. **The Human Side of Enterprise** (New York: McGraw Hill, 1960)

(27)   Yankelovich, D. **New Rules: Searching for Fullfillment In A World Turned Upside Down** (New York: Vintage Books, 1981)

(28)   Andrews, and Dubin **Human Relations** Third Edition (1984)

(29)   Ozley, Lee M. and Ball, Judith S. "Quality of Work Life: Initiating Successful Efforts in Labor-Management Organizations" **Personnel Administrator** (May 1982)

(30)   Locke, Edwin A. and Schwieger, David M. "Participation in Decision Making: One More Look" **Research in Organizational Behavior** (Greenwich, CT: JAI Press, 1979)

(31)   Sashkin, Marshall. "A Guide to Participative Management" **The 1984 Annual: Developing Human Resources** (San Diego, CA: University Associates, 1984)

(32)   Kanter, Rosabeth Moss. **The Change Masters: Innovation for Productivity in the American Corporation** (New York: Simon & Schuster, 1983)

(33)   LeBoeuf, Michael. **The Productivity Challenge** (New York: McGraw-Hill, 1982)

(34)   Schonberger, Richard J. **Japanese Manufacturing Techniques: Nine Hidden Lessons in Simplicity** (New York: The Free Press, 1982)

(35)   Dumas, Roland A. "The Shaky Foundations of Quality Circles" **Training, The Magazine of Human Resource Development** (April, 1983)

(36)   Byrum-Gaw, Beverly and Carlock, C. Jesse. "Modeling: Teaching By Living the Theory" **The 1983 Annual for Facilitators, Trainers, and Consultants** (San Diego, CA: University Associates, 1983)

(37)   Adapted from Lippitt, Ronald. "Six Problem-Solving Contexts for Intervention Decision-Making" **Clinical Sociology Review** (Vol 3, 39-49, 1985)

(38)   Trist, E., Higgins, G. W. and Murray, H. and Pollock, A.B. **Organizational Choice** (London: Tavistock, 1963)

(39)   Cherns, A. B. "The Principles of Organization Design" **Human Relations** (Vol 28, 783-792, 1976)

(40)   Gutknecht, Douglas and Gutknecht, David. **Building More Productive Organizations Through Health and Wellness Programs** (Lanham, MD: University Press of America, 1989)

(41)   Herzlinger, Regina and Calkins, David, "How Companies Tackle Health Care Costs", **Harvard Business Review**, Part 3, Jan, Feb 1986

STRATEGIES FOR ENTERING THE HUMAN RESOURCES FIELD

The strategies listed and discussed here will help the reader to better understand the HR field. Part of any career assessment relates to the process of self-assessment and the evaluation of unique skills, values, interests, needs capabilities and biases. Remember certain strategies will require more risk taking, information about costs and benefits, time, money and commitment.

Strategy 1: Informational Interview

Strategy one involves informational interviewing with people in the field. Here the individual might interview personnel directors or managers, trainers, and internal human resource development consultants to learn about various HR roles. In strategy one, you are doing your own market studies to determine the likely job prospects.

You can locate practitioners by using your own circle of friends, professional contacts, local newspaper and magazine articles, directories of companies or consultants, Consultants and Consulting Organizations Directory, Training Magazine's Directory of Consulting Services, OD Networker, Organization Development Institute, etc.

Strategy 2: Read Field-Related Literature

Numerous books, magazines, journals, computer software and cassettes exist to inform you about the HR field: examine bibliographies from college and university courses; check out the schools that offer specific programs; send in product services marketing cards from various magazines, such as Training Magazine, to get on mailing lists in order to find out what the latest HR products and services look like; browse the library at any major university and make a list of journals and periodicals under areas of management, personnel, strategic management, sociology of organizations, public administration, labor relations, economics, industrial psychology; find out which publishers have a series in the HR-OD-HRM-Management field (Addison-Wesley publishes an excellent series on HRD, OD and Stress; Jossey-Bass has an excellent organization - human resource management development series published under a joint publication agreement between the management and social and behavioral science series; John Wiley and Sons has an excellent series on organizational assessment and change; Goodmeasure, Inc. in Cambridge, Massachusetts and University Associates in San Diego, California carry a wide range of current literature; Reston, Prentice Hall, Praeger, and West Publishing Companies publish professional and academic texts in organizational studies, human resource management, organizational theory and behavior); send for tape catalogues from annual conferences of OD Network, Humanistic Psychological Association, topical conferences; get on the mailing list of an important national conference and you will soon receive other invitations. Remember you are an information scanner or scavenger, so make sure you set up a filing cabinet to keep articles, case studies, bibliographies, notes, presentations, lectures, etc. Start building your own resource library today.

Strategy 3: Exploring Degree Programs

As we have already seen, one of the hallmarks of any profession is the development of a systematic, theoretical body of knowledge regarding the field. The various theories provide the foundation for professional activities and research. The theoretical base functions to identify important academic and practical questions and research topics, while legitimizing professional practice. One might say that the theory should inform and shape research and practice, while also remaining open to modification through the feedback of results from the latter.

The need for facilitating professional skill development is rooted in the theoretical knowledge underlying basic skills. The skilled professional draws upon relevant, foundational knowledge and perspectives to identify and solve organizational problems. Any group aspiring to such a designation as professional, must provide a sound, theoretically grounded educational experience.

Theory includes the established concepts, terminology, principles and practices of the field and subfields for establishing a professional demain of knowledge. One of the most important links to building a sound theoretical foundation for the emerging professional status of HRMD are the accredited Master's and Doctorate programs in the field. Table 1 suggests the range of programs available and highlights selected schools offering the various degrees. Although generally located within one of several academic departments and disciplines (see Table 2), the degrees listed are interdisciplinary in method and scope. The general designations, thus, include HR, HR/OD, HRM, HRM/OD, HRMD, HRD, OD, OB. In addition, Table 2 suggests the range of subdisciplinary theoretical and research topics of interest and relevance to Human Resource professionals.

The advantages of obtaining advanced education, and ultimately gaining a master's or doctorate degree in the HRMD field are many: 1) access to the latest literature in the areas of theory on organizational behavior, training and development, human resource management, organization development, management, and communication, and other related applied social and behavioral sciences; 2) access to stimulating high achieving classmates from a wide variety of organizations; 3) opportunities to critically reflect upon and evaluate a systematic career development plan; 4) access to a network of alumni and contacts who have previously graduated from the program; 5) opportunities for internships and other practical experiences when trying to learn about this new field or make a career transition into consulting; 6) opportunities to talk and work with professors, many of whom are consultants or practitioners in the field; 7) the advanced degree may enhance your candidacy for promotions or enhance your credentials for professional type entry-level jobs; 8) your self-esteem may increase greatly as you accomplish academic goals and eventually achieve an important academic and professional milestone.

The disadvantages must also be weighed when deciding to attend a formal degree program: 1) the fact that a poorly prepared and low quality program may actually harm your prospects for career development; 2) formal degrees can cost a good deal of money and take time away from family and other relevant life projects; 3) your self-esteem can be challenged, particularly for those out of school for many years and during the early stages to formal coursework.

The American Society for Training and Development (ASTD) publishes a Directory of Academic Programs in Training and Development and Human Resources Development. Write for information to several of the programs that sound interesting to you.

Explore the type of educational experience to see if it matches your needs: more structured and less interdisciplinary programs allow you to become a specialist in one field of HRMD; less structured and more interdisciplinary programs allow you to become a generalist in several subfields of HRMD which allow you to keep open several job opportunities.

Strategy 4: Attending Workshops, Conferences and Seminars

One of the most practical opportunities to learn about the Human Resources field is by attending workshops, conferences and seminars. These presentations by skilled practitioners, consultants and academics will offer a good overview of the many varied opportunities and challenges facing the HR field. Good contacts can be initiated through formal and informal interviews, interaction with workshop presenters, and after-hours socializing. Also attend pre- or post-conference sessions for a more in-depth knowledge and relaxed environment.

Attend workshops on training for trainers, how to give workshop presentations, the future of Human Resources, current problems in the field, how to make the HR function relevant to your business strategy, etc., to give you a feel for the critical issues, roles, skills and perspectives in the field. Establish contact with a workshop presenter after the presentations and try to build a cordial relationship. Let him/her talk about how they earned the prestigious opportunity to organize and give their workshop or seminar: what contacts and procedures are important; what general strategies are essential for arranging and conducting a successful workshop are there different procedures for delivering a workshop in-house versus conference, versus invited guest at a local college?

Utilize the resources of other job seekers and attend conferences and workshops with a positive attitude, several specific learning goals or objectives, and room for plenty of innovative thinking. On the latter point, try some presentations or workshops that seem to go against your basic strengths, needs interests, or even personality, cognitive or learning style. Make sure you participate in formal job interviewing if the conference provides an employment service. You can even interview if you are only considering a career or job change and gain valuable experience and information, under relative stress-free conditions.

One excellent related strategy is to volunteer to assist in the planning, implementation, and registration during a conference, workshop or seminar. Often the larger HR conferences and training fairs will allow you to attend free after your volunteer hours are completed. Also volunteer for membership in various conference and professional committees concerned with conference planning, continuing education and organizational fund raising.

Workshops are offered by numerous associations, institutes, private consulting companies and educational / academic programs in local colleges and universities.

Training magazine publishes a monthly column of private - fee workshops and a yearly update (entire issue) of potential workshops and paid in-house consulting activities that run the gamut of HR topics. University Associates in San Diego sponsors workshops, as do numerous colleges and universities.

In addition, other organizations that sponsor conferences, workshops, ongoing education and training include: the National Training Laboratory (NTL) Institute, OD Network, American Management Association, Institute for Management Education, Personnel and Industrial Relations Association, Organization Development Institute, The Human Resources Institute, American Consultants League, The Clinical Sociology Association, The Association for Humanistic Psychology, The Mid-Atlantic Association for Training and Consulting, Inc., Lifework Planning, Center for Human Resources and Organizational Development, and Myers Institute for Creative Studies.

Discipline	Examples of Departments, Subdisciplines and Programs	Examples of Schools and Degrees Offered
Human Resource Management-Development and Interdisciplinary Programs	Human Resource Department Human Resources and Organization Development	George Washington U. M.A. - Ed.D. Dept. of Organ. Behavior, M.S., CASU
	Human Resource Management Development	Chapman College, M.S. in Human Resource Management Development
	Organizational Behavior and Human Resources Management	United States International University, School of Human Behavior, M.A. Ph.D.
	Organization Development	Case Western Reserve University, M.S.
	Applied Human Relations	University of Oklahoma, Human Relations Dept. M.H.R.
Business-Management	Organization Development	Pepperdine Univ., M.S.
	Human Systems Studies	U.C.L.A., M.B.A., Ph.D.
	Organizational Behavior and Organizational Development	University of New Hampshire, Whittemore School of Business & Mgt., M.B.A., Ph.D.
	Human Resource Management and Personnel	University of Georgia, M.A., M.B.A., Ph.D.
	Administrative Sciences Human Systems	George Washington U. Dept. of Science M.S., M.B.A., D.B.A., D.P.A.
	Organization Behavior	Yale School of Organization & Mgt., Ph.D. Purdue University, Ph.D. Stanford University, Ph.D.
Psychology	Humanistic Psychology and Organizational Industrial Psychology	New York University, Ph.D.
	Organization Development /Organization Behavior	University of West Florida, Faculty of Psychology, M.A., Ph.D.
	Applied Social Psychology (Joint program with School of Mgmt. in Organization Development)	Boston University, Ph.D., D.B.A.
	Human Relations Training Group Leadership/ Facilitation Organizational Psychology	Columbia University, Teachers College, Dept., of Psych., M.A., Ph.D.

Table 1. Academic Institutions and Specialities Offered in the Human Resources Field

DISCIPLINE	DISCIPLINE TOPICS
	Major Discipline Topics of Relevance to HRMD Theory and Research
Sociology	Work groups
	Group Dynamics
	Occupations
	Employee ownership-control
	Labor organization
	Unionization
	Organizational power
	Organization Development
	Socialization
	Macro organizational theory
	Social psychology
	Comparative organizations
	Industrial stratification
	Split labor markets
	Sociology of leisure and work
	Family-work linkages
	Working class conflict
	Conflict management
Psychology	Job satisfaction
	Performance assessment
	Job design
	Turnover and absenteeism
	Test validation
	Experimental research
	Personnel planning and
	Program evaluation
Management	Personnel
	Recruitment and selection
	Compensation and benefits
	Management training
	Labor law
	Executive development
	Management Information Systems
Organization Behavior*	Motivation and leadership strategies
	Organizational stress, health, safety
	Organization development
	Personality and perception
	Learning and reinforcement
	Career planning and development
	Organizational design
	Organizational change

*Some identify this as a subdiscipline of management, psychology and sociology

Table 2. Academic Disciplines and Major Topics of Relevance to HR

BIOGRAPHICAL INFORMATION

Douglas B. Gutknecht is currently an Associate Professor in the Department of Sociology/Human Resources and director of the M.S. program in Human Resources Development at Chapman College in Orange, California. He received his Ph.D. from The University of California, Riverside in 1979 and has taught at Pitzer College, The Claremont Colleges, Occidental College, and U.C. Riverside. He will be leaving Chapman College in the Fall of 1989, after teaching there for the past 11 years, to pursue other interests in education, consulting and writing. He has consulted in the areas of conflict management, communication skills, group development, creativity enhancement and organization health promotion.

Dr. Gutknecht has published four other books with U.P.A. and has most recently published **Strategic Revitalization: Managing The Challenges of Change** 2nd. edition in 1988. In the Fall, 1989 concurrent with the publication of this text, **Building Productive Organizations Through Health and Wellness Programs** will also be published by U.P.A. In addition to teaching, writing, and consulting, Dr. Gutknecht would like to explore more vigorously a career in higher education administration.

Janet R. Miller, M.S., is currently in transition from a 20 year career in Personnel, Marketing and Management within the corporate environment to consulting in the field of Human Resource Management and Development. She also teaches HRMD courses at local colleges in Southern California. She has consulted in the areas of Organizational Development, team building and group development, personality and behavior, and motivation, and plans to continue writing, teaching and consulting, as well as pursuing a doctorate in a related field.